BEFORE *UTOPIA*

The Making of Thomas More's Mind

Before *Utopia*

The Making of Thomas More's Mind

ROSS DEALY

UNIVERSITY OF TORONTO PRESS
Toronto Buffal London

Toronto Buffalo Londo
utorontopress.com

ISBN 978-1-4875-0659-9 (cloth)
ISBN 978-1-4875-3448-6 (PDF)
ISBN 978-1-4875-3449-3 (ePUB)

Library and Archives Canada Cataloguing in Publication

Title: Before Utopia : the making of Thomas More's mind / Ross Dealy.
Names: Dealy, Ross, author.
Description: Includes bibliographical references and index.
Identifiers: Canadiana 20190177713 | ISBN 9781487506599 (ha dcover)
Subjects: LCSH: More, Thomas, Saint, 1478–1535. | LCSH: More, Thomas, Saint, 1478–1535 – Knowledge and learning. | LCSH: More, Thomas, Saint, 1478–1535 – Religion. | LCSH: More, Thomas, Saint, 1478–1535 – Sources. | LCSH: More, Thomas, Saint, 1478–1535. Utopia.
Classification: LCC B785.M84 D43 2019 | DDC 199/.42 – dc2

University of Toronto Press acknowledges the financial assistance to its publishing program of the Canada Council for the Arts and the Ontario Arts Council, an agency of the Government of Ontario.

Canada Council for the Arts
Conseil des Arts du Canada

Funded by the Government of Canada
Financé par le gouvernement du Canada
Canada

For Ruth Englhart Dealy,
Anette Wydro, Nicola Lemay, and Ian Dealy

Contents

Preface

Research does not always follow a straight path. In my case, two years travelling by motorcycle from the Arctic Circle to the tip of South America and throughout Africa as an undergraduate (1952–5), led to an interest in the impact of the intellectual history of Europe on the larger world. Ford Foundation grants later allowed me to spend two years in Europe researching in the Archive of the Indies (Seville, Spain) the influence of Thomas More and Erasmus in the Spanish New World, particularly on Vasco de Quiroga – resulting in a dissertation on this subject (1975). In the 1530s Quiroga built two communities for Indians based on *Utopia* and wrote about *Utopia*, all of which forced me to look long and hard at the book. In the process I became convinced that something is fundamentally wrong (leaving aside Quiroga) with accepted interpretations. What I wanted to understand, first of all, was how More's mind worked as he went about composing the work. And was there somehow a connection to the thinking of his friend Erasmus?

Against all odds I eventually came to see that More's *Utopia* and Erasmus' war writings, free-will writings, and *Praise of Folly* are not built from rhetoric, as everywhere believed, but from a set way of thinking. And yet, for years I was unable to discover the basis of this thinking. Ultimately, however, all the uncertainty vanished when I uncovered in certain early books of Erasmus a learned and pervasive employment of the unitary two-dimensional way of thinking found in classical Stoicism – detailed in my book *The Stoic Origins of Erasmus' Philosophy of Christ* (Toronto, 2017). Further research revealed not only the Stoic methodology employed in composing *Utopia* but also the step-by-step manner in which that work had come about. While More before late 1504 had seen Christianity in dichotomous, either/or, non-worldly versus worldly, terms, and therewith had been in deep despair as to whether he should choose the monastery or the world, his outlook was radically transformed when Erasmus introduced him to the Stoic unitary two-dimensional mindset – and related this mindset to Christianity. The book at hand shows that More's work on *Lucian* (1506), Erasmus' *The Praise of Folly* (1511), and More's *Utopia* (1516) systematically work out – in social/political terms – More's new way of seeing himself and the world.

Along the way I have profited from positions at the University of Wisconsin-Marinette, Brown University (one year as Curator of Books in the John Carter Brown Library and one year as Visiting Scholar), and St John's University in New York City. I am particularly indebted to St John's in that those in charge overrode various countervailing forces and allowed time to continue research, including a research leave. As for individuals, no one has influenced my interest in research more than Professor Gerald Strauss at Indiana University. Not of little importance has been the enduring support of my life partner, Ruth Englhart Dealy, whom I met so memorably in her hometown, Aschaffenbu g, Germany.

The professionalism and good will of Suzanne Rancourt, Manager, Humanities Acquisitions, and her team are deeply appreciated, as are the helpfulness of two anonymous readers.

Abbreviations

Ac.	Cicero, *Posterior Academics*
Allen	*Opus epistolarum Des. Erasmi Roterodami.* Ed. P.S. Allen, H.M. Allen, and H.W. Garrod. 12 vols. Oxford: Clarendon Press, 1906–58
ASD	*Opera omnia Desiderii Erasmi Roterodami.* Amsterdam: Brill, 1969–
Ben.	Seneca, *De beneficiis* (On Benefits). In *Moral Essays*
C	More, *Utopia.* Ed. G.M. Logan, R.M. Adams, and C.H. Miller. Cambridge: Cambridge University Press, 1995
CN	Plutarch, *De communibus notitiis contra Stoicos* (On Common Conceptions)
Const.	Seneca, *De constantia sapientis* (On the Firmness of the Wise Man). In *Moral Essays*
CWE	*Collected Works of Erasmus.* Toronto: University of Toronto Press, 1974–
CWM	*The Complete Works of St. Thomas More.* 15 volumes. New Haven: Yale University Press, 1963–97
DL	Diogenes Laertius, *Lives of Eminent Philosophers*
De ira	Seneca, *De ira* (On Anger). In *Moral Essays*
De or.	Cicero, *De oratore* (On the Orator)
Disc.	Epictetus, *Discourses*
Ep.	Erasmus, *Epistolae* (Letters) (*Opus epistolarum Des. Erasmi Roterodami*)
Ep.	Seneca, *Ad Lucilium Epistulae Morales* (Moral Letters to Lucilium)
Fin.	Cicero, *De finibus bonorum et malorum* (On Moral Ends)
H	*Desiderius Erasmus Roterodamus: Ausgewählte Werke.* Ed. Hajo Holborn and Annemarie Holborn. Munich: Beck, 1933

Inv.	Cicero, *De inventione*
LB	*Desiderii Erasmi Roterodami opera omnia*. Ed. J. Leclerc. 10 vols. Leiden: 1703–6
Leg.	Cicero, *De legibus* (On the Laws) (*On the Republic. On the Laws*)
LS	*The Hellenistic Philosophers*. Ed. A.A. Long and D.N. Sedley. 2 vols. Cambridge: Cambridge University Press, 1987
Luc.	Cicero, *Lucullus* (*Prior Academics*)
Mur.	Cicero, *Pro Murena* (In Defence of Murena)
ND	Cicero, *De natura deorum* (On the Nature of the Gods)
Off.	Cicero, *De officiis* (On Appropriate Actions)
Or.	Cicero, *Orator* (Orator) (*Brutus. Orator*)
Ot.	Seneca, *De otio* (On Leisure). In *Moral Essays*
Par.	Cicero, *Paradoxa Stoicorum* (Stoic Paradoxes)
Rep.	Cicero, *De re publica* (On the Republic)
Rep.	Plato, *Republic*. In *Complete Works*
SR	Plutarch, *De Stoicorum repugnantiis* (On Stoic Self-Contradictions)
ST	Thomas Aquinas, *Summa theologiae*
Tr.	Seneca, *De tranquillitate animi* (On Peace of Mind). In *Moral Essays*
Tusc.	Cicero, *Tusculan Disputations*
Vit. Beat.	Seneca, *De vita beata* (On the Happy Life). In *Moral Essays*
Y	More, *Utopia*. Ed. Edward Surtz, SJ, and J.H. Hexter. New Haven: Yale University Press, 1965. Vol. 4 of CWM

BEFORE *UTOPIA*

The Making of Thomas More's Mind

INTRODUCTION

In Search of the Meaning of *Utopia*

What do we know about Thomas More prior to his writing of *Utopia*, published in 1516? It might seem that we know a lot, as considerable literature covering such things as his life in London, his study of Greek, his ties with Erasmus, and aspects of his publications exists. But how much do we really understand about his mental development and the actual workings of his mind? Why did he write *Utopia*? Was he simply performing a humanist intellectual exercise? Or could there have been something deeply personal about the work?

The book at hand is about a mind that has not been seen, a mind that was not conflicted but determined, beginning in late 1504, to embrace and represent a particular way of thinking. Prior to late 1504, More's mind, with no exception, was vacillating and polarized, either/or. Should he choose the contemplative life or the active life? But in late 1504 his outlook was suddenly and radically transformed. After that date and up to the time he wrote *Utopia* his mindset was not either/or but emphatically both/and. He had come to see – with immense relief – that he did not have to make a choice, that the contemplative life and the active life at all times require each other. And yet this discovery brought with it a challenge: What were the larger implications of this new way of seeing himself, the world, and Christianity?

What has not been seen is not just the life-altering change but what brought about this change and why it occurred so suddenly. The force behind this transformation was Erasmus, not the Erasmus commonly portrayed but an Erasmus that had himself been radicalized, beginning around 1497, by the Stoic unitary *katorthoma/kathekon* (*honestum/indifferens, honestum/utile*, contemplative/active) mindset. Erasmus' "philosophy of Christ" was built, I have demonstrated elsewhere, from this Stoic way of thinking.[1]

Textual analysis reveals that the purpose of More's work on *Lucian* (1506) and Erasmus' *Praise of Folly* (1511) was to represent for humans everywhere More's metamorphosis from an either/or, non-worldly or worldly, understanding of Christianity to a unitary both/and understanding, a Christianity that is inseparably two-dimensional, worldly and non-worldly, *honestum/utile*, contemplative/active. The book *Utopia* is built from the same frame of thought. However diverse the issue, whether discussing Utopian pleasure philosophy or Utopian warfare or the debate between Hythloday and "More," the author works out with all logic his Stoic/Christian *honestum/utile* mindset. He is determined to demonstrate the supreme applicability of this way of thinking to all situations that occur in the real world.

Consider, before going any further, current views regarding the mind that wrote *Utopia*.

"Two Minds"

Over and over it has been shown that Renaissance humanists were not systematic thinkers, much less philosophers, but rhetoricians. As rhetoricians they debated issues from opposed positions and most often did not conclusively or convincingly support one position over another. The book *Utopia* deeply reflects, it is believed, this rhetorical, vacillating, either/or, mindset. Charles Trinkaus, an expert on fourteenth- and fifteenth-century Italian humanism, once concluded an article on Thomas More's *Utopia* by stating that it is not believable that Book II, the delineation of the Utopian state, could be "programmatic," because if it were the author would not be a humanist. A humanist by very definition engages in "dialogic ambiguity."[2] "Structural ambiguity" is built into humanist thought. "If More was actually proposing Utopian communism as a programmatic solution, he would have departed from the humanist tradition." But he surely did not propose such. "In possessing this double vision, More preserved the essential dialogic ambiguity of the humanist tradition," all of which gives Trinkaus reason to support the prevailing interpretation of *Utopia*, that the true meaning is found in the Book I either/or debate between Hythloday and "More." The title of his article, "Thomas More and the Humanist Tradition: Martyrdom and Ambiguity," shows that Trinkaus, like many others, sees

1 Dealy, *The Stoic Origins of Erasmus' Philosophy of Christ*.

2 Trinkaus, "Thomas More and the Humanist Tradition," 435.

ambiguity as inhering not only in humanism and the book *Utopia* but even in More's life and martyrdom.

As we learn in the introductions to the Cambridge editions of *Utopia* (1995, 2016), the author of *Utopia* was a person of "two minds," evidenced by the two main characters, Hythloday and "More."[3] In support of this "two minds" thesis, a sizeable literature can be brought forth, most notably J.H. Hexter's classic, *More's Utopia: The Biography of an Idea* (1952), followed by George M. Logan's *The Meaning of More's Utopia* (1983, rpt. 2014); Quentin Skinner's "Thomas More's *Utopia* and the Virtue of True Nobility" (2002);[4] Dominic Baker-Smith's *More's Utopia* (1991, rpt. 2000); and Alistair Fox's *Utopia: An Elusive Vision* (1993). Hexter argues that the Book I debate between "More" and Hythloday is not an introduction but More's "second intention," his added thoughts, doubts, and concerns about Hythloday's discourse in Book II on the Utopian state. Although Logan holds, like Hexter, that it is hard to tell what More's actual views were from the Book I debate, he shows that Book II was a laborious "best commonwealth exercise" modelled primarily on Plato and Aristotle. Skinner contends that the author was a worldly Ciceronian "civic" humanist who allowed that Hythloday's Platonist best state is an ideal worth considering even if it is not implementable. Baker-Smith concludes his volume by talking about the "sphinx-like ambiguity" that forces readers to shoulder the burden of interpretation. Building rhetorically on the Hexterian viewpoint, Fox has chapters on Book II's "Eütopia" ("happy place of More's dream") and "Irony and Satire" before he discusses Book I. The final three chapters, reflecting what are perceived to be much more fundamental issues, centre on Book I and "More's Dilemma," "The Inconclusiveness of *Utopia*," and "More's Equivocal Masterpiece." More recent discussions offer further perspective, but the co e issues remain.[5]

How could it not be the case that *Utopia* was a product of the rhetorician's penchant, practised even by contemporary schoolboys, for

3 More, *Utopia*, ed. Logan, Adams, and Miller, xxiv, xxv, xxviii, xxxiii. Logan is the author of the non-textual part of the introduction. Logan's introduction to a third edition (Cambridge, 2016) represents the same thesis (xxii, passim).

4 This is a slightly revised version of Skinner's "Sir Thomas More's *Utopia* and the Language of Renaissance Humanism."

5 See Baker-Smith, "Reading *Utopia*"; Curtis, "'The Best State of the Commonwealth'"; Davis, "Thomas More's *Utopia*"; Grace, "Utopia"; McConica, "Thomas More as Humanist"; Simpson, "Rhetoric, Conscience, and the Playful Positions of Sir Thomas More"; van Ruler and Sissa, eds., *Utopia 1516–2016*; Wootton, Introduction to *Thomas More's Utopia with Erasmus' Sileni Alcibiades*; Yoran, "'Utopia and the No-Place of the Erasmian Republic," in his *Between Utopia and Dystopia*, 159–86.

debate on either side of a question, *in utramque partem*? Classical rhetoric was of three types – judicial, deliberative, and demonstrative (or epideictic) – and Renaissance humanists had employed all three.[6] Within these types of oratory, the ancients had set forth various topics for discussion, particularly important ones being *honestas* (honour) and *utilitas* (utility). Orators would support one approach or the other, but not both in the same speech. In considering a particular issue, what course of action would be the most advantageous or, on the other side of the debate, what would be the most honourable path? Or, by chance, could *utilitas* and *honestas* not be in conflict? Deliberative rhetoric tended to consider *utilitas* the ultimate end whereas demonstrative rhetoric considered *honestas* the ultimate end.[7] Throughout the Middle Ages and the Renaissance, the two main textbooks for such issues were Cicero's *De inventione*, which he wrote as a teenager (92–88 BCE), and the pseudo-Ciceronian *Rhetorica ad Herennium* (85–80 BCE).[8] A complete copy of Quintilian's massive *Institutio oratoria* (c. 96 CE) was discovered only in 1416, and intact copies of Cicero's mature works, *De oratore* and *Orator*, appeared only in 1421.[9] *Rhetorica ad Herennium* focused on expediential factors and has been related to Machiavelli's *The Prince*,[10] while *De inventione* was more moralistic in tone. *De inventione* allowed that expedience (security) could override the moral on certain occasions, but this should not be the goal.[11]

Placed within this rhetorical context, the debate in Book I of *Utopia* between "More" and Hythloday has seemed to exemplify the deliberative approach (*utilitas* or *honestas*?) and Book II, Hythloday's eulogy of the communistic Utopian state, the demonstrative approach (*honestas*).[12]

---

6 On the practice and theory of the three types of rhetoric in the classical world, see Kennedy, *A New History of Classical Rhetoric*. On their use in humanistic circles, see O'Malley, *Praise and Blame in Renaissance Rome*, esp. 36–51.

7 See Tinkler, "Praise and Advice," 204, and Cicero, *De inventione* 2.12–13, 155–75, De oratore 2.333–49, and Topica 91. Cf. Cox, "Machiavelli and the *Rhetorica ad Herennium*."

8 See Monfasani, "Humanism and Rhetoric"; Ward, "From Antiquity to the Renaissance" and "Renaissance Commentators on Ciceronian Rhetoric."

9 See Ward, "Quintilian and the Rhetorical Revolution of the Middle Ages"; Monfasani, "Episodes of Anti-Quintilianism in the Italian Renaissance"; and Walzer, "Quintilian's 'Vir Bonus' and the Stoic Wise Man."

10 Cox, "Machiavelli and the *Rhetorica ad Herennium*." Aristotle's *Rhetoric*, which was little known, also emphasized expediential factors.

11 Cicero, *De inventione* 2.156 (against Aristotle's view) and 2.174–5.

12 See Logan, "*Utopia* and Deliberative Rhetoric," and McCutcheon, "More's Rhetoric," 54–7.

There exists widespread agreement that the author never in the work resolves the contradiction between More's "indirect" approach and Hythloday's vision.[13] Nor do scholars believe that the author ever considered Utopia implementable.[14] Was Utopia even an ideal? Readers have found many Utopian practices contradictory and dystopian, most especially their restrictions of personal freedom and their foreign policy. Regarding the latter, Arthur Kinney sees a veritable "epidemic" of inconsistencies and abominable practices.[15] "They desire peace, yet they have no hesitation in annexing territory not their own; they claim selflessness yet remain imperialistic."[16] Taking pride on occasion in offensive and defensive warfare, intimidation and violence, they obtain territory for colonization, offer rewards for the assassination of enemy leaders, create disturbances in foreign lands, hire the most savage mercenaries, enslave some prisoners, are masters of cunning and deceit, and are willing to fight to the last man. Modern readers have considered this expediential ideology and behaviour the height of immorality. Surely, it is believed, More was not here representing his own views. Was he deliberately finding fault with ideals? Shlomo Avineri has concluded that the reasons the Utopians put forth for war are more objectionable than even Machiavelli's expediential strictures in *The Prince* (1513).[17] Even their discussions of moral philosophy reflect, we are told, conflicting goals [18]

"One Mind": Hythloday's or "More's"?

Recently Eric Nelson has set forth what can be called a "one mind" thesis, arguing that the author was very consciously pitting Greek thought against Roman thought. He contends in effect exactly what Trinkaus denies, that More's thinking throughout the work was "programmatic."

13 As John Guy has recently stated, "We can never know for certain to what extent the opposing views of 'Thomas Morus' and Hythlodaeus represent More's own philosophy in Book I of *Utopia*, for it was always his genius to be able to debate both sides of the question, and the *pro* and *contra* method of debate was integral to classical and Renaissance rhetoric." See "Thomas More and Tyranny," 176.

14 In summarizing the literature, James Hankins confidently concludes that Utopia was not meant to be a model for Europe. See "Humanism and the Origins of Modern Political Thought," 139.

15 Kinney, *Humanist Poetics*, 62.

16 Kinney, *Humanist Poetics*, 63.

17 Avineri, "War and Slavery in More's Utopia," 273.

18 Logan, Introduction to *Utopia*, xxxii, xxxiii (C).

In "Greek *Nonsense* in More's *Utopia*," which comprises chapter 1 of his *The Greek Tradition in Republican Thought* (2004), Nelson argues that Hythloday's support for Plato in Book I and his depiction of a communistic state in Book II reflect the actual outlook of the author. Thomas More was very explicitly rejecting the Roman way of looking at issues represented by "More," Hythloday's debating partner.

Gerard B. Wegemer has now laid out what amounts to an opposite thesis in "*Utopia*: A Model *Respublica* of Peace, Liberty, and Self-Government?," chapter 9 of his *Young Thomas More and the Arts of Liberty* (2011). He shows that "More's" argument against Hythloday in Book I is really the author's view and that Hythloday's arguments and his depictions of Utopia in Book II are full of contradictions, contradictions which illuminate what is wrong about Utopia and what by implication is right about "More's" view – which is what the author wanted perceptive readers to grasp. The book within which Wegemer embeds this thesis works out the early political and social views of More on civil and social strife and the intensity of More's early concerns with peace, liberty, and self-government – as found most especially in More's political poems and epigrams, declamation on tyrannicide, coronation ode for Henry VIII, *Life of Pico della Mirandola*, and *Richard III*. These early concerns allegedly drew More to what Wegemer sees as the worldly focused "*humanitas*" thinking found in Cicero's *De officiis* and Seneca's *Letters*. Surrounding everything was the London environment, the long tradition of law and the power of the people, and More's functions within this society.

Problems with Rhetorical Interpretations

The Difference between Rhetorical honestas *and* utilitas *and Stoic* honestum/utile

There are two very diffe ent ways of talking about *honestas* and *utilitas*. One is rhetorical, continually discussed by Renaissance scholars; the other is philosophical. In rhetoric, *honestas* and *utilitas* are separate things, even if on occasion they can be brought into alignment. In Stoic philosophy, going back to conceptualizations by Zeno (c. 300 BCE), they are not two separate things but one. Most importantly, they reflect and entail an entire philosophy. As Cicero states in *De oratore* (55 BCE), the orator would never be understood were he to use Stoic terminology: "Good and bad do not mean to Stoics what they mean to the rest of the citizens, or rather, to the rest of the nations on earth, and they also have diffe ent conceptions of honor and disgrace, and of reward and punishment" (3.66).[19] Cicero's *De officiis* (44 BCE) represents a late version of Stoic philosophy. Books 1 and 2 were very consciously influenced by the Stoic Panaetius, and Book 3, which centres on the Stoic unitary both/and, *honestum/utile*, way of solving problems, is built from Zeno and the older Stoa.[20] Fifteenth-century humanists had seen *honestas* and *utilitas* in the either/or terms represented in the works on rhetoric of Cicero and Quintilian, not the both/and philosophic terms found in *De officiis*.[21] Where they build on Stoicism, as in their "mirror-for-princes" literature, it is a top down, one-dimensional, understanding of Stoicism, not the Stoic two-dimensional *katorthoma/kathekon* (*honestum/indifferens*, *honestum/utile*, contemplative/active) frame of thought. Even contemporaries of Cicero would have been more familiar with the conflict between *honestas* and *utilitas* discussed in rhetorical works, such as Cicero's *De oratore* (2.335), than with the definition of *honestum* and the uniting of the *honestum* and the *utile* found in *De officiis*.[22] *De officiis* is not a debate about which side to support, the *honestum* or the *utile*, or even how by chance the two might be rhetorically combined. Nor is it an argument about whether honour is superior to expedience. Very consciously building on Stoic philosophy, *De officiis* shows the *honestum* and the *utile* to be two sides of one thing. However variable human problems may be, they must be addressed from a set, two-dimensional, frame of thought. There is all the diffe ence between the vacillations between *honestas* and *utilitas* in rhetoric, or even their possible union, and the actual *honestum/utile* (*katorthoma/kathekon*) union worked out in deeply philosophical terms, over hundreds of years, in Stoic philosophy. The problem is not deciding whether *utile* or *honestum* is the better approach but determining how the unitary unbending/bending frame works out in particular situations.

Cicero refers to the words *katorthoma* and *kathekon* at the beginning of *De officiis*, and his *De finibus* works out in detail their meanings – meanings

19 Translations are from printed editions found in the bibliography, unless otherwise stated. On rhetoric in antiquity see in particular Marrou, *A History of Education in Antiquity*; Kerferd, *The Sophistic Movement*; Vickers, *In Defense of Rhetoric*; Pernot, *Rhetoric in Antiquity*; Dugan, *Making a New Man*; Connolly, *The State of Speech*; and Dominik and Hall, eds., *A Companion to Roman Rhetoric*.

20 Perhaps, states Dyck, "Cicero's major contribution to Roman political thought is his radical identification of *honestum* and *utile*, with the consequences worked out in detail in *Off.* 3." "Ironically, it is in Book 3, where Cicero boasts of his independence of sources (3.34) and where the scale of values can ostensibly be either Stoic or Peripatetic (3.33), that the rigor of the older Stoa reasserts itself (cf. ad 3.62–63, 97–115, 119)." See *A Commentary on Cicero, De Officiis*, 33 and 37.

21 See Dealy, *Stoic Origins*, Part I.

22 See Long, "Cicero's Politics in *De Officiis*," 218n13.

which Cicero relates in *De officiis*, especially Book 3, not to the Stoic wiseman but to ordinary humans (3.16). The Stoics describe with these words two types of value, one perfect and the other imperfect, one unbending and the other bending. Both types of value are encompassed by their fabled wiseman. On the bending side, everything the wiseman does is "an appropriate act," *kathekon* (Latin *officium*) (*Fin.* 3.20) – a word first used by Zeno himself (335–262 BCE) (DL 7.108). An appropriate act is "an act so performed that a reasonable account can be rendered of its performance" (*Fin.* 3.58) or, stated otherwise, "an act of which a probable reason can be given" (*Off.* 1.8). What the wiseman has that others don't have is *katorthoma*, or "right action" ("rectum factum," *Fin.* 3.45). An act carried out with a virtuous disposition is a "right action," whereas the same act done without a virtuous disposition – by those not wise – is not virtuous (Seneca, *Ep.* 95.43). Those not wise can and sometimes do carry out appropriate acts, but only the Stoic wiseman consistently acts appropriately by selecting, employing reason, courses of action that are most in accord with nature and rejecting, employing reason, those that are contrary to nature. Importantly, the wiseman's selections do not in themselves contribute to virtue. Selecting is simply essential to his character and activities, his virtue and happiness (*Fin.* 3.58–9).

Kathekonta, "appropriate acts," take place in the realm of things that are "indiffe ent." From the very beginning, the Stoics had argued that everything neither good nor evil is "indiffe ent," *indifferens* (Greek *adiaphoron*) (*Fin.* 3.53),[23] and "intermediate" between virtue and vice (*Fin.* 3.58), and that some of these indiffe ents are "preferred" and others "rejected" (*Fin.* 3.15). Of the indiffe ents, some have positive value, others negative value, and others are neutral (*Fin.* 3.50). Later Stoics concentrated more and more on the real-world consequences of things indiffe ent, as can be glimpsed by Cicero's referrals in *De officiis* (following Panaetius) not to things that are indiffe ent but to things that are useful (*utile*) – while holding firm the connection to *honestum*.[24]

23 *Indifferens* is a word that occurs for the first time in Cice o's works. See Powell, "Cicero's Translations from the Greek," 296.

24 Cf. Dyck, *A Commentary on Cicero, De Officiis*: The term *utile* "refers to the relation of an act to a result and implies nothing about the ethical status of the act." "Cicero's approach is not to combat this notion but rather to reform the content of the *utile*." "Cicero's analysis thus involves two *utilia*, an apparent *utile*, which turns out on closer inspection not to be *utile*, and a true *utile*, which coincides with the *honestum*" (492–3). Prior to Panaetius, the *utile* "played only a very minor role in Stoic philosophy" (353). *Utilia* may be, as such, *indifferentia*, but now the focus is on things that are expedient or inexpedient as distinct from preferred or dispreferred indiffe ents – which subtly moves the meaning.

Reflecting in his own way the thinking of Zeno and Chrysippus, the Stoic Seneca (c. 4 BCE–65 CE) distinguishes in late letters between *decreta* – dogmas that are unchanging, absolute, and universal, requiring unflinching belief (*Ep.* 95.10, 57) – and *praecepta,* which are rules of advice and exhortation (*Ep.* 94.1, 31).[25] Neither *decreta* nor *praecepta* are functionally separable. *Decreta* require *praecepta* and *praecepta* require *decreta* (*Ep.* 94.48–50; 95.34, 41, 60).

Problems with Quentin Skinner's *Utopia*

Quentin Skinner's many writings reflect his determination to study *not* the classics of political thought as such, but rather "the place occupied by such texts in broader traditions and frameworks of thought,"[26] "trying so far as possible to think as our ancestors thought and to see things their way."[27]

And yet, is it not possible that Skinner's methodology can in some ways limit understanding? Is it really enough to give serious attention to the early modern texts alone – without serious and independent study of the classics? (a) Is there not something limiting in assuming that, whether early modern writers refer or do not refer to classic works, what matters is what these writers have to say – and not classical meanings of this or that? Is there not something limiting in believing, for historical purposes, that the meanings found in the classics by early modern writers are whatever these writers say they are? Is there not something limiting in locating *without careful study of contexts* statements in the classics that may seem to correlate with certain early modern views or that some early modern individuals may even refer to? Was Thomas More, for example, someone who in writing *Utopia* simply thumbed his way through books by Cicero, pulling out a few odd statements in passing, or was he someone who clearly recognized the context and larger meaning of these statements? Would not seeing *in context* how early modern readers were interpreting or misinterpreting particular ancient sources enhance our understanding of these readers? (b) Not of little relevance potentially, what if one or more early modern thinkers should mount an independent analysis of certain ancient

25 See Mitsis, "Seneca on Reason, Rules, and Moral Development." Cicero in *De officiis* links, without comment, *praecepta* and *admonitio* with *officia*. See Kidd, "Moral Actions and Rules in Stoic Ethics," 251. He cites *De officiis* 1.1, 7; 2.7; 3.5, 121.

26 Skinner, *Liberty before Liberalism*, 101.

27 Skinner, *Visions of Politics*, vol. 1, 47.

texts and arrive, not overtly naming sources, at radically new insights – insights not shared by contemporaries?[28] Would these insights and their sources be easily grasped employing Skinner's methodology?

Notice first that Skinner is allergic to the words "Stoic" or "Stoicism." A reader of his books would never realize that Cicero and Seneca were philosophers, much less serious and learned philosophers. Nor would a reader ever recognize that Seneca was a Stoic and what it means to be a Stoic and that Cicero was very dominantly influenced by Stoicism.[29] In focusing on the relation of Cicero's *De officiis* to *Utopia*, Skinner picks out points of comparison without realizing that *De officiis* is not just about "Cicero" but, more fundamentally, about Stoicism.[30] Nor do his writings bring into focus Cicero's many other books on philosophy, much less the role played by Stoicism in these works and in many other ancient works available to Renaissance readers.[31] He mentions Aristotle and Plato but never Stoics or Stoicism – the philosophy that Cicero in *De officiis* to a large degree modelled. What Skinner sees in Cicero and Seneca are not philosophers deeply influenced by the thinking of Zeno and his heirs but simply moralists and rhetoricians.[32]

---

28 Note Skinner's contention that, *thinking on his own*, More "intervenes" in humanist debates that were long standing. See "Thomas More's *Utopia* and the Virtue of True Nobility" (229, cf. 243).

29 It may be noted that there was little interest or understanding of Stoicism when Skinner began research, decades ago.

30 See in particular, Skinner, "Thomas More's *Utopia* and the Virtue of True Nobility."

31 Among the works then available that discuss Stoicism were Cicero's *De finibus*, *De officiis*, *Tusculan Disputations*, *De legibus*, *Academica*, and *De natura deorum*; Seneca's many essays, such as *De constantia sapientis*, *De vita beata*, and *De tranquillitate animi*, and *Epistolae morales*; Diogenes Laertius' *Lives of Philosophers*; Epictetus' *Enchiridion* and *Discourses*; Plutarch's lengthy discussions of Stoicism in his *Moralia*, especially *De Stoicorum repugnantiis* and *De communibus notitiis contra Stoicos*; and the quotations, summaries, and illustrations of Stoicism in Aulus Gellius' *Noctes Atticae* (Attic Nights). On the availability of these and many other relevant authors, such as Sextus Empiricus or Dio Chrysostom, see Hankins and Palmer, *The Recovery of Ancient Philosophy in the Renaissance*.

32 See, for example, Skinner, *Reason and Rhetoric in the Philosophy of Hobbes*, 42, 44, 76, 77 passim, and *Machiavelli*, 28, 38, 40, 44, 50. Failing to distinguish – as elsewhere – between wisdom as "ought" for the moralist and wisdom as "is" for the Stoic wiseman, Skinner comments in one article that Seneca holds (*Ep.* 85.32) that "sapientia ought above all to act 'as our mistress and ruler,'" whereas in fact Seneca states that "wisdom is [for the wiseman] mistress and ruler [sapientia domina rectrixque est]." "The wiseman's purpose in conducting his life is not to accomplish at all hazards what he tries [in contrast to the pilot's purpose], but to do all things rightly ... [He] is always in action ... His work goes on throughout his whole life." See "Ambrogio Lorenzetti and the Portrayal of Virtuous Government" (a revised version of a 1987 article), 55.

Cicero is for Skinner the exemplum par excellence of a "civic" humanist,[33] a rhetorician and moralist who opposed *negotium* (public activity) to "contemplative *otium*."[34] In arriving at this view, he focuses on Cicero's statement in *De officiis* that "to be drawn by study away from active life is contrary to moral duty. For the whole glory of virtue is in activity" (1.19).[35] What Skinner does not realize, however, is that Cicero at no time portrays the active life as separate from the contemplative life. As mentioned above, Cicero distinguishes at the very beginning of *De officiis* (1.8) the two fundamentals of Stoic philosophy: *kathekon* (mean duty) and *katorthoma* (absolute duty), opposite types of duty that for the wiseman at all times require each other. Nor does Skinner diffe entiate *honestum* from the meaning of honesty or honourableness, which he over and over links to views of early modern writers and defines as "a willingness to keep faith and deal honorably with all men at all times"[36] – rather than, as Cicero explicitly states, something that "merits praise even though it be praised by none" (*Off.* 1.14). "Though devoid of all utility, it [*honestum*] can justly be commended in and for itself, apart from any profit or reward" (*Fin.* 2.45).[37] Where Cicero sees math, astronomy, dialectics, and civil law as examples of abstruse, difficult and unnecessary endeavours (*Off.* 1.19), in that they are not tied to the active life, he is not rejecting – unrecognized by Skinner – contemplative truths. He is not thinking of the abstract philosophic precepts that comprise *honestum*. *Honestum* is a type of *otium* that exists whatever life style one leads and has four parts – wisdom (*sapientia/ prudentia*), justice (*iustitia*), greatness of spirit (*magnitudo animi*), and decorum (*decorum*) (1.15).[38] Also unsupported by *De officiis* is Skinner's

33 Skinner, "Thomas More's *Utopia* and the Virtue of True Nobility," 223.

34 Skinner, *Reason and Rhetoric*, 68; "Thomas More's *Utopia* and the Virtue of True Nobility," 216–24.

35 Skinner, "Thomas More's *Utopia* and the Virtue of True Nobility," 218.

36 Skinner, *Machiavelli*, 40–1; Cf. "Thomas More's *Utopia* and the Virtue of True Nobility," 224.

37 Long shows that Cicero attempts in *De officiis* to see the old Roman conceptions of honour in terms of this more abstract Stoic conception of honour. See "Cicero's Politics in *De officiis*," 218. Cf. Dyck, *A Commentary on Cicero, De Officiis*, 98.

38 Although Cicero found wisdom of less value than the other parts of *honestum*, even here he makes an important qualification. *Prudentia*, which is at first tied to *sapientia* (1.15), is later explicitly distinguished from it. By prudence "we understand something else, namely, the knowledge of things to be pursued and things to be avoided [expetendarum fugiendarumque]" (1.153). *Prudentia*, unlike *sapientia* but like the other virtues, is clearly, we can see, unitarily both/and, *honestum/utile*.

assertion that Cicero obtained these virtues from Plato (albeit Plato discussed them).[39] Particularly erroneous and consequential is his belief that Cicero was the source of the early modern view that *honestum* is a virtue *separate* from the four named virtues.[40] In no instance does Cicero separate *honestum* from the four virtues. If early modern authors interpreted *honestum* in this way, they were on their own.

Where Cicero states that humans should look to their own particular natures in choosing a career and practising their talents on the worldly stage with "as little impropriety as possible" (*Off.* 1.114), he is not, as Skinner would have it, contrasting "philosophical talents."[41] Humans have a particular character but they also have a universal character (*Off.* 1.107). While the first persona, the universal, consists of reason and, therewith, that which is *honestum*, the second persona constitutes our unique characters as individuals. By definition, *honestum* (like *katorthoma*) is at all times inseparable from the active life. All of which is simply a restating of the unitary both/and, *honestum/utile*, thesis argued by Stoics since Zeno. As Cicero explicitly states, the arguments found in *De officiis* are "in perfect harmony with the Stoics' system and doctrines" (3.20). What is diffe ent is Cicero's desire to relate the Stoic "system and doctrines" to the lives of ordinary humans. Holding firmly to *honestum* allows one to discover that which is truly expedient (*utile*), truly decorous, truly prudent, truly just, and truly courageous. The task for ordinary humans is to develop and acquire, in the face of life's complexities and challenges and with all seriousness and determination, rational, unitary, both/and solutions – solutions that focus on and unite two radically diffe ent types of value, the one contemplative the other active.

Regarding the dialogue in Book I of *Utopia* between "More" and Hythloday, Skinner considers "More" a person "in the guise of a good Ciceronian humanist" – and that this is the base outlook of Thomas More himself.[42] Stated otherwise, Cicero's humanism was "civic" – representing the active life rather than or opposed to the contemplative – and this was Thomas More's outlook. "*De Officiis* furnished virtually the whole framework for civic humanist discussions of the active life"

39 Skinner, *Machiavelli*, 40. All Cicero does at 1.15 is tie Plato's conception of beauty (*Phaedrus*, 250D) with Stoic *honestum*. As Cicero well knew, Stoics held *honestum* to be something inherently beautiful (*Fin.* 2.49, *Off.* 1.14, DL 7.98–101). Plato discusses four virtues in his *Republic* (4.426–35) and elsewhere.

40 Skinner, *Machiavelli*, 40.

41 Skinner, "Thomas More's *Utopia* and the Virtue of True Nobility," 219–20.

42 Skinner, "Thomas More's *Utopia* and the Virtue of True Nobility," 242, 223–4 resp.

and "More" simply mimics this outlook.[43] "More," unlike Hythloday and in line with civic humanism, argues for the "indirect" approach and for discharging one's duties "as decorously as possible" (*Utopia* 96).[44] Hythloday, in contrast, presents a Platonist ideal that lays bare the shortcomings of worldly affairs, but it was for the author only an ideal, something to think about.[45] *De officiis* 1.70, in line allegedly with civic humanism, criticizes philosophers and kings who live "just as they please," but Hythloday proudly states, "I live as I please [vivo ut volo]" (*Utopia* 50).[46] His advocating of communism as well as Plato's contention in *Republic* 6 (496D–E) that the philosopher needs to forego public affairs (*Utopia* 101) directly contradicted the "neo-roman" views on property, non-domination, virtue, and the *vita activa* held by fifteenth-century civic humanists – and by Thomas More.[47] In their antagonism to government by noble heritage and wealth, which was the *otium* they concentrated on, humanists had tended to argue for *negotium*, and Book I of *Utopia*, argues Skinner, is about this tension between *negotium* and *otium*; "More" on the *negotium* side with Hythloday and his Platonism on the *otium* side. In reworking his 1987 article on *Utopia* in 2002, Skinner doubles down on the *negotium* theme with a new title: "Thomas More's *Utopia* and the Virtue of True Nobility."[48] For humanists such as More, the virtue of true nobility lies not in the leisure (*otium*) of those possessing nobility or wealth but in the virtuous carrying out of *negotium*.[49] Virtue entails performing civic tasks that are for the common good.[50]At one point, Skinner refers to More's "philosophy" and equates this with "civic" humanism and the active life – and holds that this philosophy was what impelled him to join the court of Henry VIII in 1518.[51]

---

43 Skinner, "Thomas More's *Utopia* and the Virtue of True Nobility," 218, 221n58.

44 Skinner, "Thomas More's *Utopia* and the Virtue of True Nobility," 222. Unless otherwise indicated, I am using the 1995 Cambridge edition of *Utopia*. "Est alia philosophia civilior quae suam novit scaenam, eique sese accommodans, in ea fabula quae in manibus est suas partes concinne et cum decoro tutatur" (94/32–96/2).

45 Skinner, "Thomas More's *Utopia* and the Virtue of True Nobility," 214, 244.

46 Skinner, "Thomas More's *Utopia* and the Virtue of True Nobility," 221.

47 See Skinner, "Thomas More's *Utopia* and the Virtue of True Nobility," 243–4; *The Foundations of Modern Political Thought*, vol. 1, 255–62; *Visions of Politics*, vol. 2, chs. 5–7, 11, 12; and *Liberty before Liberalism*.

48 The 1987 title (see 5n4 above) was "Sir Thomas More's *Utopia* and the Language of Renaissance Humanism."

49 Skinner, "Thomas More's *Utopia* and the Virtue of True Nobility," 224–9, *Foundations*, 82.

50 Skinner, "Thomas More's *Utopia* and the Virtue of True Nobility," 231.

51 Skinner, "Thomas More's *Utopia* and the Virtue of True Nobility," 224, 223 resp.

A core problem is that Skinner does not recognize the actual meaning for Cicero and Seneca of "the virtue of true nobility [virtus vera nobilitas est]."[52] He states that the Utopians "forbid *otium* and require *negotium* from everyone,"[53] referencing *Utopia* 127, but what the Utopians are talking about here is aimless leisure, idleness, not contemplation as such. Failing to distinguish between leisure and *honestum*, Skinner disregards or minimizes the place of absolutes in Utopia. The cardinal virtues are not for him inherent to *honestum* and contemplative truth but simply moral ideals that need to accompany *negotium*.[54] Even more problematic is his contention that the Utopians consider their religious principles, such as belief in immortality and divine providence, "obvious," and that, leaving aside these "exceptions," their discussions indicate that "nothing about religion is certain and everything ought therefore to be tolerated."[55] But why, if this is the case, is Utopian religion "serious and strict, indeed almost stern and forbidding [quae gravis et severa est fereque tristis et rigida]" (*Utopia* 161) – an outlook that ties with that of the Stoic wiseman (*Mur.* 66)?[56] Why would the Utopians find reason, a fundamental of the Utopian state, "weak and defective" without these religious principles (*Utopia* 161)?[57] Why would Hythloday consider Utopian institutions not just extremely prudent but extremely holy, "prudentissima atque sanctissima" (*Utopia* 100/23–4)?

In actuality, virtue and true nobility are for Cicero and Seneca not one-dimensional – centred on *negotium* – but two-dimensional. The Stoic is at all times both contemplative and active, and, as Seneca

52 Skinner, "Thomas More's *Utopia* and the Virtue of True Nobility," 227–36.

53 Skinner, "Thomas More's *Utopia* and the Virtue of True Nobility," 231.

54 See page 13 above.

55 Skinner, "Thomas More's *Utopia* and the Virtue of True Nobility," 237. Cf. *Utopia* 223–5.

56 Bypassing Utopian religious absolutes and taking no notice here or elsewhere of Epicurean philosophy, Skinner sees the statement that the Utopians are "more inclined than they should" to leading a joyful and carefree life (*Utopia* 159) as reflecting the fact that Utopian happiness is based on " eason alone" – lacking Christian revelation. Leaping over the carefully worked out reasonings of the Utopians, he deduces that reason alone ultimately leads (*Utopia* 187) to the pious allowance of suicide and euthanasia when disease and the like are too debilitating ("Thomas More's *Utopia* and the Virtue of True Nobility," 238–9).

57 Not believing in rewards and punishments in an afterlife, "Who can doubt that a man who has nothing to fear but the law, and no hope of life beyond the grave, will do anything he can to evade his country's laws by craft or to break them by violence, in order to gratify his own personal greed?" (*Utopia* 225). Cf. Cicero, *Leg.*, 1.40–1.

emphasizes, this is true whether the wiseman is at leisure or not (*Ot.* 6.1, 7.2; *Tr.* 2.11). Whether he is expanding or contracting his involvement in governmental affairs, the contemplative/active mindset of the wiseman does not change (*Tr.* 5.3–4).[58] There is all the diffe ence between inconsequential abstractions and having a unitary both/and mindset. Skinner contrasts Machiavelli's outlook on virtue with that of Cicero, but the virtue Machiavelli saw and criticized in *The Prince* was the one-dimensional virtue represented by fifteenth-century humanist "mirror-for-princes" literature. He saw nothing of the two-dimensional virtue discussed and illustrated at length in Book III of *De officiis.*[59] Similarly, Skinner shows that virtue in Utopian society was a "ruling principle,"[60] but was this virtue one-dimensional or two-dimensional? The unitary *honestum/utile* outlook, two types of value that have to be worked out anew in every situation, is not just a small or odd thesis but central to all Stoic thinkers. Holding to *honestum,* the Stoic could respond to changing circumstances in multitudes of ways.

In short, Cicero never saw the world in "civic humanist" terms – however much this designation may relate to fifteenth-century outlooks. Though not a great philosopher he was a serious philosopher, never merely a rhetorician and "Roman moralist" who argued the *vita activa* against the *vita contemplativa*. For him the contemplative life – as distinct from inane or worthless leisure – was inseparable from the active life. His mindset was unitarily both/and, *honestum/utile,* contemplative/active.

Failing to grasp the mindset of Cicero and Seneca, Skinner doesn't consider the possibility (any more than have others) that the opposed views of Hythloday and "More" might demand – as they would with

58 Even should it come to complete retirement, the wiseman is still active (*Tr.* 4.8). Although Zeno, the founder of Stoicism, and Cleanthes and Chrysippus, the next two heads of the school, advocated public service, unlike the Epicureans (*Ot.* 3.2), they themselves did not become involved in politics – a fact which troubles Seneca. And yet Seneca concludes that in studying nature they were studying action as well as contemplation. When they framed laws for the entire human race, they were themselves engaging in action as well as contemplation. (*Ot.* 6.4–5, 4.1–2). Cf. *Off.* 1.70–1. Cicero well recognized the diffe ence between Plato's belief that philosophers will not assume civic duties except under compulsion (*Off.* 1.28; cf. *Rep.* 7.521b) and the Stoic belief that the wiseman by his very nature will in one way or another always be involved.

59 See Dealy, *Stoic Origins,* 39–46. I have noticed only one referral to Book 3 of *De officiis* in Skinner's many writings (*Machiavelli,* 61).

60 Skinner, "Thomas More's *Utopia* and the Virtue of True Nobility," 231–4, 242.

Stoics – reconciliation; that Hythloday's view is both right and wrong and that "More's" view (as interpreted by Hythloday) is also both right and wrong – and that there is a way in which the two views can become one view.

Problems with Eric Nelson's *Utopia*

In seeing *Utopia* as an attack on "Roman philosophy," Greek thought versus Roman thought, Eric Nelson builds on the contention of Quentin Skinner, his mentor, that Cicero was opposing the active life to the contemplative life and that Cicero's "philosophy" was a philosophy that originated in Roman culture.[61] Hythloday supports the contemplative life and relates the Utopian state to Plato's thought, so the author must have been pitting Greek philosophy, the argument goes, against Roman philosophy.

In support of his thesis, Nelson points, for one thing, to the fact that only Greek books were taken to the New World because it was thought that little in Latin literature would interest the Utopians (though in Book I Hythloday admires Seneca and Cicero as well, *Utopia* 44/1–5) (34–5). But what Nelson does not realize is that Cicero himself would have wholeheartedly agreed that Greek philosophy is entirely superior to anything found in the Roman world, where, as Cicero points out, philosophy as a discipline was highly suspect and non-existent.

> Philosophy [i.e., Greek philosophy] has lain neglected to this day, and Latin literature has thrown no light upon it: it must be illuminated and exalted by us, so that, if in the active business of life I have been of service to my countrymen, I may also, if I can, be of service to them in my leisure. (*Tusc.* 1.5, cf. 2.5)

In *De finibus* Cicero admires Cato for "teaching philosophy to speak Latin, and naturalizing her as a Roman citizen. Hitherto she has seemed a foreigner at Rome, and shy of conversing in our language; and this is especially so with your Stoic system because of its precision and subtlety alike of thought and language" (3.40).

Nowhere does Nelson take account of the many books, such as *De finibus*, *Tusculan Disputations*, *Academica*, and *De natura deorum*, in which Cicero summarizes, analyses, and relates all the major Hellenistic philosophies. Far from attacking Greek philosophy, Cicero was very

61 Nelson, "Greek *Nonsense* in More's *Utopia*," 36 and 27. Further references in text.

consciously, and with all admiration, translating Greek philosophy and relating philosophy as such to traditional Roman thought and customs (the most prominent example being *De officiis*).[62] Indeed, he had earlier gone to Athens to study philosophy and later made sure that his son did the same. As Gisela Striker states (common knowledge among philosophers): "Philosophy, for the Romans of Cicero's age, was a Greek thing, and there was no other philosophy around."[63]

Not seeing Cicero's actual outlook and goals with regard to Greek philosophy, Nelson surmises (26) that Richard Pace (in 1517) and others of the alleged "Erasmian" school go all out in their attempts to belittle Roman philosophy – whereas they are in fact only restating Cicero's view:

> Whatever seems to have originated with the Romans – history, for example, and oratory – was all taken from the Greeks as if on loan ... In philosophy it was Plato and Aristotle. To Cicero they were the most learned of the Greeks, and he often calls one of them *divine* and the other *the most wise.* But Roman philosophy is so imperfect that learned men think nothing is more stupid than to compare Roman philosophers with the Greeks. And I don't omit Cicero himself (if he'll pardon my saying so).[64]

Nelson also deduces, wrongly, that the influence of Erasmus' "Platonism" in England ("the Erasmian party line") (26) is yet another example of opposition to *Romanitas*. If Erasmus was a Platonist, this means, Nelson theorizes, that he was attacking "Roman philosophy." In fact Erasmus' outlook was not built from Plato (nor, as Nelson believes, the Florentine Platonists Giovanni Pico della Mirandola and Marsilio Ficino) but from the (Greek) Stoic *katorthoma/kathekon* way of thinking described in technical terms at the beginning of *De officiis* and at length in *De finibus*.[65]

Cicero very consciously built *De officiis*, his most original work, from Stoicism, a Greek philosophy, and Seneca was a Stoic with deep insight

62 In winning approval for philosophy, Cicero represents Roman achievement, however lacking in philosophy, as superior to the Greek in "morals, customs, family life, state organization, law, and of course, the military." See Baraz, *A Written Republic*, 106. Despite Cicero's efforts, philosophy as a discipline would emain, Baraz notes, Greek (3).

63 Striker, "Cicero and Greek Philosophy," 53. See also Powell, "Cicero's Translations from the Greek."

64 Pace, *De fructu qui ex doctrina percipitur (On the Benefit of a Liberal Education)*, 129.

65 See Dealy, *Stoic Origins*, and further below my analysis of Erasmus' *Praise of Folly* (1511).

into the writings of the originators of Stoicism, Zeno and Chrysippus. In discussing "More's" contention against Hythloday that worldly affairs require decorum, Nelson deduces that "More" is mounting "a Ciceronian [i.e., Roman] critique of Greek philosophy" (30) – not realizing that *decorum* is a core, two-dimensional, theme in Greek Stoic philosophy, the philosophy Cicero most admired (cf. *Off.* 1.93–9).[66] Decorum is one of the four fundamental aspects of *honestum*: "What is *decorous* is *honestum* and what is *honestum* is *decorous*" [quod decet honestum est et quod honestum est decet]" (*Off.* 1.94). "It is the function of justice [one aspect of *honestum*] not to do wrong to one's fellow men; of considerateness not to wound their feelings; and in this the essence of *decorum* is best seen" (*Off.* 1.99).[67] Though Nelson discusses a few statements found in Books 1 and 2 of *De officiis*, on property and "giving each his due," nowhere does he take account of or recognize the overall *honestum/utile* – Greek-based – thesis of the work.

Problems with George M. Logan's *Utopia*

In *The Meaning of More's Utopia*, George M. Logan depicts a humanist who presents "the results," laboriously worked out, of a "best-commonwealth exercise" modelled particularly on Plato and Aristotle (cf. 191, 243, 252). Although Logan's arguments are learned, they are tangled and not always easy to follow. Particularly puzzling are some of his statements about Stoicism. Fortunately, he goes into greater detail in a later article, "*Utopia* and Deliberative Rhetoric," much of which was included in his introduction to the Cambridge *Utopia*. In composing *Utopia* More was working out, Logan argues, rhetorical theory. In his reading, Book I is a rendering of deliberative rhetoric and Book II of demonstrative rhetoric. Book I is shaped by the rhetorical topics of *honestas* and *utilitas* and asks a question: should one seek *honestas* or *utilitas*? It's an either/or issue.

Logan begins by summarizing the famous debate between Hythloday and "More" on the viability of counselling those in power, which I will compress even further.

---

66 See below, 192n100.

67 "Iustitiae partes sunt non violare homines, verecundiae non offende e; in quo maxime vis perspicitur decori." Decorum includes temperance (*temperantia*) (*Off.* 1.93). What decorum and temperance have in common, Griffin an Atkins state, "are first, limit and app opriateness to context, and secondly, concern with appearance and not offending others." See *On Duties*, ed. Griffin an Atkins, 37n2.

(a) Peter Giles thinks Hythloday, who had travelled to the New World and was interested in philosophic ideas, should enter the service of some king and at the same time benefit his relatives and friends (*Utopia* 51).

"More" adds that Hythloday could with his ideals incite some prince to just and noble actions (*Utopia* 53).

(b) But Hythloday denies that he could do anything to help the public interest by becoming a counsellor. Most kings want to know only how to acquire kingdoms by hook or by crook. They are not interested in learning how to govern well the kingdoms they already have. Secondly,

> In a court composed of people who envy everyone else and admire only themselves, if a man should suggest something he had read of in other ages or seen in practice elsewhere, those who hear it act as if their whole reputation for wisdom would be endangered, and as if henceforth they would look like simpletons, unless they can find fault with the proposals of others. (*Utopia* 53)

(a) In response, "More" advises Hythloday to take the "indirect" approach and apply truth decorously. It is true that there is no place for Hythloday's rigid and abstract philosophy in the councils of kings:

> But there is another philosophy, better suited for the role of a citizen, that takes its cue, adapts itself to the drama in hand and acts its part neatly and appropriately ... If you cannot pluck up bad ideas by the root, or cure long-standing evils to our heart's content, you must not therefore abandon the commonwealth ... You must not deliver strange and out-of-the-way speeches to people with whom they will carry no weight because they are firmly persuaded the other way. Instead, by an indirect approach, you must strive and struggle as best you can to handle everything tactfully – and thus what you cannot turn to good, you may at least make as little bad as possible. (*Utopia* 95–7)

(b) But Hythloday emphatically rejects "More's" argument, stating that he doesn't know whether "it's the business of a philosopher to tell lies," but he is certain that this "indirect" approach would only result in his becoming mad and going along with the crowd. Christ commanded from the hilltops that we not dissemble truth (*Utopia* 97–9).

Logan believes "More" is clearly the orthodox rhetorician in his advocating of an "indirect" approach and winning people over tactfully. "Like rhetoricians at all times, 'More' argues for active involvement" (113). In this regard, Logan brings in the rhetorical doctrine of *decorum* in Cicero's *Orator* (21.72) and mentions relationships to a Stoic discussion of decorum in *De officiis* that advises deciding on one's natural abilities and responding to issues with "as little impropriety as possible" (1.114) (112).

Central to his argument, Logan buys into Hythloday's insinuation that "More" is advocating with his "indirect" approach the telling of lies. Quoting here the rhetorician Quintilian (*Institutes* 2.17.27–30) (111), he alleges that "More" is advocating against Hythloday "a morally dubious strategy" (111). Logan also states that "More" is arguing that *utilitas* is not always the same as *honestas*, that what is expedient may be at odds with truth, though in fact "More" never actually makes the contrast (with these words or without them) but merely points out the unworkableness of Hythloday's way of thinking in the world of affairs

As regards Hythloday's view, Logan holds that honour does not require that he join a ruler's council (110) in that Hythloday is not a rhetorician but a philosopher, a person who "studied Greek more than Latin because his main interest is philosophy" (*Utopia* 115). It is not the task of a philosopher to implement truth. Philosopher Hythloday argues in Book I that rigid and abstract contemplative truths, as exemplified by the ways thieves should be handled (*Utopia* 57, 71–5), can and should be applied *as is* to worldly affairs, and, in line with Hythloday's one-to-one view of the relation of *honestas* to *utilitas*,[68] Logan believes, from this standpoint also, that "More's" contention that truth needs to be applied indirectly and decorously is beside the point and amounts to lying.

Although the argument is not developed, Logan holds that Book II describes Platonist-type contemplative doctrines and that these doctrines exemplify the abstract one-dimensional "Stoic" thinking alluded to in Book I (103). Logan believes Skinner is entirely correct in holding that Hythloday reasserts in Book II "the Platonic case for philosophical *otium*, urged against the 'civic' – Ciceronian – humanism of 'More'" and adds to Skinner's argument a belief that Hythloday "supports this position by application of the Stoic thesis of the [one-to-one] identity of *honestas* and *utilitas*" (113).[69] Logan deduces that Hythloday is showing

68 Seneca's *De clementia*, an early work (56 CE) that appears to have inspired fifteenth-century humanists, comes close to this outlook. See Dealy, *Stoic Origins*, Part 1, 41–4.

69 In *The Meaning of More's Utopia*, Logan holds that the author "would have preferred that Hythloday be correct" but found "the results" of his best-commonwealth exercise very "disturbing" for many reasons, both rational and religious (244, 252 passim).

with his Platonist/[abstract]Stoic thesis that "More's" view, "a morally dubious expedient – a temporizing decorum – is, in a deeper view, inexpedient" (113).

A core problem, it can now be seen, is that (writing in 1983 [rpt. 2014] and 1994/5) Logan did not study Stoic writings and relied for his assessments on a secondary source now a century old, E. Vernon Arnold's *Roman Stoicism* (1911).[70] Openly reflecting Arnold's view, he states that Cicero's philosophical works "uncritically retail others' ideas" and that "Roman Stoicism embodies a logically questionable compromise between the austere posture of early Stoicism – epitomized by the figu e of the sage who cares only for virtue – and the characteristic Roman emphasis on the duties (official of practical life" (117n23). What Arnold failed to see, however, is that for early Stoics, as for late, virtue is by very definition two-dimensional, inseparably both theoretical and practical.[71] From Zeno and Chrysippus onward, Stoics had always argued that the *honestum* and the *utile* are two radically diffe ent (albeit unitary) types of value (see above, 8–11). In early Stoicism as in late Stoicism, including that represented in Cicero's *De officiis*, virtue always requires action. Unlike Plato's *Republic*, in Stoicism there are at all times two distinctive types of value at play, one unbending and abstract and the other bending and worldly – eminently decorous. The *vita activa* is inseparable from the *vita contemplativa*.

It may be that Hythloday's one-dimensional understanding of Stoicism ties (in some ways), as Logan alleges (110), with fifteenth-century humanist views – views Machiavelli was to forcefully reject – but what was Thomas More's understanding of Stoicism? What is the book *Utopia* actually about? I have shown elsewhere that More's friend Erasmus was not only the first humanist but the first person in a thousand years to grasp and see the importance of the two-dimensional nature of Stoicism.[72] If More actually understood the Stoic outlook, how would we look at *Utopia*?[73] What we would immediately see is that "More's" position is potentially as much a part of Stoicism as Hythloday's position.

---

70 Logan's introduction to the Cambridge 2016 edition of *Utopia* largely repeats his earlier views.

71 Cf. Reydams-Schils: "The question which comes first, theory or practice, is not relevant to the Stoics, because philosophy is always inextricably linked to one's being in the world and in society" (*The Roman Stoics*, 90). Cf. DL 7.130.

72 See Dealy, *Stoic Origins*.

73 As it happened, my understanding of More and his Utopia did not result from a pre-existing understanding of Stoicism but from long-term analyses of *Utopia*.

What we would also recognize is that Hythloday's position is potentially no more a part of Stoicism than is "More's" position. What we would then want to investigate is whether Book II works out, in part or in whole, the Stoic two-dimensional, unitary both/and, mindset. Should it turn out that the author had indeed grasped the Stoic frame of mind, how would we assess the role of rhetoric? Could it be that the rhetorical frame of the book, which Logan and others place at centre court, was not in the author's mind of primary importance but simply the tool by which he wanted to bring out something of vastly greater significance [74]

Problems with Gerard B. Wegemer's *Utopia*

As shown earlier, Wegemer's *Young Thomas More and the Arts of Liberty* is noteworthy in that, unlike previous studies, it focuses on More's early statements about government and relates these statement to More's life and the outlooks Wegemer finds in Cicero's *De officiis* and Seneca's *Letters*. And yet throughout there are serious problems with Wegemer's methodology and interpretations, problems which come to a head in chapter 9, "*Utopia*: A Model *Respublica* of Peace, Liberty, and Self-Government?"

We note first that Wegemer contends – at odds with other interpretations – that Thomas More's purpose in bringing in Hythloday's abstract views and Utopian outlooks and practices was merely to represent views that are essentially ironical or contradictory – and thus false. The author's view is found, he argues, in character "More's" prudential worldly outlook, and "More" uniquely embodies – unlike Hythloday and the Utopians – something called "*humanitas.*"

Humanitas is a word which Cicero adapted from Greek *paideia*, and it encapsulates ancient civic and political educational ideals. Wegemer places More and his outlook within this general context. "Cicero, Seneca, and More all included humor, charm, happiness, friendship, and civic service in their ideas of *humanitas*, of full human flourishing. Lucian and Horace did also, a factor that undoubtedly drew More's attention to them" (86). As for More's "distinctive *humanitas*," Wegemer sees in his writings "elements such as love for liberty, hatred of tyranny, and care for rhetoric and declamation" (53).

74 Not of little significance, most of the analyses of *Utopia* have been spawned (as with Logan) in literature departments, the home of rhetoric. On Logan's arguments, see also below, 33n88; 209n1; 230n52; 232n56; 271; and 313n8.

One problem stands out. Wegemer centres discussion on Cicero's *De officiis* and Seneca's *Letters*, but (like Skinner) in no instance does he imagine that Cicero or Seneca (in these works or elsewhere) was a philosopher, representative of historical positions or systematic thought. *Humanitas* is about moralizing and they were moralists. What *De officiis* and the *Letters* actually show, as do all their works on philosophy, is that Cicero and Seneca were not mere moralists and rhetoricians but representatives as well of one particular philosophy, Stoicism, and expert in many philosophies. In their philosophical works, at least, the worldly focused *humanitas* Wegemer sees was framed by something else, a unitary both/and, contemplative/active, unbending/bending mindset. *De officiis* is throughout a Stoic-framed work, and Seneca was a Stoic.

But if this is the case, how then should we understand Thomas More's thinking? Did More read Cicero and Seneca as Wegemer reads them, in one-dimensional moralistic terms, or did he grasp the actual two-dimensional mindsets of Cicero and Seneca? If More grasped the actual mindsets, it would not be possible to hold, as does Wegemer, that Hythloday's allegiance to unbending abstract doctrines was, as such, necessarily at odds with the author's outlook.

Misrepresenting the Stoic Cato

Wegemer's skewed understanding of Stoicism is evident where he equates Stoicism with Cicero's witty criticism of the Stoic Cato in a 63 BCE oration in defence of Lucius Murena – where Cato was one of the prosecutors.[75] According to Wegemer, Cicero shows that Stoicism, as evidenced by Cato, was concerned with only "an appearance of integrity," while Thomas More, in contrast, was concerned with consistency between word and deed (18).[76] In fact Cicero was not faulting, even in jest, Cato's lack of integrity but his adherence to certain counter-intuitive Stoic arguments.[77] Cato was famous for the

75 *Pro Murena* is found in *In Catilinam 1–4. Pro Murena. Pro Sulla. Pro Flacco*, 186–301.

76 For his views on Stoicism, Wegemer in *Young Thomas More and the Arts of Liberty* does not refer to the many studies of modern philosophers available but to the articles of one author, Walter Nicgorski. See for example the latter's "Cicero's Paradoxes and His Idea of Utility." Wegemer's deficient understanding is in line with that set forth by Kristeller, long ago, in *Renaissance Thought II*. The Stoics, according to Kristeller, considered most of the happenings in life "morally indiffe ent" (36).

77 See Christopher P. Craig, "Cato's Stoicism and the Understanding of Cicero's Speech for Murena"; Stem, "Cicero as Orator and Philosopher"; and Pangle, "Roman Cosmopolitanism."

very traits Wegemer denies him, unequalled integrity and unequalled consistency of thought and deed – and Stoicism was all about this integrity and consistency. Although Cicero in various works attempted to rewrite or take the edge off some aspects of Stoic thought, the fact is that he was more influenced by Stoicism than any other ancient philosophy. He and Cato remained friends, and the picture he has Cato paint of Stoicism in *De finibus* 3, written much later (45 BCE) and not in jest, is very diffe ent from that found in *Pro Murena* – and quite accurate. Cicero even points out in *De finibus* that he was only jesting, faced with a jury rather than scholars, when he criticized Stoicism in his speech in defence of Murena (4.74). However original *De officiis* may be, Cicero points at the very beginning to the relation of the work to the core Stoic concepts of *katorthoma* and *kathekon*, absolute duty and mean duty (1.8), and discusses in many locations the fact that Books 1 and 2 were modelled, though he deviates in certain respects, on the thought of the Stoic Panaetius (e.g., 1.9–10, 3.7). In Book 3, which works out the oneness of the *honestum* and the *utile*, he maintains that the arguments found in *De officiis* are "in perfect harmony with the Stoics' system and doctrines" (3.20). Nothing of this is explained or even alluded to by Wegemer.

Consider also what Seneca, who always considered himself a Stoic and had direct knowledge of the doctrines of Zeno and Chrysippus, has to say about Cato in his *Letters* – the work on which Wegemer's book swings perhaps even more that *De officiis*.

> Or take the younger Cato's behavior in warring against both Caesar and Pompey in defense of the Republic. Amid the panic no one dreamed of questioning whether Cato was free. Everyone knew that he was contemptuous of danger and the sword, that *he was the embodiment of doctrines and precepts, of the contemplative and the active.* What men asked was only whether he was still among the free. Against the false pictures men have of glory, here was true glory (*Ep.* 95.70–1,73).[78] (Italics mine)
>
> Here also was tranquility and real happiness. (*Tr.* 16.3)

78 Although the two-dimensional wiseman is a master at finding deco ous and prudent solutions to worldly situations and tries not to be a martyr, when the doctrines by which he lives are challenged martyrdom may be the only recourse (*Tr.* 11.1–6, 14.10, 16.3). Was Thomas More's later martyrdom merely a representation of the amorphous and one-dimensional worldly *humanitas* seen by Wegemer? Or did his martyrdom closely parallel the reasoning of the Stoics of old? See below, 99n33 and 298n45.

Cato was the unbending embodiment, that is, not just of one thing but of two things: on the one side abstract doctrines and on the other side worldly precepts.

Misrepresenting More's Purposes, 1500–4

At times Wegemer makes his sources fit his theses, rather than the reverse. Consider his shocking comment, near the end of his book, regarding More's relationship (1500–4) to the extremely strict Carthusian religious order.

> When More was twenty-four, he also decided to learn from the London Carthusians the arts of self-rule needed for such qualities as *fides* and *constantia* that Cicero considered necessary for the clear-sighted and courageous ruler capable of doing what *princeps* Scipio or Crasus or Regulus had done. (180)

Emphatically, the Carthusians were not about teaching political arts and the alleged *humanitas* of Cicero and Seneca. And More, equally emphatically, did not during this time look to the Carthusians for skills that would help him in worldly endeavours. He was giving serious thought to leading an ascetic life, divorcing himself from worldly affairs. Nor is there any evidence that would support a contrary view (even if to some degree More was still involved in worldly affairs). In a biography published in 1588, Thomas Stapleton reports that in his youth More "wore a hair-shirt and slept on the ground or on bare boards with perhaps a log of wood as his pillow. At the most he took four or five hours' sleep, and he was frequent in watchings and fastings."[79] According to William Roper, More's son-in-law, from 1500 to 1504 he lived without vow in the harshly strict Carthusian Charterhouse.[80] His desire was to become a monk or, according to one account, a priest. In his 1519 biography of More, Erasmus states that prior to his decision to commit to worldly affairs, in January 1505, More had engaged in fasting, watching, and devotional exercises that were extreme in their rigour[81] – and Erasmus had in 1505 lived and worked with More for around six months.

79 Stapleton, *The Life and Illustrious Martyrdom of Sir Thomas More*, 8. Cresacre More states something very similar in his *The Life and Death of Sir Thomas Moore*, 27.

80 Roper, *The Life of Sir Thomas More*, 198. Cf. Harpsfield, *The Life and Death of Sir Thomas Moore*, 62.

81 See below, 90. Earlier (*Young Thomas More and the Arts of Liberty*, 71) Wegemer actually describes Erasmus' view.

Misrepresenting the Behaviour of Utopian Priests

Consider also Wegemer's single comment – again shocking and indicative of a tendency to forcefully reconstruct or pass over inconvenient evidence – on the behaviour of the Utopian priests in the midst of war. Needing to show that Utopian views are a joke or contradictory, meant to contrast with the worldly *humanitas* represented by "More," Wegemer describes the behaviour of Utopian priests as "incredibly effective interventions" and deduces that these interventions are simply "examples of More's debt to [the humour of] Lucian" (157). In actuality, no straightforward interpretation would ever support Wegemer's contention. If the text here were to be interpreted in Lucianic terms, this would require not an assertion but major analysis. *Prima facie* what could be more moving, beautiful, and indicative of the contemplative/active mindset of Utopian priests than their behaviour in times of war – and the contrast, so evident, with European priests?

> Whenever their armies join in battle, the Utopian priests are to be found, a little removed from the fray but not far, wearing their sacred vestments and down on their knees. With hand raised to heaven, they pray first of all for peace, and then for victory for their own side, but without much bloodshed on either part. Should their side be victorious, they rush among the combatants and restrain the rage of their own men against the defeated. If any of the enemy see these priests and call to them, it is enough to save all their property from confiscation. This custom has brought them such veneration among all peoples, and given them such genuine authority, that they have saved Utopians from the rage of the enemy as often as they have protected the enemy from Utopians. (*Utopia* 233)

So again, how can Wegemer imagine that this outlook is funny, a Lucianic witticism, and contrary to the view not only of "More" but the author?

"Liberal Studies" Virtue or Stoic Virtue?

In the statement that begins his book, Wegemer ties the rebirth of "liberal studies" desired by More and Erasmus to the view of Seneca,[82]

82 The tie is not supported by the sources he cites, 1515 letters to Dorp by More (CWM 15, 18/13) and Erasmus (Allen, Ep. 337/328). Neither refers to Seneca's views and both answer critics of Erasmus' *Praise of Folly*. Nor does anything in these letters show that they are part of "their plan for international peace," contrary to Wegemer's assertion.

as expressed in his *Letters*: "Hence you see why 'liberal studies' are so called: because they are studies worthy of the free. But there is only one really liberal study, that which gives a person his liberty. It is the study of wisdom, and that is lofty, brave, and great-souled" (*Ep*. 88.1–2). Nowhere does Wegemer recognize that the view represented here is Stoic or what it means (as exemplified by Cato) for a Stoic to be "lofty, brave, and great-souled." What Wegemer sees in Seneca's *Letters*, and ascribes to Erasmus and More, is not the Stoic two-dimensional mindset but only an emphasis on liberal arts, arts that create "the best fashioned exercises to achieve the prudence that is a prerequisite for all the other arts needed by 'the leading citizens' or *principes*" (20).

Wegemer believes the virtue and *humanitas* that he finds in "More" (and Thomas More) derives from the "liberal studies" advocated by Seneca, but in fact, not recognized by Wegemer, Seneca explicitly differentiates liberal studies from virtue. "Liberal studies" contribute to our welfare, "but nothing at all as regards virtue" (*Ep*. 88.20). "'But', one says, 'since you declare that virtue [things such as bravery, loyalty, temperance, kindliness] cannot be attained without the liberal studies, how is it that you deny that they offer any assistance to virtue?' Because you cannot attain virtue without food, either; and yet food has nothing to do with virtue" (88.31). Wisdom communicates facts, not words (88.32). While the arts are "handmaids," "wisdom is mistress and ruler" (85.32). The only real honour lies with the Stoic wiseman, as elsewhere one finds only the semblance of honour, only the semblance of love, friendship, and loyalty (81.12–13). The Stoic wiseman's reason and its virtue are far above all worldly happenings. "Virtue is nothing else than right reason" (66.32). His reason is "perfect," one with divinity, the highest good (124.23). "It is a free mind, an upright mind, subjecting other things to itself and itself to nothing" (124.12). Early man saw nothing of "that philosophy which counts nothing good except what is *honestum*" (90.35). Divine virtue seeks worldly things such as health not because they are goods but because they are preferred indiffe ents (92.11). What matters is the quality of the choices we make in deciding on the most appropriate worldly actions – as we hold to divine precepts (71.32, 92.11–12).

Humanitas is a concept that applies much more naturally to rhetoric than to philosophy, much more to Cicero's *De oratore* (55 BCE) than to his *De officiis*. Seeing Seneca's *Letters* solely in rhetorical terms, Wegemer points to the role of reason but sees little diffe ence between "divine reason" and practical reason (43, 176, 181, 188), much less the relationship of divine reason to practical reason. What he sees in the *Letters* and ties with More is "prudence" (8, 9, 15, 19, 22, 189, passim) and practical morality. Thomas More's view was the view of his namesake in *Utopia*, "More," and "More" (an "orator," 159) in *Utopia* is "the prudent statesman," the person who sets forth against Hythloday's abstractions a "civil philosophy," a philosophy "which knows its stage, adapts itself to the play in hand and performs its role neatly and appropriately" (*Utopia* Y98/11–14) (34).

What Wegemer ties with the outlook of Thomas More (40) is not a two-dimensional (unbending/bending, *katorthoma/kathekon*) mindset from which all issues need to be analysed but simply ethical traits that need to be developed by liberal studies. He notes that virtue is for Seneca "man's primary art" (*Ep.* 92.10) but brings out nothing of the *honestum/indifferens* context. What he sees, at odds with Seneca, is that "All human beings are free to 'fashion' deliberately their own *ethos*, or character, by developing habits through the repetition of actions guided by a view of life considered proper to human beings" (32). Missing entirely the Stoic mindset, Wegemer refers to "a truly philosophic perspective possible only to those who have had the widest and deepest range of study" (48). Like Logan and Skinner, he sees Cicero – and in his train Thomas More – as a worldly civic humanist (34, 51). More even grew, we are told, in his secular outlook as time went on. As evidence, Wegemer shows that the 1526/7 family portrait of More and his family is "an icon of Christian civic humanism" while the 1530/1593 portrait aims at an even more secular focus (165).[83] What this scenario does not explain, for one thing, is More's martyrdom.

In summary, Wegemer fails to recognize the core outlook of Seneca and holds that rather amorphous liberal studies are what produces the ideal statesman, the *princeps*, and that it was this background – along with his legal studies and his personal involvement in London self-government – that produced the "prudential" outlook of Thomas More. Which leads again to a question: Did More read Seneca as Wegemer reads him or did he see Seneca's actual outlook?

---

83 Wegemer points out that one of More's daughters carries Seneca's Letters in a 1530 family portrait (*Young Thomas More and the Arts of Liberty*, 163, 170).

The Two Parts of Virtue

Wegemer often notes particulars in Seneca's letter 95 but nowhere mentions the lengthy and powerful rendering here of Seneca's version of the Stoic *katorthoma/kathekon* way of thinking that Cicero details in *De finibus* 3, refers to at the beginning of *De officiis*, and works out in *honestum/utile* terms in Book 3 of *De officiis*. Philosophy, states Seneca, "is both theoretic and practical; it contemplates at the same time as it acts [Philosophia autem et contemplativa est et activa; spectat simul agitque]" (95.10). "Virtue is divided into two parts – into contemplation of truth, and conduct"; "Training teaches contemplation, and admonition teaches conduct. And right conduct both practices and reveals virtue" (95.45). Honourable conduct requires, simultaneously, both *praecepta* and *decreta* (95.6–7). On the former side are "rules regarding what one should do and avoid" (95.13),[84] on the latter "a fixed and unchanging standard of judgment" (95.57). *Praecepta* are manifest, *decreta* are concealed (95.64). *Praecepta* are concerned with the tools of life (95.8) while *decreta*, though by themselves ineffectual (95.34), embrace the whole of life (95.58). *Praecepta* "add new points of view to those which are inborn and correct depraved ideas" (94.30) while *decreta* are "the means of unswerving decision" (95.62). *Precepta* need *decreta*, for "The same act may be either shameful or honorable, the purpose and the manner make all the diffe ence" (95.43). In short, *praecepta* and *decreta* comprise the inescapable components of all thought (95.60).[85] Did Thomas More see this unitary two-dimensional art of living – or only the *humanitas* Wegemer sees?

The Art of Living

Wegemer contends that, for those who would govern, the art of living is about how to pilot "the ship of state" (33, 40, 42, 188), how to sail through storms (19, 20, 24n7, 175). More used this classic metaphor often, we are told (19, 189n60), and insisted that the captain must not abandon the ship in a storm but lower the sails and fight through it – a theme represented, he points out (20), by "More" in Book I of *Utopia*

84 Inwood holds that Stoic rules are not fixed but heuristic. See "Rules and Reasoning in Stoic Ethics."

85 See Mitsis' discussion, "Seneca on Reason, Rules, and Moral Development," and Sellars, *The Art of Living*, esp. 75–8, 84.

(Y98/27–8). But what did author Thomas More actually have in mind? Seneca explicitly contrasts – not noted by Wegemer – the pilot's art with the makeup of the wiseman (85.32–40).

> The pilot and the wiseman are two diffe ent kinds of person. The wise man's purpose in conducting his life is not to accomplish at all hazards what he tries, but to do all things rightly; the pilot's purpose, however, is to bring his ship into port at all hazards. The arts are handmaids; they must accomplish what they promise to do. But wisdom is mistress and ruler. The arts render a slave's service to life; wisdom issues the commands. (85.32)

Was Thomas More thinking, like Wegemer, about the "prudence" of the pilot or was he thinking in terms of the Stoic two-dimensional mindset – a mindset that requires something of both Hythloday's abstract principles and "More's" worldly prudence?

Should it turn out that Thomas More's mindset was Stoic-based, Wegemer's thesis regarding the meaning of the book *Utopia* would collapse. It would not be possible to hold that "More's" worldly view – seen in one-dimensional terms – was the author's view and that the author's purpose in representing the outlooks of Hythloday and the Utopians was primarily to contrast jokes, contradictions, and untruths with "More's" (and Thomas More's) worldly *humanitas* – and that "sharp-sighted" readers were expected to come to this conclusion (148, 159, 187).[86]

What follows may give food for thought regarding Thomas More's true outlook and the meaning of *Utopia*.

Seneca on *Otium* and the *Vita Activa:* A Prefiguring of Hythloday and "More" – with a Resolution

Though never recognized, the unique and incontrovertible sources from which Thomas More built the debate between "More" and Hythloday – as well as, we will find, its resolution by the Utopians – are the Stoic Seneca's *De otio* and *De tranquillitate animi.*[87] In a tone entirely worthy

86 On Wegemer's views, see also below, 102 and n9; 103n12; 136n68; 138n72; 209n1; 216n14; 224n39; 272; 280; and 305.

87 Nelson asserts that Plato's *Gorgias*, 483b–486d, "largely mirrors the debate between 'More' and Hythloday" ("Greek *Nonsense* in More's *Utopia*," 41n81) – which is a long stretch.

of Hythloday and "More," these works (which may seem to comprise a unit)[88] swirl around the following themes:

(1) If one looks carefully, one will see not only that the wiseman cannot tolerate the state but that there is absolutely no human state which could tolerate a wiseman (*Ot.* 8.3) (cf. Hythloday's argument).

(2) Contrarily, Athenodorus is sharply criticized for allowing individuals to quickly withdraw from government if they discover chicanery (*Tr.* 3.2–5), and Serenus is admired because he sought high offic in order to be more useful to friends, relatives, countrymen, and all mankind (*Tr.* 1.10) (cf. "More's" argument).

(3) And yet, neither the approach that relates to Hythloday nor the approach that relates to "More," separate from the other, represents virtue (*Tr.* 2.9–10). The wiseman holds that there is no contemplation without action and no action without contemplation (*Ot.* 7.2) (cf. the Polylerites and Utopians, demonstrated in Parts VI–VIII below).[89]

(1) A Prefiguring of Hythloday's Argument

On the one hand, isn't the wiseman unfitted by his very perfection for involvement in the world of affairs – notwithstanding the teachings of Zeno and Chrysippus, the founders of Stoicism? It may be that the wiseman cannot help the state because it is too corrupt (*Ot.* 3.3). To fight against a state dominated by evil would be to no purpose. If the wiseman lacks influence or power or does not have the wealth or rank needed, what would be the point of trying (*Ot.* 6.5)? Take a long look

---

88 Both the beginning and end of *De otio* are missing (leaving eleven pages) and both it and *De tranquillitate animi* (forty-one pages) are dedicated to Annaeus Serenus. The date of neither work has been clearly established. On the issues surrounding *De otio* see Seneca, *De otio, De brevitate vitae*, 1–17. Though Seneca emphasizes in *De otio* that he is a Stoic and therewith a follower of Zeno and Chrysippus and their belief that one must be involved in worldly affairs, he he e questions the possibility of involvement only, it may appear, to detail at length the Stoic answer in *De tranquillitate animi* (and other works). Although Logan states in his introduction to *Utopia* that the two works "make the case for non-involvement" (xxiiin2; 2016 edition, xxn13), no reader of *De tranquillitate animi* would ever come to this conclusion.

89 In drawing out More's "divided consciousness," John Guy in a recent article has contrasted the possible influence of Seneca, who Guy believes advocated (consis - ently) the contemplative life, in *De otio* and other works, with Cicero, who Guy believes (like others) advocated the active life (as distinct from the contemplative) in *De officiis*. See "Thomas More and Tyranny." Neither belief is correct.

at what actually goes on in politics: the lack of good faith and the reversing, except when profitable, of values. Unrestrained ambition and pride, glory achieved in baseness, pretence, show, and masks are everywhere. Democritus laughed unendingly (rather than weep, like Heraclitus) at the folly and ridiculousness of it all (*Tr.* 15.1–3, cf. 11.10–12, 5.1). If the problem is not with the wiseman but with the state, why should not the wiseman retire from public affairs (*Ot.* 6.3)? Before getting himself contaminated it would be better to retreat and live a life of leisure and virtue (*Ot.* 3.4).

On the other hand, what state would even be willing to accept the help of the wiseman? Since what goes on in states – the envy, the sycophancy, the factionalism, the contempt for justice, the inhuman cruelty – are all totally at odds with the wiseman, what state would want to deal with him (*Ot.* 8.2)? In choosing leisure, what diffe ence does it make whether the wiseman's choice is voluntary or because the state does not want him (*Ot.* 8.1)?

It is the implications of these arguments that so disturb Seneca (and, centuries later, Hythloday). If the ideal state can nowhere be found ("nusquam est"),[90] if it is only a dream, and the wiseman has no tools to deal with any existent or previously existent state or obligation, we have a situation in which involvement is preferred but is not in fact possible. Leisure, we must conclude, is a necessity for everyone, non-wise as well as wise (*Ot.* 8.3):

> If anyone says that the best life of all is to sail the sea, and then adds that I must not sail upon a sea where shipwrecks are a common occurrence and there are often sudden storms that sweep the helmsman in an adverse direction, I conclude that this man, although he lauds navigation, really forbids me to launch my ship. (*Ot.* 8.4)

(2) A Prefiguring of "More's" Argument

Serenus, the addressee of *De tranquillitate,* had the right idea. Following the advice of Zeno, Cleanthes, and Chrysippus,[91] he had taken on high office He had taken this step not because of the purple robes, but to be

90 Parrish has seen a possible tie here to Hythloday's view and More's referral to Utopia as "nowhere" in a 3 September 1516 letter to Erasmus. See his "A New Source for More's *Utopia.*"

91 See 17n58 above.

more useful to friends, relatives, countrymen, and all mankind (*Tr.* 1.10; cf. *Ot.* 3.5).[92] Athenodorus (we know little about him) was right in holding that whenever the stated purpose is to help one's countrymen a person should set himself in the very midst of public and individual affairs and become involved (*Tr.* 3.1–2). The discovery that in public affair right is twisted into wrong and that it is not safe to be simple and direct (3.2–5) is not in itself sufficien reason to withdraw to leisure and studies. The wiseman does not whine or complain, he knows that there are problems everywhere, that in one way or another "all life is servitude" (10.4). Although one must sometimes retire when faced with obstacles, any retreat must be gradual, "without surrendering the standards, without surrendering the honor of the soldier" (4.1; cf. *Ot.* 3.5).[93] Then too there are myriad ways in which one can be involved in public affairs. One does not have to be at the top. One does not have to be a general. Virtue is active even in expressions, gestures, the way one walks (*Tr.* 4.2–7).[94]

Non-perfect persons such as Serenus (*Tr.* 11.1), persons suffering waverings and pangs of conscience regarding proper actions, should follow rules (*praecepta*), rules based not on custom but on nature. These rules include looking to one's own nature for guidance in deciding whether to become involved in the world of affaris (6.1–2); choosing for friends those "least bad," avoiding in particular complainers (7.5–6); establishing limits to advancement (10.6); confining wealth to that which is not poverty but close to it (8.9); dressing simply and in accord with one's mode of life (9.1–4). Although there is some danger in speaking frankly, with simplicity, without a mask, this is the course to pursue – in moderation.[95] Living naturally does not mean living carelessly (17.1–2). Neither laugh like Democritus nor cry like Heraclitus at the crass duplicity everywhere evident in the world but calmly accept the way things are (15.2).

---

92 In Book I of *Utopia*, Peter Giles, a man of affairs and worthy of highest honour (43), and "More" criticize Hythloday for not serving friends, relatives, and the public by joining the counsels of some great prince (50/6–12, 52/4–14). Cf. Stobaeus, LS p. 433, W.3.

93 Compare "More's" answer to Hythloday in Book I of *Utopia*: "That's how things go in the commonwealth, and in the councils of princes. If you cannot pluck up bad ideas by the root or cure long-standing evils to your heart's content, you must not therefore abandon the commonwealth. Don't give up the ship in a storm because you cannot hold back the winds" (*Utopia* 97).

94 Cf. *Off.* 1.126.

95 Griffin comments on Seneca's position at the court of N o and shows that Seneca's *De clementia* and De *beneficiis* advise – while recognizing the difficulty – fran advice rather than flatter . See "Political Thought in the Age of Nero."

(3) A Prefiguring of the Polylerites and Utopians, Parts VI–VIII below

The wiseman recognizes that nature has created us for both contemplation and action and, more than this, that the active life is attached to the contemplative. Although contemplation alone may be pleasant and charming, just as, on the other side, action alone may seem quite adequate, the reality is very diffe ent (*Ot.* 6.1). Neither approach, separate from the other, represents virtue. When things do not work out, the person concerned only with public affairs and action suffers from dissatisfaction, boredom, mental vacillations, mourning, melancholy, and wavering; he becomes bitterly jealous of others and desires their ruin (*Tr.* 2.9–10). As for contemplation, it is against nature to reject society (*Tr.* 3.7). Were virtue to consist of leisure without action, it would be "an imperfect and spiritless good" (*Ot.* 6.3). Contemplation should not labour for useless ends (*Tr.* 12.1). Claiming for virtue the entire earth (*Tr.* 4.4), the wiseman holds that there is no contemplation without action and no action without contemplation (*Ot.* 7.2). Among those not wise, the active life may exist without the contemplative, but the active life embodied by the wiseman can represent moral virtue only where contemplation is fully engaged. Although there is a great diffe ence between the chief aim of life and something attached to the chief aim, between, that is, contemplation and action, they are, for the wiseman, two parts of one thing (*Ot.* 5.8). At no time does the wiseman make an either/or choice between the contemplative and the active. By its very nature the mind is active (*Tr.* 2.11).[96] Never retreating before Fortune, the wiseman performs his duties "as a devout and holy man" (11.1–2).

An indispensable and ever-present tool of the wiseman in his dealings with the world are "reservation" clauses:

> Say "I will set sail unless something happens," and "I shall become praetor unless something hinders me," and "My enterprise will be successful unless something interferes." This is why we say that nothing happens to a wiseman contrary to his expectations ... (*Tr.* 12.2–3)

The wiseman is determined to sail and will sail unless events beyond his control make this impossible. Reservation clauses guarantee that he will never be surprised, that nothing will happen to him unexpectedly (*Tr.* 13.3). He knows that the sea is often not calm and

96 The Stoics held that humans ought to choose the rational life over the contemplative alone or practical alone because, states Diogenes Laertius, "a rational being is expressly produced by nature for contemplation and for action" (DL 7.130).

is sometimes swept by great storms (11.7). He knows that everything in life is changeable, that what can happen to one person can happen to anyone (11.8–11). Those who expect nothing but good fortune are bound to experience anguish and unhappiness (11.6). The wiseman is an expert at coping with evil and change, at recognizing and dealing with the uncertainty of events, the possibilities of error, the obstacles that confront him (14.1). Far from restricting or making action impossible, the reservation clause opens up the wiseman. He has no reason not to be involved in public affairs and no reason not to take appropriate action, for he can never fail (*Ben.* 4.4–5).[97] All of which, in effect answers the pessimistic final sentence (*Ot.* 8.4, above, 34) of the incomplete *De otio* manuscript[98] – and remedies therewith Hythloday's argument.

Seneca lived out this Stoic mindset in a very real world. Gifted in both oratory and philosophy, he became tutor to the young Nero around 49 CE and then, after Nero became emperor in 54 CE, principal advisor, writing speeches and influencing appointments.[99] He ended his life, in 65 CE, by committing suicide on the command of Nero.[100]

Late 1504: More's Life-Changing Insights

Unlike his readers, Thomas More had deeply imbibed core Stoic doctrines. *Before Utopia* demonstrates that in late 1504 More's mind was radicalized by the Stoic two-dimensional way of thinking – after reading Erasmus' *De taedio Iesu* and *Enchiridion*. He saw what moderns have not seen, that these books are groundbreaking in that they show – building on the Stoic mindset – that Christianity is not one-dimensional but unitarily two-dimensional.

97 Perhaps the Stoic Marcus Aurelius (emperor 161–80 CE) said it best: "We have the power of acting conditionally and changing: for the mind converts and changes every hindrance to its activity into an aid; and so that which is a hindrance is made a furtherance to an act; and that which is an obstacle on the road helps us on this road" (*Meditations* 5.20).

98 See 33n88 above.

99 See, for perspective, Rawson, "Roman Rulers and the Philosophic Adviser."

100 Although the Stoic is a master at finding deco ous solutions and holding to reservation clauses, martyrdom may be the only resort if things come to a point where his unitary both/and mindset is challenged (*Tr.* 11.1–6, 14.10, 16.3; *Ep.* 95.70–1, 73). (Compare the meaning of More's martyrdom, below, 99n33 and 298n45.) Beginning in 62 CE, following Stoic abstentions from the senate and the resultant threat to the powers that be, being a Stoic became a crime. See Griffin, Seneca *A Philosopher in Politics*, 363.

More was profoundly affected by *De taedio Iesu* and the *Enchiridion* because these works, particularly *De taedio Iesu*, provided answers to issues that had for years tormented him. While it has long been recognized that More as a young person was deeply disturbed by his bodily and mental proclivities and tormented over whether he should commit to things of the world or pursue a religious life, what has never been seen is that Erasmus' youth had been consumed by these very issues – issues that were resolved when he came to see (around 1497) the true, two-dimensional, nature of Stoicism and to relate what he discovered to Christianity. What More learned from Erasmus, by reading his books and then a few months later (in 1505) by working with him, is that Christianity is not an either/or proposition. There is no need for anguish as to whether to join the Carthusians and lead a religious life or wholeheartedly commit to worldly activities, for spirituality and worldliness are two sides of one coin. There is no necessary contradiction between deep involvement in worldly affairs and the contemplative life. More specificall , More learned (1) that natural instincts (including sexual desire) and character traits are ineradicable and inherent to the human condition (Stoic *oikeiosis*), inseparable parts of truth, philosophy, and Christianity, and (2) that worldly involvements do not as such give reason for guilt in that one can adapt to social and political circumstances using a type of prudence and decorum (here philosophical – not rhetorical) that is not evil but entirely Christian.

Not understanding Erasmus' mindset, much less his early writings, scholars have repeatedly contrasted the outlook and personality of Thomas More. Building on the fact that More, unlike Erasmus, early on had political aspirations,[101] J.H. Hexter long ago contended that Thomas More was a worldly, "hard-headed," "open-eyed" realist while Erasmus was "unattached" and, this being the case, merely an idealistic intellectual, comparable to the Platonist Hythloday in *Utopia*.[102] Seeing the diffe ences in this way, scholars have puzzled over the personal relationship of Erasmus and More. If they were so diffe ent, what could explain their friendship? Using a deconstructionist methodology, one biographer has recently sought to take away even their friendship, opinionating that More and Erasmus hardly knew each other and were not really friends.[103] Puzzlement over the abiding friendship of

101 See for example Mermel, "Preparations for a Politic Life," 65.

102 Hexter, *More's Utopia*, 131, 136, 143. Wootton, to give one example, repeats the theme: "As we listen to Hythloday it is Erasmus's voice that we hear." See *Thomas More's "Utopia" with Erasmus' "Sileni Alcibiades,"* 33.

103 Guy, *Thomas More*, 211.

Erasmus and More evaporates once it is seen that it was not just built on shared humanistic interests but had, above all, a deeply philosophical and emotional foundation.

More first worked out his new way of thinking within one year of his January 1505 decision to marry and commit to worldly affairs. Never realized, his rendering of Lucian, published in 1506, develops very consciously and with all determination a Stoic/Christian *honestum/utile* frame of mind. He begins by describing two polar, either/or, perspectives, only to set forth the solution: a unitary both/and, *honestum/utile*, mindset. Also never understood, Erasmus followed up on More's *Lucian* by describing the outlook of More, the real-life person, in unitary both/and, unbending/bending terms, in his introduction (1510) to *The Praise of Folly* (published 1511). What Erasmus then does in composing *The Praise of Folly* is of enormous significance, though again never recognized – notwithstanding that the work is a classic and has been discussed, mainly from rhetorical standpoints, in many books. He silently works out opposite issue after issue the implications of More's transit from an either/or mindset to a unitarily two-dimensional mindset, showing that the latter outlook is epitomized by the person Folly, rightly understood – and by Christ. In *Utopia* (1516), More himself works out this outlook – in very diffe ent, non-European, contexts. The mind that created the either/or debate in Book I between Hythloday and "More" did not debate. He knew the answer before picking up his pen.

Up until late 1504, More had deeply experienced both positions presented in Book I of *Utopia*. His obsession at that time with Carthusian and contemplative ideals relates to Hythloday's rigid absolutism and Platonism. His deep interest, at the same time, in political affairs, humanistic studies, and sex relates to character "More's" advocating of worldly prudence and decorum. The problem had been that he found the two positions contradictory and believed his entire life depended on making a choice – a choice between being a true Christian and not being a true Christian.

Readers have seen Book I as comprising an either/or debate between Hythloday and "More," but what has not been seen is that Book I also sets forth a unitary both/and outlook, an outlook that the Utopians were to develop at greater length. We are presented with a positive and a negative side to Hythloday's outlook (positive in that he unbendingly holds to truth; negative in that he doesn't believe that truth is applicable in the real world) and a positive and a negative side to "More's" outlook (positive in that he sees that truth requires the "indirect" approach; negative in that he doesn't explicitly say that the indirect approach requires absolutes), but we are also shown, particularly with the lengthy discussion resolved by the Polylerites (55–77), that the positive side of Hythloday and the positive side of "More" are actually inseparable. And in Book II the author details, at great effort, precisely how in situation after situation these two types of value unite. In the section on Utopian pleasure philosophy, for example, the author works out, as with his *Lucian* and Erasmus' *Praise of Folly*, Stoic-framed solutions. Step by step he resolves the opposition between Stoic absolutes and Epicurean relativism in terms of the Stoic unitary *honestum/utile* mindset. Here as elsewhere there is nothing of the imaginative and rhetorical "play of spirit" readers have seen. The extensive discussions of Utopian warfare – which readers have found contradictory and Machiavellian – are worked out from the same vantage point. On the abstract side of their minds, the Utopians "utterly loathe" warfare, while on the worldly side they exhibit unrivalled expertise in the tools of war – all held together by a Stoic unitary both/and way of dealing with issues. *Their ways of handling warfare would be impossible lacking their absolute precepts.* Even the Utopian understanding of communism is described and worked out in Stoic terms.

In short, all the evidence indicates that the Utopians were pagans who had mastered, in their own terms, the Stoic *honestum/utile* way of thinking and living – a way of thinking and living that Christianity perfects. Hythloday may talk the talk about Plato, and may even paraphrase him, but the Utopians place Plato – just as had Erasmus in the *Enchiridion* and *The Praise of Folly* – solidly within a Stoic-based frame.

Encapsulation of the Argument of the Book

Detailed analysis of the sources reveals that before late 1504 More's mind was always polarized. He saw Christianity in starkly either/or terms. A choice had to be made between that which is worldly and that which is non-worldly (Part I).

But his outlook was suddenly radicalized upon reading Erasmus' *De taedio Iesu* and *Enchiridion* (published together in 1503) in late 1504 and then within months working with Erasmus directly (Part II).

More's *Lucian* (1506) and his *Utopia* (1516) both espouse – reconciling two seemingly contradictory positions – a Stoic unitary both/and, *honestum/utile*, view of truth and Christianity. Erasmus' introduction (1510) to *The Praise of Folly* pinpoints More's unitarily two-dimensional mindset, while his *Praise of Folly* (1511) works out issue after issue in terms of More's transit from either/or thinking to both/and thinking – showing that this is the path Christianity demands.

In each of these writings, beginning with *Lucian*, there is a singular pattern of thought. This pattern in each instance begins with seemingly contradictory viewpoints, viewpoints in their own ways reflected by Hythloday and "More" (as seen by Hythloday) in Book I of *Utopia* (Part VIII below).

Hythloday's abstract view of truth in Book I of *Utopia* relates to:

a *Cynicus* in *Lucian* (Part III),
b the Democritus side of More the real-life person (Part IV),
c the abstract side of Folly (Part V),
d the *honestum* side of Utopian pleasure philosophy (Part VI), and
e the "utter loathing of war" side of Utopian warfare (Part VII).

"More's" worldly view of truth (as seen by Hythloday) in Book I of *Utopia* relates to:

a *Menippus* in *Lucian* (Part III),
b the "man for all seasons" side of More the real-life person (Part IV),
c the worldly side of Folly (Part V),
d the pleasure (*utile*) side of Utopian pleasure philosophy (Part VI), and
e the expedient and decorous side of Utopian warfare (Part VII).

But in each instance the apparent contradictions are resolved by an actual working out – not by mere words or the forced interjection of a thesis – of a Stoic-based unitary both/and mindset:

a The opposition between *Cynicus* and *Menippus* is resolved by *Philopseudes* (Part III).
b The opposition between Democritus and the "man for all seasons" is resolved by More, the real-life person (Part IV).
c The opposition between the positive (as not the negative) abstract side of folly and the positive (as not the negative) worldly side of folly is resolved by the person Folly (Part V).
d The discussions of Utopian pleasure philosophy in Book II reveal that the *utile* (pleasure) requires the *honestum* and the *honestum* requires the *utile* (Part VI).
e The discussions of Utopian warfare in Book II reveal that Utopian expedient and decorous solutions require the "utter loathing of war" absolute and that the latter requires the former.

Part VIII below will show that even the debate between Hythloday and "More" is actually resolved in that "More," unlike Hythloday, implicitly grasps the two-dimensional Utopian way of thinking.

Clearly, after late 1504 Thomas More was never of "two minds," the standard view (Hexter, Skinner, Logan, et al.). Nor did he see, an alternate view (Nelson), abstract precepts in one-dimensional "Platonist" terms or see, an opposite alternate view (Wegemer), worldly expedience in one-dimensional "Ciceronian" or "Senecan" terms. Stoicism – which prefigu ed, More believed, Christianity – is about the application of two radically diffe ent but inseparable types of value to all the issues of life, no matter how diverse in nature, place, or time, and the Utopians in Book II work this out in a New World context. Against what is so often asserted, Thomas More was himself a Utopian.[104] He was a Utopian in that – far from the meaning of our word "utopian" – the Utopian state is built from a particular philosophical mindset, and it was precisely this mindset, as filled in by Christianity, that More was to transfer two years later to Henry VIII's court.

Themes

Part I ("The Mystery of More's "Either/Or" 1505 Decision: Bodily and Mental Issues before Late 1504") demonstrates with unprecedented evidence – not least being his lectures on Augustine's *City of God* in 1501 – that prior to late 1504 More always saw himself, the world, and Christianity in polar, either/or, terms. He was torn between a desire to join the rigid Carthusian order and lead a contemplative life and a desire to marry, have sex, develop his knowledge of Greek and other humanistic interests, and become fully involved in legal and political affairs. He considered any type of compromise with his one-dimensional Christian ideal a breakdown in faith, jeopardizing one's eternal life.

In seeking to discover what it was about *The City of God* that in 1501 interested More, I evaluate Stapleton's Comments on More's lectures (1588) and show that More was not focused on the theology found in *The City of God* but only on the history and philosophy discussed in the early parts (31 per cent of the work). The statements of Ro Ba (1599) and W.E. Campbell (1949) do not hold. I then work out what More's lectures likely dealt with, that he related Augustine to the tyranny he found in his own world, that of Richard III (1483–5) in particular, and contrasted

104 Hankins repeats (seeing Utopian as equivalent to our word "utopian") the accepted view: More "was, himself, no Utopian." See "Humanism and the Origins of Modern Political Thought," 140.

a Christianity seen as abstract and one-dimensional. Therewith he saw no way to become involved in worldly affairs without becoming contaminated. And he held firmly to Augustine's one-dimensional contention, augmented by monasticism, that the Christian is distinguished from the non-Christian by "love of God extending even to contempt of self."

More's outlook in his translations of Pico in 1504 was also one-dimensional. Of even greater significance is his despairing, either/or, October 1504 letter to John Colet, his spiritual advisor. Without question, More here as earlier accepted Colet's rejection of marriage, the human body, and worldly involvement.

All of which leads to a core question: Did More in January 1505 make an either/or choice in favour of the active life over the contemplative, as is widely believed?

Part II ("More's Radically New, Both/And, Paradigm: Erasmus' *De taedio Iesu* and the *Enchiridion*, 1503") begins by discussing the reasons why it has seemed obvious, not worthy even of comment, that More's January 1505 decision to marry and commit to worldly affairs was unrelated to Erasmus. I then point out that Erasmus' *De taedio Iesu* is from cover to cover a criticism of the either/or, non-worldly/worldly, outlook of More's spiritual advisor, Colet, and that his *Enchiridion* depicts throughout a two-dimensional type of Christianity directly at odds with not only Colet's outlook but also the outlook of More himself, at least through the time of his letter dated October 1504 to Colet. Analysis shows that there is every reason to believe that More first read *De taedio Iesu* and the *Enchiridion*, published together in 1503, between his October letter and his January 1505 marriage.

More would have been astonished and transfixed on learning from *De taedio Iesu* that Christ was not a martyr and that Christ did not try to go beyond his human nature and natural instincts. From the *Enchiridion* he would have learned in addition that Christianity requires a unitary both/and, non-worldly/worldly, mindset – and would have seen example after example of the application of this thinking to real-world situations. I then show that Erasmus' 1519 biography of More supports, though unrecognized, everything deduced regarding More's January 1505 decision. More's mind had been radically transformed. At odds with everything he had previously believed, he now saw himself, the world, and Christianity in unitary both/and – non-worldly/worldly, contemplative/ active – terms.

Part III ("More's *Lucian*, 1506 – and *Utopia*: Teaching Stoic Two-Dimensional Christianity") demonstrates that More's introduction and translations of three of Lucian's dialogues in late 1505 and early

1506 – no more than a year after his decision and while he was working directly with Erasmus – reveal throughout the ways in which his mind had been radicalized. His discussions and translations of *Cynicus* and *Menippus* represent either/or views – his previous outlook – while *Philopseudes*, the last in order and longest, shows that truth is unitarily both/and. There are two ways of thinking about absolute values and two ways of thinking about worldly values. Truth is found only where the valid type of absolute value and the valid type of worldly value are inseparable.

Chapter 1 in Part III contrasts More's 1506 introduction to *Lucian* with both Lucian's text and More's despairing 1504 letter. Detailed also is the tie between More's Stoic two-dimensional conclusion and Cicero's *Tusculan Disputations*. Chapter 2 shows that More rewrites Lucian's *Philopseudes* in Stoic two-dimensional, *honestum/utile*, terms. Those responsible for defiling "truth unadorned" with certain false Saints' Lives include, most prominently, members of the London Carthusians – the very order More before late 1504 had longed to join. Chapter 3 shows that a great number of Lucian dialogues were available to More and that he chose the three dialogues and sequenced them in a certain way in order to illustrate a thesis. Chapter 4 shows that More was modelling Books I–III of *De officiis*. Chapter 5 asks a question: Did the structure, methodology, and meaning of the Lucian work (1506) prefigu e the structure, methodology, and meaning, ten years later, of *Utopia* (1516)?

Part IV ("Thomas More as *Unitarily* 'Democritus' and 'The Man for All Seasons': Erasmus' Preface to *The Praise of Folly*, 1510") shows that Erasmus in his introduction to *The Praise of Folly* does not see More – contrary to both popular and scholarly opinion – as simply a person who could adapt to all sorts of situations. More than "a man for all seasons," as such, Thomas More inseparably – and without contradiction – represents at all times the non-worldly and rigid truth of Democritus (460–370 BCE). In short, Erasmus is set on depicting the real-life More as embodying at one and the same time two opposite types of value, one absolute and unbending and the other eminently bending. Seen in one-dimensional terms, More was *not* "a man for all seasons."

Part V ("A Stoic/Morean *Praise of Folly*, 1511: *The Praise of Folly* Works Out More's Stoic-Framed Transformation") shows that Erasmus' *Praise of Folly*, everywhere considered one of the great works of literature, was actually built from a philosophy and therewith represents throughout the life and outlook of Thomas More. Scholars (most of them found in literature departments) have gone astray in believing that Folly's base thinking is rhetorical and represents a conglomeration of ironical and contradictory theses, a supposition embedded in the conviction that there is no firm foundation to Erasmus' writings or mindset or life, that he vacillated from one viewpoint to another, at ease, as a rhetorician, with inconsistency – and that all this is magnified by *The Praise of Folly*.

There is positive and negative abstract folly and there is positive and negative worldly folly. Folly the person shows that positive abstract folly and positive worldly folly, correctly understood, are one and the same. Hardly noticed by the secondary literature, the abstract and Democritean side of More's personality, as depicted by Erasmus, is paralleled by discussions of Democritus within *The Praise of Folly* itself. Like More, Folly accepts people on equal terms, with all their diversity and foolery, but prudence and flattery can be either positive or negative depending on their relationship to abstract truth. Plato's myth of the cave [*Republic*, 7.514a–520a] is very deliberately turned into a two-dimensional Stoic myth. What is "real" is not just the "form" or "idea" of the good but the everyday realities, however ridiculous, that we see around us. Working out the Stoic unitary both/and mindset, Folly shows us that truth is "truer than truth itself." Epitomizing all this, Christ was "the wisdom of the Father," that which is perfect, yet he inseparably "took on human nature." Thomas More embodies this two-dimensional mindset and so too should other humans.

Part VI ("Utopian Philosophy, 1516: Epicureanism within a Stoic *Honestum/Utile* Frame") shows that the Utopians employ in their philosophy the same framework, methodology, and understanding of Stoicism and Christianity found in More's *Lucian* and Erasmus' *Praise of Folly*. Epicurean pleasure philosophy is at all times reworked within a Stoic *honestum/utile* frame. *Voluptas* is merely an augmentation of *utile*. The Utopians are able to distinguish positive pleasure calculations from negative because – and only because – they hold unbendingly to *honestum*. Reflecting their Stoic mindset, and more immediately *The Praise of Folly*, "happiness," "virtue," "the supreme good," "nature," and "reason" are unitary *voluptas/honestum* words. The Utopians don't just assert that *honestum* and *voluptas* are unitary, they demonstrate that this is the case by working out with all logic, in situation after situation, why this is the reality. Even their communistic lifestyle is explained in eminently Stoic – as not Platonist – terms. What their *honestum/voluptas* mindset lacks is only the infusion of Christ's *honestum/voluptas* teachings.

Part VII ("Utopian Warfare: A Unitary Two-Dimensional Mindset") shows that, in both their warfare games and actual warfare, the Utopians hold unbendingly to an "utter loathing of war" absolute at the same time as they develop, employing the indirect approach, eminently decorous and expedient ways of carrying out war. Contrary to the large and virtually unanimous secondary literature, going back to the nineteenth century, Utopian actions in warfare are in no instance contradictory or evil. Correctly understood, their cunning, stratagem, and ferocity are at all times righteous. Indeed, their clever and brilliant methods of warring would be impossible lacking the absolutes that govern everything they do in life. At the conclusion of Part VII, the Utopian way of thinking and solving problems is compared and contrasted with Machiavelli's *Prince* (composed in 1513).

Part VIII ("What Wiseman Hythloday Did Not Understand") reveals that the ostensible hero of the book, Hythloday, was never, in the author's mind, wise. Although Hythloday well represents the need for truth in all situations, he fails to see what truth entails. In his Book I criticisms of "More" and discussions of the Polylerites, as in his Book II descriptions of the Utopian commonwealth, Hythloday in no instance grasps the two-dimensional, *honestum/utile*, nature of truth – a truth that is workable in all situations and eminently Christian. Seeing truth in one-dimensional terms, Hythloday emphatically and self-righteously rejects "More's" decorous "indirect approach" but fails to observe – like modern scholars – the obvious, that the Polylerites and Utopians in all instances employ the indirect approach – along with unbending precepts. The author's whole purpose in writing the book was to show what is lacking in Hythloday's one-dimensional view of truth – the view he himself held before late 1504. They have assumed that "More's" indirect approach is rhetoric-based and contradicts abstract truth, whereas in fact it is Stoic-based – and as such cannot be separated from absolute and unbending truths.

All of which shows that our word "utopia," derived from More's work, is based on a misunderstanding. The book *Utopia* is not about an ideal state, as such. It is about a mindset and the methodology that flows from this mindset. The book can be considered "utopian" only if we do not agree with the author's conviction that the methodology Utopians employ in solving problems is a methodology that needs to be – and can be – applied everywhere. What the methodology entails are not static solutions to problems but solutions that are in a continual state of flux – as issues and situations change. Solutions valid and workable in the Utopian world are not solutions that are necessarily valid in very diffe ent societies and situations. What does not change is the two-dimensional frame of mind. For Thomas More, the *honestum/utile* mindset and its methodology are not simply the epitome of realism, they frame Christianity. In 1518 Thomas More was to transfer this unitary both/and, unbending/bending, way of thinking directly to the court of Henry VIII.

PART I

The Mystery of More's "Either/Or" 1505 Decision: Bodily and Mental Issues before Late 1504

At the time Erasmus was writing *De taedio Iesu* and the *Enchiridion* (1499–1503), More was torn between two polar alternatives: Should he take a Christian route and join the most rigid of monastic orders or should he commit to marriage and involvement in worldly affairs? What we know is that in January 1505 he married and became ever more immersed in legal, political, and humanistic activities. Scholars have not imagined that More's thinking at the time, much less his life-changing decision, had anything to do with Erasmus or any views of Erasmus. But was this actually the case? And was it the case, as everywhere believed, that More's thinking even at the time of his decision was ambivalent, that in deciding to marry he made a choice between two polar, worldly/non-worldly, alternatives?

More's 1505 decision clearly marked a decisive turning point in his life, but what kind of thinking had led him to make this decision and what was the nature of the decision? The secondary literature shows us a mind that had long vacillated between two poles of thought, worldly and otherworldly, and that in making his decision he chose one pole over the other. What is striking is that this interpretation, which has seemed so obvious, ties in with the way the book *Utopia*, written ten years later (1515), is interpreted. *Utopia* vacillates, it is held, between two opposed views, and here too one view, this time not the worldly but the abstruse and rigid, ultimately trumps the other. Vacillations or contradictions are also seen in More's joining the court of Henry VIII in 1518, two years after *Utopia* was published. In accord with the pattern, More's martyrdom in 1535 was yet again preceded, we are told, by a mental swing – this time to the non-worldly pole. But are these interpretations viable?

1 Religion, Law, and Humanism

The broad outlines of More's life before his 1505 decision seem clear. He had indeed been considering an ascetic life for himself. Noted earlier, Thomas Stapleton reports in a biography published in 1588 that in his youth More "wore a hair-shirt, and slept on the ground or on bare boards with perhaps a log of wood as his pillow. At the most he took four or five hours' sleep, and he was frequent in watchings and fastings."[1] According to William Roper, More's son-in-law, from 1500 to 1504, when More would have been twenty-two through twenty-six, he lived without vow in the harshly strict Carthusian Charterhouse.[2] His desire was to become a monk or, according to one account, a priest. By January 1505, however, a new reality had emerged. For at this time More married and gave up his monastic and priestly goals. Sex played a major role in his decision. In deciding to marry he acknowledged that he needed an outlet for his sexual desires. As Stapleton words it, More chose marriage because he "feared, even with the help of his practices of penance, that he would not be able to conquer the temptations of the flesh that come to a man in the vigor and a dor of youth."[3]

And yet many aspects of More's personality and previous life seem incompatible with the Charterhouse. Of major significance, he had already spent considerable time around official at the highest levels of government. From 1490 to 1492, between the ages of twelve and fourteen, he had served as a page in the household of John Morton, Lord Chancellor of England 1487–1500, Archbishop of Canterbury 1486–1500, Cardinal 1493–1500. Behind the king, Henry VII, Morton was the most important person in England. He was deeply involved in the intrigues of court and worldly affairs generally. Morton's personality, including, most importantly, his ability to make the best of all situations, had a great impact on young More – evidenced most of all by Book I of *Utopia* and the *History of King Richard III* (c. 1513–18).

Before 1505 More had also spent many years studying the common law. After a stint at Oxford, 1492–4, sponsored by Morton, he returned to London in 1494, studying law at New Inn and then in 1496 at Lincoln's Inn. His father, whom he always venerated, was a senior member of the latter. In 1501 he was "called to the bar." Related to this training in law was an interest in politics. According to Roper's account, More was

1 Stapleton, *Life*, 8. Cresacre More states something very similar in his *The Life and Death of Sir Thomas Moore* (London, 1627), 27.

2 Roper, *The Life of Sir Thomas More*, 198. Cf. Harpsfield, *The Life and Death of Sr Thomas Moore*, 62.

3 Stapleton, *Life*, 8.

a member of the Parliament of January–March 1504.[4] If this is true, we must conclude that More's involvement in politics preceded by at least a year his decision to marry and give up his monastic goals.

Also long standing was a deep interest in humanism, the study of grammar, rhetoric, history, poetry, and moral philosophy. First-year students at Oxford studied not only logic, a subject at the core of scholastic thought, but grammar and rhetoric, and we can well believe that the fifteen-year-old More took a great interest in the latter subjects. In the years that followed, he relished, like so many other humanists, writing poems. Particularly indicative of a dedication to humanistic interests was his study of Greek. Importantly, his teachers had all studied in Italy, the fountainhead of Renaissance humanism. For a period prior to 1500, William Grocyn (d. 1519) was his tutor. Grocyn had lived and studied in Italy from 1488 to 1491 and in 1496 became rector of the Church of St Lawrence Jewry in London. By 1500 More was working on Greek with Thomas Linacre (d. 1524). Linacre had lived in Italy from 1487 to 1499, studying Greek and Latin in Florence and obtaining a medical degree from the University of Padua. Later he was to become physician to Henry VIII (1509) and would be famous for his translations of the Greek physician Galen. More and William Lily (d. 1522), who had lived in Italy (c. 1488–92), made rival versions of eighteen epigrams, probably around 1503, mainly from the *Greek Anthology*.[5] More's epigrams, along with others he later wrote, were to be published with the March 1518 Basel edition of *Utopia*. Although Colet was not knowledgeable in Greek, his moral teachings, exemplary behaviour, and opposition to scholastic ways of reading the Bible were very much a part of More's early mental world. Colet was an Oxford doctor, a traveller in Italy from 1492 to 1995, a Neoplatonist, and he later, inspired by humanistic educational methods, founded St Paul's School. His lectures on St Paul's epistle to the Romans, around 1497, and his sermons and writings up until his death in 1519 had a considerable impact on contemporaries.[6]

More (born 1478) met Erasmus, approximately ten years his senior (born 1466 or 1469?), when Erasmus first visited England in the summer of 1499 (staying until January 1500). One thing we know about the visit is that More took Erasmus to meet the royal children, including the

---

4 Roper, *Life*, 199.

5 An edition of the *Greek Anthology*, in Greek (as revised by Planudes in 1299), was published in Florence in 1494, edited by Janus Lascaris.

6 On the dating of Colet's lectures and writings, see Jonathan Arnold, "Humanist Ecclesiology in Theory"; also Gleason, *John Colet*, 67–92. Arnold believes Colet's lectures on 1 Corinthians and Romans, his treatise on the Mystical Body of Christ, his commentary on Romans 1–5, and his letter to Radulphus were written from 1496 to 1505.

future Henry VIII, then aged eight.[7] The first surviving letter is that of Erasmus to More, dated 28 October 1499. Other letters that do not survive, going both ways, preceded this one. In his October letter, Erasmus refers to More as "sweetest Thomas [mellitissime Thoma]."[8] More thought of Erasmus in a similar way. Even in 1532, when their lives had long taken radically divergent paths, he refers ten times, in response to a taunt, to Erasmus as "my derlynge."[9] In a 1506 letter, Erasmus remembers that Richard Whitford, a mutual friend, used to describe Erasmus and More "as so similar in mind, character, outlook and pursuits that no pair of twins on earth could be more alike."[10]

On Erasmus' second visit to England, summer of 1505 to June 1506, shortly after More's marriage, he and More prepared and published translations from Greek into Latin of some of Lucian's dialogues. In addition, each prepared a *declamatio* in response to Lucian's "Tyrannicida." In 1509 Erasmus wrote *The Praise of Folly* in More's house in Bucklersbury, London. The work is dedicated to More, and the title, *Moriae encomium*, is a play on More's name – *moria* being the Greek word for folly. Erasmus lived with More for many weeks, possibly much of the time, between the summer of 1509 and the spring of 1511 and remained in England, lecturing at Cambridge, until 1514.[11] In December 1516 he edited (along with Peter Giles) and saw through the press, in Louvain, More's *Utopia*.

Observance of harsh religious practices at the same time as involvement in exciting political, legal, and intellectual matters might seem, in itself, to require a disturbed soul. However this may be, considerable evidence indicates that before 1505 More was indeed very troubled about his purposes in life. As Harpsfield states in his biography of 1557, More had serious doubts as to which of two contrary lives he should lead. Should he lead a worldly life or become a monk and take on a very strict and regulated life or at minimum become a priest?[12] Added to More's quandary was tension with his father. A lawyer and a person deeply involved in governmental affairs, his father was unhappy

---

7 *Ep.* 1341A (1523). Allen 1, 6/4–28, CWE 9, 299–300/172–96.

8 *Ep.* 114 (October 1499). Allen 1, 266/8.

9 More, *The Confutation of Tyndale's Answer*, CWM 8, Pt. 1, 177/10–179/17. On the context see Stewart, "The Trouble with English Humanism."

10 *Ep.* 191. Allen 1, 423/28–32, CWE 2, 113/38–9.

11 Although Erasmus was in England during this period, there is a curious lacuna in the records of his activities. Sowards surmises that Erasmus destroyed his letters because of bitter comments in them regarding Pope Julius II. See "The Two Lost Years of Erasmus."

12 Harpsfield, *Life*, 62.

because More's religious and humanistic interests threatened to take away the legal career that he had mapped out for him.[13]

In January 1505, however, More married and became fully involved in the active life. His legal and governmental career took off. His advice was much sought after in private legal practice and as a result he was able to command substantial fees.[14] In 1507 he became financial accountant for Lincoln's Inn – followed by various honours at this Inn.[15] He became under-sheriff of London in 1510, commissioner of sewers in 1514, and royal commissioner to Flanders in 1515 – on which mission he wrote the Discourse on the Utopian state (Book II of *Utopia*). In 1518 he joined Henry VIII's court.

Harpsfield and Stapleton were perplexed by More's 1505 decision. Since both considered the contemplative life superior to the active, they found it necessary to find excuses and rationalizations for More's choice. Harpsfield points out that no one is bound to pursue the contemplative life and suggests, in addition, that God himself wanted More to take the worldly path for the good of his soul and the state of England.[16] Stapleton thinks it possible that More was not able to aspire to the more perfect state of life because (here not mentioning his sexual drives) monasticism was then in a bad state or because God had planned for him to lead a lay life of great sanctity.[17]

Can we find more insightful explanations for the choice? Can we better understand the nature of the decision? The place to begin is with More's intellectual output before his marriage, focusing in particular on his lectures on *The City of God*, his translation of *The Life of John Picus*, and a 1504 letter to John Colet.

2 The Lectures on Augustine's *City of God* (c. 1501)

Erasmus, Roper, Harpsfield, and Stapleton all note that More gave lectures on Augustine's *City of God* (written 413–26).[18] The lectures took place in the Church of St Lawrence Jewry, at the invitation of Grocyn, it seems, around 1501. They were said to be excitedly attended and much

---

13 Erasmus, *Ep.* 999, to Ulrich von Hutten, 23 July 1519 – a short biography of More. Allen 4, 13/12–23, CWE 7, 19/16–25.

14 Erasmus, *Ep.* 999. Allen 4, 17/150–6, CWE 7, 21/160–7.

15 Guy, *The Public Career of Sir Thomas More*, 4–5.

16 Harpsfield, *Life*, 62.

17 Stapleton, *Life*, 8–9.

18 Erasmus, *Ep.* 999. Allen 4, 17/156–60, CWE 7, 21/168–72; Roper, *Life*, 198; Harpsfield, *Life*, 59–60; Stapleton, *Life*, 7–8.

esteemed by the most important and most learned men of London,[19] favoured even over lectures given concurrently by Grocyn at St Paul's on Dionysius the Areopagite (a Neoplatonist wrongly thought to have been converted by St Paul). More's youth – he was around twenty-three – added to the marvel. But what were these lectures about? In the first place they were almost certainly about two polarities, the Earthly City and the Heavenly City. The central purpose of *The City of God* was to diffe entiate, on an immense scale, between these two cities:

> Two cities, then, have been created by two loves: that is, the earthly by love of self extending even to contempt of God, and the heavenly by love of God extending to contempt of self. The one, therefore, glories in itself, the other in the Lord; the one seeks glory from men, the other finds its highest glory in God, the Witness of our conscience. (14.28)

While those in the earthly city deny their dependence on God, those with heaven as their goal take their cue at all times from God. The division between the two cities did not in fact begin with the coming of Christ or even with Moses but has been evident throughout all human history. Angels, signs, and symbols proclaimed the mystery of eternal life from the beginning (7.32). Throughout history the story of Cain and Abel, two irreconcilable alternatives, has played itself out over and over (15.1, 17, 18). Cain was the first-born of Adam and Abel the second-born. The worldly successful Cain, founder of the earthly city, slew his brother Abel because of envy. He was envious not because Abel wanted worldly things but because Abel was a believer in the City of God. While those who belong to the earthly city will reap eternal punishment with the devil, those who belong to the heavenly city will reap eternal life.

Although the book is about the contrast between the two cities, it is also about what it means for a Christian to live in the world. Most of the advantages and disadvantages of worldly living are shared by good men and bad. The two groups hold in common many worldly goals. All men, for example, desire worldly peace (19.12). Members of both cities seek security by organizing society in such a way as to attain things that are helpful in life. As long as God's truth is not an issue, there is little diffe ence in the worldly goals of Christians and pagans. Both groups seek those things which are either necessary for life or make life less burdensome. Christians will even go to war alongside the reprobate to attain and enjoy earthly goods (15.4). But virtue and vice are not at all the same

19 Baker-Smith gives a provisional list of those who might have been present and believes the lectures speak to "a native tradition of lay piety." See "Who Went to Thomas More's Lectures on St. Augustine's *De Civitate Dei*."

(1.8). Individuals belonging to the two types of cities have entirely different motivations. With regard to peace, therefore, members of the City of God have a radically diffe ent perspective. They know that real peace is found only in the City of God. They know that even where there is order and respect and "that virtue which everywhere gives everyone his due," what is due to God is not considered (19.21). True justice is found only in the commonwealth of Christ (2.21). Consequently, they enter into worldly affairs "like captives and strangers" and "only because they must" (19.17). Their overriding goal is eternal peace (19.14). Happiness in this life without hope of that which is beyond is a false happiness (19.20).

Considering that the lectures were given at or near the beginning of More's association with the Charterhouse, there is reason to believe that he was greatly impressed by the dichotomy between the two cities and by the fact that the heavenly city entailed "love of God extending to contempt of self." Struggling to figu e out whether he wanted to become involved in worldly affairs or join the Charterhouse, young More was assuredly drawn to this book because it addressed in its own way the two sides of his concerns.

That More had not focused on odd particulars but the basic either/or frame of the work and what it means to be a Christian within this context is indicated not only by the nature of the work and his own needs but also by the manner in which he read it. What we know with some certainty is that he did not read the work through scholastic binoculars. He had little background or interest in the logical methods of scholastics. Humanists such as himself were interested in reading and investigating sources in a literary and contextual manner, while scholastics minutely dissected and placed statements of a host of authors in logical contexts for and against particular points. John Colet, More's older friend and spiritual mentor, learned theologian, humanist, and Neoplatonist, had already by 1497 challenged tradition by reading the Pauline Epistles in a non-scholastic, straightforward, literary manner.[20] Colet disdained Thomas Aquinas' writings in particular, claiming that Aquinas had not only arrogantly and rashly defined things but had corrupted the whole of Christ's teachings with a worldly philosophy – referring, it appears, to Aquinas' use of Aristotle and the intricate pro and con scholastic method.[21] Although Italian humanists had sometimes seen value in

20 Erasmus, *Ep.* 108. Allen 1, 247–8/64–74, CWE 1, 204/74–82.

21 Erasmus, *Ep.* 1211 to Justus Jonas, 13 June 1521. Allen 4, 520/425–41, CWE 8, 238–9/467–83. For an example of what Colet was objecting to, see Aquinas' use of Augustine's "two cities" statement quoted above (from *The City of God* 14.28) in a complex pro and con debate as to "Whether an Angel by Natural Love Loves God More than He Loves Himself?" (*ST* I, q.60, a.5).

scholastic philosophy, there is no reason to believe that any of this was reflected in More's lectures. Not only were bows to scholasticism out of sync with his immediate environment, but he also expresses at length utter contempt for Peter of Spain and modern "logic-choppers" in his letter to Martin Dorp[22] and in his *Utopia* (Y159/20–35), both written in 1515. There is every reason to believe, therefore, that More, like predecessors such as Petrarch (d. 1374), was deeply cognizant of the fact that Augustine's method of writing was at the opposite pole from scholastic methodologies.[23] And he would have related to Augustine's training in grammar and rhetoric the fact that, unlike scholastics, with their rooting in Aristotle and logic, Augustine admired above all philosophies the one-dimensional outlook provided by Platonism, most especially Neoplatonism. In short, More would have been acutely aware of the larger either/or parameters of *The City of God*.

Stapleton's Comments: History and Philosophy, Not Theology

Granting that More focused on Augustine's either/or frame, what was it within this frame that most interested him? Researchers appear to have passed over evidence that allows us to greatly limit More's interests. Consider Stapleton's comments in his biography, published in 1588:

> He [More] did not treat this great work from the theological point of view, but from the standpoint of history and philosophy; and indeed the earlier books of St Augustine's work deal with these two subjects almost exclusively.[24]

Analysing closely, we can see here (1) what subjects More was concerned with, (2) what subject he was not concerned with, (3) what parts of the work he concentrated on, (4) the part he did not concentrate on, and (5) that his interests were two-pronged.

Initially, however, these comments may seem puzzling. The first part of the statement may seem puzzling because Augustine never separated his theological views from his discussions of history and philosophy.

22 CWM 15, 1–127, esp. 25–41.

23 On Petrarch's use of *The City of God* to combat scholasticism, see Quillen, *Rereading the Renaissance*, 166–9 passim.

24 Stapleton, *Life*, 7–8. "Eodem etiam tempore Londini in Ecclesia D. Laurentii Augustinum de civitate Dei publice docuit, non quidem ejus operas theologica discutiens, sed philosophica tantum atque historica, qualia sunt priorum ejus Operis librorum sola fere argumenta" See Stapleton, *Vita Thomae Mori*, 6.

Indeed his extensive discussions of history and philosophy are all for the purpose of divulging his views regarding the Christian religion and theology. The second part may seem puzzling because Stapleton contends that the early books of the work deal almost exclusively with history and philosophy. The later books also depend on discussions of history, and philosophy plays a significant role. If the earlier books are not clearly distinctive, how can Stapleton justly contend that More dealt with these books "almost exclusively"?

In fact, the earlier books are clearly separable from the later books. Augustine himself saw the work as consisting of two parts (as at 10.32). Of twenty-two books, he considered Books 1–10 the first part and Books 11–22 the second. While the first part is polemical, the second attempts to resolve abstruse theological issues. Against pagan charges to the contrary, the first part contends that Christianity had nothing to do with the fall of Rome in 410 and, at the same time, contrasts the one true religion with the many Roman religions and philosophies. The second part discusses in order the origin, development, and ends of the City of God. Throughout, the second part expands on statements found in scripture, beginning with Genesis. As Augustine states at the beginning of Book 11, "The City of God of which we speak is that to which the Scriptures bear witness." Accordingly, Part II is all about the exegesis of scripture, the theological point of view that Stapleton says More was not concerned with.

Knowing that More did not delve into Part II and Augustine's theological discussions of the origin, development, and ends of the City of God is important in that it greatly narrows the parameters of More's lectures. We will also see below that he almost certainly was not concerned with Books 6 and 7 of Part I. Spacewise, this means that he focused on only 31 per cent of the work. Commentators have long imagined that he took as his domain the entire work and that he was thinking as a theologian as well as a historian and philosopher – or, if they have noted Stapleton's statement, they have made little of it. In his *The Lyfe of Syr Thomas More* (completed 1599), for example, Ro Ba simply read into More's lectures Part II of *The City of God*. "More in his reading proved him selfe a divine, a philosopher [and] historian; for he must be furnished with these arts that will read and expound these books of St. Augustines as he did."[25] W.E. Campbell, among more recent authors, states that More gave listeners "a lesson in divinity."[26] Not being able to see what in particular interested More about *The City of God*, readers have not been able to

25 Ro Ba, *The Lyfe of Syr Thomas More*, 23.
26 Campbell, *Erasmus, Tyndale and More*, 81.

consider what in this massive work More studied and what might have been his deeper motivations in giving the lectures.

The Meaning of "History" and of "Philosophy"

Regarding Part I and the material that More did focus on, according to Stapleton, it is important to consider again the fact that Augustine very consciously separates Books 1–5 from Books 6–10 (as at 10.32). Books 1–5 detail the ineffectiveness of the Roman gods in worldly affairs and the inadequacies of the Roman search for glory and dominum – vis-à-vis Christianity. They show us that Roman history, however horrible or virtuous, has always lacked a higher purpose. Pagans may be concerned with bettering worldly affairs, but what they have not seen is what it takes to win eternal life. Books 6–10 focus not on social and political matters but on philosophy. They detail the ineffectiveness of the Roman gods as a goal of the afterlife and likewise the limitations of even the most admirable philosophic thought – vis-à-vis Christianity. While Books 6 and 7 centre on the falsities of Roman mythical and civic religions, Books 8–10 reveal that the highest philosophies, most particularly Plato's, have anticipated Christianity in many of their theses but nonetheless lack the essential core, Christ.

All of this allows us to see precisely what "history" and what "philosophy" More's lectures dealt with. More was interested in *The City of God* from two standpoints. He was interested in "history" (Books 1–5) and he was interested in "philosophy" (Books 8–10). Contrary to what could be imagined and has been imagined, the "history" and "philosophy" Stapleton refers to are not found in the same books. More was interested in two distinct subjects, history and philosophy. Stapleton does not state or imply that More was interested in "the philosophy of history." There is no support, therefore, for T.E. Bridgett's assertion that More's lectures were about "history and Divine philosophy of history."[27] The "philosophy" that Stapleton sees More focusing on was the academic philosophy found in Books 8–10. What is discussed in these books is not a philosophy of history but the relation of various ancient philosophies to Christianity. And when More focused on history he was not, again, thinking about history as philosophy or theology but about Roman history and the relationships to Christianity.

27 Bridgett, *Life and Writings of Sir Thomas More*, 23. Nor, to give a more recent example, does any evidence support Richard Sylvester's statement that More got "his philosophy of history" (equated with a "first vision of an harmoniously o dered society") from *The City of God*. See CWM 2, lxxxii.

Stapleton's Credibility

There is every reason to consider Stapleton's statements knowledgeable and eminently believable. Stapleton's forte was theology and *not* history or philosophy. Unless Stapleton had had reason for making such a distinction, he would not have pointed out that More, unlike himself, did not take up theology. Stapleton was a Catholic in exile, beginning in 1563, and he, unlike his hero, had had a very solid training in scholastic modes of argument and was at ease with a plethora of medieval and Renaissance theologians.[28] He had been a professor of theology at Louvain and Douai since 1571 and had written weighty, scholastically rooted tomes against Calvin, Luther, and Protestantism.[29] In 1590, Philip II made him Professor of Scripture at Louvain. Not only was Stapleton's interpretation not self-motivated, he had the expertise, unlike lesser intellects, to appreciate and understand exactly what More concentrated on in his lectures. And Stapleton obviously knew much about St Augustine. In his writings he scolded his opponents for their over-simplified use of Augustine[30] and even referred at times directly to *The City of God*.[31] Not unrelated to his interpretation, we should note the plethora of sources available to him. Not only did he have at hand the biographies of Erasmus, Roper, and Harpsfield but he was also in contact with other exiles who knew More and had lived in or around More's household. And he is the singular source for some letters written by More.

More's Theological Interests and Abilities in 1501

Crucially important, Stapleton's account agrees with what we know about More's mind, most especially his 1501 mind. Contrast in this regard Harpsfield's interpretation of the lectures. Harpsfield was impressed by the difficult of *The City of God* and the fact that only those expert in both divinity and profane knowledge can profitably study it.[32] Lacking Stapleton's intellectual acumen, he may well have referred to the difficult of the work because he himself had little grasp of what

28 See O'Connell, *Thomas Stapleton and the Counter Reformation*, 78–81. A perusal of Schutzeichel's *Wesen und Gegenstand der kirchlichen Lehrautorität nach Thomas Stapleton* makes plain Stapleton's ease with both Augustine and scholastic sources.

29 Stapleton, *Principiorum fidei doctrinalium demonstratio methodica* (1578) and *De universa justificationis doctrina hodie controversa* (1582). He also published a translation of Venerable Bede's (d. 735) *A History of the Church of England* (Antwerp 1565).

30 O'Connell, *Thomas Stapleton*, 101–2.

31 O'Connell, *Thomas Stapleton*, 79n47.

32 Harpsfield, *Life*, 59.

was contained in it. However that may be, in imagining that More was the equal or more of doctors of divinity, his thinking is at odds with the evidence. More had spent years studying the intricacies of law, not scholastic theology. Outside of law, what had inspired him was humanistic studies. Nor was he seriously interested in scholastic theology as such. There is good reason why he was not inclined to delve into specific arguments found in Part II of *The City of God*. He was interested in the history and the philosophy, but only tangentially interested in the theology (as distinct from the larger two-cities theme). Arguing from scripture, Part II takes up multitudes of abstruse issues, such as "Whether the bodies of women will retain their sex in the resurrection" (22.17).

It is possible that Harpsfield was influenced by a statement in Erasmus' short 1519 biography of More. Lauding More's extempore speaking abilities, Erasmus states that "In disputations nothing more acute can be imagined, so that he has often taken on even the most eminent theologians in their own field and been almost too much for them."[33] What does this statement really tell us? Although Erasmus was not thinking here of More's youth, much less his lectures on *The City of God*, did he imagine that More had acquired a vast knowledge of scholastic theology? Richard Pace, another friend of More (and Erasmus), gives a similar description, dated about the time *Utopia* was composed, of More's abilities.[34] That More could shrewdly dissect and ridicule the logicizing of *modernista* theologians cannot be questioned. Pace shows that More had this ability even as a boy ("puer"), and More exemplifies the ability, we can see, in his lengthy 1515 letter to Martin Dorp.[35] And yet there is no reason to believe that More's knowledge of scholastic theology was anywhere near that of the more learned theologians – and even less so, not discounting his precocity, in 1501.

All of which is not to say that More was not deeply interested in certain theological issues and theology broadly considered. In his later polemical works he presents the fathers of the church, Augustine being a favourite, as foils to Protestant doctrines.[36] But in 1501 this was far away. Nor is there evidence that he knew about or was interested in the debate between his mentor Colet and Erasmus at Oxford in 1499 – a key reason surely was that Erasmus' radical development and rewriting of that debate in *De taedio Iesu*, published only in 1503, had not come to his attention.

---

33 Erasmus, *Ep.* 999. Allen 4, 21/265–7, CWE 7, 24/289–92.

34 See Pace, *De fructu qui ex doctrina percipitur*, 103–7 and Surtz, "Richard Pace's Sketch of Thomas More."

35 CWM 15, 50/1–54/13 passim.

36 See Marius, "Thomas More and the Early Church Fathers."

The History More Studied

Looking more closely at the history More studied, what stands out, first, is the ending of the short preface to Book 1 of *The City of God*. The earthly city is "that city which, when it seeks mastery, is itself mastered by the lust for mastery even though all the nations serve it." The rise of Rome came about through lust for domination (3.14) and desire for material reward and glory (5.12–20). Rome, like other empires and kingdoms, was created by pride, plunder, and treachery (5.18). What is called robbery elsewhere was here called justice (4.4) (cf. Cicero, *Rep.* 3.14). True justice is found not in the Roman state but only in the commonwealth of Christ (2.21). The desire for liberty and human praise has resulted in many admirable deeds among the Romans, but true virtue is found only in "the most glorious city of God" (5.18). Terrible calamities have happened to Rome in the ages before the arrival of Christianity. War, disease, captivity, killings, and great suffering have occurred over and over, yet in no instance were the Roman gods a help (Books 2 and 3). Nevertheless, pagans want to impute the destruction of Rome in 410 (immediately before Augustine wrote *The City of God*) to Christ. In fact it was God's clemency, the fact that the invaders had been touched by Christianity, that moderated the ruin of Rome (1.34). Nothing happens without God's providence, but the empire would have been very different had there existed worship and faith in the true God (4.28). Those who focus on heaven hold earthly goods in contempt (5.18). This being the case, they do not see life as the search for pleasure, unlike others, but make use of earthly goods modestly, soberly, and with godliness. They know that they are only pilgrims (1.29–30). The conclusion to Book 5 considers whether or not good men who have the skill to rule should also have the power (5.19). That they should is demonstrated by the behaviour of the Christian emperors Constantine I (306–37 CE) and Theodosius (379–95 CE). Virtuous and pious, they did not rule from a love of power, or to gratify their own enmity, or out of a craving for worldly glory, but from a sense of duty. They were slow to punish and often demonstrated mercy (5.24–6).

The Philosophy More Studied

Although Book 1 mentions in passing that the greatest philosophers agree with Christianity regarding the immortality of the soul and providence (1.36), it is Books 8–10 that discuss the contributions of philosophy to religion and the diffe ences with Christianity. Books 6 and 7 discuss at length the shortcomings of the theologies described by Varro (116–27 BCE), most especially the mythical theologies held to by common people and the civil theologies held to by priests. Book 8 centres on Plato. Platonist theology is preferable to that of all other philosophers. More than any other philosopher, Plato anticipated many precepts of Christianity. "Plato said the wiseman is an imitator, knower and lover of this God, and is blessed by participation in Him" and the Platonists "have said that the true God is the author of all things, the illuminator of truth, and the giver of happiness" (8.5). Unlike the natural philosophers, such as Thales and Epicurus, the Platonists saw that God is not a body and diffe entiated that which is immutable from the mutable. In Book 9 Augustine discusses the soul and mental disturbances as seen not only by Platonists such as Plotinus (d. 270) and Porphry (d. 305) (he made no distinction between Neoplatonists and Plato) but also by Peripatetics (Aristotelians) and Stoics.[37] He also considers at length the nature and place of the demons that are alleged by some philosophers to be mediators between man and the gods. Christianity differs, Book 10 shows, in the incarnation. The invisible God has made himself visible (10.13). Christ, beyond Platonism, is the mediator between humans and God (10.20).

The History That Surrounded More: Richard III, Morton, and English Law

Compare the history that Augustine saw with the history that was close to More's experience and concerns. We know from Erasmus that even at a young age More had conceived a hatred of tyranny and a love of equality.[38] We know also that by 1501 More had spent seven years studying English law. This is significant, for one thing, because it relates to his hatred of tyranny. As one biographer surmises, the most important thing English law taught More was that kings are limited in the power they may exercise justly.[39] And More's earliest political actions were to be in full accord with this outlook. Roper describes at some length how More ran afoul of Henry VII at the beginning of 1504.[40] As a member of the Parliament of January–March 1504, More argued so well against Henry's exorbitant taxation demands that these demands were entirely denied. On hearing that "a beardless boy had

37 Cicero was a significant sou ce for Augustine's view of Plato (leaving aside the *Timaeus*) and the Stoics. See van Oort, *Jerusalem and Babylon*, 242.

38 *Ep.* 999. Allen 4, 15/87–91, 21/253–4, CWE 7, 18/88–92, 23/275–7.

39 Marius, *Thomas More*, 33. Sir John Fortescue detailed the workings and ideals of the Inns of Court in his *De laudibus legum anglie*, written around 1470.

40 Roper, *Life*, 199–200.

disappointed all his purpose," the king became indignant and set on revenge. One result was that More's father was imprisoned in the Tower until such time as he could come up with a hundred-pound fine. More was himself in fear of his life and would have fled the realm, according to Roper, had not the king died. At the accession of Henry VIII in 1509, More not only praised the new king in a long poem but bitterly attacked what he saw, like many others, as Henry VII's tyrannical taxation policies.[41]

According to Erasmus, it was More, not himself, who suggested in 1505 that he and More write competing declamations in response to Lucian's "Tyrannicida."[42] In his declamation, More depicted the tyrant as "cruel and violent by nature," a person who "trampled on the laws of men, scorned those of the gods, and had no respect for life," a person "puffed up by pride, driven by the lust of power, impelled by greed, provoked by thirst for fame." "Why mention heirs to me? Why remind me of laws in a tyranny? They are laws in name only."[43] Even More's Latin poems, some of which predate the 1501 lectures,[44] strongly attest to a deeply rooted hatred of tyranny. Repeatedly he chose to translate, epigrammatically, poems from the *Greek Anthology* which dwell on the despicable nature of tyrants, the contrast between their pretensions and reality, and what it is that separates good and bad rulers.[45] While More's epigrams on kingship express common themes (though the subject is entirely original for an epigrammatist),[46] what comes out strongly is the danger posed by contemporary tyrants. Take, for example, the epigram on the joy that cruelly persecuted subjects take in the death of a tyrant. According to the modern editors, the theme "is expressed with such bitter and sardonic hatred as to leave no doubt that More is here giving vent to his own emotions."[47]

---

41 CWM 3, Pt. 2, 101–3.

42 *Ep.* 191. Allen 1, 422/3, CWE 2, 112/5–6.

43 CWM 3, Pt. 1, 94–127 at 101 and 105. Considering the other evidence available, Craig R. Thompson's contention that More's focus on tyranny in his declamation was simply a literary exercise is untenable (CWM 3, xxiii, xxxix). Robert P. Adams demonstrated long ago that More was utterly serious in condemning tyranny. See *The Better Part of Valor*, 35–6. Dermont Fenlon relates the theme to More's entire life, including his martyrdom, in "Thomas More and Tyranny."

44 Erasmus states that More wrote many of the poems as a boy. "Epigrammata lusit adolescens admodum ac pleraque puer." See *Ep.* 635. Allen 3, 57/9–10. Some of the poems, however, are as late as 1520.

45 On tyranny, see Epigrams 80, 110, 114, 120, 121, 142, 162, 198, 201, 227, 238, and 243, in CWM 3, Pt. 2.

46 CWM 3, Pt. 2, 62.

47 CWM 3, Pt. 2, 62. When this epigram was composed has not been determined.

What needs to be underscored, considering all the above, is that More's brilliant *History of Richard III*, composed between 1513 and 1518, is the outcome of a long-held focus on tyranny.[48]

What was it, however, that had originally inspired this obsession with tyranny? Critical in explaining the strength of More's focus on tyranny were his stay when only a youngster with Morton and the influence of his father. Morton was a player in the kingships of Henry VI (1422–61), Edward IV (1461–83), Richard III (1483–5), and Henry VII (1485–1509).[49] Indeed, Morton's role was pivotal in Richard's demise and the ascension to the throne of Henry VII. That More admired Morton above all political actors, and as a person, is well attested to in Book I of *Utopia* (1516) and in *Richard III* (1513–18). Without question, Morton was the hero of the latter work. And the esteem went both ways. Roper reports that Cardinal Morton, delighting in young More's wit and presence of mind, "would often say of him unto the nobles that divers times dined with him, 'This child here waiting at the table, whosoever shall live to see it, will prove a marvelous man.'"[50] Not of little significance, More had begun his stay at Morton's residence only five years after Richard III's downfall. Undoubtedly it was Morton, who had died in 1500 only shortly before the lectures, who truly sparked More's feelings about tyranny and the world of Richard III.[51] It is widely recognized that some of the topics discussed in *Richard III* could only have come from Morton's first-hand knowledge. Some historians have gone so far as to claim, though this view is now discredited, that, considering the details

48 More wrote both an English and a Latin version of *Richard III*, both unpublished at his death. See R.S. Sylvester's edition of these works: *The History of King Richard III*, CWM 2. Daniel Kinney has more recently discovered a more complete edition of the Latin version. See *Historia Richardi Tertii*, text and translation, in CWM 15, 313–485. On More's *Richard III*, see Baker, "Jacobean Historiography and the Election of Richard III"; Leonard F. Dean, "Literary Problems in More's *Richard III*"; Paul Dean, "Tudor Humanism and the Roman Past"; Donno, "Thomas More and Richard III"; Grant, "Thomas More's Richard III"; Hanham, *Richard III and His Early Historians, 1483–1535*; Kendall, ed., *Richard III*; Kincaid, "The Dramatic Structure of Sir Thomas More's History of Richard III"; Logan, "More on Tyranny: *The History of King Richard the Third*"; Pollard, *Richard III and the Princes in the Tower*; Ross, *Richard III*; Richard S. Sylvester, CWM 2, lix–civ; Warnicke, "More's Richard III and the Mystery Plays"; and Weir, *The Princes in the Tower*.

49 No book on Morton, notwithstanding his importance, exists. To date the best discussions are found in Seward, *The War of the Roses*.

50 Roper, *Life*, 198.

51 Sometime between 1496 and 1500, More contributed the introductory and concluding verses for John Holt's *Milk for Children*, a Latin grammar dedicated to Cardinal Morton and intended for the use of his pages at Lambeth palace, where Holt had been appointed schoolmaster (CWM 3, Pt. 2, 65–6, 294–7, 417–18).

brought up in the work, Morton must have been the real author.[52] In fact, More was acquainted with many individuals who had first-hand knowledge of events relating to Richard.[53] One immediate source was his father, for whom he displayed throughout his father's long life deep attachment. In *Richard III* his father is the only person named as a source of information. From "long ago," More recalls a conversation reported to his father, a conversation that foretold Richard's usurpation.[54] As evidenced by his will and other factors, his father had a special attachment to the memory of Edward IV, Richard's predecessor.[55] More's work likewise sees Edward IV in a very favourable light.

From all these sources, More would have learned about a world more horrific and very diffe ent in mental set from anything described by Augustine. How he saw his world is illustrated by his characterization of Richard:

> He [Richard] could adopt any role, then play it out to perfection, whether cheerful or stern, whether sober or relaxed, just as expediency urged him to sustain or abandon it. There was modesty in his countenance when in his heart there was arrogance, uncontrollable, boundless, and monstrous. He would speak flatteringly to those whom he inwardly loathed, and would not hesitate to embrace those whom he had decided to kill. He was cruel and inexorable, not always from anger, but more often because of ambition, as he sought to augment or secure his own fortune; he had equal regard for a friend and for an enemy in comparison with his own advantage.[56]

Note the utter contrast between body language and motivations. Richard's real purposes were not observable and, thus, unpredictable. He at all times played out roles to suit his own advantage.[57] Expedience governed everything, and in this context his role-playing was magisterial. In his heart there was nothing of Christian precepts, nothing of the City of God, but only "arrogance, uncontrollable, boundless, and monstrous." He was a master of rhetoric, but it was evil rhetoric. More than

52 George Buck, who had family reasons for seeing Richard III as a hero, famously argued that Morton was the real author in his *The History of King Richard III* (1619).

53 See Pollard, "The Making of Sir Thomas More's Richard III," Richard S. Sylvester, CWM 2, lxv–lxxx, and Weir, *The Princes in the Tower*, 10–11.

54 CWM 15, 327, 329.

55 The entire will is found in Hastings, "The Ancestry of Sir Thomas More." See 101.

56 This is Daniel Kinney's translation of the Latin manuscript, CWM 15, 325. For the variant of my quotation found in More's English version, see CWM 2, 8/7–13.

57 Machiavelli's *The Prince* (1513) is sometimes related, though often incorrectly, to *Richard III*.

simply a tool, Richard's rhetoric reflected the very core of his being. No higher principles governed any statement or any action. He was a person incapable of true friendship or true feeling for others. Ambition encompassed everything. His cruelty was all the more potent precisely because it did not necessarily result from the emotion of anger. Perceived worldly self-interest governed every detail of his life. He was thus at all times double-faced, totally lacking in the ideal of openness and friendship so often espoused by ancients such as Cicero, humanists such as Erasmus, and, according to many sources, More himself.[58]

Much has been made of the literary and dramatic nature of *Richard III* and the fact that it became the prime source for Shakespeare's play. According to Richard Sylvester, during 1509–14 More had deeply studied the ancient Roman histories, most particularly those of Sallust, Suetonius, and Tacitus, and his brilliant character portrayals and renderings of the complexities and uncertainties of motives, causes, and interpretations were significantly influenced (though Sylvester finds no direct borrowings) by these histories.[59] That More had acquired an expertise in all the tools of rhetoric by the time he wrote *Richard III* has also been amply demonstrated.[60] Beyond the ancient histories and beyond contemporary Italian humanist historiography, however, More used rhetoric to unveil and exhibit not simply Richard's character and decisions but the nature of tyranny.[61] The humanist Polydore Vergil's assessment of Richard in his *Anglica Historia* (1534), written 1506–13, is not out of sync with that of More, but the methodology and motivation are very diffe ent. While Vergil's investigative methods have much in common with previous humanist writings (style, structure, criticism of sources), as well as medieval chronicles,[62] More's account, which

58 Erasmus is one of those who sees More in this way. *Ep.* 999. Allen 4, 16/97–125, CWE 7, 18/98–19/131. See also the introductions to *Utopia*. On Erasmus' view of the indispensabilty of friendship, see *The Praise of Folly* (*Moriae encomium*), 30–3, ASD IV-3, 92/377–94/410. The 1500 edition of Erasmus' *Adages* includes "Between friends all is common [Amicorum communia omnia]." Erasmus made this the first adage beginning with the 1508 edition. See CWE 31, 29–30. Cicero refers to this "Greek proverb" at *Off.* 1.51, but he denies that this means holding property in common (1.21). Vogt shows that early Stoics did not see holding all goods in common as having anything to do with property or material possessions (*Law, Reason, and the Cosmic City*), 152. See also Eden, *Friends Hold All Things in Common*, 78–108.

59 Richard Sylvester, CWM 2, esp. xc, xciv–xcvi. See also Ronnick, "A Note Concerning Elements of Tacitus' Depiction of Nero in Thomas More's *Historia Richardi Regis Angliae*."

60 See in particular Donno, "Thomas More and Richard III."

61 Cf. Gransden, *Historical Writing in England*, vol. 2, 443–53.

62 See Gransden, *Historical Writing in England*, vol. 2, 430–43 and Hay, *Polydore Vergil*.

covers only a small period of time, is, above all, high drama. We learn about motivations, the contrast between what is seen and reality, the complexities of events and their settings. And there are feelings, human joys, witticisms, and pathos (the plight of the courtesan, Jane Shore, stands out).

In fact, however, More's outlook on Richard III and tyranny did not originate in the ancient historians and a high-level development of rhetorical tools. First of all, the depiction of Richard and surrounding events has now been largely corroborated, most importantly by *The Crowland Chronicle Continuation, 1459–1486* and Dominic Mancini's *The Usurpation of Richard III* – both near contemporary.[63] Nigel Saul well sums up the importance of these sources and where research now stands in *The Three Richards: Richard I, Richard II and Richard III* (2005), ch. 1. "The Tudors did not invent the character of black Richard. The blackening of Richard was begun by his contemporaries" (19).[64]

In short, More did not make up the central reality. Even as a youngster, as indicated above, More had been fixated – undoubtedly infl - enced by Morton – on the evils of Richard III and tyranny. Adding to this picture, there is every reason to believe that his 1501 lectures centred on tyranny. Consider what follows.

History in More's Lectures

How did More's social, political, and intellectual experiences and concerns impact the way he read Books 1–5 of Augustine's work? The range of possibilities is far less than could be abstractly imagined. This is the case because we can now see the particular parts of *The City of God* that More was looking at and can compare and contrast the tyranny found in More's – very diffe ent – world.

How did the Roman lust for domination to which Augustine constantly refers in his five "history" books filter through More's mind? More did not after all analyse these books and lecture on them by chance. He chose them and he had reasons for choosing them. And these reasons were not derived from abstract scholarship. He was impelled by his own deeply held concerns about contemporary tyranny. What he wanted to think about was what Augustine had to say about the place of tyranny in

63 See *The Crowland Chronicle Continuations, 1459–1486*, and Mancini, *The Usurpation of Richard III*.

64 See also Hanham, *Richard III and His Early Historians, 1483–1535*. Logan shows that More and his contemporaries were correct, considering contemporary meanings of the word, in labelling Richard a "tyrant" ("More on Tyranny," 179–80).

the earthly city. Is it a necessary phenomenon? What is the relationship of tyranny to Christianity? How should the Christian respond?

In line with Augustine, he would have been at pains to show that Christianity itself was not responsible for tyranny. It was not Christianity that brought about Richard III, nor were Richard's acts in any way Christian. But there were important diffe ences between the contemporary situation and that witnessed by Augustine. Is it possible to postulate how some of these diffe ences affected the lectu es?

It seems safe to say that More would not have failed to recognize that, unlike the world described by Augustine, the world from which Richard III emanated was nominally Christian. Nominally Christian and yet a world governed throughout not only by unchristian killings and unchristian brutality but, at the root of everything, unchristian and pervasive deceit and self-interest. Augustine denied, against the charges of pagans, that the fall of Rome in 410 had anything to do with Christianity and argued that the history of Rome is a history of tyranny, but how relevant was this to the world More witnessed? Now the tyrants were all nominally Christian. Modern instances of tyranny are so much worse, More could well have argued, precisely because they have been carried out by persons claiming to be Christian. And while Augustine had contended that the Christianity of the invaders of Rome lessened the carnage, what would have been very evident to More and others was that modern tyranny, carried out by so-called Christians, did not mitigate but increased the carnage.

Contrast also the positive traits Augustine saw in Roman tyranny with the tyranny More saw in Richard III. Augustine thought the Roman Empire was a great advance over everything preceding (2.21) and he admired the traits that in his view had made this possible. In particular, he admired the Roman emphasis on virtue and the desire for praise and glory. Love of praise and glory are vices, but they restrain greater vices (5.13). It was a combination of the desire for liberty and the desire for human praise that motivated the Romans to perform admirable deeds (5.18). Indeed, the Roman desire for virtue and glory foreshadowed the infinitely higher virtue and glory of the City of God. In Peter Brown's words, "Augustine drains the glory from the Roman past in order to project it far beyond the reach of men, into the 'Most glorious city of God.'"[65] If he saw the rise of Rome as demonstrating lust for domination, it was only within this larger frame of thought. Even when, as Sallust described it, the virtue of a Cato was lacking, giving way to deceit and treachery, glory and honour were still motivators

65 Brown, *Augustine of Hippo*, 310 (commenting on 5.18).

(5.12). What was truly horrible, in Augustine's mind, was the lack, as with Nero, of even the desire for honour and glory. "He who is a despiser of glory, but is greedy of domination, exceeds the beasts in the vices of cruelty and luxuriousness" (5.19). But this was the exception.

However More assessed the positive traits of the Romans, as described by Augustine, he did not in 1501 find any such positive traits in contemporary tyranny. And while Augustine mentions Nero as a minor aside, More's Nero, Richard III, was to be the subject of an entire book. A work consisting of eighty-six pages in a modern edition of the Latin version (CWM 15), *Richard III* is driven throughout by More's powerful depictions of chameleon contrivance and deceit. Honour, not to mention godliness, is nowhere to be found. Nothing in Augustine's monumental coverage of human history, not even his referrals to Sallust's history of the moral decline of Rome (2.19), compares with this all-pervasive and diabolical portraiture of a world where nothing but evil expediency governed and deceit had become highest art. The most emphasized and repeated word in the work is "pretext." Related words, skimming through the work, are "cunning," "design," "secretly," "strategy," "trickery," "flatter ," "contrive," "pretence," "corrupt intent," "convenience," "envy," "pride," "words," "stir up," "trap," "evil counsel," "blindness," "feigned friendship," "dissembling," "crafty," "perverse," "prudence," "pre-arranged," "hypocrisy," "malice," "schemes," "malignant intelligence."

There is also reason to believe that More would have been much more concerned than Augustine with the place and role of worldly action. Augustine wrote *The City of God* as a scholar looking at the whole of history. More, in contrast, was a lawyer and expert on English law. He saw tyranny in this context. Even in 1501 More had a great deal of peripheral acquaintance with politics and was seriously considering personal involvement in politics – the other option of course being the monastic life. Augustine had no such interest or goal. What in 1501 did More think involvement in worldly affairs meant for a Christian? Was he entirely satisfied with Augustine's view? If for Augustine the goal of the Christian is always otherworldly, "love of God extending even to contempt of self," what did More think this entailed for worldly behaviour? Augustine saw Christians as strangers in the world who nonetheless work with members of the earthly city to achieve common worldly goals, but is this working together possible if the political horizon is governed, as there is reason to believe More saw it, by unsurpassed deceit and contrivance? Augustine had contended, against those who had blamed Christianity for the fall of Rome, that Christianity had had a very positive effect on world affairs. But More would have now seen a very diffe ent situation. What effect was Christianity now having on worldly affairs? The Roman pagans no longer existed, but what could be more horrendous than the likes of Richard operating within a society formally Christian? Is Christianity without effect on the world of affairs? How can Christian ideals ever deal with someone like Richard or even with milder political situations? How is it possible for a Christian to work with the powers that be, awaiting the City of God? Augustine saw Christians as fighting wars alongside the reprobate for the common good, but what could this mean in the world of Richard III? Wouldn't this necessarily mean direct involvement with evil?

Regarding Christian leadership, Augustine lauds the lack of self-interest and the merciful attitudes which he sees in the performances of the Christian emperors Constantine I and Theodosius. But how applicable would this have been to the tyranny More was confronted with? Did More think Christianity was exemplified only by traits such as these? Did he think that lack of self-interest and mercy would alone produce results in the world that surrounded him, a world epitomized by the pervasive and brilliant duplicity of Richard? It seems likely that More's mental struggles from 1501 to 1504 had much to do with the fact that he saw no solution to worldly evils considered in Augustinian terms and thus believed that Augustine's rather benign conception of leadership could not be adhered to in the contemporary world – the Charterhouse being the only solution. If this was the case, More was not torn between worldly and otherworldly endeavours simply because on the one hand he considered monasticism the highest form of Christianity and on the other was driven by native political instincts. He was torn because he was convinced that the political world surrounding him, as epitomized by Richard III, was irredeemable, antithetical by its very nature to Christianity. Joining this world would have been not a second-best choice, merely a less admirable type of Christianity, but for all eternity a condemnation of his soul. We can well believe that this outlook motivated More's lectures and that this is why his learned audience was transfixed

Philosophy in More's Lectures

Although More would have been little interested when reading Books 6–10 of *The City of God* in the discussions of Roman mythical and civil theologies, he would have been intensely interested in the discussions of Plato and the relationship of his thinking to Christianity. Consider here too the milieu surrounding More. Centred in Florence, the Platonist revival had recently spread to the rest of Europe, including England.

Although Aristotelianism remained strong in the universities, among humanists Platonism was the vogue at the time of More's lectures. While a number of Plato's dialogues had been translated from the Greek in the early fifteenth century, among them the *Republic* (1402, 1439), nothing matched the achievements of Marsilio Ficino (1433–99), who in 1484 published translations of all of Plato's writings.[66] Humanists were very much aware of Plato's long-standing reputation for divinity and much was made of Augustine's contention that Platonists were closer to Christianity than other philosophers.[67] Here too no intellectual had an influence comparable to that of Ficino. In James Hankins' words, Ficino's achievement was "the most powerful and sophisticated attempt of the age to reconcile the works of Plato with the values of Christian society in the Renaissance."[68] And yet, like Augustine before them (who had not read Plato directly), the Florentine Platonists little distinguished between Plotinus and Plato. What particularly interested Ficino and others in Florence was demonstrating the immortality of the soul. His *Platonic Theology: On the Immortality of Souls*, consisting of eighteen books and composed around 1469–74, was printed in 1482.

More would also have recognized that his older friend and spiritual mentor Colet was a Platonist (i.e., Neoplatonist).[69] Colet was exceedingly proud of a few communications with Ficino, making extensive notes on one of them, and even made some use of Ficino's *Platonic Theology*.[70] Not able to meet with Ficino during his stay in Florence, as a result of political events it seems, he expressed great disappointment and the hope that such a visit would be possible in the future.[71] As early as 1499 Erasmus explicitly connected Colet with Plato: "When I hear Colet it seems to me that I hear Plato."[72] In short, in 1501 More would not have questioned the common view that Plato's thought was related to the essence of Christianity, albeit Plato knew nothing of Christ. Whether or not More believed that the immortality of the soul was demonstrable, he certainly believed, as do his Utopians (C160/7–8), that belief in the immortality of the soul is a sine qua non of the faith.

---

66 Ficino, *Opera Omnia*.

67 See Kraye's discussion in the *Cambridge History of Renaissance Philosophy*, 356–9.

68 Hankins, *Plato in the Italian Renaissance*, vol. 1, 359.

69 See Miles, *John Colet and the Platonic Tradition*.

70 See Jayne, *John Colet and Marsilio Ficino*, and Trapp, *Erasmus, Colet and More*, 138.

71 See Gleason, *John Colet*, 47–52.

72 *Ep*. 118 to Fisher, 5 December 1499. Allen 1, 273/21, CWE 1, 235/24–5. Now that we know that Erasmus was even at this date not a Platonist but a Stoic, it can be seen that this statement is not as adulatory as readers have imagined.

Also indicative of More's abstract one-dimensional outlook in his lectures, in a letter written about the same time (1501) he states with admiration that Grocyn, his teacher of Greek, had recently begun giving lectures at St Paul's Cathedral on *The Celestial Hierarchy* of Dionysius the Aeropagite.[73] Contemporaries, including Pico and Ficino, were greatly interested in Dionysius because it was thought that he was an Athenian converted by St Paul and that his mystical and hierarchical type of thinking reflected St Pau 's thinking.[74]

In summary, however much More may have compared and contrasted Augustine's outlook with his own experiential and intellectual world – and found Christianity inapplicable or, worse, necessarily involving a practitioner in evil – he still held firmly to Augustine's one-dimensional contention, augmented by monasticism, that the Christian is distinguished from the non-Christian by "love of God extending even to contempt of self." His Charterhouse years, 1501–4, prove the point.

3 The Translations of Pico's Writings (1504)

Certainly no new outlook is found in More's translation into English of Gianfrancesco Pico's *Life of John Picus* (CWM 1, 47–75), completed around 1504 according to Stapleton.[75] In accord with More's Charterhouse years, the work has much to say about heavenly values and little positive to

73 Thomas More, letter to John Holt, c. November 1501. *The Correspondence Of Sir Thomas More*, 4 and *St. Thomas More: Selected Letters*, 2.

74 During the course of his lectures, Grocyn came to realize, correctly, that Dionysius could not have been alive in St Paul's time (we now know he lived in the early sixth century) and was thus not Paul's disciple. And yet Colet and many others were to pass over or deny this discovery.

75 Stapleton, *Life*, 9. Of core importance, and not previously noticed it appears, Stapleton refers to More's work on Pico (9) *after* discussing More's desire to become a Franciscan (8) and *before* quoting in its entirely More's despairing letter to Colet (below, 74–5), a letter which is dated by More 23 October 1504 (10–12). In this context, the *terminus ad quem* for More's *Life of Pico* is 23 October 1504. What needs to be taken account of here is (a) what I have shown regarding Stapleton's unequalled expertise on More's lectures on *The City of God* (above, 54–7), (b) the fact that More was involved with the London Carthusians from 1500 to 1504, (c) the fact that More dedicated the work to a nun (and gave her a manuscript copy, apparently around 1 January 1505), (d) the fact that Pico at the end of his life decided to become a Dominican, (e) the fact that Pico refused to consider marriage, and (f) the fact that More's 23 October 1504 letter, which follows the *Life*, is otherworldly in the extreme. Then too, Colet was More's spiritual advisor during this period, and it was almost certainly Colet who introduced More to Pico (see below), a role Erasmus had clearly taken over by January 1505 (see Part II below).

say about worldly values.[76] The work is dedicated, accordingly, to Joyce Lee, who had entered the strict Poor Clares Convent.

Giovanni Pico della Mirandolla (1463–1494) was a key figu e, along with literary and artistic notables such as Lorenzo di Medici, Leon Battista Alberti, Angelo Poliziano, Cristoforo Landino, Marsilio Ficino, Sandro Botticelli, and Michelangelo Buonarotti, in the late fifteenth-century Florentine Renaissance.[77] More's translation is made from the *Life* written by Pico's nephew Gianfrancesco, first published in 1496. A child prodigy, Pico had early on contended that the multitude of philosophies that exist are in fact just diffe ent expressions of a singular truth and that philosophy is in accord with Christian teachings. In 1486 Pico announced that he would publicly defend nine hundred theses drawn from Christian, Jewish, Muslim, Platonic, Aristotelian, Hermetist, Orphic, Zoroastrian, and Cabalist thought, not to mention

---

In 1505 More worked with Erasmus for months on Lucian. The fact that Stapleton states that More chose Pico because he wanted to "put before his eyes the examples of some prominent layman, on which he might model his life" can be easily explained: Stapleton knew that More had married *after* his work on Pico (see also Cresacre More, *Life*, CWM 1, xxxviii) and assumed that Pico's contemplative ideals were seen as a way of compensating for what would be the downward pull of worldliness. Although George B. Parks does not notice the significance of whe e Stapleton locates *The Life of Pico*, he is very correct in concluding that More's work on Pico should be dated between 1499 and 1503 or 1504, at a time when he was "inspired to adopt Pico's pattern of life." See "Pico della Mirandola in Tudor Translation," esp. 357–9. For many valid reasons, Parks rules out the period between 1505 and 1509. In Part V below I will demonstrate that *The Praise of Folly*, written at More's home in 1509, works out from beginning to end More's mindset, a mindset that at that time could not have written *The Life of Pico*.

All of which shows that A.S.G. Edwards' contention that More wrote the work around 1510, which has often influenced modern discussions, is not viable. Edwards' argument is based solely on the fact (well known) that the *Life* appears to have been published by John Rastell around 1510 and that John's son William states in the *English Works* of 1557 that the work was translated by More around 1510 (CWM 1, xxxvii–xxxix). Employing the 1510 dating, Furey builds up a very misleading (heavenly versus worldly) picture of More's mental state in the years following his marriage. See *Erasmus, Contarini, and the Religious Republic of Letters*, 15–16 passim.

76 Semler relates the work to Augustine's *Confessions*, Petrarch's *Secretum*, and Erasmus' *De contempt mundi* (c. 1485–8), a work which precedes, as I have shown, the radicalization of Erasmus'mind by Stoicism. Semler sees More's *Life of Pico* as throughout a contrast of worldly and otherworldly. See his "Virtue, Transformation, and Exemplarity in *The Lyfe of Johan Picus*." Other works include Lehmberg, "Sir Thomas More's Life of Pico della Mirandola"; Copenhaver, "Studied as an Oration," 157–68; Curtright, *The One Thomas More*, 15–41; and Wegemer, *Young Thomas More*, 70–87.

77 On Pico see Hankins' summary and bibliography in "Pico della Mirandola, Giovanni (1463–94)."

other sources. The goal was to set forth a theological system that took into account all past and present philosophies and theologies. But the Pope condemned the theses, and thereafter Pico became ever more religious and otherworldly. Before his untimely death a few years later, at age thirty-two, Pico came under the sway of the harsh and apocalyptic sermonizing of Girolamo Savonarola (d. 1498). Gianfrancesco's *Life* emphasized the pious and ascetic Pico.[78]

More did not just translate the *Life*, he severely edited it. The resulting product comprises less than half of the original.[79] Throughout we fin omissions, extending in length from words, phrases, and sentences to pages, and sometimes additions, comments, or summaries.[80] By far the most important effect of this editing is that it increases the contemplative focus beyond even that found in the original. This is due most of all to the fact that More leaves out much of the discussion of Pico's philosophical thought and writings. At CWM 60/17–61/1, for example, he summarizes a large block of the philosophical material with a paragraph of his own. Very near the beginning of the translation he adds a long statement contrasting honour given because of one's ancestry and the virtue and resultant honour exemplified by Pico (52/25–53/28), a theme that had been set forth in various contexts and with various meanings by humanists.[81] What stands out in the body of More's work is Pico's replacing of his earlier desire for praise and glory, as evident in his nine hundred theses, with the desire for heavenly joys and the glory and profit of Christ. Overcome in the process was his "volupteouse vse of women" (59/9).

Many themes tie in, we can see, with issues in More's own life. Consider Pico's desire for freedom from a life at court and freedom from marriage. Although he fled both palaces and marriage, he considered marriage the lesser evil: he would "leuer take him to marriage/ as y[t] thing in which was less seruitude & not so moche ieopardie" (69/12–25). Reminding us again of More (above, 48), we learn that Pico whipped himself in remembrance of Christ's passion (64/27–65/3). Significant also is More's comment on the fact that, near the end of his

78 On Gianfrancesco's severe distortions of Pico's life and thought, see Farmer, *Syncretism in the West*, 150–79.

79 The Latin original, accompanied by a modern translation that shows the parts More did not translate, is found in CWM 1, 294–341.

80 See CWM 1, 209–28 and Lehmberg, "Sir Thomas More's Life of Pico della Mirandola."

81 Among those who had contrasted virtue and true nobility with inherited nobility were Niccolo Niccoli (d. 1437), Alberti (d. 1472), Landino (d. 1498), and Platina (d. 1481). See Skinner, *Visions of Politics*, vol. 2, 224–9, and Rabil, ed., *Knowledge, Goodness, and Power*.

life, Pico had decided to become a Dominican. More inserted into the original that this had come about "by the especiall commaundement of god" (70/18–19; cf. 330/13–14).[82] At its conclusion, More's *Life* discusses Pico's early death and Savanarola's sermonizing on its meaning. Since he had delayed joining a religious order, his death should be seen as punishment by God, and God was sending him, for a time, to purgatory (73/8–75/20). Did More feel that he likewise would be punished if he did not dedicate his life to the Charterhouse?

What seems likely is that More's choice of Pico as a subject to translate was inspired by Colet, More's most important spiritual advisor in the period preceding his decision to marry. Colet is reported to have stated that there were many able intellects in England but only one true genius, Thomas More.[83] This being his view, we can easily imagine that he tied in England's genius, More, with Italy's genius, Pico. Colet had not only been to Florence but had gone to great lengths to curry favour with the Neoplatonist Marsilio Ficino.[84] And he was clearly familiar with Pico's writings. In a letter of unknown date, Colet shows, approvingly, that "the Platonist" Pico had divided the universe into four parts: divine, angelic, heavenly, and earthly.[85] Colet here refers to the introduction to Pico's *Heptaplus* (1489), an interpretation of the creation myth in Genesis inspired by the mystical oral traditions of Cabalism and pseudo-Dionysian theology.[86] Although not translated by More, the *Heptaplus* is referred to three times in Gianfrancesco's *The Life of John Picus* (CWM 1, 304, 306, 316).

More also translated at this time three of fifty letters written by Pico. The three that he chose all place the contemplative life far above the active. In one of the letters, written to Andrea Corneo in 1486, Pico replies to Corneo's admonition "not so to embrace Martha [the active life] that ye should utterly forsake Mary [the contemplative]" (CWM 1, 85–8).[87] Although not denying the value of business affairs

82 See Lehmberg, "Sir Thomas More's Life of Pico della Mirandola," 62.

83 Erasmus, *Ep.* 999. "Ioannes Coletus, vir acris exactique iudicii, in familiaribus colloquiis subinde dicere solet Britanniae non nisi vnicum esse ingenium: cum haec insula tot egregiis ingeniis flo eat." Allen 4, 21/267–70, CWE 7, 24/292–5.

84 See Miles, *John Colet and the Platonic Tradition*; Jayne, *John Colet and Marsilio Ficino*; Trapp, *Erasmus, Colet and More*; and Gleason, *John Colet*.

85 See Colet, *Letters to Radulphus on the Mosaic Account of the Creation*, 10.

86 *Heptaplus* is found in Pico's *Opera Omnia* vol. 1, 1–62.

87 As with his *Life*, More does not translate more than half of the letter. Note that More did not include Pico's comment, near the end, regarding a person, Pico it seems (236), who had been involved in a sexual escapade (354/5–28). Since this person is sorry, he should be excused. "Nothing is weaker than man, nothing stronger than love." Even Jerome, a hermit, was present at the dances of girls.

and involvement at court, Pico sees worldly affairs as evil and fie cely defends the contemplative life.

> [Philosophers] dwell with them selfe and be content with the tranquillite of their owne mynde. Thei suffic them selfe & more/ they seke nothing owt of them selfe: the thingis that are had in honoure amonge y[e] commune peple: amonge them be not holden honourable. All that euir the voluptuouse desire of men thirsteth for: or ambition sigheth for: they set at nought and despyce ... I therefore abyding fermely in this opinion: set more bi my little house/ my study/ the pleasure of my bokes/ y[e] rest and peace of my mynde: then by all your kingis palacis/ all your commune besines/ all your glory/ all the aduauntage that ye hawke aftir/ and all the fauoure of the court. (CWM 1, 87/ 5–11, 20–4)

So why did More get married and become deeply involved in worldly affairs shortly after these translations

4 The Despairing Letter to Colet (1504)

A letter of 23 October 1504 from More to Colet is important and unusual in that it expresses despair at the course of his life – and this only three months away from his marriage. Here again truth is located in the contemplative life.[88]

More begins the letter by stating that he had come upon Colet's servant while strolling along in the law courts, "unbusy where everybody else was busy [inter aliena negotia]." Upon learning from the servant that Colet would not be returning to the city for some time, he states that he has become depressed. He is saddened by the loss of Colet's companionship, advice, intimacy, sermons, and righteous living. Without Colet's help he is falling away from a Christian life:

> By following your footsteps I had escaped almost from the very gates of hell, and now, driven by some force and necessity, I am falling back again into gruesome darkness. I am like Eurydice, except that she was lost because Orpheus looked back at her,[89] but I am sinking because you do not look back at me.[90]

88 Preserved by Stapleton, the letter is found in *The Correspondence of Sir Thomas More*, 6–9.

89 Cf. Virgil, *Georgics* 4.453–525.

90 The translation is that of Rogers, *St. Thomas More: Selected Letters*, 4–6.

In the city, as contrasted with the simple life in the country where Colet was residing, that person who is "straining in his own power to climb the steep path of virtue" is turned back by a thousand devices. Everywhere one finds deceit, including feigned love, false flatter . Everywhere there are fie ce hatreds and quarrels, exemplified by the buzz of the law courts. Emphasized is the contention that preachers are false physicians, prescribing cures when they themselves are covered with ulcers, their lives contrasting with their words. Colet epitomizes everything this worldliness is not. Hoping that Colet will return and nurture both his own Christianity and that of London, More contrasts the evils of city life, where even buildings block out heaven, with the bucolic country life presently surrounding Colet. Although the contrast between city and country life is old, the emotions expressed by More are very real and unusual. More was not prone to express personal feelings.[91] Just as important is the fact that he indisputably locates truth in the contemplative life.[92] Christianity is about a hierarchical climb from evil to virtue.

Analysing the world from an abstract position, "unbusy where everyone else is busy" (the importance of which will become even more evident in Parts IV and V below), More sees two opposing outcomes on the table. He can sink down into the worldly muck, with all its deceits, "the very gates of hell," as is presently occurring, or he can, with Colet's help, escape from all this. He sees the world, as represented by the city (a city surely coloured by his rethinking of Augustine's Earthly City), as evil and Christianity as something over and against this worldly condition. It is an either/or situation.

Again, why did More choose – within two to three months of his letter to Colet – the world and marriage? The letter to Colet as well as the translations of Pico might have led one to expect an opposite outcome. Is it not evident that More in January 1505 turned away from his ideals, turned away from contemplative truths, turned away from his conception of highest Christianity?

The Views of More's Spiritual Advisor, Colet: A Rejection of Marriage, the Human Body, and Worldly Involvement

What kind of consolation was More looking for from Colet, his long-standing spiritual advisor? How did he imagine Colet could help him cope with the evils of worldly affairs? Did he think Colet would

91 Clarence Miller states the same in referring to More's epigrams, prayers, and devotional works. See CWM 3, Pt. 2, 55.

92 Marius begins his biography by discussing the old city/country contrast found in the letter but fails to mention the real point of the letter, More's despair. Nor does he notice the "contempt of the world" context. See *Thomas More*, 3–4.

have some practical, worldly-wise, advice? Was Colet a person More could talk to, heart to heart, about his sexual desires and thoughts about marriage? Would Colet have talked positively about the appropriateness of marriage and advised marriage and involvement in the evils and hurly-burly of everyday affairs? John B. Gleason, without mention (or probably even knowledge) of More's letter to Colet, makes the matter utterly clear: "In all his writings he [Colet] has not a single favorable thing to say of the world here below."[93] Colet advised "forsaking the lively bustle of society for motionless incorporatedness."[94] In line with his Neoplatonism, he not only scorned marriage, he was intensely hostile to the flesh as such. He thought in one-dimensional, absolutist, ascetic, either/or terms; damnation or salvation, Satan or heaven. The imitation of Christ meant, for him, forsaking the world altogether.[95] Indeed, More's late 1504 letter shows that he takes for granted that Colet's message is all about a hierarchical climb to virtue – and that he, More, entirely agrees with this view, the only problem being that without help he cannot do what is required.

At the very time More was faced with making a decision, Colet was writing a treatise on St Paul which holds that human nature is bestial and unchristian.[96] Never neutral, flesh is for him always opposed to spirit, always something to be crucified [97] Marriage is a disease, lacking all positive value, something to be avoided.[98] Following St Paul and Jesus, the ideal should always be the heroic life of celibacy. "The law of nature is a law beneath man; the law of Moses is a law on the level of man; the law of grace is a law above man."[99] Such views were tied in with the Neoplatonism of Ficino (especially his translation of Plotinus) and Pico, which Colet equated with opposition between the sensible and intelligible worlds and the nothingness of man.[100]

93 Gleason, *John Colet*, 17.

94 Gleason, *John Colet*, 193.

95 Gleason, *John Colet*, 185–94. See also Trapp, "An English Late Medieval Cleric and Italian Thought"; Jayne, *John Colet and Marsilio Ficino*, 60–70, and Rice, "John Colet and the Annihilation of the Natural."

96 Colet, *An Exposition of St. Paul's Epistle to the Romans* (16-ch. version), Rom. 7, p. 22, Latin, p. 150. Gleason dates the work (the 16-chapter version) late 1504 or early 1505. See *John Colet*, 92. On the dating of this and other writings of Colet, see also Jonathan Arnold, "Humanist Ecclesiology in Theory."

97 Gleason, *John Colet*, 186.

98 Gleason, *John Colet*, 17, 94, 95, 187, 192, 213, 313.

99 Colet, *An Exposition of St. Paul's Epistle to the Romans* (5-ch. version), Rom. 5, p. 162, Latin p. 279. Cf. Rom. 4, p. 135, Latin p. 260.

100 Gleason, *John Colet*, 194, 198. On Colet's use of Pico and Ficino, see Miles, *John Colet and the Platonic Tradition*; Jayne, *John Colet and Marsilio Ficino*; Trapp, "An English

For Colet, the martyrs were following the pattern established by Christ. "Holy deaths, and God-pleasing sacrifices for others, had their beginning in Christ." "The holiest of all deaths, even Christ's, which is hallowing as well as holy, wrought the fullest redemption; and other deaths of saints work redemption in His death."[101] We need to die rather than give in.[102] "Origen affirm that one chief cause of the fall and abandonment of the world is the failing of human sacrifices; that is, of martyrs, who are propitiatory sacrifices for sin."[103] Utterly unappreciative of Erasmus' criticism of the martyrs' joy (*alacritas*) as an ideal, in their 1499 debate at Oxford,[104] Colet shows over and over, in effect, that joy in martyrdom is the ideal for Christians and that Christ led the way.[105] At odds with the law of the Jews, the Christian's soul needs to be deeply inflamed, so that "being wholly on fi e, and rapt, as it were, into flame, it might leave the darksome body and attach itself to God alone."[106] "The whole life, in truth, of Jesus Christ on earth was nothing else than a continual ascending to heaven; its whole aim being there, and not here." "He had his body in complete obedience and subjection to his blessed soul."[107] "He confessed that the world hated him, and he the world; and that his own were hated by the world, or else they could not be his own."[108] Not without reason Colet states in a 1514 letter that he is thinking daily of his retirement among the Carthusians.[109]

Late Medieval Cleric and Italian Thought" and *Erasmus, Colet and More*, 79–141; and Gleason, *John Colet*. Note also Erasmus' 1499 comment tying Colet and Plato, above, 69.

101 Colet, *An Exposition of St. Paul's Epistle to the Romans* (5-ch. version), Rom. 5, p. 155, Latin p. 274.

102 Colet, *An Exposition of St. Paul's Epistle to the Romans* (16-ch. version), Rom. 12, pp. 89–90, Latin p. 197.

103 Colet, *An Exposition of St. Paul's Epistle to the Romans* (5-ch. version), Rom. 4, p. 121, Latin 250.

104 Dealy, *Stoic Origins*, Part III, Ch. 3.

105 Nowhere does Colet ever discuss or even acknowledge, after the initial letters, the lengthy counter-arguments set forth by Erasmus in *De taedio Iesu*, a work which (according to Gleason, *John Colet*, 117) was to go through twelve reprints during Erasmus' lifetime. I have shown elsewhere that Gleason misjudges the nature and meaning of Erasmus' criticisms of Colet. See *Stoic Origins*, 49n5, 154nn6 and 7.

106 Colet, *An Exposition of St. Paul's Epistle to the Romans* (16-ch. version), Rom. 7, p. 24, Latin p. 151.

107 John Colet, *An Exposition of St. Paul's First Epistle to the Corinthians*, 1 Corin. 7, pp. 71–2, Latin, pp. 209–10.

108 Colet, *An Exposition of St. Paul's First Epistle to the Corinthians*, 1 Corin. 7, p. 69, Latin, p. 208.

109 *Ep*. 314 from Colet. Allen 2, 37/9–10, CWE 3, 48/11–12. Cf. Erasmus, *Ep*. 1211. Allen 4, 518–19/371–7, CWE 8, 237/404–6.

Allegory and hidden meanings pervade Colet's hierarchical thinking. Following Dionysius the Aeropagite, albeit in his own terms, Colet correlates categories of spiritual beings with the soul's rise to God. When he read scripture, this was the way his mind worked.[110] In his *Letters to Radulphus*, Colet divides the universe, "as is done by the Platonist Mirandola [Pico] in his *Hexameron*," into four worlds, at the bottom of which is, of course, the world inhabited by man.[111] Believing that Dionysius was the pupil of St Paul (a view which contemporaries, including Erasmus, were beginning to reject), he composed abbreviations of Dionysius' *Celestial Hierarchy* and *Ecclesiastical Hierarchy*, replete with tables and diagrams. Everything had to have a fixed place. Christ, at the top of the human hierarchy, came into the world "to support the angels."[112] As Dean of St Paul's Cathedral from 1505 until his death in 1519, Colet attempted to implement this perfectionist, fixed place, type of thinking, often meeting resistance. According to Jonathan Arnold, "Colet's vision of the Church as a single corporate entity relied on hierarchy, discipline, unity and devotion. All of these characteristics are found in Colet's interpretation of Dionysian theology, and in his convocation sermon (1510)."[113] While Erasmus reveals a Christ who draws and wins humans over by demonstrating that he has the same emotions and natural instincts as they, and suffers therewith incomparably,[114] Colet sees Jesus as at the top of an authoritative hierarchy: "He commanded men to follow him."[115]

110 Cf. Jayne, *John Colet and Marsilio Ficino*, 28–34, 62–3, and Gleason, *John Colet*, 153, 166, 200.

111 John Colet, *Letters to Radulphus*, 10, Latin 170–1.

112 Colet, *An Exposition of St. Paul's First Epistle to the Corinthians*, 1 Corin. 12, p. 125, Latin, p. 250. Colet discusses nine orders of angels at length in his *Celestial Hierarchy*. On the complex problems regarding dating the *Ecclesiastical Hierarchy* and the other works by Colet, see now Lochman and Nodes, eds. and trans., *John Colet on the Ecclesiastical Hierarchy of Dionysius*, 32–43. On Dionysius see Rorem, *Pseudo-Dionysius*; Perl, *Theophany*; and Hathaway, *Hierarchy and the Definition of Order in the Letters of Pseudo-Dionysius*.

113 Jonathan Arnold, "John Colet, Preaching, and Reform at St. Paul's Cathedral, 1505–19," 465. See also his *Dean John Colet of St. Paul's*. According to Gleason, the ideas found in Colet's only surviving original treatise, *De sacramentis* (c. 1512–16), "are the conceptual expression of dark certainties that possessed him early on and never lost their hold on him." See *John Colet*, 185. Gleason shows, as do others, that Colet was little affected even by his travels in Ital , 1492–6 (62). On *De sacramentis* see also Kaufman, "John Colet's *Opus de sacramentis* and Clerical Anticlericalism."

114 See Dealy, *Stoic Origins*, 147–8, 179–80.

115 Colet, *An Exposition of St. Paul's First Epistle to the Corinthians*, 1 Corin. 12, p. 123, Latin p. 248.

One thing stands out in the above: Colet would have had no sympathy for More's worldly goals. And we know that, up through his October 1504 letter, More entirely agreed with Colet's negative assessments of worldly involvements, agreed that Christianity is strictly hierarchical and one-dimensional.

5 January 1505: An Ambivalent Decision?

In vacillating regarding which type of life he should live, the active or the contemplative, the worldly or the Carthusian Charterhouse, More was not debating the nature of Christianity. The Christianity that he saw was essentially one-dimensional, otherworldly, and unquestioned. His lectures on *The City of God*, his editing and translation of *The Life of John Pico*, and his despairing October 1504 letter to Colet have two things in common: (1) Each focuses on what are seen as two utterly contrasting ways of life and (2) each expresses an uncompromisingly abstract view of the Christian message. If there is reason to believe that More's lectures on *The City of God* compared and contrasted Augustine's social and political concerns with contemporary evils, those epitomized in his mind by Richard III, there is also reason to believe that he, far more than Augustine, saw the situation facing him in polar terms: either join the world and become part of its deceits or retreat to the Charterhouse. And if his lectures related Augustine's admiration for Plato to the contemporary Platonist movement, as there is reason to believe, here too his purpose was to work out the relationships to highest truth, the precepts of the Christian faith – and with it Augustine's "love of God extending even to contempt of self." Demonstrably, his translation of *The Life of John Pico* portrays the world (including marriage) as essentially evil and focuses on heavenly values. In accord with the lectures and the translation, his anguished letter to Colet of 23 October 1504 sees Christianity as something over and against the world. The earthly city is everywhere filled with deceit (feigned love, false flatter , words contrary to actions), hatred, and quarrels. Virtue lies elsewhere. Seeing himself sinking ever more deeply into this worldly muck, "the very gates of hell," he asks Colet, in despair, to help him take the opposite path. The problem he sees has nothing to do with Colet's conception of Christianity. Colet's conception was his conception. The problem is only with himself and the world.

Worldly living presented problems for More not found in relevant parts of *The City of God*, the parts he lectured on. English tyranny, I have shown, was very diffe ent from the Roman tyranny described by

Augustine. More would have seen that there is nothing comparable to a Richard III in Augustine's discussions. And More had had, unlike Augustine, direct experiences with government and secular leadership. Not only had he observed at close hand, through his residence and acquaintance with Morton, the workings of government at the highest level, Roper (our only source for this) holds that he himself had been a key figu e, earning Henry VII's wrath, in the Parliament of January–March 1504. Also not a part of Augustine's résumé or interest, the many years spent in legal studies had deeply attuned More to particular real-world issues and distinctions. Sexual desires (which Augustine had overcome) added to this worldly mix.

While Part I of *The City of God* asks individuals to make a choice between earthly goals and a heavenly goal, the choice on the table for More, it appears, was more stark. How is Christian action in an evil world possible? Augustine presented the matter as rather simple. One chooses to make heaven rather than the world the goal. In worldly affairs one seeks the same things as the reprobate – while holding to the faith. In search of the good life, war and the like are not contraventions of the faith. Should a leadership role become possible, one is a do-gooder, a person who rules justly and dispenses mercy. But for Thomas More, it appears, the burning question was: How is it *possible* to live in the world – Richard III's world – and remain a Christian? There is reason to believe he thought it impossible. Not only was a diffe ent either/or ideology on the table, More had experienced ground-level angst. In his work on Pico, the admirable thing is not so much to work with the world, while firml holding to Christian otherworldly truths, as to escape worldly involvements entirely. The letter to Colet is profoundly anti-world and escapist.

All of which greatly amplifies modern belief that More's mind was torn between the desire for marriage and worldly involvements and an all-consuming belief that Christianity is entirely at odds with this desire – and that he needed to make a choice. The mystery remains, however, why he would choose, opposite to his long-standing ideals, the worldly path. How could he so suddenly, so at odds with his anguished letter to Colet, embrace marriage and a worldly life? And consider again the outlook of the person to whom he sent the letter – Colet, his spiritual advisor. As shown in large above, and as Colet's biographer has stated, "In all his writings he [Colet] has not a single favourable thing to say of the world here below."[116] In his letter to Colet, More condemns those around him who live lives at odds with their words, but had he not embarked on a like path? Puzzlement regarding

116 Gleason, *John Colet*, 17.

More's decision has existed, as I have already shown, from early on. Harpsfield and Stapleton were perplexed because they believed, like More himself prior to January 1505, at least, that the contemplative life is the highest form of Christianity. Moderns now have the explanation provided by Richard Marius, in his influential biography: More went against his own highest religious instincts and beliefs because, we are told, he had to. Although no new evidence is brought forth, biological and psychological factors are said to have made the decision inevitable. Focusing on the hair-shirt and the whippings to subdue sexual desire, Marius deduces that More had an extraordinary sex drive. This being the case, More did not choose to give up on the idea of becoming a monk or priest; he was forced to give it up. His sexual nature simply could not cope with such demands. A leitmotif, also based on conjecture, is that More experienced in choosing marriage and a worldly life a deep, psychological, sense of failure. Far more than simply a decision, the choice had life-long consequences. Thereafter he was always haunted, Marius theorizes, by guilt and a sense of defeat. Everything amounted to an either/or struggle between the desire for worldly involvement and the desire to be an ascetic, resulting ultimately in his stand against Henry VIII. His was a life about sin and redemption.[117]

Even without Marius' explanation, there exists a widespread belief that More vacillated mentally throughout his life, that the 1505 decision was not clearcut but represented one side of an unstable polar mind. Most scholars see the vacillation of his Charterhouse years as intrinsic to his personality, not something that relates to merely one period in his life. His mind always oscillated, we are told, between two antithetical goals. In effect, he could not decide between the Earthly City and the Heavenly City. He both chose the world and did not choose the world, the latter impulse culminating in his martyrdom. Dominic Baker-Smith thus speaks of "a sphinx-like ambiguity" and "an ambivalence which More clung to stubbornly" throughout his life.[118]

117 Marius, *Thomas More*, xxi–xxiv, 14, 42–3. Cf. Guy, *Thomas More*, 102. Peter Ackroyd imagines that More simply made a common-sense response to his sex drive. He knew the consequences of lechery, so he married. See *The Life of Thomas More*, 111.

118 Baker-Smith, *More's Utopia*, 15. Ackroyd speaks similarly of "a consistent doubleness or ambiguity of mind" (*Life*, 55). The editors of the Cambridge *Utopia* also see a "persistent dividedness of mind" (xxiv). Guy holds not only that More did not resolve his contradictory goals in 1505 but that the basis of the decision he actually made at this time will be forever unknowable (*Thomas More*, 181, 214, 38 resp.). According to Greenblatt, *Utopia* demonstrates throughout that More "remains ambivalent about many of his most intensely felt perceptions" (*Renaissance Self-Fashioning*, 54). See also Daniel Kinney, CWM 15, lxxxix and my Introduction above.

PART II

More's Radically New, Both/And, Paradigm: Erasmus' *De taedio Iesu* and the *Enchiridion*, 1503

Never envisioned by scholars is the possibility that More's decision was not ambivalent, uncertain, or indecisive, not a result of conflicting feelings or thoughts – but a resolution. Never considered is the possibility that his decision was not either/or but both/and, that he had suddenly seen a paradigm that made sense of both polarities, a paradigm that showed that they were in fact inseparable and that truth is one thing, that spirituality can never be separated from worldly situations, including one's bodily and mental instincts and traits. In short, nothing has led scholars to entertain the possibility that something other than simply a decision within a see-sawing state of mind might have taken place, something other than merely the decision to marry and have sex, other than the decision to practise law and become ever more involved in politics and humanistic endeavours. It is assumed that the question before More was simply how he would respond to Christianity, whether he would commit himself to a monastic existence or join the world. Nowhere is it imagined that the question was ultimately about the nature of Christianity, that More's decision did not represent failure but liberation.

But why should More's decision be considered both/and rather than either/or? Does not everything brought out in Part I augment the accepted view? Considering his long-standing prior outlook, how could his decision have been anything other than a swing of the pendulum from one side to the other – from the otherworldly ideal to worldliness?

Scholars have recognized that within months of his marriage, from mid- (or late) 1505 through the first four or five months of 1506, More was working with Erasmus on humanistic endeavours, but no one considers the possibility that Erasmus had anything to do with his decision. Working with Erasmus is seen as a consequence. The idea that Erasmus' thinking was causal is never imagined. There are many reasons why it has seemed obvious, not worthy even of comment, that More's decision was unrelated to Erasmus:

- More had become somewhat acquainted with Erasmus during the latter's first visit to England in 1499, but what inte ested him, it appears, was simply Erasmus the humanist.[1]
- No evidence now exists of interactions between Erasmus and More between 1500 and January 1505.
- Nothing in More's comments or writings before his January 1505 decision relates to anything in Erasmus' writings.
- It is assumed that More's anguish and polarization between a one-dimensional view of Christianity and his bodily and worldly desires had no counterpart in Erasmus' experience.
- Most important is the fact that Erasmus' *De taedio Iesu* and *Enchiridion* have been considered unoriginal and lacking in substance – whatever rhetorical or personal particulars Erasmus may have incorporated.
- Nowhere is it recognized that Erasmus' thinking was not either/or but unitarily both/and.
- Nowhere is it seen that Erasmus' mind had been radicalized by Stoicism.
- What could the work of Erasmus and More on the Greek satirist Lucian (b. c. CE 120), of all persons, have to do with More's decision or larger intellectual issues? There is wide agreement, in this regard, that More's introduction to his translations of Lucian (early 1506) is humanistic hocus-pocus.
- A long-standing view is that More was essentially a "hard-headed" and "open-eyed" realist while Erasmus was merely an "unattached" idealistic intellectual.[2]

On the other hand, where is the evidence that actually shows the nature of More's 1505 decision? What was it that impelled him to choose marriage and the world? In the secondary literature we find

1 One small piece of evidence is the poem Erasmus was forced to compose as a result of being "carried off by Thomas Mo e" from Mountjoy's estate, where he was staying (not More's house, significantly), to see the eight-yea -old boy who was in line to become Henry VIII. While More came prepared with a writing (probably a poem), Erasmus was embarrassed at having nothing, and at the urging of the boy went home and composed a poem within three days. *Ep.* 1341A (1523). Allen 1, 6/4-28, CWE 9, 299–300/172–96.

2 Hexter, *More's Utopia*, 131, 136, 143. Passing off Erasmus as "medieval," Ackroyd talks repeatedly about the influence of Augustine, Pico, and Ficino on More. See *Life*, 65.

only speculation. No evidence has been found as to why he picked one option over the other. In the absence of evidence, it is believed that he must have chosen what was for him the less Christian path, giving in to his sexual and worldly impulses. His choice represented a defeat. If we look at his life up to October 1504, there is every reason to believe this scenario. In fact, however, we know nothing of More's mental state between his desperate and despairing letter to Colet of October 1504 and his marriage in January 1505. Can we be sure about the actual meaning of his decision? Did he vacillate in making it, as is unanimously believed? Did he really make a choice between the monastic ideals set forth in his prior intellectual output and his worldly desires, not only sex and marriage but social, political, and humanistic involvements?

1 Thomas More's Transformation: A First Reading of *De taedio Iesu* and the *Enchiridion*

Is it only of coincidental interest that *De taedio Iesu* (*On the Distress of Jesus*)[3] is from cover to cover a criticism of the outlook of More's spiritual advisor? Is it only a chance relationship that the *Enchiridion militis Christiani* (*Handbook of the Christian Soldier*)[4] depicts throughout – as demonstrated in my *The Stoic Origins of Erasmus' Philosophy of Christ* – a two-dimensional type of Christianity directly at odds with not only Colet's outlook but the outlook of More himself, at least through the time of his October 1504 letter to Colet?

In fact there is every reason to believe that More read *De taedio Iesu* and the *Enchiridion* for the first time between his October letter and his January 1505 marriage. In late 1504, around December, Erasmus himself transmitted the two works (published February 1503) along with a letter to Colet.[5] It would have been entirely natural for Colet to loan the works to More, either personally or through an intermediary. In

3 *Disputatiuncula de taedio, pavore, tristitia Jesu, instante supplicio crucis: Deque verbis, quibus visus est mortem deprecari, Pater, si fieri potest, transeat a me calix iste* (Antwerp, Th. Martens, 15 February 1503), LB 5, 1265A–1292A; trans. Michael J. Heath, *A Short Debate Concerning the Distress, Alarm, and Sorrow of Jesus As the Crucifixion Drew Nigh; and Concerning the Words in Which He Seemed to Pray for Deliverance From Death: "Father, If It Be Possible, Let This Cup Pass from Me,"* CWE 70, 13–67.

4 *Enchiridion militis christiani* in *Desiderius Erasmus Roterodamus, Ausgewählte Werke*, ed. Hajo and Annemarie Holborn, 22–136; trans. Charles Fantazzi, *Handbook of the Christian Soldier*, CWE 66, 24–127.

5 *Ep.* 181. Allen 1, 405/42–5, CWE 2, 87/49–52. We may presume that the books and letter were sent to Oxford, but London is a possibility.

his despairing October letter to Colet, More notes that he had come across Colet's servant, who seems to have given him some message from Colet. However this may be, it was the same servant who must have carried his letter to Colet. In the letter More begs Colet to return from the country to London. We know also that Colet was in the process of moving from Oxford to London, where he was to become within months Dean of St Paul's Cathedral. In Part III it will be shown that More was not only working with Erasmus within months of his decision but also was intent on setting forth, against his former either/or way of thinking, a Stoic/Christian unitary both/and outlook – which clearly indicates that his decision resulted directly from reading Erasmus' writings and that it was these writings, above all, that explain his bonding with Erasmus.

As he read *De taedio Iesu* More would have quickly recognized Colet's outlook, but what would have been new and eye-opening was Erasmus' thinking, the actual subject of the treatise. More would have immediately seen that Erasmus' focus on natural instincts was relevant to his own situation. He would have been surprised and altogether taken by the arguments showing that natural instincts and character traits are outside the realm of human control – and yet all-important, indispensable components of what it means to be human and Christian. And he would have been thunderstruck, and deeply moved, on seeing the relationships to Christ himself unfolded; that Christ not only chose human nature but in so doing accepted involuntary natural instincts; that even in the state of innocence Christ experienced not only physical instincts, such as hunger and thirst, but emotional instincts, including sadness and fear of death; that Christ had no means, unlike other humans, of even mitigating his natural fear of death.

More would have also found both astonishing and enlightening the idea that Christ was not a martyr. There is no way that More could have missed the relationship to himself and the issues that had torn him apart. Martyrs, *De taedio Iesu* makes clear, attempt to blot out their fear of death and other physical and mental pains. But Christ, in contrast, did not try to go beyond his human nature and natural instincts and thus did not feel in his Passion the joy, *alacritas*, that martyrs feel. Erasmus drives home the import of Christ's example by showing that the martyr mentality is inappropriate for virtually all human beings. Before this time, More had in fact seen Christ and Christianity in terms of the martyr mentality. Previously, his concerns had all centred on whether or not he was going to be able to drum out of himself his worldly urges, particularly his desires for sex and for political and humanistic involvements. What *De taedio Iesu* would have shown him is that he had no need to try to be a martyr, no need to join the Carthusians. Christ experienced to the full natural instincts. He did not escape, did not try to go beyond them. Joining the Carthusian monastery would have been counter to everything Christ felt and stood for.

In short, *De taedio Iesu* would have set before More's eyes a picture of Christ and the meaning of Christianity that he had never imagined. What an immense relief, what an exhilarating experience, to see – argued, spelled out, and exemplified – that Christ does not expect his followers to go beyond nature, that they must learn to live and deal with their particular natures. As applied to himself, he would have seen that his sexual urges and desires for political and humanistic involvements were genetic and ineradicable, essential aspects of what it means to be a Christian; that Christianity is not one-dimensional but both/and.

The *Enchiridion militis Christiani* explains why joining a religious order, even the strictest, does not in itself make one holy and, for most people, is unsuitable. Spirituality depends on "each person's physical and mental constitution," a constitution that must be studied in depth and then built upon. As stated near the conclusion:

> Being a monk is not a state of holiness [not something attained by a title or by engaging in ceremonies] but a way of life, which may be beneficial or not according to each person's physical and mental constitution [as one resolutely holds to the unbending precepts of the faith]. (127)

Rejected, in effect, was More's assumption that joining the Carthusians would be the highest possible expression of his Christianity. More had long recognized that joining the Carthusians was at odds with his proclivities and he had seen these proclivities in very negative terms, especially, it appears, his sexual impulses, but the *Enchiridion* shows at length that one's particular instincts and character traits are not in themselves evil. More than this, these instincts and traits need careful attention. Spirituality is all about developing and building on the elements of one's constitution as one holds unbendingly to the precepts of the faith. Holiness does not depend on joining an order, and living in a monastery does not make one holy. Holiness is something else, something that hinges on how a person develops his physical and mental makeup. Holiness can be present in every type of life. More would have recognized that the work is dedicated not to a theologian or religious but to a lay person and that the examples given of ways to live a Christian life relate to ordinary humans.

As he read on, all the reasons More had had for thinking his own impulses were unacceptable would have evaporated. He would have seen that persons born with ideal character traits are no more worthy of admiration than persons born with negative character traits, in that humans are not responsible for the traits they are born with. Some humans come into this world in a very flexible and agreeable state while others are born with "a rebellious body," one example being a passion for sex (another being, as with Erasmus, a problem with fasting) (45). While some men have a passion for women and love things sensual, others (perhaps Erasmus himself) never have any particular desire for pleasures of the flesh and the like (53). Others are constitutionally geared towards things such as anger, or sluggishness, or envy. One may have a good trait in one area along with very bad traits in another area. However varied, these inborn characteristics are all indiffe ent. One temperament is not better than another but only more or less fortunate (45). What matters is only what a person does with his particular traits. Natural urges and traits of character are not things that contrast with highest Christianity but are part and parcel of being human and of the Christian life. The desire for sex and marriage is not in itself a negative thing, any more than is the penchant for involvement in politics and humanistic studies. In short, the anguish so evident in More's October 1504 letter was entirely unnecessary. There is no need to feel defeat or guilt about things that are inherent to one's very being. Our struggle, Erasmus emphasizes, is not with nature.

Comments on sex and marriage comprise only small pieces of the *Enchiridion*, but More would certainly not have missed them. Most importantly, he could not have helped but see that these comments are not odd opinions but are supported by a central argument of the entire work. Notably, Erasmus explicitly warns against either celibacy or marriage where such is against one's nature:

> The myth of the giants admonishes us that we must not do battle with the forces of heaven,[6] but that we should refrain from those desires from which nature recoils [a quibus natura abhorret] and should set our minds on those things to which our nature is more inclined [ad quae natura propensior es],

6 Cf. Erasmus' *De taedio Iesu* (1501): "It is no sign of bravery to take arms against nature, like the Giants" (LB 5 1272A) and his edition of *De officiis* (1501), p. 57 (1.110). In Cicero's *De senectute* (*On Old Age*), the Stoic Cato asks: "To rebel against nature – is not that to fight like the giants with the gods?" (2.5). It is likely that Erasmus was looking at Gellius' similar Stoic comment on the giants at 12.5.13. Hesiod's *Theogony* (c. 700 BCE) seems to have been the inspiration behind many ancient versions of the myth. See Price, *Religions of the Ancient Greeks*, 13. Clay argues that the Giants were "the ancestors of the human race." See *Hesiod's Cosmos*, 154.

> provided they are morally acceptable [modo honesta sint]. Thus, do not entangle yourself in marriage if celibacy is more suitable [utilior] to your character, and conversely, do not vow yourself to celibacy if you seem more adapted to the married state, for whatever you attempt against your natural inclination usually turns out to be unsuccessful. (68, H 70/30–71/1)

Imagine Thomas More's reaction to this statement. Joining the Carthusian order would mean (a) doing battle with the forces of heaven, (b) taking part in a goal which his nature abhors, (c) not focusing his mind on things to which his nature was more inclined, and (d) being unsuccessful even if he joined the order. What he would also have noted is one very crucial condition: In following our nature the path that is found more suitable ("utilior") cannot be at odds with that which is morally right ("honesta"). Christianity comprises a unitary both/and. What would have transfixed More is not, however, the restriction, which he would have immediately accepted, but the need to decide on marriage or celibacy based on one's natural inclinations.[7]

Immensely relieving also would have been the contention in both *De taedio Iesu* and the *Enchiridion*, built on but going beyond Stoicism, that the greater the handicap – whether physical or mental or circumstantial – the greater the opportunity for virtue. In *De taedio Iesu* Erasmus demonstrates that Christ himself, counter to Colet's view, is the unparalleled example. His handicaps, including fear of death, were incomparably greater than ever experienced by a human – which gave him the opportunity to exhibit incomparable virtue. Far from being evil or diminishing a person, defects of nature augment the possibilities for spirituality. The person born with unyielding sexual desires, for example, need not lose heart. He must realize that this gives him "a richer opportunity for the practice of virtue" (*Enchiridion* 45, *De taedio Iesu*, 1275B). Since the problem is greater than for others, dealing with it takes greater effort and the achievement is consequently greater. Persons who do not have a particular handicap get no points for their good fortune.

---

7 On the Stoic wiseman's approval of marriage, see Diogenes Laertius 7.121, *De finibus* 3.68, Schofield, *The Stoic Idea of the City*, 119–27, and Reydams-Schils, *The Roman Stoics*, 143–76. The secondary literature tends to see Erasmus' thinking on marriage in terms of rhetorical debate *in utramque partem*. See van der Poel, "For Freedom of Opinion," and Leushuis, "The Mimesis of Marriage." However valuable these discussions, nowhere is it understood that a non-rhetorical (Stoic) frame of thought (centring on things indiffe ent and motivation) underlies his thinking here as elsewhere. Other works include Pabel, "Reading Jerome in the Renaissance"; Reese, "Learning Virginity"; Rummel, ed., *Erasmus on Women*; and Telle, *Érasme de Rotterdam et le Septième Sacrement*.

2 Erasmus' Biography of More

Erasmus' short but detailed 1519 biography of More supports, though this is unrecognized, everything deduced above regarding More's January 1505 decision.[8] Lacking an understanding of the origin, nature, and meaning of the *Enchiridion*, Morean and Erasmian scholars have simply read into the biography what they think Erasmus must be saying rather than what he actually states.[9] They do not see that Erasmus' biography not only nullifies their either/or assumptions and arguments regarding More's decision but also clearly explains how we should understand that decision – and many events that followed. Nor does the biography support the common view that there was a wide gulf between Erasmus' outlook and More's. Many historians hold that Erasmus' biography is not simply a compendium of more or less true facts, as some believe, but that he deliberately distorted More's character to make him fit his own very diffe ent ideal.[10] According to one recent biographer, Erasmus was simply "a spin doctor" not interested in the truth but in constructing – employing his "showmanship" abilities and "a 'simple' philosophy of Christ" – what he considered a rhetorically viable and decorous ideal.[11]

In fact the biography is extraordinarily believable, and the problems scholars find result from a failure to grasp the thinking of either More or Erasmus. There is no reason to dispute Erasmus' claim that he gives here "an outline sketch of the whole man based on long-standing and intimate acquaintance, as far as my observation and memory will serve" (lines 29–31).[12] Consider, for example, the comments on More's

---

8 Erasmus, *Ep*. 999. Allen 11, pp. 13–23, CWE 7, 16–25.

9 In his classic, *Thomas More* (1935), Chambers nowhere mentions the *Enchiridion* or even the philosophy of Christ.

10 Ackroyd, *Life*, 139; Reynolds, *The Field Is Won*, 33. Chambers mines the biography for more or less true facts in his *Thomas More*.

11 Guy, *Thomas More*, 45, 48, 66, 73, 80, 175, 213, passim. The irony is that Guy is himself the true "spin doctor." Throughout this work Guy mixes serious research with faddish "deconstructionist" theses (far more applicable to literature than history). Nothing could be more perversely counterfactual than his opinionating that More and Erasmus were acquainted but were not really friends (211). True friendship would have been impossible, considering that they had "incompatible philosophies" (48) and numerous other diffe ences. Guy's view was preceded by that of Geoff ey Elton and Richard Marius. See also Schoeck, "Telling More from Erasmus."

12 Jardine has shown the extent to which Erasmus ("the model for the detached and disinterested pursuit of learning") and those associated with him in actuality consciously packaged ("cunningly contrived") for maximum effect, using the media of

bodily characteristics and his attitudes towards his body. Among numerous details, we learn that his right shoulder appears to be a little higher than his left (36–62); that he is not a good singer, "though he is fond of music of all kinds" (75–8);[13] that he spends little time on niceties of his appearance (52–5) (a lack of concern which can perhaps be seen in the unshaven Holbein portrait);[14] that he dresses unpretentiously, very simply, never wearing (unlike others of his status and position) silk or scarlet or a gold chain, except on occasions when he has to (compare in this his Utopians, C166/23–168/23); that he is not interested in the "ceremonies" which others associate with good breeding (80–92); that he tends to eat simple, basic types of food, such as eggs, "though in other ways he was by no means averse from all the things that bring harmless pleasure, be it only to the body" (72–3). Illustrating the fact that Erasmus is not assessing More in terms of himself, he points out that More is a person less particular about food than anyone he has ever known (62–3). Erasmus had been and always would be – unlike "the friend I love best" (22–3) – obsessed by concern about types of food and the ability of his body to digest food.

Regarding More's 1505 decision, Erasmus makes four points (172–9):[15]

(1) More had engaged in fasting, watching, and devotional exercises that were extreme in their rigour.

(2) Unlike many others, however, he had made a careful study of himself before committing to the monastic or priestly way of life.

(3) What he discovered was that his constitution was not up to this. He "could not shake off his wish to marry." Nothing stood in the way of his devoting himself to the monastic or priestly life other than this fact.

(4) "And so he chose to be a god-fearing husband rather than an immoral priest."

---

print, their letters and publications. As one example, she points to Erasmus' biography of More and his statement at the beginning that More deserves immortality as much as Alexander the Great or Achilles, even if he himself lacks the painting skills of Apelles. What a reader may not realize in all this is that the "portrait" Erasmus actually paints of More is not idealistic bombast but eminently realistic and detailed. See Jardine, *Erasmus, Man of Letters*, 6 and 58.

13 Carpenter shows that More's adult life "reflects everywhe e a deep interest in and knowledge of music" – and music of all kinds, as "most clearly expressed" in his *Utopia*. She cites, respectively, Y140, 145, 129, 223, 222, 159, 237. See "A Song for All Seasons," 118 and 128–9.

14 See Morison, *The Likeness of Thomas More*. The portrait is in the Frick collection in New York.

15 "Interim et ad pietatis studium totum animum appulit, vigiliis, ieiuniis, precationibus aliisque consimilibus progymnasmatis sacerdotium meditans. Qua quidem in

The first thing to notice is that Erasmus in no way sees More's decision in negative terms. He does not imagine that More had become a lesser person by making the decision – or that More was indecisive by nature. Nor does he intimate that More in any way felt bad about the decision. He does not see that the decision was damaging to More's psyche either in the long term or in the short term. In fact the tone is thoroughly positive. More's decision, he believes, was well taken and very admirable.

Let's look closely at each of the statements.

(1) The fact that More had engaged in fasting, watching, and devotional exercises that were extreme is not at odds with Erasmus' "philosophy of Christ." Being rigorous and rigid regarding the precepts of the faith is an inherent part of the philosophy of Christ. What matters is the motivation. Are these exercises mere "ceremonies" or do they have a spiritual two-dimensional, real-life, meaning?

(2) The fact that More had made a trial of himself before committing to a monastic or priestly way of life was not in Erasmus' mind merely an odd fact. Nor did it represent a failure, a giving in to worldliness, a triumph of sexual desires over Christian truths. Erasmus argues at length in the *Enchiridion* that spirituality cannot begin where there is not deep analysis of one's natural instincts and character traits. He shows how difficul this endeavour is – that humans constantly deceive themselves rather than begin the journey – and it is in this context that he finds More's trial of himself so admirable, so unlike many others. Those who do not practise Christianity from the vantage point of their own unvarnished natural state, whether priest or other, inevitably engage in mere "ceremonies" – blotting out not only the realities of who they are but the precepts of the faith. Indeed, this was for Erasmus not just a philosophy but how he saw his own experiential and spiritual journey.

(3) According to a major theme of the *Enchiridion*, the fact that More's constitution was not up to a monastic existence was not, in itself, a negative. Nor does the fact that one has sexual desires (or other traits) that are much more extreme than is common make one a lesser person. What matters is only how one responds to a particular handicap or

re non paulo plus ille sapiebat quam plerique isti qui temere ad tam arduam professionem ingerunt sese, nullo prius sui periculo facto. Neque quicquam obstabat quo minus sese huic vitae generi addiceret, nisi quod vxoris desyderium non posset excutere. Maluit igitur maritus esse castus quam sacerdos impurus" (Allen 4, 17–18/160–7).

shortcoming. In fact, deviations in one's constitution offer greater opportunity for virtue than does a more normal or agreeable constitution.

(4) That More "chose to be a god-fearing husband" is another way of saying that his decision was unitarily both/and. More decided to be a married person, have sex, and engage in worldly activities, but this did not entail his giving up any of his Christian beliefs. He now saw that worldliness is an inseparable part of Christianity, that Christianity is not just one-dimensional but two-dimensional, that, indeed, worldly activities are the proving ground of Christianity. Even monks cannot get away with being one-dimensional. Spirituality at all times requires a both/and mindset – no matter one's station in life.[16]

In stating that, "rather than [being] an immoral priest," More chose to be a god-fearing husband, Erasmus is bringing out two things:[17] (a) Persons with uncontrollable sexual urges, such as More, should not become part of a situation that requires them to be something they cannot be. This is not what Christianity is about. In such a situation they are bound to engage in immorality, to deceive themselves as well as others. (b) Many priests and monks neither understand nor practise Christ's message. These priests have not come to grips with their bodily and mental situation and consequently cannot progress spiritually – and as a result cling to "ceremonies." Ceremonies allow them to cover up at one and the same time both the reality of who they really are and the precepts of the faith.

Nor does Erasmus' description of More's religiosity at Henry VIII's court support the modern belief that in deciding for the active and worldly life in 1505 More rejected the contemplative and non-worldly life.[18]

> True piety finds in him a practicing follower, though far removed from all superstition. He has his fixed hours at which he says his prayers, and they are not conventional but come from the heart. When he talks with friends about the life after death you recognize that he is speaking from conviction, and not without good hope. And More is like this even at court. *What*

16 Ackroyd, like many, sees two separate sides to More's life after the 1505 decision, one spiritual and one decorous and worldly, the "Contrast between a secret inner life and a rhetorical public role creating this enigmatic and inscrutable figu e." See *Life*, 219 and 266.

17 Guy imagines More's alleged choosing to be a god-fearing husband rather than an immoral priest was merely a playful "quip" by Erasmus. See *Thomas More*, 32–4.

18 Guy claims, for example, that More "irrevocably abandoned 'contemplation'" in favour of the "active" life when he entered royal service in 1518. See *Thomas More*, 39.

becomes then of those people who think that Christians are not to be found except in monasteries? (296–302; italics mine)

Here too Erasmus sees More as holding to a rigid type of thinking when it comes to the ultimate truths of Christianity at the same time as he is involved in all the hurly-burly and dangers at court. "Even at court" – not in some separate location – he practises true Christianity, a Christianity not rooted in superstitious ceremonies but in the heart. Against what Erasmus sees as a common opinion, More's Christianity is as valid as anything found in monasteries. Action and contemplation, worldly and otherworldly, are inseparable.

Critics have long been particularly disturbed by Erasmus' statement at one point that More was "dragged" into Henry VIII's court. They believe this contention is clearly untrue and gives further reason to deny the trustworthiness of Erasmus' biography.[19] Erasmus himself ran from all church or political involvement and saw that More's involvement was a loss to humanist scholarship, so he simply manufactured his account. More had to have been "dragged" into court because if he were not "dragged" Erasmus' ideals would have been jeopardized. In fact, the critics argue, More enjoyed worldly affairs and went willingly to court. Here again, however, researchers have thoroughly misunderstood Erasmus' meaning – resulting from their failure to understand the *Enchiridion* and *The Praise of Folly* (1511) (see below, Part V) – much less More's own thinking as found in his translations and *Introduction to Lucian* (1506) (see below, Part III), *Richard III* (1513–18), and *Utopia* (1516) (see below, Parts VI–VIII). Let us look at the relevant statements:

> Court life and the friendship of princes were formerly not to his taste, for he has always had a special hatred of absolute rule and a corresponding love for equality. You will hardly find any court, however modest, that is not full of turmoil and self-seeking, of pretence and luxury, and is really free from any taint of despotic power. Even the court of Henry VIII he could not be induced to enter except by great efforts, although it would be difficul to wish for anything more cultured and more unassuming than the present king [as assessed in 1519]. By nature he has a great love of liberty and leisure; but dearly as he loves to enjoy leisure when he can, no one displays more energy or more endurance at the call of duty. (88–97)

19 See Elton "Thomas More, Councilor"; Suzuki, "Thomas More on Politics as a Profession"; Ackroyd, *Life*, 90; Guy, *Thomas More*, 48, 54, 58, 67 passim; and Furey, *Erasmus, Contarini, and the Religious Republic of Letters*, 26–8, 32–3, 37–8.

> He had made up his mind to be content with this station in life (as a judge in civil cases, 1510–18), which gave him quite sufficien standing and at the same time was not exposed to serious risks. More than once he was forced to go on a diplomatic mission;[20] and as he conducted these with great intelligence, his serene Majesty King Henry VIII would not rest until he had dragged the man to his court. I use the word "dragged" advisedly, for no man was ever more consumed with ambition to enter a court than he was to avoid it. (234–40; italics mine)

I will begin by making two points:

(1) More's long-standing hatred of the pretence, self-seeking, luxury, and despotism found at court is not contestable. More had even written a highly original book on the subject, *Richard III* (above, 62–5) – so powerful that it would carve a place in Shakespeare's mind. And in 1505–6 at his suggestion, Erasmus tells us, he and Erasmus wrote competing essay replies to Lucian's *Tyrannicida* (277–9). As shown earlier (61), More expresses in his essay unmitigated contempt for the tyrant, a person cruel, violent, and lawless. The flip side of his disparagement of tyranny was a "love for equality." In his youth More had "even worked on a dialogue in which he supported Plato's doctrine of communalism, extending it [as did Plato, *Rep.* 5.449–61] even to wives" (275–7). The radicalness of this proposition comes into focus if we consider that in Florence, the epicentre of the spread of Platonism in the latter fifteenth century, better-born citizens found Plato's community of women even more distasteful (allegorizing it away) than his acceptance of homosexuality.[21] Further illustrating this focus on equality and disdain for tyranny, considerable evidence supports the view that More "was the first Englishman seriously to consider the education of women, whom he considered not a jot less intelligent or scholarly than men."[22] And a relationship between More's admirable family life, to which Erasmus refers (180–215), and family life among the Utopians has long been recognized.[23]

(2) No evidence indicates that More was not content with being a judge in civil cases from 1510 to 1518. This was true not only because,

20 It is Erasmus who tells us that More wrote Book II of *Utopia* before Book I while at leisure on a mission in 1515 to Antwerp (282–4).

21 See Field, *The Origins of the Platonic Academy of Florence*, 269. Ficino thoroughly distorted Plato's thinking on communism, seeing the common life in simple moralistic terms. Rich persons should take care, protect the poor, and distribute wealth. See Letter 73, in *The Letters of Marsilio Ficino*, 119–20.

22 Ackroyd, *Life*, 146.

23 Bridgett, *Life and Writings of Sir Thomas More*, 138.

according to Erasmus, he enjoyed it, was highly respected, and received a large income (165), but because in this position he was "not exposed to serious risk." There was every reason why a man of principle (and even one without) should find being a king's councillor risky in the extreme. *Richard III* is all about this risk: the deceit that everywhere reigns in a king's court. Smiles and alleged friendship, and even doing good, mean nothing when the perceived self-interest of the king or other councillors is at stake. More's own execution shows just how right he was in seeing the danger inherent in involvement in the court of a king – notwithstanding his enjoyment of politics and the law.

In short, when Erasmus states that More could not be induced to enter Henry VIII's court "except by great efforts" and that "no man was ever more consumed with ambition to enter a court than he was to avoid it," he was describing exactly why, from rational self-interest, More of all people would have been extremely apprehensive about joining the court. Compare also the reasoning found in Book I *Utopia*, C81–95.[24]

But there are even more important reasons why Erasmus holds that More was "dragged" into court – relating directly to the person More had become and the philosophy of Christ.

(1) A core theme of the *Enchiridion* is that "We should strive after Christ, our only goal [scopum], with such great ardor that we have no time to attend to any of these (worldly) things, either when they are given to us or when they are taken away" (63, H 65/18). From the standpoint of Christ's precepts – one side of the unitary both/and – worldly acts are in themselves indiffe ent (as seen from the first type of value in Stoicism, not the second type). While others would have relished being at court because of ambition, wealth, power, and the like, More was above all this. He had no ulterior motives. What matters – as with the Stoic wiseman – is only the goal, the intention. Things indiffe - ent, as Zeno and all Stoics contended, should never be sought after on their own account (DL 7.101–7).

(2) Although Erasmus does not refer to Plato in this connection, he and More would have likely recognized that Plato had argued: "Only if the city is ruled by those who do not wish to rule but have other things that they would prefer to do can the city be well ruled" (*Rep.* 520E–521A). They would have seen this contention as relating to the unbending side of the Stoic unitary both/and.

24 See also Seneca's discussions of the reasons why Stoic philosophers were apprehensive about joining the councils of heads of state. See Introduction, 33–4. These reasons compare closely to the objections of Hythloday in Book I of *Utopia*.

(3) More looked at involvement from two radically diffe ent but inseparable perspectives – just as in his 1505 decision. On the one hand, he loved by nature liberty and leisure, all the variables of life, and, on the other hand, was unmatched in his response to "the call of duty" – precepts. Critics not only do not see a relationship to the *Enchiridion,* they do not see that the thesis of the *Enchiridion* is not Platonist and one-dimensional but through and through Stoic and two-dimensional.

(4) In saying that More was "dragged" into court, Erasmus cannot be supporting a non-worldly ideal against a worldly reality because Erasmus' own ideology – which he in fact gave to More – is profoundly worldly. The *Enchiridion* is all about the mindset that should govern in worldly situations, no matter what these situations might be. Whether involved in humanistic endeavours or life at court, Christianity requires the same unitary both/and mindset. Worldly matters are to be considered simultaneously from two types of value; from the unbending side they are utterly indiffe ent, while from the bending side the diffe ences between these indiffe ents are all-important. When Erasmus regrets that More's involvement at court took him away from humanism, in a letter that served as an introduction to the 1518 edition of *Utopia,* he was not imagining that there was something wrong about More's involvement but simply recognizing – contrary to what is so often contended – that this was an undeniable consequence (C 4/9–11). Indeed, Erasmus praises in his biography More's performance at court.[25] Whether More joined the court or did not, Christianity required for Erasmus, and in his footsteps More, the same mindset.

3 The Unexplained Explained

Why readers have seen nothing of the radically new paradigm that suddenly encased More's mind in late 1504 – much less the effect of this paradigm on the writings and life that followed – can now be easily explained.

Around ten years older than More, Erasmus had been radicalized beginning around 1497 by Stoicism. Unlike any of his humanist

25 "Happy indeed a commonwealth would be if the prince would appoint to each post a magistrate like More" (248–50). "Had you lived in this court, my dear Hutten, I have no doubt you would ... cease to be a professed enemy of court life" (311–13). Often difficult issues demand an authoritative and able judge, and M e – with "absolute integrity" (227–8), free of pride (250) or love of money (216) – can settle these in such a way that both parties are grateful (245–7).

predecessors, he had come to see the true nature of Stoicism and had transferred the Stoic two-dimensional way of thinking to Christianity. His edition of *De officiis* (1501), *De taedio Iesu* (1501), and *Enchiridion militis Christiani* (1503) work out this newfound outlook. What had led Erasmus to Stoicism was not abstract intellectualizations but deep concerns about the nature of his body and mind and relationships to society and Christianity.[26] Thomas More, as we have seen, had closely related concerns. And just as Erasmus before his Stoic-based transformation had contrasted worldly concerns with Christianity, a Christianity seen in abstract one-dimensional terms, so too had Thomas More.

In short, we can now understand both the nature of More's decision and why it had come about so abruptly. Erasmus' *De taedio Iesu* and *Enchiridion* spoke directly to everything that had so disturbed him – and provided answers. In January 1505 he did not make a choice between two polar views. Worldly and otherworldly, he now saw, are not two separate things. Joining the Carthusians would have been for him not a greater thing but a lesser thing. Even Christ himself had found that physical, mental, and situational factors are ineradicable starting points. There is no necessary contradiction between highest Christianity and wholehearted commitment to worldly affairs – worldly affairs that include marriage, humanistic studies, lawyering, and politics.

We can now also comprehend how it came about that More was working with Erasmus, filled with joy and good spirits, within months of his January 1505 marriage. His prime purpose in so quickly developing his relationship with Erasmus and working with him on a day-to-day basis would have been to more deeply gauge the mind and thinking of an author who had decisively changed the course and meaning of his life. And this bonding would have deepened as he worked with Erasmus. He would have learned that Erasmus had once shared More's former one-dimensional understanding of Christianity, that in *De contemptu mundi* he had held that highest Christianity is about vigils, fasts, and silence and that the world is evil and marriage an affliction but that, inspired by Stoic discussions of "the law of nature," he had long before changed his views completely – even composing, mainly in 1497 or 1498 (though it was not printed until 1518), a book on marriage, *Encomium matrimonii* (*The Praise of Matrimony*).[27]

---

26 See Dealy, *Stoic Origins*, Part II, Ch. 4.

27 ASD I-2, 400–29, CWE 25, 129–44.

He would likely have brought to More's attention statements in that work such as the following:

> Wedlock is called honorable, and the marriage bed undefiled by the apostle Paul, but celibacy is never even named there. Nor is it excused except by the compensation of a greater good. In all other respects one who follows the law of nature and procreates children is to be preferred to one who perseveres in the single state simply in order to have a more independent life.
>
> *For if, as the Stoics, the most perceptive of philosophers, maintain, to live rightly is to follow the instigations of nature, what is so consistent with nature as marriage?* (Italics mine)
>
> I have no patience with those who say that sexual excitement is shameful and that venereal stimuli have their origin not in nature, but in sin.[28]
>
> *"But [they say] one must obey virtue rather than nature." As if anything which is at variance with nature could be called virtue!* (Italics mine)[29]

Not of little significance, reflections of *De taedio Iesu* are found in More's last major work, *De tristitia Christi* (*On the Sadness of Christ*), written in the Tower of London shortly before his execution in 1535 (CWM 14). Standing out is his use of the word *alacer* (eager joy) and cognates. Germain Marc'hadour shows that he employs this word at least thirteen times; in one instance, late in the work, even discarding in handwriting *alacritatem*.[30] What Marc'hadour and others have not seen, in their attempts to understand why he would use this word, a word not found in the New Testament, is that More is building on Erasmus' all-out criticisms of *alacritas* in *De taedio Iesu* – in rejecting, building on negative Stoic employments of this word, the martyr mentality.[31] Not cognizant of this heritage, Marc'hadour does not grasp the significance of his own research, most especially where he finds that "Nowhere is it

---

28 Contrast Augustine, who, in Peter Brown's words, "held that the most humble details of the body's experience of sexuality – erection, impotence, orgasm, and instinctive shame – mirrored a failure of the will more drastic and irrevocable than [even] Cassian [who greatly influenced estern monasticism] had been willing to admit." See *The Body and Society*, 433.

29 See ASD I-2, 406/3–5, 409/5–7, 414/11–12, 415/44–5, CWE 25, 132, 134, 136. This work and others aroused much criticism from theologians. In 1526 he published his lengthy *Institutio christiani matrimonii* (*Institution of Christian Matrimony*) (LB V, 613–724, CWE 69, 215–438).

30 Marc'hadour, "Thomas More on the Agony of Christ."

31 See Dealy, *Stoic Origins*, 146–8.

[the word *alacritas*] construed as a note of true sanctity."[32] In *De tristitia Christi* More even brings in, without attribution, Erasmus' distinction in *De taedio Iesu* between the person with a martyr mentality, who experiences *alacritas* at the expense of his natural instincts, and the person whose bravery is like Christ's in that it does not overleap his human nature. "He [Christ] wished His followers to be brave and prudent soldiers, not senseless and foolish. The brave man bears up under the blows which beset him; the senseless man simply does not feel them when they strike" (CWM 14, 59/3–6).[33] In this context – as he faced execution – he also brings in Erasmus' "greater handicap thesis": "But before the actual engagement, fear [for Erasmus a natural instinct, Stoic *oikeiosis*] is not reprehensible, as long as reason does not cease to struggle against fear – a struggle which is not criminal or sinful but rather an immense opportunity for merit" (CWM 14, 73/1–4). Nothing in *De tristitia Christi* ties in with Colet's outlook.[34]

Although from 1520 onwards the lives and outlooks of Erasmus and More had increasingly diverged, the bond between them remained – and considering all the above we can now well understand why this was the case. On hearing in 1534 that More was in jail, Erasmus stated, simply, that he was "the greatest friend I ever had."[35] This was not mere hyperbole. In a 1506 letter (noted earlier, 50) Erasmus remembers that Richard Whitford, a mutual friend, used to describe himself and More "as so similar in mind, character, outlook and pursuits that no pair of twins on earth could be more alike."[36] In *De Copia*, published in 1512, Erasmus had given two hundred ways of saying, centring on More,

---

32 Marc'hadour, "Thomas More on the Agony of Christ," 498. Marc'hadour does note (497), without finding an explanation, Erasmus' employment of the wo d *alacritas* ("at least twelve times") in his late 1499 letter (*Ep*. 109) to Colet.

33 In facing execution, made inevitable by a "scruple of conscious" (reminding us of the Stoics of old), More did not exhibit *alacritas* and did not attempt to abrogate his physical and mental instincts. Even moments before ascending the platform, talking to his daughter Margaret, his fear was manifest. See Ackroyd, *Life*, 346, 381, and 401 (Cresacre's report). Even the effort Mo e took to defend himself at his trial, and before, demonstrates that he was in no way seeking martyrdom. In this regard, Guy's discussion is convincing. See *Thomas More*, 190–7. The Stoic Seneca, we may note, considered political martyrdom necessary only when incessant attempts to rectify issues by unitary both/and methods have failed. See *Tr*. 5.2–4, 11.1–6, 14.3, 7, 10, 16.1, 3; *Ep*. 95.70–1, 73, 120.12.

34 Clarence H. Miller's belief (CWM 14, 1007) that More combined at 47/3–49/2 the positions of Colet and Erasmus in *De taedio Iesu* reflects a misunderstanding. The theses he mentions are both represented by Erasmus.

35 *Ep*. 2965. Allen 11, 39/26–7.

36 *Ep*. 191. Allen 1, 423/28–32, CWE 2, 113/38–9.

"Always, as long as I live, I shall remember you." One example is: "My beloved More is so closely embraced in my soul that he cannot escape while I live."[37] In Part V below I will demonstrate, something never heretofore recognized, that his *Praise of Folly* (1511) is from beginning to end a play on More's Stoic/Christian unitary both/and personality. More, for his part, defended Erasmus and *The Praise of Folly* in a lengthy 1515 treatise, *Letter to Martin Dorp*,[38] written about the same time as Book II of *Utopia*, and in 1519 in another lengthy treatise, *Letter to a Monk*,[39] defended Erasmus' life and works and attacked monastic abuse – against, not of little significance, a prominent resident of the London Charterhouse, John Batmanson. In the last years of his life More endorsed all of Erasmus' writings[40] and in 1532 (noted earlier, 50) refers ten times, in response to a taunt, to Erasmus as "my derlynge."

One point needs emphasis. In late 1504 More came to think about himself, the world, and Christianity in terms of a philosophy, not a philosophy of his own making but a philosophy that had a long and distinguished ancient heritage. While modern scholarship has always seen the thinking of Erasmus and More in rhetorical terms, in actuality Erasmus built his "philosophy of Christ" from Stoicism, and More, we will see in Parts III–VIII, was to build on both the "philosophy of Christ" and his own deep studies of Stoicism. While fifteenth-century humanists had made philosophy serve rhetoric, Erasmus made rhetoric serve philosophy – and so too does Thomas More. Contrary to what has been believed, *Utopia* is not a rhetorically inspired work. It is rhetorical only in the sense that rhetoric works out a deep-seated philosophical way of thinking.

Part III below demonstrates that More's late 1505 to early 1506 translations and introduction of Lucian are throughout carefully built from his new Stoic-based, two-dimensional, way of thinking – and poles apart from anything he had previously written.

37 CWE 24, 354/22–364/26 at 361/20–1.

38 CWM 15, 1–127.

39 CWM 15, 198–311.

40 See McConica, "The Recusant Reputation of Thomas More."

PART III

More's *Lucian*, 1506 – and *Utopia*: Teaching Stoic Two-Dimensional Christianity

Erasmus arrived in London in the summer of 1505, his second visit, and stayed until June 1506.[1] During this period he and More prepared translations from Greek into Latin of some of the dialogues of Lucian of Samosata, the second-century satirist and social commentator.[2] The resulting work was published in late 1506.[3] During More's lifetime none of his writings, not even *Utopia*, was printed as many times as his Lucian compositions.[4]

---

1 There exists no precise dating for Erasmus' arrival in England. He could have arrived any time between March 1505 and the fall of 1505. See Allen 1, p. 414.

2 Lucian wrote around eighty prose works, a great many of them dialogues. See the Loeb edition of *Lucian*, vols. 1–8. His writings are not easy to categorize and his purposes are often unclear. See Bompaire, *Lucien, écrivain, imitation et création*; Anderson, *Lucian*; Hall, *Lucian's Satire*; Jones, *Culture and Society in Lucian*; Branham, *Unruly Eloquence*; Whitmarsh, *Greek Literature and the Roman Empire*; and Goldhill, *Who Needs Greek?* 60–107.

3 *Luciani opuscula ... ab Erasmo Roterodamo et Thoma Moro ... in Latinorum linguam traducta*. On 1 November 1506 Erasmus presented to the printer seven of his translations and four of More's. An addendum to the work includes more of his translations and later editions added to this. All in all Erasmus translated twenty-eight dialogues, eighteen of them brief and ten longer. See Christopher Robinson, ASD I-1, 370–1. Erasmus' contributions are found in ASD I-1, 361–627 and More's in CWM 3, Pt. 1.

4 The Lucian compositions were printed nine times during More's life and *Utopia* fiv times. See Gibson and Patrick, *St. Thomas More*, and Constance Smith, *An Updating of R.W. Gibson's 'St. Thomas More: A Preliminary Bibliography'*. On the Latin translations and impact of Lucian before More, beginning around 1400, see Marsh, *Lucian and the Latins*. A listing of editions of Lucian printed in the fifteenth and sixteenth centuries is found in Lauvergnat-Gagnière, *Lucien de Samosate et le lucianisme en France au XVIe siècle*, 352–431. The importance of Lucian's influence on Erasmus – in his translations *Adages*, *Praise of Folly*, and, most of all, *Colloquies* – is demonstrated by Robinson, *Lucian and His Influence in Europe*, 165–97. See also Goldhill, *Who Needs Greek?* 49–54.

The secondary literature has tended to see More's Lucian compositions as mere "literary recreations" and, compared with his mind in later years, "remote irrelevancies."[5] The editors of the Cambridge *Utopia* consider his short introduction to the three dialogues he translates a rhetorical and vacillating mishmash, displaying, as in his previous writings and later the *Utopia* (1516), "persistent dividedness of mind."[6] This assessment was influenced by Alistair Fox's *Thomas More: History and Providence*.[7] According to Fox, the dialogue *Cynicus* reflects in More's introduction one side of an either/or while *Menippus* reflects the other. More simply could not make up his mind whether to be holy or merely wise.[8] Gerard Wegemer, on the other hand, has decided that More's real view is found in *Menippus*, where it is argued that "the life of the ordinary citizen is best."[9]

Hard analysis uncovers an entirely diffe ent picture. There is in Thomas More's mind no rhetorical nonsense, no game playing, no vacillating, and no contradicting. He sets forth thoughts at the very centre of the way he viewed the world and Christianity. And his arguments are anything but traditional. The introduction gives us compelling proof, documentary evidence, of a radically changed mind no more than a year after his life-changing decision – and shows us much about the particulars of that mind. Nothing in his previous thinking is even remotely relevant to what is found in these few pages. Nothing earlier indicates knowledge or even interest in Stoicism. And the perception of Stoicism that existed in the humanistic culture that could have touched him, at odds with everything his introduction is about, was only one-dimensional – further proof of the influence of Erasmus.

5 Craig R. Thompson, CWM 3, Pt. 1, xxiii.

6 Cambridge *Utopia*, xxiv. For More's introduction see CWM 3, Pt. 1, pp. 2–9 (Latin, modern English). His translations of the three dialogues are found on pages 10–77 (Greek, Latin) and pages 159–96 (modern English). He also translated (not mentioned in his introduction) Lucian's *Tyrannicida* (78–93; modern English 197–204) and composed a declamation, in competition with Erasmus, in response (Latin/modern English, 94–127). Erasmus translated *Tyrannicida* separately (ASD I-1, 506–13), and his declamation is considerably longer than More's (ASD I-1, 516–51). Regarding More's translations, see Pawlowski, "Thomas More's Mis-translations of Lucian's *Cynic, Menippus,* and *Tyrannicide.*"

7 Fox, *Thomas More*, 35–44. Goldhill shows that Lucian was at the time (and even for centuries thereafter) of central importance for those wishing to learn Greek. See *Who Needs Greek?* 43–9 passim.

8 Fox, *Thomas More*, 38. A theme is that More's introduction is "a deceptive document," "provocatively disingenuous," "a piece of propaganda pleading," "deliberately elusive," "entirely harmless," a "red herring," spoken "tongue in cheek."

9 Wegemer, *Young Thomas More*, 67–8. Beyond comprehension, Wegemer finds su - port for More's worldly focus in his despairing 1504 letter to Colet – a letter which is profoundly non-worldly in focus. See above, 74–5.

Not least, the introduction is a first statement of the unitary both/and (non-rhetorical and non-Platonist) thinking that I had found long ago, but could not explain, in *Utopia* – published ten years after the introduction to *Lucian*, in 1516.

Although the first sentence of the introduction lauds Lucian for fulfilling the Horatian maxim that pleasure and instruction be combined, More's interest throughout is in instruction.[10] The fact that Lucian was a pagan and doubted his own immortality does not detract, More stresses, from the relevance of what he has to say. "What diffe ence does it make to me what a pagan thinks about those articles contained in the principal mysteries of the Christian faith?" (5/19–20).[11] He found Lucian relevant in that he refrains from "the arrogant pronouncements" of (certain types of) philosophers as well as "the wanton wiles of the poets" and yet censures common human frailties (3/7–11). But for More this setting provided only a platform. Analysis reveals that the central purpose of his introduction and of his translations is to rewrite Lucian in Stoic/Christian unitary both/and terms. Previously unseen, the introduction digs deeply into *Tusculan Disputations* and *De officiis* and reveals that it was not for odd or rhetorical reasons that More chose the three dialogues he translates. Nor was the way he orders the three dialogues capricious. *Cynicus*, the first dialogue, describes Stoic *honestum* in Christian terms. *Menippus*, the second dialogue, describes Stoic *utile* in Christian terms. *Philopseudes*, the third dialogue, describes the oneness of the *honestum* and the *utile* – and the accompanying emotional and mental well-being – in Christian terms. The either/or positions of *Cynicus* and *Menippus* reflect More's outlook before his life-altering January 1505 decision, while *Philopseudes* reflects the radicalized way he had come to see the meaning of Christianity. His criticisms of insertions and additions to saints' lives show how this way of thinking is worked out vis-à-vis a particular issue.

1 Joy and the New Frame of Mind

More has most to say about the dialogue *Philopseudes sive Incredulus* (*The Lover of Lies, or the Doubter*),[12] a work that had previously aroused

10 Whether or not Ackroyd is correct in alleging that Lucian's focus on laughter had a "permanent and profound" influence on Mo e (*The Life of Thomas More*, 94), the actual message of More's introduction is anything but funny.

11 The numbers in these references are to pages and lines respectively.

12 CWM 3.1, Greek and Latin pp. 44–77; modern English pp. 180–96. Incredibly, Fox declines even to discuss *Philopseudes*, commenting, without giving a single reason, that this dialogue is "not immediately relevant to an understanding of More's

little interest among humanists.[13] Near the beginning he states (the numbering here and elsewhere is mine) the following:

> Hunc certe fructum nobis affe et iste dialogus ut neque magicis habeamus praestigijs fidem, & superstitione careamus, quae passim sub specie religionis obrepit, tum uitam ut agamus minus anxiam, minus uidelicet expauescentes tristia quaepiam ac superstitiosa mendacia. (4/17–21)

> Surely the dialogue will teach us this lesson: (1) that we should put no trust in magic and that we should eschew superstition, which obtrudes everywhere under the guise of religion and (2) that we should live a life less distracted by anxiety; less fearful, that is, of any gloomy and superstitious untruths. (5/21–5)

Component (1) betokens an intellectual issue, the need to reject magic and superstition. But what are magic and superstition? All we learn at this point is that magic and superstition are not religion, and that, notwithstanding, superstition is always set forth "under the guise of religion." Component (2) tells us that fear and gloom inhere in "superstitious untruths" and that anxiety is the result, which is another reason why "superstitious untruths" must be overcome.

An immediate problem is More's assertion that "the dialogue will teach us" (1) and (2). Is he intimating that (1) and (2) reflect "as is" the lessons the dialogue teaches, or is he thinking that (1) and (2) are implications that can be drawn or developed from what the dialogue teaches? We can begin to answer this question by placing (2) opposite, on the one hand, what Lucian actually argues – which More had carefully studied in the act of translating – and, on the other hand, More's October 1504 letter, written one year earlier, before the mindset that emerged in January 1505 (above, 74–5). What can be demonstrated is

---

intellectual development." See *Thomas More*, 44. In fact most of More's discussion of the dialogues is about *Philopseudes*. *Philopseudes* takes up 44 lines (4/10–6/20) in the CWM edition while *Cynicus* and *Menippus* together take up only 20 lines (2/20–4/10). Imagining that More overlays *Cynicus* and *Menippus* with "familiar Christian pieties," Branham likewise passes over *Philopseudes*. See "Utopian Laughter," 25. Wegemer comments on *Philopseudes* but does not recognize that it resolves, as I will demonstrate, the issues debated in *Cynicus* and *Menippus*. See *Thomas More on Statesmanship*, 84–8 and *Young Thomas More*, 65. Ogden has now worked out the heritage of each of the tales found in *Philopseudes* in *In Search of the Sorcerer's Apprentice*. See also Ebner, Gzella, Nesselrath, and Ribbat, *Lukian*.

13 See Marsh, *Lucian and the Latins*, and Lauvergnat-Gagnière, *Lucien de Samosate et le lucianisme en France au XVIe siècle*.

that More's emphasis on the relief of anxiety gives a radical twist to both Lucian and the letter.

Contrast (2) with Lucian

At the end of *Philopseudes*, Philocles jokes about a story that a person bitten by a mad dog goes mad and fears water and that if such a person bites someone else that person will have the same type of fears ("eodem modo formidaturum") (77/21, 196). Philocles wonders if Tychiades has not passed the bite on to him and filled his soul with spirits, to which Tychiades replies:

> At bono animo simus amice, quum magnum aduersus huiusmodi res remedium habeamus, ueritatem rectamque omnibus in rebus rationem, quo si utamur, nullis huiusmodi uanis stultisque mendacijs turbabimur. (77/24–7)

> Well, never mind, my dear fellow; we have a powerful antidote to such poisons in truth and in sound reason brought to bear everywhere. As long as we make use of this, none of these empty, foolish lies will disturb our peace. (CWM 3.1, 196)

That our peace will be disturbed by foolish untruths is not a contention made elsewhere in *Philopseudes*. Nor is Tychiades making a statement about the nature of distress. He is merely commenting, as a conclusion to the work, on the mysterious ways in which superstitious nonsense moves from one person to another and affirmin that the elimination of such, using common sense, will take away the clutter from our minds. Belief in magic and superstition, such as a statue walking at night (188), creates fear, and this fear is contagious. Once one person alleges something, others believe the same. Eliminating magic and superstition by truth and common sense means that irrationalities will no longer disturb our minds.

More is talking about a very diffe ent type of superstition and mental disturbance:

(a) He is not talking merely or even primarily about mental disturbances brought on by "superstitiously" holding to irrational and contagious beliefs, such as a statue walking, but about mental and emotional anguish brought about by "superstitiously" holding to false conceptions of religion. Tychiades nowhere distinguishes between true and false conceptions of religion. Nor does he anywhere allow the validity of *faith*.

(b) More's statement is not tacked on at the end of his discussion but is at the very beginning. Here and in what follows he makes a major issue of the idea "that we should live a life less distracted by anxiety; less fearful, that is, of any gloomy and superstitious untruths."

(c) The deep feelings brought out in More's statement have no counterpoint in *Philopseudes*. In his concluding remark, Lucian is not discussing or thinking of or delving into a discussion of emotions as such. Nowhere does Tychiades talk about "anxiety" and "gloomy untruths," the need to live life "minus anxiam, minus uidelicet expauescentes tristia quaepiam ac superstitiosa mendacia." Getting rid of superstition doesn't simply clear our minds, as with Lucian: it deeply affects our emotional state.

Contrast (2) with More's 1504 Letter

In the letter More very explicitly states that he is suffering from extreme anxiety brought about by the fact that he sees himself sinking down, hopelessly, into worldly muck – unable to come up to the one-dimensional ideals he and Colet espouse. Now, however, we find not only a focus on anxiety as such but the belief that anxiety can be overcome. Now, anxieties, fear, and gloom are not the result of holding to the otherworldly demands of the Christian faith – though not able to come up to them – but "superstitious untruths." Somehow a positive mental and emotional state is connected with the elimination (yet to be defined) of magic and superstition that "obtrudes everywhere under the guise of religion." In the letter More is in despair because he has no solution to his dilemma and Colet is not helping him. Now he has a solution. But what is it? In the letter, anxiety is brought about by the demands of Christianity, whereas now anxiety is brought about by "superstitious untruths." In the letter, he imagines that joining the rigid Carthusian order and living up to the ideals of that order would eliminate anxiety. Now it is the overcoming of "superstitious untruths" that can eliminate anxiety.

What accounts for this apparent reversal in outlook? It cannot be that this new outlook and spirit are merely the response of a rhetorician to Lucian's dialogues, for throughout the introduction More is very clearly talking about the relation of the dialogues he translates to a particular view of Christianity. Nor is it helpful here to engage in psychoanalytic theorizing. Without a trace of evidence, Marius speculates (taking no note even of More's October 1504 letter and his previous intellectual output) that More's opposition here to gloom, fear, and anxiety "may have represented a counterattack against the anxiety he felt [in Marius' imagination] for his married condition and the opportunity it gave him to have sexual intercourse anytime he wanted."[14] In other words, (2) is not what it seems. It is just words, a mirage covering deeper psychological problems, one side of the polar mentality that ostensibly characterized More throughout his life. More allegedly made his decision to marry fuelled only by sexual disturbance, and this decision was accompanied by a deep feeling of failure, a failure that resulted in vacillations between worldly involvements and abstract ideals that were always to accompany him.

Or, could it be, as I will demonstrate below, that More had come to see – in accord with what was uncovered in Part II – his earlier anxieties as reflecting a false view of Christianity and that as a result his life had dramatically changed?

The Role of *Tusculan Disputations*

Note the carefully worded statement by which More concludes his introductory discussion of *Philopseudes* (and the other two dialogues). The argument here is central to the entire introduction. This is the case because it is a rewording with much greater detail of the two theses, one intellectual and one emotional, that begin his discussion – analysed above. Look closely at the words:

> Quamobrem quas scriptura nobis historias diuinitus inspirata commendat, eis indubitata fides habenda est. Caeteras uero ad Christi doctrinam, tanquam ad Critolai regulam, applicantes caute & cum iudicio, aut recipiamus, aut respuamus, si carere uolumus, & inani fiducia, & supersticiosa formidine. (6/15–20)

> (1a) We ought to place unquestioning trust in the stories commended to us by divinely inspired Scripture, (1b) but testing the others carefully and deliberately by the teaching of Christ (as though applying the rule of Critolaus), (1c) we should either accept or reject them (2a) if we wish to free ourselves both from foolish confidence and superstitious dread. (7/17–22)

What are we to make of these assertions?

(1a) advises "unquestioning trust" in a hard type of truth, the accounts found in "divinely inspired Scripture."

(1b) contends that other, non-scriptural, types of allegations should be judged in accordance with the hard truth that comprises scripture, "the teaching of Christ." But how precisely did More understand

14 Marius, *Thomas More*, 85.

Christ's message? This is not by any means obvious. More immediately problematic is the manner in which the judging of non-biblical stories, accounts, or arguments should take place. There are true non-scriptural stories as well as false non-scriptural stories. Determining which stories are true and which false must be done in a particular way, "as though applying the rule [regulam] of Critolaus." What is this rule? What does this rule entail? More seems to assume we know.

(1c) Testing the secondary, non-scriptural, types of allegations in terms of hard truth, as though applying the *regula*, we should then "either accept or reject" their claims to truth. We must not, that is, just leave these stories, views, or allegations hanging.

(2a) makes the freeing of ourselves "both from foolish confidence and superstitious dread" central to this enterprise. Why would emotional liberation be an inextricable outcome of applying the *regula* to the teachings of Christ?

Compare the earlier statement:

> Surely the dialogue will teach us this lesson: (1) that we should put no trust in magic and that we should eschew superstition, which obtrudes everywhere under the guise of religion. (2) It teaches us also that we should live a life less distracted by anxiety; less fearful, that is, of any gloomy and superstitious untruths. (5/21–5)

The concluding statement (7/17–22) carefully develops the earlier statement and, we will see, encapsulates what the entire introduction is about. While the beginning (1) simply castigates magic and asserts that the dialogues teach us that superstition always presents itself "under the guise of religion," the concluding (1a–c) gives us a methodology by which such deceit can be overthrown. While at first glance the beginning (2) sounds similar to the ending (2a), it merely states that the dialogue teaches that we should live a life with less anxiety and fear as a result of superstition. (2a) tells us not only that we *should* live such a life but shows us *how*. Freedom from "foolish confidence and superstitious dread" is a *direct result* of the *methodology* detailed in the concluding (1a–c).

Demonstratively, More's beginning statement and conclusion are in no way manifestations of some type of rhetorical game. What stands out are the outlines of a set frame of thought, a frame of thought that combats contentions that are not religious but are set forth "under the guise of religion." Nothing in the October 1504 letter even hints at problems he finds with conceptions, seemingly widesp ead, of Christianity, much less sets forth a correct way of thinking about Christianity and a methodology for countering the false contentions. In 1504 More saw Christianity and his shortcomings in starkly either/or terms. It was only Colet's one-dimensional view of the world that was in focus.[15] (1a–c) obviously represents, in contrast, a both/and. There is divine truth and there is human truth – as well as human untruth. The human truth cannot exist lacking a direct tie to absolute truth. What could be the meaning and implications of this both/and? And why would carrying out (1a–c) result in (2a), a solution to one's emotional problems? More's introduction thus ends, as it begins, by pointing to a solution to gloom and foreboding, the gloom and foreboding he so strongly felt when writing the October 1504 letter. Let us underline the point: In October 1504, three months before his marriage, he had no solution to his mental anguish; in 1505–6 he does, and he is determined to make an issue of this solution.

Nor is there any serious relationship between More's thesis and what Lucian's *Philopseudes* – closely studied by More in preparing his translation – actually argues. At most, *Philopseudes* can be considered a starting point. Tychiades, the hero, ridicules all allegations of abstract truth. The only thing he sees and values is common sense. Tychiades sees people everywhere spouting superstitious untruths, sometimes covered by a veneer of religion, but nowhere does he imagine or allow that *a true religion* is being subverted by superstition, "which obtrudes everywhere under the guise of religion." For Tychiades, Christian precepts would compare to "statues walking" and the like, simply another type of magic and superstition. He would have no patience with discussions of worldly values that relate or do not relate to divine values. He would not be interested in even considering a method of reasoning or a frame of thought that should accompany reason. Nor would he accept that getting rid of "superstitious dread" depends on holding to abstract conceptions as one distinguishes between true and false stories. All one needs is worldly experience and common sense.

Standing out in the concluding statement is More's referral to "the rule of Critolaus." On the one hand there are stories found in the Bible and, on the other, stories that are not. While the former should be trusted absolutely, the latter need to be carefully analysed in terms of Christ's teachings, "as though applying the rule [regula] of Critolaus," and then be either accepted or rejected. What process is he actually advocating? What in this context is the *regula* and where did he get this word? Clearly there is a connection between this *regula* and the assertions surrounding it and the thinking going on in the entire

15 Nor would Colet have ever dreamed of relating Lucian to the issues at hand.

introduction. Puzzling also is his contention that the *regula* can help "free ourselves both from foolish confidence and superstitious d ead."

Critolaus' Rule

Without question, More had been studying Cicero's referral to Critolaus' "balance [libra]" at 5.51 of *Tusculan Disputations*. Critolaus' "rule" – no other ancient source for this referral exists[16] – goes to the very heart of Cicero's argument in Book 5, and analysis of the discussions surrounding 5.51 proves that More was not simply picking out an odd statement but had a deep familiarity with Book 5.

Before calling attention to Critolaus' balance, Cicero argues that vice produces misery while virtue produces happiness. The Peripatetics (Aristotelians), unlike the Stoics, admit not just one good but three goods, not just virtue but bodily and external goods, but, if this is the case, assurance of virtue is necessarily lacking, for the good that is virtue is necessarily competing with bodily and external goods, not to mention the existence of bodily and external evils. Such goods and evils would be beyond the control (as the Stoics contended) of the wiseman. How can a wiseman lacking assurance of virtue be happy? (5.40). He cannot. Virtue depends on the wiseman being always free and undefeated, never having to repent, doing everything consistently, soberly, rightly ("constanter, graviter, honeste") (5.52). The lives of noteworthy individuals demonstrate, Cicero shows, at length, what is praiseworthy and what is not praiseworthy (5.49, 54–67). Antiochus decided that happiness is relative, that the sage who has bodily and/or external goods in addition to virtue is not just happy but supremely happy. But if being *simply* happy is a lack, how, asks Cicero, can it be happiness? (5.23). If a virtuous life is not a happy life, then there is something better than a happy life. But this is impossible to believe, considering that virtue produces happiness (5.50). In short, the possessor of bodily goods or/and external goods is miserable if he is unjust, intemperate, fearful ("timidus"), or of sluggish or nonexistent intelligence (5.45). *Honestum*, as the Stoics saw, is the only good. "The man then who is temperate, steadfast, without fear, without distress, without any eagerness, without lust, is he not happy?" The happy man is free not from just a little fear ("metus") but from all fear (5.41). All things depend on himself (5.42). Wretchedness is produced only by disturbances of the soul (5.43).

16 Cf. Glucker, "Critolaus' Scale and Philo." *Fin.* 5.92 and *Off.* 3.11 refer to the balance without mentioning Critolaus.

It is within this context that Cicero turns to the balance ("libra") of Critolaus – which More refers to as a rule ("regula"):

> Quo loco quaero quam vim habeat libra illa Critolai, qui cum in alteram lancem animi bona imponat, in alteram corporis et externa, tantum propendere illam putet, ut terram et maria deprimat. (5.51)

> And at this point I ask for the meaning of the famous balance of Critolaus, who claims that if in one scale he puts the good that belongs to the soul, and in the other the good that belongs to the body and good things which come from outside that man, the first scale sinks so far as to outweigh the second with land and seas thrown in as well.

Critolaus had been head of the Peripatetic school in the mid-second century BCE, and Cicero sees his balance as a way of making the Peripatetic three-goods argument compatible with the Stoic view that virtue is the only good.[17] While the Stoics see *honestum* as the only good and yet hold to a second type of value, comprising indiffe ents (which can be preferred or dispreferred), Critolaus contends that bodily and external goods exist but are nothing in comparison to *honestum*. Later Cicero expands on the argument without reference to Critolaus. Setting aside Stoic subtleties, he grants that there are three kinds of good things, "provided only that goods of the body and external goods lie groveling on the ground and are merely termed good because they are 'preferred'" (5.76). He agrees with Carneades (fl. 150 BCE) that what determines is the thing, not words, so there is no factual disagreement between Stoics and Peripatetics regarding "preferreds" and "goods" (5.120). Putting all the weight on virtue, like Critolaus, Cicero thinks it allowable to say that anyone who has acquired bodily and external goods is not just happy but extremely happy (5.34). Whether happy or extremely happy, virtue is undefeated.

But how, many contemporary and modern scholars have asked, can virtue be so highly valued that happiness is guaranteed even if (against the traditional Stoic view) poverty, ill health, pain, and the like are not simply dispreferred indiffe ents but the opposite (as with Peripatetics) of that which is good (5.76ff.)? Although Cicero's argument here is weak, it is Stoic *honestum* (a fixed disposition) and Stoic *disdain* for

17 On Critolaus, about which rather little is known, and speculations regarding his relationship to Aristotelian and Antiochean arguments, see Annas, *The Morality of Happiness*, 413–15 and 422n51, and Hahm, "Critolaus and Late Hellenistic Peripatetic Philosophy." Along with Diogenes the Stoic and Carneades the Academic, Critolaus had visited Rome in 155 BCE as an Athenian ambassador.

pain and the emotions that drive the entire discussion. Following the referral to Critolaus, it is emphasized that virtue depends on the wiseman being always free and undefeated – never having to repent (5.53), doing everything consistently, soberly, rightly ("constanter, graviter, honeste") (5.81).[18]

The Tie between More's Conclusion and Tusculan Disputations

It remains to be shown just how closely the frame of thought encapsulated in More's conclusion relates to Critolaus' balance, Book 5 of *Tusculan Disputations* as a whole, and the Stoic mindset. As shown above (107), his conclusion reads as follows:

> (1a) We ought to place unquestioning trust in the stories commended to us by divinely inspired Scripture, (1b) but testing the others carefully and deliberately by the teaching of Christ (as though applying the rule of Critolaús), (1c) we should either accept or reject them (2a) if we wish to free ourselves both from foolish confidence and superstitious dread. (7/17–22)

The meaning can now be clearly discerned.

(1a) refers to stories that are embedded in "divinely inspired scripture" and are absolutes of the faith. These truths are beyond question and must be held to with "unquestioning trust." In the context of Cicero's referral to the balance of Critolaus, we can see that "divinely inspired scripture" is More's version of *honestum*. The happy person, the person who unvaryingly lives in accord with virtue and nature (*honestum*), is, by definition in Stoicism, obedient to the creator of the universe (*Fin.* 3.61). We must put all the weight of that which is good and virtuous, as Critolaus advises, on these scriptural stories. Other goods are in comparison infinitesimally small

(1b) "Testing the other stories" clearly refers to a very diffe ent, worldly, type of story. These stories or contentions are not absolute and not found in scripture. Although humanly created, they are by no means equal. Some are true and some are false. Humanly created stories tie in with Cicero's incessant concern, encapsulated by the balance of Critolaus, with the second side of the Stoic both/and – in Book 5 of *Tusculan Disputations* as also in *De finibus* and *De officiis*. How can one

18 Cf. Erasmus, *De taedio Iesu*, LB5 1268A–B, 1273C, 1280F, 1288B. And note again Cicero's contention, in Book 4, that the Stoics may in fact be the only real philosophers (4.53).

make no distinction between Stoic preferreds/dispreferreds and Peripatetic goods/evils and yet hold to *honestum* and happiness? More is here clearly following Cicero in not making a distinction between preferreds and goods or between dispreferreds and evils. And it is in this context that we should see the humanly created stories that concern More. While the stories in scripture do not need testing (but only "unquestioned trust"), worldly stories do. They must be tested "carefully and deliberately." But how? On their own merits? Against each other? Not at all. The point of this testing, in the first place certainly, is to see if these stories are in accord with the absolutes of scripture, Christ's teachings (Christian *honestum*). False stories are stories not in sync with the absolutes.

Clearly, there is a method in play here. No humanly created story can be evaluated lacking comparison and analysis in terms of the absolutes. More is not saying, any more than Cicero, that the content of human contentions is found, as such, in the absolutes. He is stating that worldly contentions are radically diffe ent from divine precepts and yet true worldly contentions, as distinct from false worldly contentions, are one with the divine precepts.

And yet there is more to evaluating the humanly created stories than passing the test of acceptability. What the *regula* adds, in More's mind, is the prescription that the humanly created stories be considered as nothing in comparison with Christ's teaching – "as though applying the rule of Critolaus." Christ's teachings are for More an extension and higher form of what Cicero sees as virtue and *honestum*. The *regula* relates to preferreds or goods as not dispreferreds or evils. It is a statement of the place of humanly created stories, *even where deemed true*, opposite the absolutes. Whether we describe these humanly created stories as preferreds or goods or both, they are of minuscule importance compared to divinely inspired scripture. This is true even if it is allowable to say, as More certainly believed (see (2a) below), in accord with Cicero, that these stories not only are necessary components of life and thought but also contribute to happiness.

(1c) states that we must either accept ("recipiamus") or reject ("respuamus") the non-biblical stories. While the first side of the both/and is not problematic, the second side is. We must make choices between contentions on the second side. We cannot waver between accepting and rejecting or simply ignore an issue, but must decide one way or the other. If we find that a story or argument is in accord with scripture, it must be accepted. If we find that it is not, it must be unhesitatingly rejected. The false stories are found to be such not by direct comparison with worldly stories judged to be true but by direct contrast with the absolutes. Accept/reject, it seems clear, is simply another way of talking about and distinguishing between preferred/good and dispreferred/bad. Preferreds or goods we should accept and dispreferreds or evils we should reject.

Why is making a choice so imperative? Why not let some issues slide? The Stoic answer, from Zeno onwards, is clear. The purpose of "preferred" and "rejected" indiffe ents was "to admit a certain principle of choice among things" (*Fin.* 3.14, 4.43) while holding that *honestum* is inseparable from these choices. The fact that holding to *honestum* entails worldly choices means that those who do not make such choices abolish virtue itself (*Fin.* 3.12). Book 3 of *De officiis* closely relates to the way More is here looking at the issue, the need even where this is difficul to make a choice. Throughout, Cicero's goal is to show how to resolve conflicts between what *appears* to be useful but is not and what is *actually* useful – and thus one with *honestum* (cf. 3.50). And he gives example after example of real-world situations. As one authority states, summarizing the role of *utile* in Book 3, "Cicero's analysis thus involves two *utilia*, an apparent *utile*, which turns out on closer inspection not to be *utile*, and a true *utile*, which coincides with the *honestum*."[19] In chapter 2 below I will show that More's diffe entiations between true and false saints' lives were modelled on the methodology of Book 3.

(2a) may seem strange, on the surface. Why does More imagine that in carrying out (1a–c) we "free ourselves both from foolish confidence and superstitious dread"? Clearly More is intimating that he himself has been so freed. The fact that this statement is found not only at the end of the encapsulated frame of thought but is at the same time at the end of the entire discussion of the dialogues gives us particular cause for reflection. Our mind wanders back to the October 1504 letter and the extreme angst expressed there. Now, between late 1505 and early 1506, he shows us a way out. Steps (1a–1c) free us from anxiety and fear of the future. And yet, however personal the message, (2a), like (1a–1c), is central to the frame and meaning of *Tusculan Disputations*. As shown above, a theme of Book 5 – fundamentally Stoic – is that happiness depends on virtue while vice is synonymous with misery. Falling away from *honestum* has devastating consequences for one's mental state. Bodily and external goods without virtue entail wretchedness. In a wretched life nothing is praiseworthy, while in a happy life something is praiseworthy and that something is virtue. That happiness depends on virtue while vice is synonymous with misery is emphasized

19 See Dyck, *A Commentary on Cicero, De Officiis*, 493.

both immediately before and immediately after Cicero's referral to Critolaus' balance, at 5.51. There are very deleterious emotional consequences to not holding to the happy life. At 5.50 we are warned that vice ("vitium") makes life wretched while virtue makes life happy. At 5.53 Cicero contends – a thesis at the very heart of Stoicism – that the virtue that produces happiness depends on the wiseman being always free and undefeated, never having to repent, doing everything consistently, soberly, rightly ("constanter, graviter, honeste") (5.81). At 5.41 the happy man, "impregnable, fenced, and fortified," is said to be free from not just a little fear ("metus") but from all fear.[20] At 5.48 he is said to be "temperate, steadfast, without fear, distress, excitability, or lust." "Vir igitur temperatus, constans, sine metu, sine aegritudine, sine alacritate ulla, sine libidine, nonne beatus?" (*Tusc.* 5.48).

(2a) indicates not only that Christianity comprises simultaneously two types of value (1a–c) but that the result – here too building on *Tusculan Disputations* – is happiness and peace of mind. "If we wish to free ourselves both from foolish confidence and superstitious dread," we must either accept or reject the non-biblical stories (or contentions) in the manner above discussed (1a–c). Seeing Christianity in unitary both/and terms takes away "foolish confidence and superstitious dread." Both/and truth holds unswervingly to the absolutes, judges worldly stories in terms of the absolutes, and puts all the weight on the absolutes. "Foolish confidence" is holding to worldly conceived stories that are not in accord with Christ's teachings. "Superstitious dread" likewise results from the failure to hold to scriptural teachings. Humans suffer from the emotion of fear because they do not adhere to the happiness represented by Christ's truth. Were all the weight placed on the divine teachings, one would accept or reject the humanly created stories in terms of these precepts. Dread of the future results when the humanly created stories are considered without regard to the absolute standard. Fear of the future also results where humans do not have a perspective, do not see that even the "true" human stories are as nothing compared to the central precepts of the faith. In short, happiness depends on holding firmly at all times to a Stoic/Christian *honestum/utile* state of mind. In this way we are free and undefeated and never, whatever the ultimate outcome, do we have to repent.

Note the word "supersticiosa" in (2a). We must carry out steps (1a–1c) "si carere volumes, & inani fiducia, & supersticiosa formidine [if we wish to free ourselves both from foolish confidence and superstitious

20 Cf. Seneca, *Vit. Beat.* 4.3.

dread]." What is particularly interesting in the present context is the word which "superstition" modifies. "Formido" directly relates to one of the four basic Stoic emotions, and discussion of this word immediately surrounds the referral to Critolaus' balance at 5.51 of *Tusculan Disputations*. At 5.52 "formido" (dread or fright) is shown to be a subdivision of "metus" (fear), the anxious anticipation of coming distress.[21] At 5.52 we are told that "aegritudo" is a disorder that arises from an opinion about a present evil, while "formido" is, like "metus," the anxious anticipation of coming distress. The person susceptible to distress is, necessarily, also susceptible to fear, dread, nervousness, panic, cowardice ("metus, formido, timiditas, pavor, ignavia"). While virtue always remains free and undefeated, "formido," like the other emotions, represents defeat and enslavement.

Why did More chose to use the word "formido," fear in anticipation of future distress, rather than "aegritudo," distress regarding what is considered a present evil? These words, and most especially "aegritudo," hold a very prominent place in *Tusculan Disputations*, and both are discussed, as I have noted, even with regard to the balance of Critolaus. More chose "formido," it appears, because this word was at the very centre of his personal concerns. Only a year or less before, he had been filled with foreboding regarding his future. Prior to late 1504, he had been tormented by the need, as he perceived it, to choose between a worldly and an otherworldly path. But now the situation was entirely diffe ent. Now he had found a solution, a path to the future, and peace of mind. And his introduction shows us precisely what that solution was and why he was filled with joy. Christianity, he now saw, is not an either/or proposition but – as in Stoicism – unitarily both/and. And he now knew – and had experienced the fact – that he who employs the methodology inherent to this both/and will be, as in Stoicism, not disturbed and fearful but filled with happiness

In short, More encapsulates in the conclusion to his introduction everything his January 1505 decision had been about – and brings into focus yet again the life-changing influence of Erasmus of Rotterdam. What More works out in the above, modelling the Stoic way of thinking, is what he had first learned from reading *De taedio Iesu* and the *Enchiridion* – and from conversations with Erasmus. And we can well believe that More was actually, in real life, happy. He was happy because not only had he replaced his tormented either/or way of thinking with a Stoic/Christian two-dimensional mindset but because – building

21 In *De finibus*, *formido* is not shown as a subdivision but replaces *metus* (3.35).

on Erasmus' expansion and correcting of Stoicism – he had accepted his desire for sex and politics and the like as ineradicable natural instincts and had recognized that these desires are not the problem; that they are merely things indiffe ent. What matters is only how these indiffe ents are dealt with, whether or not they are carried out in ways inseparable from the precepts of the faith.

2 A New Analysis of Saints' Lives

But how does the new-found Stoic way of thinking that More insists on work out when placed opposite the issue that it answers to, the problems he finds with discussions of lives of saints and martyrs

In his October 1504 letter, More berates preachers for living in opposition to their words, but now, one year later – working with Erasmus and setting forth a Stoic *honestum/utile* way of thinking – the concern is with the words themselves, the meaning of Christianity. As stated in an opening sentence and carefully developed in what follows, false views of Christianity, "superstitions," are rampant and "everywhere" set forth "under the guise of religion." Unnamed persons have added and inserted material into the authentic (whatever that might be) lives of saints, martyrs, and virgins (i.e., female saints and martyrs). On the one hand they have made up or embellished aspects of the stories surrounding the achievements of saints and martyrs and on the other have found ingenious ways to augment descriptions of hell – and terrorize people.

> They think they've done a great work, and put Christ in their debt forever, if they've feigned a story about a saint or a horrendous tale of hell to drive some old woman to tears or make her tremble with fear. And so there is scarcely a martyr's or a virgin's life which they have passed over without inserting some falsehoods of this kind. (5/34–7/1)

Relating the magic and superstition described by Lucian to a Christian context, unnamed individuals have attempted to build up the lives of saints and martyrs by inserting and adding in things – presumably miraculous powers – and in doing so have deliberately instilled in the minds of "the common herd" (5/33) the idea that those carrying out certain practices in honour of saints and martyrs will reap a heavenly reward, "put Christ in their debt forever." On the other side, they have augmented the picture of hell by depicting ever more horrific punishments for wrongdoing. In short, the problems that More sees do not come from the mere fact that material is added. What is added is false, and the views set forth are not simply mistaken, honest errors, but are set forth "under the guise of religion." These stories represent "magic" and "superstition" because in the first place they are not in accord with Christ's teachings and in the second place they are set forth deceitfully.

In attacking the creators of the additions and insertions, was More simply restating existing criticism, or does his thinking have a diffe - ent basis? And why, at this particular time, was he focusing on and criticizing these books? Was he reacting to recent developments in the interpretation or employment of saints' lives? Was he exemplifying a new "rationalistic" spirit?[22] Was he engaging in the humanist tendency to accuse previous writers of adding and inserting falsehoods – while employing non-classical Latin – into the original sources?

What about Saints' Lives Was More Criticizing?

It takes some effort to appreciate just how deeply saints and martyrs permeated More's world. The routine of life at work, in church, and in social activities was directly related to saints. Local devotion to saints had proliferated throughout the Middle Ages, so much so that by the late Middle Ages much of local religion pivoted around veneration of the saints.[23] Saints were tied not only to admired ideals, miracles, and the hope for divine help but also to particular professions, particular worldly endeavours, and particular days in the calendar.[24] Local communities also had their own saints. And there were saints for special situations, such as childbirth. Not including church days, over fifty days a year were dedicated to saints. Not surprisingly, stories of saints and martyrs permeated this world.[25] As Alison Knowles Frazier notes, "a

22 C.R. Thompson imagines that More's criticism of saints' lives is simply an exemplification of rationalit . "He [More] is too sensitive and too scholarly to be patient with the palpable fictions so common in saints' lives." See CWM 3.1, xli , and also Trapp, *Erasmus, Colet and More*, 54.

23 French, *The People of the Parish*, 194.

24 Who became a saint, and how, had societal as well as ideological aspects. Changing economic, social, political, intellectual, and institutional realities resulted, we now know, in variations throughout the Middle Ages. Within the church the roles played in the descriptions of saints by the Pope, regulars, secular clergy, and laity were very diffe ent and continually changed. See Abou-El-Haj, *The Medieval Cult of Saints*; Vauchez, *Sainthood in the Later Middle Ages*; and Weinstein and Bell, *Saints and Society*.

25 Relating to More's surroundings, see, among other works, Cartwright, ed., *Celtic Hagiography and Saints' Cults*; Clayton and Magennis, *The Old English Lives of St*

sizable proportion of all the written texts in premodern Europe were about saints."[26] In England the most influential sources for saints' lives, in More's time, were Jacobus Voragine's *Legenda aurea* (*The Golden Legend*) (c. 1260),[27] the anonymous *South English Legendary* (1270–85),[28] *Speculum Sacerdotale* (early fifteenth century), and John Mirk's *Festial* (c. 1390). In 1483 Caxton printed in seven volumes his English translation of the *The Golden Legend*. *The Golden Legend* and *South English Legendary* were thirteenth-century abbreviations of much more lengthy stories, while *Speculum Sacerdotale* and Mirk's *Festial* were more recent collections that were abbreviated and organized for insertion into sermons. Parishioners heard or read many versions of the stories. Very popular were verse lives of the saints, plays based on the lives, and calendars found in *Books of Hours*, all available from the 1490s in cheap printed versions.[29]

Like everyone in his time, More believed in supernatural events and not only those surrounding Christ.[30] In *The Stripping of the Altars: Traditional Religion in England 1400–1580* (1992), Eamon Duffy has shown that magic and "superstition" were not mere pagan rites but part and parcel of Christianity and that elites shared views and practices with commoners, even if they sometimes had a larger perspective. The supernatural was everywhere thought to be active in the material world. Among the sophisticated and those of undoubted orthodoxy, as well as among simple people, could be found "verse legends of the saints, or the signs of the end of the world and its attendant horrors; a circumstantial version of the legend of the 'Fifteen Oes', charms for making angels appear in

---

Margaret; Coletti, *Mary Magdalene and the Drama of Saints*; Delany, *Impolitic Bodies*; Duff , *The Stripping of the Altars*; Heffernan, *Sacred Biography*; Ramsay, Sparks, and Tatton-Brown eds., *St. Dunstan*; Love, ed. and trans., *Goscelin of Saint-Bertin*; Ridyard, *The Royal Saints of Anglo-Saxon England*; Rollason, *Saints and Relics in Anglo-Saxon England*; Julia M.H. Smith, "Oral and Written"; Winstead, *Virgin Martyrs*; Winterbottom and Thomson, ed. and trans., William of Malmesbury, *Saints' Lives*.

26 Frazier, *Possible Lives*, 8.

27 See Reames, *The Legenda Aurea*.

28 See Gorlach, *The Textual Tradition of the South English Legendary*; Jankofsky, ed., *The South English Legendary*; and Thompson, *Everyday Saints and the Art of Narrative in the South English Legendary*.

29 Duff , *The Stripping of the Altars*, 165.

30 In *A Dialogue Concerning Heresies* (1529), More states "that many miracles there be whiche no good crysten man maye deny to be trewe" (CWM 6, Pt. 1, 85/19–20). He takes for granted that there is nothing wrong with praying to saints, going on pilgrimages, or worshipping relics and images. The problem is only that some persons carry these practices out in evil ways and for evil purposes (235/24–31). "The

a child's thumbnail, the Charlemagne prayers."[31] Sophisticated persons not only said the same prayers but also sometimes had collections of relics. This tie between simple folk and elites existed notwithstanding the criticism at times by theologians and others of the excesses found in the beliefs and practices of simple persons.[32] It was all one religion.

Although adding and inserting was prevalent in saints' lives, what in particular was More thinking in making his criticisms? Even medieval writers often recognized the difficult of corroborating details about the original events. Clearly, the stories that had sprung up regarding these events diffe ed greatly. Lacking a settled foundation, writers found it particularly easy to build up happenings surrounding a favourite saint, and scholastic methodology greatly abetted this enlarging of interpretation. Writing glosses on biblical passages and listing arguments for and against particular theological interpretations expanded the sources in many ways. In his vastly influential *Historia scholastica* (c. 1173), Peter Comestor – taught by Peter Abelard and a close adherent of Peter Lombard (whose *Sentences* he had glossed) – made use of a great variety of Jewish, pagan, and Christian sources as well as myriads of non-biblical historical and geographical tidbits.[33] Biblical accounts were seen to invite, if you will, "adding," and "inserting." Comestor saw the martyr Methodius, for example, as simply enlarging a theme stated more briefly in Genesis.[34] More than a staple among academics,

---

calendar of saints," states Germain P. Marc'hadour, "was, in More's view, an integral truth, like church doctrine as a whole" (CWM 6, Pt. 2, 483). As for relics, More states that he was present thirty years before when some relics were discovered which seem to go back to the time of Christ, albeit relics may sometimes be mistaken or fraudulent (CWM 6, Pt. 1, 221/17–223/16).

31 Duff , *The Stripping of the Altars*, 278. On magic, see also Flint, *The Rise of Magic in Early Medieval Europe*; Kieckhefer, *Magic in the Middle Ages* and "The Specific Ratio - ality of Medieval Magic"; Peters, *The Magician, the Witch and the Law*; Scribner, "The Reformation, Popular Magic, and the 'Disenchantment of the World'"; Thomas, *Religion and the Decline of Magic*; and *Witchcraft and Magic in Europe: Volume 3, The Middle Ages*, ed. Jolly, Raudvere, and Peters.

32 Duff , *The Stripping of the Altars*, 277, 298.

33 See Daly, "Peter Comestor"; Dean, "The World Grown Old and Genesis in Middle English Historical Writings"; Hindman, "Dutch Bible Illustration and the *Historia Scholastica*"; Kurz, "Filippino Lippi's Worship of the Apis"; Luscombe, "Peter Comestor"; Morey, "Peter Comestor, Biblical Paraphrase, and the Medieval Popular Bible"; Ogle, "Petrus Comestor, Methodius, and the Saracens"; Shereshevsky, "Hebrew Traditions in Peter Comestor's *Historia Scholastica*"; Smalley, *The Study of the Bible in the Middle Ages* and *The Gospels in the Schools, c. 1100–c. 1280*; and Twomey, "Falling Giants and Floating Lead."

34 Twomey, "Falling Giants and Floating Lead," 145–6.

material from the *Historia scholastica* was tied to or woven into pieces of vernacular translating of the Bible in France and England through the fifteenth century. The work was also extensively versified, used in plays, and incorporated into some paintings and sculptures.

Could More's criticism of horrific descriptions of hell give us some clues to his underlying motivation? Descriptions that could scare an old lady (above, 5/34–5) are well represented, it would appear, in the *South English Legendary*. Consider the vivid account of the knight Owen's pilgrimage, as penance for his sins, to St Patrick's Purgatory, a cave on an island in Ireland. Stepping through a physical gateway into the otherworld – cf. Lucian's exemplifications of magic in *Philopseudes* – Owen visits "four fields of punishment where, as in earlier visionary and apocalyptic accounts, sinners are devoured by dragons, set upon by serpents and toads, fixed to the ground with red-hot nails, baked in furnaces, immersed to various degrees in boiling cauldrons, and hooked to a flaming version of Ixion's wheel."[35] The story of St Patrick's Purgatory was well known in Europe and England beginning around 1250. Note its pictorial nature. Depictions of judgment and punishment in purgatory and hell had become increasingly detailed in the later Middle Ages.[36] While Dante's poetic representation in the *Divine Comedy* (c. 1308–21) stands out, as does the Dutch painter Bosch's *Garden of Earthly Delight* (c. 1500),[37] the trend is found at the local level also. Visualizations of hell had become ever more prominent in the church decorations and book illustrations seen by ordinary persons. In the late fifteenth and early sixteenth centuries, specific punishments were popularized by the printing press. In 1505, for example, at the time More was writing his introduction, Wynkyn de Worde added woodcut illustrations of such punishments in *The Arte or Crafte to Lyve Well*.[38]

35 Zaleski, "St. Patrick's Purgatory," 475. See also *The South English Legendary*, vol. 1, 88/89–110/716; *St. Patrick's Purgatory: Two Versions of "Owayne Miles" and "The Vision of William of Stranton" together with the Long Text of the "Tractatus de Purgatorio Sancti Patricii"*; and Haren and de Pontfarcy, eds., *The Medieval Pilgrimage to St. Patrick's Purgatory*.

36 Bernstein, *The Formation of Hell*; Bynum and Freedman, eds., *Last Things*; Delumeau, *Sin and Fear*, esp. 373–400; Dinzelbacher, *Vision und Visionsliteratur im Mittelalter*; Morgan, *Dante and the Medieval Other World*; Newman, "On the Threshold of the Dead"; Patch, *The Other World, According to Descriptions in Medieval Literature*; Spencer, "Chaucer's Hell."

37 On pictorial representation of hell see Baschet, *Les justices de l'au-delà*; Davidson and Seiler, eds. *The Iconography of Hell*; Hughes, *Heaven and Hell in Western Art*; Schmidt, *The Iconography of the Mouth of Hell*; and Turner, *The History of Hell*.

38 Duff , *The Stripping of the Altars*, 339–41.

At one point More emphasizes that the fiction found in the false lives often closely resembles what is found in sacred scripture (6/12–15). Could his outlook have had something to do with a belief, as Thomas J. Heffernan argues, that in saints' lives portrayal of the joining of the human and the divine "was dangerously close to an acknowledgment that the mystery of the Incarnation had taken place more than once in a particular man or woman"?[39] Not only were saints tied in with the ultimate in divinity, but it was also commonly believed, as noted above, that devotion to the saints would magically deliver one from particular earthly travails and even win a heavenly reward. This notwithstanding that churchmen had now and then criticized not only various outlandish stories in the lives of the saints but belief in the power of saints to help a person win acceptance into heaven. In 1455, for example, Nicholas of Cusa forbade his clergy to teach *superstitiosa* as found in *The Golden Legend*. According to Sherry L. Reames, the chapters singled out "have one thing in common: they promise in unequivocal terms that acts of devotion to the saints in question will magically guarantee one's deliverance from certain evils, among them illnesses, poverty, and damnation itself."[40]

Humanist Influences?

It could be imagined – wrongly – that More was somehow responding to the more positive assessments of human nature and human prospects evident in some writings of leading Italian humanists, including Giovanni Pico della Mirandolla and Marsilio Ficino. Giannozzo Manetti had written a book *On the Excellence and Dignity of Man* (1451–2), in opposition to Pope Innocent III's work *On the Misery of Man* (c. 1198).[41] At the conclusion Manetti brings up hell as the opposite of heaven but states that humans have nothing to worry about as long as they practise virtue, the virtue, it appears, they were born with. And "all those who prove themselves careful observers of God's commandments are blessed from the moment of their birth and are, as we see, happy in this

39 Heffernan, *Sacred Biography*, 30. On the expansion of the miraculous in the later Middle Ages, see in particular Vauchez, *Sainthood in the Later Middle Ages*, 444–77.

40 Reames, *The Legenda Aurea*, 50. Regarding virgin saints, Winstead shows that *The Golden Legend* focused more on a saint's exploits than on her faith. Miracles are sometimes listed with no mention of God (*Virgin Martyrs* 66f). Although the reasons are unclear, demand for *The Golden Legend* in Europe was falling by the 1490s. See Reames, *The Legenda Aurea*, 4, 28, 41.

41 Manetti, *De dignitate et excellentia hominis* and *De miseria humane conditionis*, both translated by Murchland in *Two Views of Man*.

world and will be happy forever."[42] Whether or not More could have been influenced indirectly by such views, the tone of his introduction is definitely not that of Manetti. He is not rhetorically glossing hell but alleging that horrendous tales of hell are widespread and that there is a problem here. The problem has to do with the fact that those who set forth these stories ("magic" and "superstition") do so "under the guise of religion" and to scare people.[43] Nor, it can be noted, do More's translations of Pico (see above, 70–4) relate to the positive assessments of human nature found in Pico's early thought.

More directly pertinent, could More have been imitating, responding to, or developing ideas found in fifteenth-century Italian humanist lives of saints and martyrs? Alison Frazier shows that the authors of these works considered Jacobus de Voragine, who had put together the ever-popular *Golden Legend* in the thirteenth century, ignorant in both manner of writing and doctrine.[44] Not surprisingly, their criticism closely related to their training in the *studia humanitatas* (rhetoric, grammar, poetry, history, and moral philosophy) – and a growing lay orientation. This meant that these humanists looked down on the non-classical Latin of medieval writers and focused on grammar, emotional impact, and audience. And yet their substantive achievements were small. Although they, like other humanists, were interested in getting back to the original sources, in practice they did not find it possible to find corroborating evidence for the actual lives of martyrs and saints and thus simply looked for the sources that seemed most authentic – and to relics. In fact, some medieval authors had worked harder than they at uncovering sources. Nor, surprisingly, were they interested in collating and emending texts. Often they did little more than reproduce older medieval manuscripts. And while *The Golden Legend*, which they often used, was itself an abbreviation of much larger accounts, they

42 Murchland, *Two Views of Man*, 102.

43 Nor was More somehow talking about the relationship between natural magic and religion, which in the years surrounding 1500 excited Giovanni Pico and other humanist intellectuals, such as Marsilio Ficino, Gianfrancesco Pico, Jacques Lefèvre, Johannes Reuchlin, Johannes Trithemius, and Henricus Cornelius Agrippa. On this subject see Borchardt, "The Magus as Renaissance Man"; Brann, *Trithemius and Magical Theology*; Copenhaver, "Scholastic Philosophy and Renaissance Magic in the *De Vita* of Marsilio Ficino"; Mebane, *Renaissance Magic and the Return of the Golden Age*; Walker, *Spiritual and Demonic Magic from Ficino to Campanella*; and Yates, *Giordano Bruno and the Hermetic Tradition*.

44 Frazier, *Possible Lives*, 193. See also Reames, *The Legenda Aurea*, 49–52; Vitz, "From the Oral to the Written in Medieval and Renaissance Saints' Lives"; and Webb, "Eloquence and Education."

abbreviated even further. Their contributions in terms of argument were also meagre. Giovanni Garzoni, a layman, composed far more saints' lives than any other humanist, yet he had little or nothing to add to the arguments found in his sources. He thus defended the discussions of miracles found in *The Golden Legend*.[45]

In translating Lucian from the Greek, More was deeply engaged in developing his ability to deal with original sources, a humanist goal, but his criticism of the false stories does not appear to originate in typical humanist concerns about language, style, or audience. And considering that he states that those responsible for the false stories have corrupted virtually every saint's life they have considered (5/37–7/1), it would appear that he is talking about saints' lives in general – and not particular collections or odd contemporary versions of the stories.

Differentiating More's Criticism

What diffe entiates More's evaluations of lives of saints and martyrs from all the above is his Stoic-based *honestum/utile* frame of thought. He was not merely following some church leaders, such as Nicholas of Cusa, in criticizing the belief that honouring the lives of saints and martyrs can magically deliver one from certain evils or allow entrance into heaven. Nor was he simply glossing – with his criticisms of "adding" and "inserting" – humanist interest in abbreviating medieval accounts of the saints and going back to more authentic sources. He looked at the issue from the vantage point of a particular mindset.

Rewriting *Philopseudes*

We can begin by showing the ways in which More's thinking on magic and superstition contrasts with the arguments on magic and superstition set forth at length in Lucian's *Philopseudes*. Not only is the magic and superstition More finds in many lives of saints and martyrs of a diffe ent genre, he very deliberately and carefully rewrites Lucian's perspective – which was contextualized in second-century society and a non-Christian world – to make it fit his own outlook

Why People Lie

How Lucian saw the "lying" behind the magic and superstition he describes and how More sees the lying behind insertions and additions

45 Frazier, *Possible Lives*, 97, 95, 211, 107, 25, 201 resp.

to lives of saints and martyrs differ throughout. Lucian saw gullibility, More sees deceit.

Tychiades and Philocles are mystified, Lucian shows, as to why people lie (CWM 3, Pt.1, 180). If lying served a purpose, such as to deceive an enemy or save one's life or make money, it might be pardoned. Were making money from tourists the goal, we might, for example, excuse the Cretans for exhibiting the tomb of Zeus. Somewhat less easy to excuse are poets such as Homer who concocted stories about the doings of the gods, such as how Prometheus, bound to a pillar, hurled defiance at Zeus, or stories about the castration of Uranus or how a love affair impelled Zeus to turn into a bull or swan (181). But none of this explains the type of "lying" that Tychiades and Philocles see. One can find people everywhere, we are shown, who delight in lying about apparitions, spells, and magical happenings. Even otherwise sensible persons lie about such things. Nothing illustrates this more than the lying of philosophers, ostensibly the wisest of persons. Their various formal philosophies going virtually unmentioned, the lies – which Lucian finds in his second-century world[46] – of a Peripatetic, a Stoic, and a Platonist are illustrated at length. They are said to have no qualms about asserting, for example, that a Babylonian magician brought a person bitten by a snake back to life and then, after repeating seven sacred names out of an old book, called out of hiding and destroyed all the offending snakes in a whiff of fi e – or that a foreigner was seen flying (182–5). Observed not by just one individual but by everyone living in a certain house, a statue comes down from its pedestal at night and walks (187–8). Not even open to question, spirits, phantoms, and souls float above ground (192). Described at length are journeys with a holy man from Egypt who had learned magic by living for twenty-three years in underground sanctuaries (193–5).

While Tychiades ostensibly describes the pervasive "lying" in his time of so-called philosophers and others but actually demonstrates only their gullibility, More shows that in his time unnamed intellectuals are bona fide liars. Far from being themselves gullible, they feed on and take advantage of the gullibility of others. Masters of cunning and deceit, they create the magic and superstition that "the common herd"

46 On declining ethical standards in philosophy and the commercialization of education, satirized by Lucian, see in particular Whitmarsh, *Greek Literature and the Roman Empire*, chapter 5: "Satirizing Rome: Lucian." On the changeover from pagan to Christian heroes, sites, and other aspects of the supernatural world, see in particular Brown, *The Cult of the Saints*; Delehaye, *The Legends of the Saints*; and Flint, *The Rise of Magic in Early Medieval Europe*.

falls for (5/33). These "crafty, wicked wretches, and heretics" (7/11) "think they've done a great work, and put Christ in their debt forever, if they've feigned a story" (5/34–5). Claiming pious intention, they bolster truth with lies (7/1–3). They take joy in deceiving simple persons and, worst of all, they are set on counterfeiting the Christian message (7/11–14). It is they who are responsible for the "superstition which obtrudes everywhere under the guise of religion" (5/22–3).

What explains this emphasis, so at odds with Lucian, on pervasive deceit? With Lucian intellectuals are gullible idiots, while with More intellectuals deceitfully take advantage of the gullibility of others. The fact that those responsible for the false stories do so "with such a show of confidence and authority" (5/26) seems to indicate, in addition to their expertise in deceit, that the persons More is thinking of are respected leaders or intellectuals and do not represent merely odd or minority opinions.

Rectifying Tychiades on Abstract Truth and Religion

Tychiades sees belief in the gods in naturalistic terms, exemplified by the ability of physicians such as Aesculapius and Hippocrates to heal with drugs and other remedies (184, 189). Of philosophers he has praise only for Democritus, who believed, in the midst of those who would distract him with foolery, "that souls are nothing after they have gone out of their bodies" (193).[47] It goes without saying that Tychiades is not concerned with establishing the nature of religion, much less fundamentals of faith. Nor is there mention of any type of abstract principles or abstract truth. Reason and truth are equivalent to worldly experience and common sense alone (190). What concerns him is only irrationality, unreason versus common sense. Indeed, Tychiades complains that those who do not use reason go so far as to accuse him of being a sacrilegious fool for doubting what they consider evident and genuine facts – such as where Tychiades denies that cures can be effected by repeating holy names ("ut per sacra nomina remedia morbis adferantur") (53/1–3, 184).[48] Alternately, he is accused of being a mere layman or of not believing in the gods. Tychiades replies that he does believe in the

47 Democritus, of course, believed that in nature there is nothing but atoms, that all things happen by necessity, and that fear and superstitions should be rejected. See DL 9.45; also *Tusc.* 1.82.

48 Compare a statement in More's *Letter to a Monk* (1519): "After a lengthy exchange, all I finally achieved was that the friar was praised to the skies whe eas I was laughed down as a fool" (CWM 15, 289/21–3). On the "repeating of holy names,"

gods but this is not the issue: Outlandish tales should call forth experience, not imaginings about the gods.

In contrast to Tychiades, More considers abstract truth, comprising "the principal mysteries of the Christian faith" (5/20), an irreducible necessity of thought, not something in any way dependent on the worldly experience that Tychiades touts. And worldly and non-worldly *are* bridgeable; reason cannot be separated from faith. Some supernatural events exist. He sees no connection at all between Christian claims that Christ arose from the dead and the magic and superstition that Tychiades over and over describes. For Tychiades such faith and such reason would be just another preposterous and risible example of superstition and credulity. Even the formal and abstract arguments of philosophers are for Tychiades, it appears, worthless.

Stoic/Christian *Honestum*

More does not simply contrast "Christianity" with Lucian's outlook. He sets forth a particular two-dimensional understanding of Christianity. On one side he develops the *honestum* thesis described in his conclusion (1a), discussed in the previous chapter: "We ought to place unquestioning trust in the stories commended to us by divinely inspired Scripture."

"Truth Unadorned"

While Lucian rejects any idea of abstract truth, those responsible for the false lives of saints and martyrs give verbal support to such, but in actuality this is only a disguise. Christian *honestum*, "truth unadorned," is neither conceptualized nor held to:

> They (the authors of the lives) have not shrunk from defiling with their tales that religion which Truth itself established and which it intended to consist of truth unadorned. *Nec ueriti sunt eam religionem contaminare figmentis, quam ipsa ueritas instituit, & in nuda uoluit ueritate consistere.* (6/3–5)

Christianity is not about adornments but about naked ("nuda") truth, "truth unadorned" – also referred to as "divinely inspired Scripture"

---

compare Erasmus' *The Praise of Folly*. Many believe that "if they address a statue or Barbara with prescribed words they will return from battle unharmed" – and that by such means they will ultimately breach the portals of heaven. See ASD IV-3, 122/5–6, Miller trans., 63.

and "the principal mysteries." The problem is that this truth is being undermined by fictions ("figmentis," 4/28, 6/4), "additions" and "insertions" that go for truth but are not.[49] But what precisely, we may ask, do the fictions take away from "truth unadorned"? What is "truth unadorned" without the "fictions"? Had More mentally worked out components of "truth unadorned"? He certainly believed that, in deciding on which humanly created stories are true and which not, a person is of necessity deciding on aspects of absolute truth and making statements (verbalized or not) about the content of absolute truth.[50] In *Utopia*, we will find, he carefully sets forth many components of absolute truth.[51]

It is because intellectuals do not want to acknowledge "truth unadorned" that they produce false stories. While Tychiades is mystifie as to why people "lie," seeing only an inexplicable propensity for irrationality, More sees no mystery at all. Persons who are not in reality Christians deliberately make up false stories about saints and martyrs in order to avoid recognizing and accepting "truth unadorned, "the principal mysteries." Those who contrive this nonsense do so "with pious intent, to be sure, for otherwise there was danger lest truth could not stand by its own strength but had to be bolstered with lies! [pie scilicet, alioqui enim periculum erat, ne ueritas non posset sibi ipsa suffic e, nisi fulciretur mendacijs]" (6/1–3). Note the sarcasm. Not wanting to see the singularity of the Christian message, they imagine that such additions will win favour with Christ, "put Christ in their debt forever."

More than even blinding people to truth, fictions cause people to doubt truth. Those responsible "have not considered that fables of this kind, so far from helping at all, do more deadly harm than anything else" (7/5–7). "Deadly harm" results because, as Augustine pointed out, falsehood diminishes the authority of truth (7/7–9).[52] A thing believed and then found false leads to unbelief in what is true.[53]

---

49 Duffy shows at length, as have others, that "Late medieval Catholicism was a b oad Church." See *The Stripping of the Altars*, 298.

50 In a lengthy 1515 letter to Martin Dorp, in which he defends Erasmus and *The Praise of Folly*, More refers to "that living gospel of faith [vivum evangelium fidei]" which is the "unbending standard of truth [inflexibilem veritatis egulam]" – something that goes beyond the written word. See CWM 15, 1–127 at 88/2–6.

51 See below, 283.

52 See Augustine, *De mendacio* (*On Lying*) 10.17.

53 Of course Tychiades would see that More has it backwards, that "deadly harm" is found in the original belief.

Fiction Often Resembles Truth

Since superstition "everywhere" obtrudes "under the guise of religion," it is often difficul to distinguish truth from fiction. The problem is that those who have created the falsehoods do so with all deliberation.

While Lucian's *Philopseudes* does not distinguish pious intellectuals from evil intellectuals, but only the diffe ence between common sense and the nonsense of intellectuals and others, More's introduction pivots on the diffe ences. Those responsible for defiling truth, "certain crafty, wicked wretches and heretics [uafris ac pessimis quibusdam nebulonibus, haereticisque]" (6/9–10), have maliciously concocted false stories, and for two reasons. They do it (a) partly to amuse themselves at the expense of simple-minded people[54] and (b) "partly to undermine trust in the true stories of Christians by traffi in mere fictions, since they often invent things so nearly resembling those in sacred scripture that they easily reveal that by playing upon those stories they have been ridiculing them" (7/13–17).[55]

Even careful and well-meaning scholars can on occasion be fooled by the cleverness and conspiracy of those who make up, "with such a show of confidence and authority," false stories. Notwithstanding, for example, that Augustine was "a man of complete sobriety and a zealous enemy of lies" (5/28), even he was once fooled by a story – which More found in Augustine's tract on "Care for the Dead" (*De cura pro mortuis gerenda*, 12.15) – that had in fact already been ridiculed by Lucian in *Philopseudes* employing diffe ent names (5/29–32). In Lucian's account, Cleodemus, one of the philosophers present, reported that he was once in fever and dying when he was taken to Pluto, in Hades. Pluto, in anger, overrode the death that was certain to occur and gave him back life. In exchange, however, Pluto foretold that a certain blacksmith would have to die – which, Cleodemus claimed, actually happened (190–1).[56]

In short, superstition always comes camouflaged in the clothes of religion, often even "nearly resembling" scripture. There are two types of abstractions: one is false, one is true. Fictions blind people to "truth

54 Cf. Erasmus, *The Praise of Folly*. "Or what about those who rely on certain little magical tokens and prayers thought up by some impious imposter for his own amusement or profit." ASD IV-3, 124/3–4, Miller trans., 64.

55 Compare the consummately dissembling fictions by which, in Mo e's view, Richard III governed.

56 More accepted Lucian's ridicule of this supernatural event, but, had the context been supernatural events in Christianity, such as the resurrection of Christ, his response would of course have been entirely diffe ent.

unadorned." Far from seeing, like More, a "resemblance" between lies and truth – truth accepted on faith – Tychiades emphasizes that a chasm separates lies and truth and that the diffe ence is obvious. "Lying" is just another word for gullibility and truth is found in common sense (reason devoid of all abstractions). One does not have to work at untangling magic and other nonsense from truth, nor does untruth have a similar appearance.

Stoic/Christian *Utile*

The second side of the *honestum/utile* mindset also stands out when applied to the lives of saints and martyrs. Worldly truths and divine truth are two utterly diffe ent types of value, and yet some worldly values are one with divine truth while others are not. On this basis Christians need to distinguish the diffe ence between false and true saints' lives. As More states in his conclusion (1b–c): "testing worldly values carefully and deliberately by the teaching of Christ (as though applying the rule of Critolaus), we must either accept or reject them."

Deciding between Apparently Utile *and Actually* Utile, *False and True Saints' Lives*

However necessary it may be to distinguish what is false as well as what is true in the stories, contentions, or arguments set forth by humans, exemplified by lives of saints and martyrs, this can be extremely difficul because, as shown above, the false stories often sound much like true stories. Nor is Lucian's *Philopseudes* of any help. While Tychiades would have us use worldly reason against lies (what we would consider credulity), More has a much more difficul problem. For him, highest reason, "truth unadorned," is not open to Lucian's common sense. It must be accepted on faith. And the true humanly created stories More sees are not such because they are common sense, as such, but because and only because they are one with "the principal mysteries" of the faith. For More, unlike Tychiades, "reason" can never be something obvious. Stories that seem true, that seem "reasonable," but are not in total (both/and) accord with the gospel are not true and represent false reason. In short, More's mindset, unlike Tychiades', is not one-dimensional but two-dimensional. Abstract truth and faith are no more a part of Tychiades' mental baggage than is judging humanly created stories in terms of these yardsticks. More's frame of thought, however much he may laud Lucian, has nothing in common with Lucian's frame of thought.

From Zeno onwards, of course, Stoics had been greatly concerned with the second side of the both/and, distinguishing in various ways things that are "preferred indiffe ents" and things that are "dispreferred indiffe ents." In Book 3 of *De officiis*, Cicero takes this thinking yet one step further. Developing a goal of the Stoic Panaetius, he distinguishes in case after case the diffe ence between things that are apparently *utile* and those that are actually *utile*. More applies this thinking to saints and martyrs. Christians must test worldly stories (or other contentions) "carefully and deliberately" because some are true and some are false and the diffe ence has to be worked out. Everything rides on discovering whether a saint's or martyr's life is or is not in sync with the precepts of the faith (Christian *honestum*). This is the case notwithstanding that worldly values can never be divine values – and that worldly values, in accord with Critolaus' rule, are minuscule in comparison. Christians, like Stoics, do not have the option of not deciding between the worldly stories. They must meticulously work out the diffe ences between true and false stories. A particular story must be either accepted or rejected. The saints' stories that are valid are at the same time useful, while those that are not have no beneficial role. Not choosing – or choosing the non-Christian story – is evidence of depravity of soul, one result being unhappiness, "superstitious dread."

Contrast again this worldly two-dimensional Christianity with More's outlook only one year earlier. A standard theme in the lives of saints and martyrs – one example in *The Golden Legend* is St Augustine – is the scorning of sex, marriage, riches, public activity, companionship, and all sensual delights.[57] A year earlier this theme had been fully in accord with Thomas More's view of highest Christianity. Now he sees, his mind revolutionized by Erasmus, that religion by its very nature is worldly and can encompass all these things. Now he argues that the only thing that will advance one in religion is carefully deciding either for or against the particular worldly stories or contentions that everywhere confront a person – while holding firm to the unbending precepts of the faith. A Christian cannot escape worldliness. The difficult – and necessity – of this enterprise, the combining at every step of two types of value, one worldly and the other non-worldly, is not mitigated but emphasized.

57 See Reames, *The Legenda Aurea*, 157. Illustrating the gulf which separates saints from worldliness, it was held that St Bernard "could consume raw blood without noticing that it is not butter" (161).

Deceit: Building on the Stoic Conception

Note carefully the place of deceit and here too the relationship to Stoicism. As shown in Part I, considerable evidence indicates that, in his 1501 lectures on Augustine and earlier, More was fixated on the role of deceit in society. He saw deceit as central to worldly ills and he contrasted – either/or – this worldliness with the rigid one-dimensional view of Christianity represented in their own ways by Colet and Carthusian monasticism. Those modern critics who have seen something suspicious or merely rhetorical in More's 1513–18 representation of Richard III as a brilliant and unparalleled exemplar of deceit (see above, 64–5) have a foil to their arguments not only in More's lectures on Augustine, and sources near contemporary with the events surrounding Richard's reign, but in More's introduction to Lucian, written in early 1506. Pervasive deceit governs worldly activities in the introduction to Lucian just as it does in *Richard III*.[58] The diffe ence is that here deceit explains great numbers of religious writings, the work of respected intellectual leaders, whereas in *Richard III* deceit explains the political world from 1483 to 1485, most particularly Richard III.

What distinguishes the Lucian work from the lectures on Augustine, five years earlier, is that now deceit is fully implanted within a Stoic frame of thought. In Stoicism, we remember, *honestum* is the only good and *turpe* is the only evil (*Fin.* 3.11). Virtue and vice reflect fixed – and opposed – intentionalities. That which is base, dishonourable, disgraced, evil, sinful, or foul ("turpe, inhonestum, indecorum, pravum, flagitiosum, foedum") has absolutely no tie to virtue (*Fin.* 3.14). Evil deceit pervades *turpe*.[59] Since the false saints' lives could not be such were "the principal mysteries" held to, anyone setting forth such stories is guilty (tying with Stoicism) not simply of an error in judgment but of deliberate and heretical deceit (7/11). But in Stoicism that which contrasts with *turpe, honestum*, is not one-dimensional (in line with the outlook of a Colet or the Carthsians) but two-dimensional. And this is the way More now sees Christianity. In 1501 he saw no worldly solution to the evils of Richard III, while now, against those responsible for the false lives, he has a solution. Now he knows that Christianity

58 We need to study more carefully the relationship of More's deep-seated belief that deceit is everywhere with his later harshness (towards Protestants in particular). See Wood's incisive description of More's harshness in "Sir Thomas More."

59 In *De officiis* Cicero demonstrates, in actual cases, how one can determine whether such deceit is present (cf. *Off.* 3.64–74). Where wrong is done, deceit is more contemptible than even the use of force (the diffe ence between the fox and the lion) (1.41, cf. 3.60).

is indistinguishable from a certain type of worldliness, that there is all the diffe ence between true worldliness and the deceits found in false worldliness. As in the *Enchiridion*, his thinking is not just either/or but profoundly both/and.

In short, no previous criticism of lives of saints and martyrs had a comparable conceptual basis. More does not simply criticize "additions" and "insertions," he also shows how an evaluator needs to think about the issue, the frame of mind that should govern how a decision about what is valid and what is not should be made. Lacking a Stoic/Christian *honestum/utile* mindset, one cannot distinguish between true and false lives, much less the creators of these lives. More than this, the evaluator who lacks this mindset is himself not a Christian.

Note one thing more. In line with Stoic *honestum*, divine truths do not dictate in More's thinking the particular content of humanly created stories or contentions. There are two types of value, not just one, and divine values are only – opposite worldly values – the *sine qua non*. Absolute truth allows as well as disallows. This recognition not only brought false human stories and contentions to light but also made possible the consideration of points of view that had been previously downgraded or not seen. In working out in *Utopia*, ten years later, exemplifications of the working of the Stoic *honestum/utile* way of thinking, More shows that many practices that on the surface appear outlandish do not in fact contradict the absolutes, while practices that seem entirely normal may contradict the absolutes (see Parts VI–VIII below).

A Mystery Resolved: Pinpointing Those Responsible for Defiling "Truth Unadorned" with False Stories

What seems evident is that More was working out in his own way Erasmus' pervasive criticism of "superstitious ceremonies." In his *Enchiridion*, Erasmus often criticizes those who honour saints with "superstitious" and "magical" ceremonies at the expense of Christ and being a Christian.[60] While "ceremonies" such as honouring saints are not in themselves wrong but simply things indiffe ent, "superstition" is evident when so-called Christians imagine that such practices in themselves win points. Venerating saints and the like can have value only if placed within a spiritual context – worked out in terms of a Stoic-based two-dimensional, unitary both/and, mindset.[61]

60 See for example H 77/15–16 and 80/4, CWE 66, 74 and 76.

61 See Dealy, *Stoic Origins*, Part VII.

Compare More's thesis. Those who create and fall for the false saints' lives, lives set forth "under the guise of religion," imagine that they are practising religion, but this is an illusion, "foolish confidence." They think that the insertions and additions will help them get into heaven, but such practices are merely superstition. What they do not see and do not want to see is that, pending analysis, worldly stories or contentions have no status. Choices must be made (as in Stoicism, distinguishing preferred indiffe ents from dispreferred). The true worldly stories can be identified and worked out only by those who think in spiritual unitary both/and terms. For people lacking such a mindset, genuine Christianity does not exist.

In fact even the particular individuals More was attacking in his criticisms can be, almost certainly, identified. Corresponding with his criticisms in the Lucian work are the charges he levels against John Batmanson in *Letter to a Monk*, a long 1519 treatise in defence of Erasmus and Erasmus' thinking, most especially in *The Praise of Folly*.[62] Batmanson was a prominent member of the London Carthusians, the very order More before late 1504 had longed to join, and More's criticisms are aimed not just at Batmanson but at the order itself – which he still considers the most religious of the orders (283/16–18). What he repeatedly objects to is the one-dimensional outlook of Batmanson and other religious. Here, as in his introduction to *Lucian*, we read: "You think you put all the saints forever in your debt by protesting that they were never wrong" (217/13–14) – a "superstitious piety" (217/18). And just as in his *Lucian*, though with diffe ent examples, he demonstrates that even St Augustine could be wrong (213/19–215/11).[63] Also repeated, authority figu es or intellectuals – deceiving themselves as well as others – are spreading falsities regarding saints' lives: "Some of your brethren suppose they put all of the saints in their debt every time that they honor their memory with such foolish jingles that not even a rogue trying his hardest to mock them could muster more foolish ones" (259/21–6).

So-called Christians conveniently use saints to support their own "ceremonies" against others – and in doing so prize their own ceremonies more than God's precepts (281/16–18). Although ceremonies are not bad in themselves, people "superstitiously" abuse them at the expense of God's commandments (277/24–6). Even a person chosen head of the Carthusian monastery went from one crime to another: "Paying less attention to God's precepts than to monastic ritual," he

62 CWM 15, pp. 197–311.

63 More also demonstrates that Augustine could be wrong in a 1515 letter to Dorp. See CWM 15, pp. 1–127, at 67/24–69/16.

even planned a murder and recruited killers (283/11–13). And under the influence of an ignorant but pretentious and influential friar, "the very worst people were those who recited the Psalter most religiously, and they did so precisely in order to secure themselves a licence to do anything at all, since they thought it a sin to retain any doubts about heaven when so weighty an authority as that friar had dropped out of heaven to promise it to them with so much conviction" (285/24–8). Equally Erasmian, More refers to those who think they will go directly to hell if they change any item in their dress whereas they feel no regrets about amassing money or fighting with their abbot (281/24–7). More knows of one monk who spewed out, indulging like so many his own vices, all sorts of verbiage about miracles – "under a pretext of piety" (289/23–4).[64] Comparable to those criticized in his *Lucian*, those in religious orders have a lofty opinion of themselves and thus, lacking all charity, tend to look down superciliously on others (279/7–13). Going to the core of the *Enchiridion*, as well as *The Praise of Folly*, More tells us that Erasmus, in contrast, tries "to make us see ourselves as we really are" (291/16–18).

More's discussion here of Mary and Martha (Luke 10:38–42) also illuminates his Stoic/Christian *honestum/utile* mindset. Mary's other-worldly approach may be "better," but members of religious orders need to realize that God observes everything in our hearts and he "may find that what you have been doing is avoiding responsibility, dodging work, cultivating the pleasure of repose in the shadow of piety, looking for a way out of life's troubles, and wrapping your talent up in a napkin, thus wasting it inside for fear of losing it out-of-doors" (301/23–303/10).[65] And we may tie in here Erasmus' ever-present contrast in *De taedio Iesu* of the *alacritas* (eager joy) of martyrs with Christ's life and mental state. Christ did not experience the one-dimensional *alacritas* of martyrs but a worldliness that exceeded that of any human. So-called Christians want to believe that Christ was a martyr, but this belittles Christ's achievement and entirely misrepresents the nature of Christianity. Christ's experience and outlook was unitarily both/and – and in a unique way.[66]

64 Duffy concludes that in *A Dialogue Concerning Heresies*, published in 1529, More "was undoubtedly prepared to tolerate a good deal that Erasmus deplored as 'superstition.'" More considered "pilgrimage, the veneration of relics and images, and the hope of miracles worked by their intercession" as ancient as the church and inseparable from that church. See "'The comen knowen multytude of crysten men,'" 201 and 197 resp. See also 119n30 above.

65 Compare the two types of religious in the Utopian state (C229).

66 See Dealy, *Stoic Origins*, Part III, Ch. 3.

3 The Role of *Cynicus* and *Menippus*

Neglected in chapters 1 and 2 were discussion of *Cynicus* and *Menippus*, the two dialogues that precede *Philopseudes*. Why did More include these dialogues? Considering that they set forth one-dimensional and opposed positions, should we not see them in rhetorical terms, as representing simply a debate *in utramque partem*? Don't they contradict the unitary both/and thinking so evident in More's rewriting of *Philopseudes*?

More states that he chose the three dialogues not randomly (from dozens Lucian had written) but because he had a particular interest in them (3/16–23). Analysis reveals just how true this statement is and that his prime interest was not rhetorical but philosophic. The first and second dialogues, as presented by More, are essential prerequisites to his rewriting of *Philopseudes*. The purpose of *Cynicus*, the first dialogue, is to build up what will become with the third dialogue, as rewritten, the hard and non-worldly side of truth. The purpose of *Menippus*, the second dialogue, is to build up what will become with the third dialogue the bending and worldly side of truth. Neither the non-worldly values nor the worldly values are valid in themselves. The issue is not either/or but both/and.

More did not just happen on the arrangement of the three dialogues in perusing Lucian's works. He created it. The recently published Greek editions of Lucian (1496 and 1503), which More used,[67] do not put the dialogues in this sequence.[68] Nor did Lucian compose *Menippus* with the specific purpose of contradicting *Cynicus*, or vice versa. And it goes without saying that Lucian would not have dreamed that the theses of the two dialogues actually require each other. What More does by bringing in the two opposite dialogues is to open our eyes by yet another route to the reality of his newly acquired Stoic/Christian *honestum/utile* understanding of Christianity. His goal was to rewrite *Philopseudes*, but how the goal is reached was for More of great importance. He wanted above all to demonstrate, it will become evident, the diffe ence between his old dichotomous way of thinking about life and Christianity and his new Erasmian-inspired outlook.

67 C.R. Thompson shows that he was using the more widely available 1503 edition rather than the 1496. See CWM 3.1, p. xl.

68 CWM 3.1, p. xxix. The editor finds no explanation other than the possibility that More wanted to put the shortest first. Like others, egemer does not imagine that the order of the dialogues has anything to do with the meaning of the dialogues. See *Young Thomas More*, 65.

Cynicus (and Abstract Truth)

Answering in the dialogue itself the question of why he lives in utter simplicity, with long hair and bare feet, lacking clothes, food, and housing, the Cynic points to all the worries and havoc brought on by the desire for money, prestige, a big house, extravagant eating, and outward display.[69] At odds with what others call civilization, he has based his life on principles. There is a direct relationship between holding to principles and simplicity of life. "Neque quicquam ergo mirandum est, si ab his differimus habitu, a quibus tantum differ - mus instituto" (21/8–10, 166). While others live life in terms of habit and appetite, wherever pleasure, ambition, avarice, anger, or fear takes them, he bases everything on rational judgment (167). What he desires is virtue and association with intelligent and decent men. He considers the golden crowns and purple robes of the so-called fortunate mere pride and laughs at those who wear such. Like the gods, he has no needs.

In his introduction, More relates *Cynicus* – said to be of great weight, notwithstanding its shortness (3/24–8) – to St John Chrysostom (d. 407), in his view not only a man of acute judgment but also the most learned of all Christians (2/26–7).[70] There is good reason why Chrysostom incorporated this dialogue, according to More, into a homily.[71] Grave and truly Christian as well as excelling in learning, he would have greatly appreciated the message of *Cynicus*, for in this dialogue, "while the severe life of Cynics, satisfied with little, is defended and the soft, enervating luxury of voluptuaries denounced, by the same token Christian simplicity, temperance, and frugality, and finall that strait and narrow path which leads to life eternal, are praised"

69 CWM 3.1, Greek and Latin pp. 10–23; modern English pp. 159–68. The most famous Cynic was of course Diogenes of Sinope (c. 403–321 BCE). See DL 6.20–81. On the development of Cynicism to the time of Lucian, see Branham and Goulet-Cazé, eds., *The Cynics*; Moles, "The Cynics and Politics"; and Schofield, *The Stoic Idea of the City*. Zeno was greatly influenced by Cynicism, befo e founding Stoicism and inaugurating the two-value system. On Cynicism in the Middle Ages and the Renaissance, see Matton, "Cynicism and Christianity from the Middle Ages to the Renaissance," and Kinney, "Heirs of the Dog."

70 In his 1518 *Letter to the University of Oxford*, More contrasts the subtleties of scholastic theology with the theology of "the oldest and holiest fathers," one of those named being Chrysostom, who saw that holy scripture is the proper home of theology. CWM 15, 129–49 at 141.

71 No evidence that Chrysostom incorporated this dialogue into a homily has been found. See CWM 3.1, pp. 138–9.

(5/2–6). Ultimately, as More probably recognized, Chrysostom became a hermit.[72]

In short, More (1) relates the Cynic's severe life, his principles, use of rationality, and oneness with practices of the gods to "that strait and narrow path which leads to life eternal" and (2) ties the Cynic's disdain for worldly goods and what is called civilization with "Christian simplicity, temperance, and frugality."[73] The picture that emerges here is that of hard, unbending, one-dimensional truth on the one side – an offshoot being simplicity, temperance, and frugality, monastic ideals – and worldliness seen in negative terms on the other.

Menippus (and Worldly Truth)

While the Cynic looks at the world from the top down, Menippus, as described by Lucian, looks at the world from the bottom up.[74] Uncertain in his youth what he should believe, considering that the gods engage in adultery and the like, Menippus had gone to the underworld for help. There, as in the worldly arena, he found stealing, lying under oath, extortion, fighting over pennies, adultery, the invoking of spirits by magicians, and, particularly evident, pride in wealth and place. The rich plunder and oppress without regard for law or the poor. But among philosophers, "the ignorance and perplexity was greater than elsewhere, so that they speedily convinced me that the ordinary man's way of living [vita idiotarum] is as good as gold" (27/38–29/1, 171). Using clever syllogisms and discussing final and first causes, the philosophers everywhere contradict each other. And yet there is no way of deciding in favour of one view over another. Each argument sounds plausible. Most unreasonable of all, their practices directly contradict their preaching (172). They scorn money but are avaricious; they oppose

---

72 Believing (in accord with the overriding thesis of his book) that More's real view is found in *Menippus*, where referral is made to the "life of the ordinary private citizen," Wegemer fails to mention Chrysostom in discussing *Cynicus* and believes that Lucian attacks philosophers in all the Lucian dialogues More translated. See *Young Thomas More*, 63–5, 84.

73 Regarding "atque eneruata delicatorum hominum luxuria reprehenditur" (4/3–4) and the contrast with the severity of the Cynics, note Cicero's relentless criticism, in his philosophical works, of the soft pleasure-loving philosophy of Epicurus – opposite the hard principles adhered to by Stoics.

74 CWM 3.1, Greek and Latin pp. 24–43; modern English pp. 169–79. On the person Menippus, of whom little is known, see the *Oxford Classical Dictionary*, rev. 3rd ed, (2003), 959. Relihan has nothing to say about More's Menippus in "Menippus in Antiquity and the Renaissance."

pleasure but indulge in it. Underscored is the fact that life is like a pageant where various costumes are worn and then given back, as Fortune dictates.[75] Even kings are ultimately reduced to poverty. All this being the case, the best thing, Menippus concludes, is to be concerned only with the present, "laughing a great deal and taking nothing seriously." "The life of the common sort is best" (179).

In a short comment on *Menippus*, More states that Lucian here refrains from the arrogant pronouncements and "fruitless contentions" of philosophers, "the jugglery of magicians," and "the silly fictions of poets" (5/9–10). By implication, More here agrees that common sense is better than philosophy, magic, or poetry. Three further observations are in order: (1) Tying in with More's own background, the context is Menippus' youthful struggles regarding how he should think and the course of his life considering all the contradictions of laws and gods (171). (2) Menippus' attack, as More sees it, on the arrogant pronouncements and "fruitless contentions" of philosophers ties in with the syllogisms and extreme logicizing of late scholastic philosophy – not with how More and humanists saw ancient philosophy. (3) Menippus' further disdain for philosophers on the grounds that their practices are at odds with their teaching relates not only to the moral focus of humanists but, more specificall , to More's criticism of preachers in his 1504 letter.

Rhetoric?

Importantly, if we step back from More's description of the first two dialogues, we can see that there is both a positive and a negative type of abstraction and both a positive and a negative type of worldliness at play. Chrysostom and the Cynic represent positive abstractions, while the philosophers and their methods of philosophizing represent negative abstractions. Living a simple Christian life in this world, as in *Cynicus*, and using common sense, as in *Menippus*, represent positive worldliness, while things such as cheating, lying, avarice, and pride, described in both dialogues, represent negative worldliness. What are we to make of these contradictory positions? Does More not care about consistency or logic? That which is unseen is true, that which is unseen is false; that which is seen is true, that which is seen is false. Abstractions are positive, abstractions are negative; worldliness is positive, worldliness is negative. Abstractions are praised, abstractions are criticized; worldliness is praised, worldliness is criticized. Abstractions

75 Cf. Erasmus, *The Praise of Folly*, below, 173–4.

are opposed to worldliness; worldliness is opposed to abstractions. Worldliness is entirely superior to abstractions; worldliness is inferior to abstractions.

It could be imagined that a rhetorical game is being played here at the reader's expense or possibly for the reader's enlightenment. For Lucian, in the context of second-century intellectual and social life, the dialogues may well have represented a type of game playing. Was More simply demonstrating his rhetorical abilities? Was he vacillating, either/or, between positions? Was he engaging in a debate *in utramque partem*, simply throwing out positions for the reader to ponder? In the one case worldliness wins while in the other case abstract principle wins. The worldliness approved in the one case differs greatly from the worldliness disapproved in the other case. The philosophy approved in the one case differs greatly from the philosophy disapproved in the other case.

Notice, however, what happens if we take away the two negatives, negative worldliness and the negative abstractions of philosophers and philosophy. We are left with two positives, the obvious problem being that they are polar and contradictory positives. On the one hand, certain worldly values are entirely superior and should be followed. On the other hand, certain otherworldly values are entirely superior and should be followed.

The Relationships to *Philopseudes*

Cynicus and *Menippus* illustrate false ways of thinking. Their purpose is not to pose a rhetorical question, whether one should choose worldly values or non-worldly, but to lay out the ways of thinking that need to be overcome. The two dialogues represent the contemplative life and the active life respectively, the non-worldly and the worldly, and each contends that the contrary way of life is faulty – but neither of these outlooks, More is intent on showing, is in itself valid. Positive non-worldly values always have a worldly dimension; positive worldly values always have a non-worldly dimension. He rewrites Lucian's *Philopseudes* to show – as set forth in his conclusion (see above, chapter 1) and detailed in his discussion of saints' lives (see above, chapter 2) – that Christianity is not either/or but comprises unitarily two utterly diffe - ent types of value.

In rewriting *Philopseudes*, More very consciously and deliberately rejects *Cynicus* and *Menippus* in the following ways:

(1) Against *Menippus* he shows that abstract values are real and indispensable. His interpretation of *Cynicus* added to the Cynic's severe

life and principles Chrysostom's straight and narrow path to eternal life, and now, with *Philopseudes*, we learn, developing the thesis, that Christianity is that religion "which Truth itself established and which it intended to consist of truth unadorned [quam ipsa ueritas instituit, & in nuda uoluit ueritate consistere]" (6/4–5).

(2) On the other hand, we know from his employment and interpretation of *Menippus*, above, that he did not agree with the Cynics' demeaning of worldliness. Worldly values are inextricable aspects of Christianity. Christianity is about worldliness, not just the worldliness of monks but true worldly involvement, making decisions that relate to the hurly-burly of life, "the ordinary man's way of living."

(3) But the worldliness of Christianity is of a particular type. Worldliness is not simply a matter of choosing one view over another based on innate common sense, as Lucian's *Philopseudes* (which attacks the "fruitless philosophizing" of philosophers even more insistently than *Menippus*) has it. Common sense can be very wrong. In his rendering of *Philopseudes*, More shows that a methodology is required, and this methodology cannot work without abstract standards. Some worldly contentions are true and some false, and, lacking principles, it is not obvious which is which. The truth or falsity of statements can be discovered only by meticulously working out the unitary both/and methodology.

(4) Neither of the two types of value set forth by More is "common sense." On the one hand, true reason cannot exist lacking "unquestioning trust" (7/17) in "the principal mysteries" of the faith (4/16–17). On the other hand, the lesser, humanly created, truths cannot be simply common sense because their legitimacy depends on their not being out of sync with the absolutes even though they are utterly different.

(5) Not only is it the case that views considered "common sense" or "common opinion" can never be valid in their own right, it follows that views or assumptions considered "not common sense" or "not common opinion" can be entirely valid, should analysis reveal that they are one with the absolutes. More was to ingeniously illustrate this point, I will demonstrate in Parts VI–VIII, in his *Utopia*.

(6) While Tychiades explicitly connects "right reason [rectam rationem]" (77/24–7) with one-dimensional common sense, More sees "right reason" as Stoics see it, in *honestum/utile* terms.[76]

(7) Lucian would have found More's thinking doubly ridiculous. In the logic of Lucian's *Philopseudes*, Christian faith in things not seen

76 For Stoic referrals to "right reason" see DL 7.88, and Stobeaus, LS 61G (2).

would not be truth but just another example of magic and superstition, and, this being the case, More's worldly type of truth would also be magic and superstition (since in More's view there are no worldly values separate from non-worldly values).

4 Modelling Books I–III of *De officiis*

It seems clear that More was thinking of the frame and central theses of *De officiis* in his choosing of the dialogues (from the dozens of Lucian dialogues available), the way he arranges them, and the meanings he gives them. *De officiis* comprises three books, and More correlates the meanings and arrangements he gives to the three dialogues he translates with these books. Book 1 discusses the *honestum*, Book 2 the *utile*, and Book 3 the oneness of *honestum* and *utile*. More makes the first dialogue, *Cynicus*, represent the *honestum*; the second, *Menippus*, represent the *utile*; and the third, *Philopseudes*, represent the oneness of the *honestum* and the *utile*.

Chapters 1 and 2 above show that More rewrites *Philopseudes* in terms of the Stoic *honestum/utile* mindset and that his thinking is clearly built – Lucian's *Philopseudes* merely providing a platform – from Book 3 of *De officiis*. Book 3 builds throughout on the Stoic *honestum/utile* theme, worded by Cicero in various ways:

> That which seems expedient [utile] must not be morally wrong [turpe]; or, if it is morally wrong, it must not seem expedient. (3.81)
>
> As to the claim that what is extremely beneficial becomes honorable – it does not *become* so; rather it is so. For nothing is beneficial [utile] that is not honorable [honestum]; but it is not honorable because beneficial, but beneficial because honorable. (3. 10)
>
> Expediency [utilitas], therefore, must be measured by the standard of moral rectitude [honestate], and in such a way, too, that these two words shall seem in sound only to be diffe ent but in real meaning to be one and the same. (3.83)
>
> The *utile* and the *honestum* are two conceptions that nature has made one. (3.75)

What is particularly striking about *De officiis* is that it transfers the Stoic wiseman's frame of thought to the lives of those not wise (3.13–17). Book 3 illustrates over and over how this unitarily two-dimensional way of thinking can be applied to contemporary social and political problems.[77] A stated purpose is to correct the deficiency of the Stoic Panaetius, who, notwithstanding his promise, failed to discuss how one should decide when something that has the appearance of *honestum* conflicts with something that seems *utile* (3.7). Accordingly, Book 3 demonstrates throughout why and how it is that what is actually *utile*, as distinct from what is only apparently *utile*, is never separate from the *honestum*.[78]

Employing the same mindset and methodologies, More shows in his discussion of the lives of saints and martyrs that what seems to many beneficial is not, that what is actually beneficial is never separate from Christian *honestum*, "truth unadorned."[79]

Regarding More's pervasive insistence that deceit is always present where a person does not act and think in unitary both/and terms, Cicero insists that there can be "no more pernicious doctrine" than the belief that has gradually come to be accepted that a thing may be *honestum* without being *utile* and *utile* without being *honestum* (2.9). Deceit is never allowable (3.71). Anyone who does not accept that what is *utile* and what is *honestum* are one and the same "will be capable of any sort of dishonesty, any sort of crime" (3.74). Mere debate as to whether something is *utile* or whether it is *honestum* or more one than the other shows, according to Cicero, the workings of a non-moral mind. "Those who are accustomed, in considering any question, to weigh the morally right [honestum] against what they think the expedient [utile], good men are not" (3.18). In short, either/or thinking or debate *in utramque partem* – whether for worldly, philosophical, or rhetorical purposes – is in this context very wrong and can lead to all sorts of evil.[80] In this regard, Peripatetic thinking is faulty (3.20). One rule governs.

---

77 Perhaps, states Dyck, "Cicero's major contribution to Roman political thought is his radical identification of *honestum* and *utile*, with the consequences worked out in detail in Off. 3." See *A Commentary on Cicero, De Officiis*, 33.

78 More dedicates his translations (7/26–37), "these first f uits of my Greek studies," to Thomas Ruthall, an experienced diplomat and since 1503 bishop of Durham. He sees Ruthall as having both "distinction in learning" and "unsurpassed wisdom in practical affairs." Rega ding the latter, he cites his "numerous diplomatic missions carried out in various lands with such difficult negotiations and with such success. More was to write Book II of *Utopia*, it may be noted, while carrying out a similar diplomatic mission in 1515. But there is all the diffe ence between humanistic admiration for both experience and learning and the *honestum/utile* mindset.

79 Compare Erasmus' *Enchiridion*. See Dealy, *Stoic Origins*, Part VII.

80 Only where it is accepted that the *utile* and the *honestum* are inseparable can one justly debate issues from two sides, *in utramque partem* (cf. Diogenes of Babylon and Antipater, *Off.* 3.51–5, and Hecato of Rhodes, *Off.* 3.89). The principle always holds (*Off.* 3.98).

Note also the relation between *De officiis* and More's referral in his conclusion to Critolaus' "rule" ("regula"), *Tusculan Disputations* 5.51 (above, 110–12). Cicero makes very clear in *De officiis* that Critolaus' rule takes away nothing from the unitary both/and. It may be that expedient things are infinitesimally small, as contrasted with the *honestum*, but it is still the case that the *utile* and the *honestum* can never conflict

> For whether moral goodness [honestum] is the only good, as the Stoics believe, or whether, as your Peripatetics think, moral goodness is in so far the highest good that everything else gathered together into the opposing scale would have scarcely the slightest weight, it is beyond question that expediency can never conflict with moral ectitude.[81] (*Off.* 3.11)

In line with the social and political examples in *De officiis*, More's discussion of lives of saints and martyrs demonstrates that even the true human stories are infinitesimally small in comparison to divine truths and yet that worldly and non-worldly can nonetheless never conflict. Holding to saints' lives that are not one with *honestum* (spirit) is as inexpedient as it is dishonourable (*inhonestum*).

Differences between Books 1 and 2 of *De officiis* and *Cynicus* and *Menippus*

While More's rewriting of *Philopseudes* closely accords with Book 3 of *De officiis*, his polar, either/or, method of developing his first and second dialogues – within themselves and between each other – is not paralleled in Books 1 and 2 of *De officiis*. *Cynicus* represents the *honestum* described in Book 1 and *Menippus* the *utile* described in Book 2, but Cicero does not show in these books that the *honestum* contradicts the *utile* or the *utile* contradicts the *honestum*. In Book 1 the four parts of *honestum* – wisdom/prudence, justice, magnanimity, and propriety/temperance – are described at length and their opposites brought into focus, but rejection of the *utile* is not a consequence. Book 2 describes aspects of that which is truly *utile*, such as various administrative abilities, and what happens when such abilities are not in play, but nothing is taken away from the *honestum* as such.[82]

81 Cf. also *Fin.* 5.91.

82 Early in Book 1, Cicero mentions Plato's criticism of philosophers for being so absorbed in pursuit of truth that they will not assume civic duties except under

What can explain the fact that More's rewriting of *Philopseudes* aligns with Book 3 while his brief interpretations of *Cynicus* and *Menippus* deviate from Books 1 and 2? The essential explanation lies close at hand. The polar, either/or, outlook represented by *Cynicus* and *Menippus* epitomizes the way More himself had assessed reality and Christianity until some time shortly before his January 1505 decision. He had seen his worldly and non-worldly goals as mutually contradictory and had vacillated precipitously between these two outlooks. In choosing and interpreting *Cynicus* and *Menippus*, he was talking about not only Books 1 and 2 of *De officiis* but also this earlier struggle between two irreconcilable polarities. Should he commit himself irretrievably to marriage, worldly affairs, and humanistic studies or should he become a real Christian and join the Carthusian monastery? From the standpoint of monasticism and the Carthusians, the world was nothing and he himself was wallowing in muck and evil. From the standpoint of worldly affairs, his many involvements in political and legal activities, humanistic studies, learning Greek and the like, what could the monastic life accomplish? It followed that there were two ways of looking at worldly affairs, one negative and one positive; two ways of looking at abstract ideals, one negative and one positive. Not only, that is, did he see a worldly/non-worldly either/or, he saw worldliness as both negative (as in *Cynicus*) and positive (as in *Menippus*) and non-worldliness as both positive (as in *Cynicus*) and negative (as in *Menippus*).

Philosophy, Not Rhetoric

One thing is clear: Thomas More's either/or thinking before late 1504 did not originate in rhetoric. It originated in existential moral quandaries built, however uniquely, from the surrounding social, political, intellectual, and religious world. *Cynicus* and *Menippus* employ rhetorical tools, but More's mindset here too was not rhetorical. Although his mind had once vacillated, unendingly, between worldly desires and otherworldly ideals, this was no longer the case. Inspired by Erasmus of Rotterdam, he had come to see Christianity in an entirely new way – as the highest expression of a particular ancient philosophy. His rewriting

compulsion and contrasts non-philosophers who seek only their own self-interest at the expense of larger social concerns (1.28–9) (cf. Hythloday, Book I *Utopia*, C81–3, 101). But philosophers in Cicero's comment do not contend that what goes on in the world is nothing but evil and those who pursue self-interest do not here show up the worthlessness or evil of abstract concerns.

of *Philopseudes* resolves the issues raised by *Cynicus* and *Menippus* and in doing so illustrates the workings of that philosophy.

5 A Relationship to *Utopia*?

Did the structure, methodology, and meaning of the Lucian work (1506) prefigu e the structure, methodology, and meaning, ten years later, of *Utopia* (1516)? Otherwise stated, is the frame of thought that governs More's choice of particular Lucian dialogues and the meaning he gives them found in the book *Utopia*? Should the answer turn out to be affirmative all modern interpretations of *Utopia* would be at risk in that the Lucian work sets forth two polar opposite views only to show with *Philopseudes* how they are resolved. As shown in my introduction, most modern scholars have argued that the real meaning of the work is found in the Book I "either/or" debate between worldly "More" and Platonist Hythloday and that the author did not clearly side with either view. Book II, it is believed, does not resolve the issues.

In Book I of *Utopia*, the position of Hythloday ties, it may now seem apparent, with Thomas More's rendering of *Cynicus*, and the position of character "More" (as seen by Hythloday) ties, it may also seem apparent, with Thomas More's rendering of *Menippus*. Hythloday holds heroically to abstract truth and is contemptuous of the discordant and self-serving behaviour found in worldly affairs. "More" sees positive aspects of worldly actions, contending that much can be accomplished by decorum (an "indirect approach"), and points to faults in Hythloday's outlook. But the problem comes when we try to correlate the unitary both/and message of More's *Philopseudes* that follows his either/or rendering of *Cynicus* and *Menippus* with Book II of *Utopia*, which follows the either/or debate in Book I between Hythloday and "More." In his description of the Utopian state in Book II, Hythloday takes no account of the view represented by "More" in Book I. Indeed, he sees "More's" "indirect approach" as contrary to the "Platonist" outlook of the Utopians. In contrast, *Philopseudes* had presented, ten years before, an outlook that is not one-dimensional but two-dimensional, at once both abstract and worldly, contemplative and active. So what can this unitary both/and view have to do with Book II of *Utopia*? If Book II represents Hythloday's abstract and Platonist outlook, as Hythloday contends, and scholars believe, there can be no significant relationship to the fundamental message of the Lucian work.

But what if analysis should reveal that the debate between Hythloday and "More" is not built from rhetoric, as scholars everywhere believe, but from a philosophy – the Stoic-based thinking More had developed in his work on Lucian? Could it be, corresponding to *Philopseudes*, that author More shows with his Utopians that there is a valid type of absolute value, but it is not one-dimensional, and a valid type of worldly value, but it too is not one-dimensional; that wiseman Hythloday's position lacks a necessary relationship to worldly prudence and decorum while "More's" position (as seen by Hythloday) lacks a necessary relationship to abstract value; that the Utopians work out at length in an imaginary New World setting the Stoic unitary both/and way of thinking the author had outlined in *Philopseudes*? What if, that is, analysis should reveal that in composing *Utopia* the author's mind did not vacillate between the two opposed positions found in Book I but shows in Book II how the contradictions are resolved; that truth is not either/or but unitarily both/and? In Parts VI and VII below, I will demonstrate that this is exactly the thinking that governs in Book II the Utopian discussions of pleasure philosophy and the Utopian discussions of warfare. And in Part VIII, I will show that this unitary both/and outlook in fact surrounds even the Book I debate between Hythloday and "More."

Going even further back in time, it may appear that there is a trajectory from Book 3 of Cicero's *De officiis* to More's rendering of *Philopseudes* to the Utopian state. It may appear that behind *Cynicus* and Hythloday is Book 1 of *De officiis*, which deals with the *honestum*, and that behind *Menippus* and "More" is Book 2 of *De officiis*, which deals with the *utile*. And yet we can see that *De officiis* differs in that Book 1 describes the *honestum* without contrasting the *utile*, unlike *Cynicus* and Hythloday, and Book 2 describes the *utile* without contrasting the *honestum*, unlike *Menippus* and "More." What explains this diffe ence? It seems likely that the author's either/or mental suffering prior to his reading *De taedio Iesu* and the *Enchiridion* led to a principles-versus-worldly casting of *Cynicus* and Hythloday and a worldly-versus-principles casting of *Menippus* and "More." More's *honestum/utile* representation of *Philopseudes* clearly ties with Book 3 of *De officiis*, and my analyses in Parts VI and VII below will show that this same unitary both/and thinking is developed at length in Book II of *Utopia*.

Crucially important, it will be found, *Utopia* was directly influenced not just by the frame and message of Cicero's *De officiis* but also by the Stoic Seneca's related way of thinking, worked out in *De otio* and *De tranquillitate animi*. The basic either/or outlooks of Hythloday and "More" in Book I of *Utopia* were modelled from the latter two works (see my Introduction, 32–7, and Part VIII below). And yet the goal of both *De otio* and *De tranquillitate animi* is to show that the contemplative and active lives, correctly understood, are inseparable – just as, I will demonstrate, is the case with the Utopians.

Hythloday admires what he sees as the Platonist-based outlook and practices of the Utopians, but what he does not grasp is that the Utopian way of thinking is not Platonist but Stoic. What the author shows us, in all detail, is that the Utopian mindset is unitarily both/and, *honestum/utile*, and that this way of thinking, though unrecognized, is fundamental to Christianity; that Christians don't discern the hard side of the Christian faith any more than they discern the workings of the bending side; that the Utopian state is not a finished "utopian" product, and neither, in this life, is Christianity; that just as in Stoicism, the particulars that arise in life have to be continually confronted and dealt with on their own terms, while holding unflinchingly to unbendable principles; that the Utopians show the reader how to make choices between things only apparently useful and things truly useful – and as such inseparable from unbending principles; that solutions vary according to situations and more than one solution may be possible; that what is most admirable about Utopian society is not particular doctrines, rules, customs, or practices but the spiritual two-dimensional way of thinking and living – an outlook that applies even more to Christianity.

In summary, my analysis in Part I shows that in the years before his January 1505 decision More had deeply experienced both positions presented in Book I of *Utopia*. The problem had been that he found the two positions contradictory and believed his entire life depended on making a choice. His earlier obsession with Carthusian and contemplative ideals relates to Hythloday's rigid absolutism and Platonism – as well as to *Cynicus*. His earlier preoccupation with political affairs, humanistic studies, and sex relates to character "More's" advocating of worldly prudence and decorum – as well as to *Menippus*. What will be shown with the discussions of philosophy and warfare in Parts VI and VII is that the way of thinking that came to dominate his life beginning in January 1505, after he read *De taedio Iesu* and the *Enchiridion*, is represented by Book II of *Utopia* – as well as *Philopseudes*. Stoicism is about the application of two radically diffe ent but inseparable types of value to all the conditions that may occur in life, no matter how varied, and the Utopians – expanding the thinking found in More's rewriting of *Philopseudes* – work this out in an imagined New World context.

PART IV

Thomas More as *Unitarily* "Democritus" and "The Man for All Seasons": Erasmus' Preface to *The Praise of Folly*, 1510

As described by Erasmus in 1510 and 1519, More's personality correlates with the *honestum/utile* way of thinking that More delineated in his 1506 analysis of *Philopseudes* and worked out at length in 1516 – as will be exemplified by Parts VI and VII below – in Book II of *Utopia*.

Not only did Erasmus' *De taedio Iesu* and *Enchiridion*, followed by study of Stoicism, radically change More's perception of his mission in life and his writings, it also deeply affected, Erasmus shows, his personality. Although there may always have been two very diffe ent sides to that personality, what can be seen is that by January 1505 a personality that was vacillating between two poles of thought, non-worldly and worldly, was suddenly replaced by a both/and mental state. Very much aware of the seismic shift in More's outlook, Erasmus makes a point of describing, in a 1510 letter to More which prefaces *The Praise of Folly*[1] and in a biographical sketch published in 1519,[2] two opposite sides of More's mind which, far from conflicting, comprise a unitary whole

Near the beginning of the preface, Erasmus states that he got the idea of writing an encomium of Folly from the correspondence of the name "Morus" with the Greek word for folly, "Moria," and because More normally appreciates jokes of this sort. He adds to these reasons two fundamental, unusual, and – to his mind – altogether admirable sides to More's personality. (The numbering here and elsewhere is mine.)

> et omnino in communi mortalium vita Democritum quendam agere. Quanquam tu quidem, vt pro singulari quadam ingenii tui perspicacitate, longe lateque a vulgo dissentire soles, ita pro incredibili morum

1 *Moriae encomium*. ASD IV-3, 67–70, translated by Clarence H. Miller, *The Praise of Folly*, 1–5. On the dating of the letter see ASD IV-3, 15.

2 *Ep*. 999. Allen 4, pp. 12–23 and CWE 7, 15–25.

suauitate facilitateque cum omnibus omnium horarum hominem agere, et potes et gaudes.[3]

(1) You habitually play the role of Democritus by making fun of the ordinary lives of mortals. Although, to be sure, because of a unique perspicacity in your make-up you are accustomed to dissent sharply from the crowd,

(2) at the same time because of your incredibly affable and easy ways you can play the man for all seasons with all men, and enjoy doing so.[4]

Scholarly as well as popular accounts of More (notably Robert Bolt's play and film) describe him, building on Erasmus' account, as "a man for all seasons," but what is largely passed over is Erasmus' referral to More, at one and the same time, as "Democritus." What do these two characteristics actually tell us about More's personality, and why does Erasmus imagine in a follow-up that they make More's appreciation of the work at hand, *The Praise of Folly*, a foregone conclusion and that, this being the case, More will henceforth accept and defend the work as his own? Researchers have heretofore seen no serious relationships between More and the content of *The Praise of Folly*.

What can be seen is that More exhibits both (1) an all-seeing abstract perspective entirely superior to and at odds with worldly outlooks and behaviour and simultaneously (2) an ability to enter into and enjoy all the variables that are found in life, to be a "man for all seasons [omnium horarum hominem]."[5] Most persons are not able to separate their outlook from common opinion, but this is not the case, the first remark indicates, with More. He "dissents sharply from the crowd" and, like the philosopher Democritus (460–370 BCE), habitually laughs at what goes on in the world. Although what goes on in the world is complex and far from abstract truth, the second remark expresses admiration for More's ability to engage with and even enjoy that world. He does not rigidly confront worldly affairs but enters into the lives of others on their own terms. Being "incredibly affable" and easygoing, he can "play the man for all seasons with all men, and enjoy doing so."

But why does Erasmus not consider the two traits contradictory? How can More "dissent sharply" and ridicule the lives of humans and

3 *Moriae encomium*. ASD IV-3, 67–8/15–19.

4 Compare the translations of Miller, *The Praise of Folly*, 2, and Hudson, *The Praise of Folly*, 2.

5 In 1520 Robert Whittington applied the phrase "omnium horarum hominem" to More and translated it as "a man for all seasons." See his *Vulgaria*, 64–5 and Sylvester, "The 'Man for All Seasons' Again." Erasmus had discussed historical meanings of the phrase in his 1508 edition of the *Adages* (I iii 86).

also, "at the same time," happily enter into the lives of humans, no matter how varied? Why do the two polarities not compare with the either/or outlook held by More before January 1505 or More's contraposing of *Cynicus* and *Menippus* in 1506? Readers have most often simply passed over the text as if there were no difficul .[6] Editors have noted diffe - ent sources for the two statements but do not comment.[7] Some readers have imagined that the two characterizations are really the same, that Democritus' laughter at the affairs of man is somehow one with More's worldly affabilit .[8] Others have seen a portrayal that merely idealizes, as they interpret it, Erasmus' own outlook.[9]

What the text clearly describes, however, are two distinct sides to More's personality, one Democritean and the other worldly. "The man for all seasons" does not represent all aspects of More's personality but only a half of that personality. Democritus was not "a man for all seasons." Whereas Democritus was above and alien to the game of life, "the man for all seasons" enters into this game.[10]

Nor would contemporary intellectuals have considered Democritus "a man for all seasons." Quite the contrary. In the late Middle Ages and among

---

6 Chambers, in his classic biography of More, takes no note of what Erasmus states here (or in 1519) regarding More's personality, concentrating instead on what he sees as great diffe ences between *The Praise of Folly* and More. See *Thomas More*, 101. Marc'hadour lists many translations of "omnium horarum hominem" but, regarding Erasmus' meaning, mentions only some obvious misinterpretations and misapplications. No mention is made of the referral to Democritus. See "*Omnium Horarum Homo*" and "Latin Lives of Thomas More," 24.

7 See Clarence H. Miller, ASD IV-3, 67n16 and 69n19 (1979), and Betty Radice, CWE 28, 466nn3 and 4 (1986).

8 Surtz, "Richard Pace's Sketch of Thomas More," 185, and Yale *Utopia*, cxlix; Boyle, "Folly Plus," 442; and Grace, "*Utopia*," 180. Placing Democritus within "the man for all seasons," Kay sees a "genial criticism of the world." See "Erasmus' Learned Joking," 262.

9 Gordon, *Humanist Play and Belief*, 158. Democritus represents for Erasmus, we are told, the Christian view, while "the man of all seasons" is about joy and the ludic. Furey believes that "the man for all seasons" portrayal is "subtly subversive" in that Erasmus frequently separated the sacred from worldly ambition. Indeed, the label "has an ironic undertone – a subtly condemnatory comment on More's ability to please everyone." See *Erasmus, Contarini, and the Religious Republic of Letters*, 36–7. Joanne Paul wants to show in her recent book that More was not just "a man for all seasons," as Erasmus called him, but "also a thinker for his time" – assuming, like others, that there is no necessary connection between the latter and the former. See *Thomas More* (Cambridge: Polity Press, 2017), 141.

10 In a 1521 letter to Guillaume Budé, Erasmus again describes More as a "man for all seasons," something distinct from but, with him, united with real wisdom. *Ep*. 1233. Allen 4, 577–8/82–112, CWE 8, 296–7/89–111. The context is somewhat diffe ent in that Erasmus is here not contraposing a "man for all seasons" with a Democritean outlook but with humanistic studies.

fifteenth-century humanists, Democritus was known as "the laughing philosopher" (often coupled with Heraclitus "the weeping philosopher") because he was thought to have always laughed at the foolishness of people.[11] Seneca was one of many sources for this view. "Democritus, it is said, never appeared in public without laughing; so little did the serious pursuits of men seem serious to him."[12] In 1517, Richard Pace, who knew More and who was possibly influenced by Erasmus' preface, stated that More's favourite philosopher was Democritus and that More went beyond even Democritus by considering human affairs not just ludicrous but ridiculous.[13] Emphatically, Renaissance readers did not see Democritus as a person engaged with life and worldly affairs but the contrary, a person who sees and judges things from high above.[14] Tychiades, the spokesman in Lucian's *Philopseudes*, translated and interpreted by More, states that he admires no philosopher other than Democritus because Democritus, unlike others, including other philosophers, was not distracted in his view of the soul by foolishness.[15] Democritus laughed because he saw things in terms of truth. Although he went blind, according to Cicero, he could still "distinguish good from bad, just from unjust, honourable from disgraceful, expedient from inexpedient."[16] Some contemporaries

11 Attention to Democritus' genuine doctrines, most importantly his thinking on atoms, came only later. See Luthy, "The Fourfold Democritus on the Stage of Early Modern Science."

12 *De ira* 2.10.5, cf. *Tr.* 15.1–3. See also Horace, *Ep.* 2.1.194; Juvenal, *Satyra* 10.28–53; Lucian, *Philosophers for Sale* 13–14; Cicero, *De or.* 2.235. Rütten distinguishes sources that see Democritus in terms of the Stoic wiseman and sources that see him in terms of Diogenes the Cynic (c. 412–323 BCE) and his followers, such as Lucian. He imagines that Erasmus' comparison of More with Democritus is a joke that relates to the latter tradition. See *Demokrit – Lachender Philosoph und Sanguinischer Melancholiker*, 50–1. Goldhill, also, imagines that the relating of More with Democritus is Lucianic. See *Who Needs Greek?* 48.

13 Pace, *De fructu qui ex doctrina percipitur*, 104. On Pace's outlook, methodology, and relationship to Erasmus and More, see Curtis, "Richard Pace's *De fructu* and Early Tudor Pedagogy." Like Pace, Curtis sees the relationship of Democritus to More, and Erasmus' description of More as Democritus, in one-dimensional terms. See Curtis, "From Sir Thomas More to Robert Burton."

14 Compare the one-dimensional wiseman described by Seneca in *De otio*: If the problem is not with the wiseman but with the state, why should not the wiseman retire from public affairs? (6.3). Befo e getting himself contaminated it would be better to retreat and live a life of leisure and virtue (3.4). See my Introduction, above, 32–7.

15 See above, 126.

16 *Tusc.* 5.114. According to *De finibus*, Democritus sought freedom from care (5.23). Rütten shows that Democritus' laughter was often laced with sadness, as with the Neoplatonist Marsilio Ficino (1433–99). See *Demokrit – Lachender Philosoph und Sanguinischer Melancholiker*, 109–15.

of Erasmus wanted to hitch him to divinity and even Christianity. One example of this is a widely acclaimed poem published in 1505, composed by Antonio Fregoso, a Florentine. Presenting Democritus as a hermit who observes from high above the follies of worldly behaviour, Fregoso laments that he is not of the Christian sect.[17] In *Dulce bellum inexpertis* (War is sweet to those who know it not) (1515), a lengthy adage, Erasmus imagines Democritus arriving on the scene from far-away worlds only to discover that Christians live in a way entirely at odds with the life and precepts of Christ.[18]

Erasmus' biographical sketch of More, published in 1519, restates and even expands on the dual nature of More's personality and behaviour. More is both aloof and worldly, unbending and bending, but he does not vacillate between one pole and another, nor are the two sides contradictory. He embodies, at one and the same time, both poles:

> (1) You would think More was Democritus reborn, or rather that Pythagorean philosopher who strolled in a disengaged mood through the market-place, contemplating the turmoil of those who buy and sell. There is no one less guided by the opinion of the multitude.
>
> (2) and yet nobody is closer to the feeling of ordinary men[19]... He is disposed to be merry rather than serious or solemn ... [Whether a person be educated and intelligent or ignorant and stupid] he adapts himself to the disposition of anyone.[20]

(1) On the one hand his outlook is entirely remote from the worldly drama, those who obtain the necessities of life by buying and selling. He sees everything that goes on but is uninvolved in the hurly-burly of life. Nor are his views in any way guided by common opinions. The comparison with Pythagoras (c. 582–500 BCE) simply reinforces the likeness to Democritus.[21] Diogenes Laertius reports that Pythagoras

17 See Luthy, "The Fourfold Democritus," 456–7. On Fregoso's poem see also Garcia Gomez, *The Legend of the Laughing Philosopher and Its Presence in Spanish Literature (1500–1700)*, 74–94, and Pyle, *Milan and Lombardy in the Renaissance*, 217–19. On Democritus as a Christian in the Renaissance see Wind, "The Christian Democritus."

18 Adage 3001 (IV.i.1). ASD II-7, 28/469–91, CWE 35, 418–19. Democritus appears in the woodcut initial of Erasmus' edition of St Ambrose (1513). See Luthy, "The Fourfold Democritus," 457–8.

19 "Diceres alterum quendam esse Democritum, aut potius Pythagoricum illum philosophum, qui vacuus animo per mercatum obambulans contemplatur tumultus vendentium atque ementium. Nemo minus ducitur vulgi iudicio, sed rursus nemo minus abest a sensu communi." *Ep.* 999. Allen 4, 16/126–30, cf. CWE 7, 19/132–6.

20 *Ep.* 999. Allen 4, 14/46–8, 16/124–5, cf. CWE 7, 17/47–8, 19/130–1.

21 According to Diogenes Laertius, Democritus greatly admired Pythagoras (DL 9.38).

"compared life to the Great Games, where some went to compete for the prize and others went with wares to sell, but the best as spectators; for similarly, in life, some grow up with servile natures, greedy for fame and gain, but the philosopher seeks for truth."[22] (2) "And yet," states Erasmus, More is deeply affected by the ways of the world. "No one is closer to the common feelings of men." He is unrivalled in his ability to adapt to his surroundings, to identify with all the varieties of character, ability, intelligence, situation, feeling, and motive.[23] And he is disposed to be merry rather than overly serious. The Democritean More may laugh and the worldly More may be in good spirits, but in the one case there is abstractness and alienation from common feelings, opinions, outlooks, and activities, and in the other case extreme involvement and empathizing with all that goes on in the human scene.

Late in the biographical discussion Erasmus points to the very different personality that had existed before late 1504. Emphasizing both More's extreme piety and the fact that he is now a member of Henry's court, Erasmus exclaims: "What becomes then of those people who think that Christians are not to be found except in monasteries?"[24] But More himself had once been just such a person – as Erasmus so well knew! We can clearly see something of this earlier view, together with that of Democritus and Pythagoras, in More's despairing October 1504 letter (above, 74–5). He begins the letter by stating that he had come upon Colet's servant while strolling along in the law courts, "unbusy where everybody else was busy [inter aliena negotia]." His mood is entirely negative and his outlook one-dimensional. The situation he sees is either/or. He can either sink into worldly muck or rise up – and join the Carthusians. And he begs Colet to help him take the upward path.

---

22 DL 8.8. *Tusculan Disputations* discusses the same at more length (5.8–10). In Renaissance Florence, much was made of the notion, introduced by Iamblichus (c. 245–c. 325), that Pythagoras was sent down by the gods as a divine guide. See Celenza, *Piety and Pythagoras in Renaissance Florence*, 18ff and Joost-Gaugie , *Pythagoras and Renaissance Europe*. Beginning with the 1508 edition of the *Adages*, the first adage, "Friends Hold All Things in Common," swirls around Pythagoras – and the relationship to Christ. Holding things in common was first imagined by Pythagoras and then supported by Plato. See Eden, *Friends Hold All Things in Common*.

23 Compare Utopian music. In one respect "they are beyond doubt far ahead of us, because all their music, both vocal and instrumental, renders and expresses natural feelings and perfectly matches the sound to the subject. Whether the words of the prayer are supplicatory, cheerful, serene, troubled, mournful or angry, the music represents the meaning through the contour of the melody so admirably that it stirs up, penetrates and inflames the minds of the hea ers" (C239). See Carpenter's discussion, "A Song for All Seasons."

24 Ep. 999. Allen 4, 21/275–6, CWE 7, 24/301–2.

Not one statement in either the biographical sketch or the preface to *The Praise of Folly* indicates that Erasmus saw any conflict between the two opposite sides of More's personality. On the contrary, he sees the two polar characteristics as essential aspects of a personality that is one. He does not show that More vacillates from the Democritean side to "the man for all seasons" side, or vice versa. Nor does he reveal a More who rhetorically debates issues from these two opposite types of value, *in utramque partem*. The personality described is cohesive. And there is no reason to believe that Erasmus was imposing his own ideological thinking on More.[25] In accord with one type of value, More ridicules and dissents sharply from what goes on in worldly affairs, and in accord with another type of value, he enters into worldly affairs – and yet the two types of value are inseparable.[26]

Considering the above evidence and what has been revealed in Parts II and III above, it seems clear that Erasmus is describing a person who embodies the Stoic unitary, *honestum/utile*, both/and. Thus, we can set forth the following chronology: A Stoic-based unitary both/and outlook is found in (a) More's rendering of *Philopseudes*, 1506; (b) Erasmus' description of More's personality in the preface to *The Praise of Folly*, 1510; (c) More's framing of the Utopian state in Book 2 of *Utopia*, 1516, as outlined in Part III.4; and (d) Erasmus' 1519 biographical description of More's personality.

But how are we to assess *The Praise of Folly* (*Moriae encomium*), written in 1509? Surely this work, everywhere considered a rhetorical tour de force and one of the great works of literature, cannot be Stoic-based or seriously represent Thomas More's personality. Or can it?

25 Guy imagines that Erasmus' biographical sketch is not about More but a mere "façade," "a rhetorical triumph." "He [Erasmus] wrote to construct an ideal." See *Thomas More*, 32, 66, 80. Actually, it is Guy himself who constructs "a rhetorical triumph." See above, 89n11.

26 The editors of *A Companion to Thomas More* state that More "was not a man for all seasons, political or religious," in that there were many things he did not advocate (13) – which entirely misses the point. Erasmus never imagines that being "a man for all seasons" entails agreement with all views (see below, 190n95, 322n20, 325). If More represented in his life the Stoic unitary both/and, unbending/bending, *honestum/utile*, mindset, he was "a man for all seasons" no matter the worldly context – and even in martyrdom.

PART V

A Stoic/Morean *Praise of Folly*, 1511: *The Praise of Folly* Works Out More's Stoic-Framed Transformation

A Stoic/Morean outlook consciously frames Erasmus' *Praise of Folly* (*Moriae encomium*), written three years after the Lucian volume in 1509 and published in 1511. Although it is everywhere considered a rhetorical tour de force, only tangentially related to Thomas More, deeper analysis reveals something else: a philosophy and a working out of Thomas More's newfound outlook and personality.

1 The Rhetoric Is Brilliant but Secondary

Readers everywhere consider *The Praise of Folly* a literary masterpiece, a classic.[1] They see in the work a brilliant mishmash of inconsistent or contradictory theses that reflect, among other things, the ancient

1 *Moriae Encomium id est Stultitiae Laus*, ed. Clarence H. Miller, ASD IV-3, *The Praise of Folly*, trans. Miller. See Baker, *Divulging Utopia*, Ch 1; Boyle, *Christening Pagan Mysteries* and "Folly Plus"; Chomarat, "L'Eloge de la Folie' et Quintilien"; Christ-Von Wedel, *Erasmus of Rotterdam*, Ch. 6; Christian, "The Metamorphoses of Erasmus' 'Folly'"; Colie, *Paradoxia Epidemica*; Gavin and Walsh, "*The Praise of Folly* in Context"; Gordon, *Humanist Play and Belief*; Grassi and Lorch, *Folly and Insanity in Renaissance Literature*; Griffiths, "Glossing the Spoken ord"; Haarberg, *Parody and "The Praise of Folly"*; Kahn, *Rhetoric, Prudence, and Skepticism in the Renaissance*; Kaiser, *Praisers of Folly*; Kay, "Erasmus' Learned Joking"; Könneker, *Wesen und Wandlung der Narrenidé im Zeitalter des Humanismus*; Martin, *Truth and Irony*; McDonagh, "Holy Fools, Witty Fools, Depraved Fools"; Miller, "The Logic and Rhetoric of Proverbs in Erasmus' *Praise of Folly*"; Rebhorn, "The Metamorphoses of Moria"; Screech, *Erasmus: Ecstasy and the Praise of Folly*; Stenger, "*The Praise of Folly* and Its Parerga"; Swain, *Fools and Folly during the Middle Ages and the Renaissance*; Geraldine Thompson, *Under Pretext of Praise*; Watson, "Erasmus' Praise of Folly and the Spirit of Carnival"; Wesseling, "Dutch Proverbs and Ancient Sources in Erasmus' *Praise of Folly*."

paradoxical encomium and Menippean satire.[2] According to A.H.T. Levi, the work "exults in deliberate ambiguity and in the end communicates its message without ever allowing that message to be pinned down."[3] Rosalie L. Colie contends that Erasmus deliberately leaves interpretation up to the reader.[4] Jon Haarberg considers the work "a hybrid of epideictic rhetoric and inappropriate colloquialisms," deeply influenced by Menippus (third century BCE). "Every attempt to reduce the text to a single, unambiguous meaning can only be detrimental to its literary merit."[5] Exemplifying the enormous complexity of the literary referrals, Clarence Miller has shown that "there are 285 proverbs and proverbial expressions, an average of one in every 86 words."[6] Erasmus' preface ties the work to the mock encomiums of Homer, Virgil, Ovid, Polycrates, Isocrates, Glauco, Favorinus, Synesius, Lucian, Seneca, and Plutarch.[7] Many readers have made much of three divisions that can be found in the work. Wayne Rebhorn describes a metamorphosis from irony to satire to Christian mysticism.[8] According to another critique, "The last part of Folly's speech is completely inconsistent with the first part, but it is equally ironical."[9] The word *irony* – with its multiple meanings – is everywhere at centre court.[10]

Without doubt the work is a rhetorical tour de force, but is that all? My research, undertaken without preconceptions but with many unanswered questions, shows something else. The work is not built from rhetoric but from philosophy. The rhetoric is only a tool. Represented is the two-dimensional way of thinking worked out earlier by Erasmus

---

2 On the paradoxical encomium see Burgess, *Epideictic Literature*, 157–66; Pease, "Things without Honor"; Marsh, *Lucian and the Latins*, 167–76; and Henry Knight Miller, "The Paradoxical Encomium with Special Reference to Its Vogue in England, 1600–1800." On Menippean satire see Relihan, *Ancient Menippean Satire*; Blanchard, *Scholars' Bedlam*; and De Smet, *Menippean Satire and the Republic of Letters, 1581–1655*.

3 Levi, Introduction to *The Praise of Folly*, CWE 27, xxii.

4 Colie, *Paradoxia Epidemica*, 20.

5 Haarberg, *Parody and "The Praise of Folly,"* 243, 255.

6 Miller, "The Logic and Rhetoric of Proverbs in Erasmus' *Praise of Folly*," 84. Erasmus had brought out a second edition of his *Adages* in 1508.

7 According to Goldhill, *The Praise of Folly* appropriates and adapts Lucianic strategies. See *Who Needs Greek?* 49–54 at 52.

8 Rebhorn, "The Metamorphoses of Moria."

9 Miller, *The Praise of Folly*, xvii. Erasmus has Folly "play off one i ony against another." Cf. Kaiser, *Praisers of Folly*, 38 and, especially, Martin, *Truth and Irony*.

10 On the many meanings of the word *irony* see Dilwyn Knox, *Ironia*; Norman Knox, *The Word "Irony" and Its Context, 1500–1755*; Muecke, *The Compass of Irony*; and Reiss, "Medieval Irony."

in his editing of *De officiis* and in *De taedio Iesu*, and the *Enchiridion*.[11] Erasmus' mind did not oscillate as he composed the work and he did not contradict himself. Folly, the character, slides from one contention to another – from various types of unbending values to various types of bending values – but Erasmus' mind did not slide. Far from being a mishmash, the picture Folly paints is eminently rational. Scholars have discussed unendingly the ironies they find, without seeing the systemic reasoning that undergirds these ironies. The multitudes of sources and arguments develop major philosophical theses. Even the three divisions that researchers have found in the work have much less meaning than has been imagined in that a particular philosophical frame of thought surrounds everything. Near the beginning Folly warns against "the common herd of rhetoricians." Her power, she avers, extends far beyond the definition and division of hetoricians.[12]

The brilliant display of sources and disputation was made possible not only by Erasmus' rhetorical skills but, most of all, because he had spent years thinking about and being personally affected by the two utterly diffe ent types of value represented by Stoic thought – and how they unite. He doesn't tell us that he is building on a philosophy, much less what that philosophy might be. Instead he shows us his meanings, expounding philosophy by rhetoric. Folly discloses by multitudes of one-dimensional theses what is wrong and what right about concepts relating to each of the two types of value. Platonists, and scholastics (theologians as well as philosophers), see only abstract conceptions and imagine they can be applied to worldly affairs as is, but in fact truth comprises not just one type of value but two. Christianity goes nowhere lacking worldly values, values deriving from natural instinct, character traits, and all the variables of worldly situation. The goal is to distinguish valid worldly values from invalid ones and valid non-worldly values from invalid ones and to show that Christian spirituality can never occur where the two valid types, albeit radically diffe ent, do not comprise a unit.

Throughout much of the treatise, the fabled "Stoic wiseman," that remote, unbending, and unfeeling wiseman so ridiculed by fifteenth-century humanists, is at the centre of attack and ridicule. This being the case, readers everywhere have always imagined that the work is clearly anti-Stoic – and that Erasmus, being a good rhetorician,

---

11 I studied *The Praise of Folly* long before these works. I could see that there was a set way of thinking but did not grasp at that time the Stoicism.

12 Miller, trans., *The Praise of Folly*, 12.

is simply making arguments by picking and choosing, rather helter-skelter, from many literary and philosophic sources.[13] In fact, Folly's one-dimensional Stoic wiseman is only a straw man. *The Praise of Folly* is from cover to cover a Stoic-framed work. As I have shown in *The Stoic Origins of Erasmus' Philosophy of Christ*, no one since late antiquity had come near Erasmus' grasp of Stoicism. It had become deeply entrenched in how he viewed himself and all the issues of life. Stoicism was not just one of multitudes of sources that an encyclopaedic mind chose from. His youthful physical, mental, and social problems were resolved by Stoicism, and *De taedio Iesu*, his edition of *De officiis*, and the *Enchiridion* all testify to this imprinting – as does *The Praise of Folly*.

Relationships to More's Personality and Methodology

Within the confines of Erasmus' Stoic mindset, two factors explain the work, with rhetoric playing only a secondary role: (1) The ideal set forth is that embodied by More's Stoic/Christian, unitary both/and, personality (represented by More in his interpretation of *Philopseudes* and portrayal, later, of the Utopian state). (2) Folly employs the methodology used by More in his rendering of Lucian (and, later, in *Utopia*), presenting issues in either/or terms only to show more forcefully the Stoic-based unitary both/and resolution.

Even in the preface there is much to be learned about the overriding thesis and More's relationship to it. Besides showing that More has a personality that is unusual and entirely admirable, in that it is unitarily both/and, Erasmus alleges that More has every reason to appreciate *The Praise of Folly* and even to consider it his own. Indeed, he claims the work was entirely due to More. The following points stand out: (a) The idea of writing it had come to Erasmus as he thought of More while travelling by horseback over the Alps from Italy to London.[14] (b) It was

13 Chomarat, for example, assumes that Erasmus' assessment of Stoicism goes no deeper than Folly's criticism of the Stoic wiseman. See *Grammaire et rhétorique chez Erasme*, vol. 2, 989–90.

14 Among other friends in England, "my dear More, you were one of the first to come to mind, for I have always enjoyed you as much in my memory when we have been apart as I have delighted in your presence when we were together – and rest assured nothing in my whole life could be sweeter than your company" (*The Praise of Folly*, 1). According to Clarence Miller, Erasmus' claim that the idea of the work came while riding over the Alps should be considered fact, not convention (ASD IV-3, 13). In his 1519 biographical sketch, Erasmus states that it was More who persuaded him to write the work (after an early version had circulated?). *Ep.* 999. Allen 4, 16/119–20, CWE 7, 19/124–5.

written at More's house.[15] (c) It is addressed to More. (d) The title, *Moriae encomium*, plays on the relationship between More's name and the Greek word for fool, "Moria." (e) It is dedicated to More. (f) More is admonished to consider the work his own. (g) Immediately following the description of his both/and personality, Erasmus avers that, More's personality being such, he will readily accept the work as an object of his "patronage and defense" (p. 2).

Regarding the title, Erasmus insists that More is actually as far as can be from folly (p. 2). But this allegation tells us only what More is not, which leads to two questions: (1) What is it about More that is the opposite of folly, that is wise rather than foolish? If More epitomizes wiseness, what is the nature of this wiseness? I have in fact already answered this question (in Part IV). Erasmus' description of More's personality shows exactly why More is as far as can be from folly. There are two distinct sides to that personality, and each is unique and admirable, but what is most amazing is his ability to practise both sides at the same time. (2) But is there a relationship of this wiseness to *The Praise of Folly*? The task that remains is to discover the relationship or non-relationship of that personality to *The Praise of Folly*.

If the treatise is about foolishness, why did Erasmus owe the very conception of the work to thoughts about wise More? Why is the work dedicated to him? Why would More want to consider the work his own and even defend it? Readers have noticed Erasmus' statement that More likes jokes of this type, provided they do not lack learning and wit, and have imagined that Erasmus was simply having fun. More's primary interest in the work, according to this reading, would have been amusement.[16] Another explanation for More's alleged tie to the work is that Erasmus wanted to obtain More's "professional assistance" in defending it against all the criticism that he (rightly) expected – most especially from scholastics.[17] As it turned out, More did defend *The Praise of Folly* at length, in a letter to Martin Dorp (CWM 15, 1–127), at the very time he was writing Book II of *Utopia*,

15 *Ep.* 337 (1515). Allen 2, 94/126–7, CWE 71, 10. How long Erasmus remained at More's home is unknown. See Sowards, "The Two Lost Years of Erasmus."

16 Cf. Levi, Introduction to *The Praise of Folly*, CWE 27, 7. According to Hudson, Erasmus was being "playfully ironical." See *The Praise of Folly*, xxxii.

17 Thomas I. White, "Legend and Reality," 499. Marsh thinks that Erasmus dedicated the work to More "in a spirit of humanist collegiality" See *Lucian and the Latins*, 168.

in 1515.[18] Against the logicizing, "supersophistical trifling" of the theologians (26/26), More highlights in his defence of the work the need for real-world language skills (16/21–4), staying within nature's bounds (30/14–16), and, from another angle, holding to "that living gospel of faith [vivum evangelium fidei]" which is the "unbending standard of truth [inflexibilem veritatis regulam]" (88/2–6). Why did he defend *The Praise of Folly* by arguing for nature and real-world language skills on the one hand and for unbending truth on the other?

Erasmus contends that the "amusements" and "trifles" found in the work lead to "serious ideas" (p. 3). "Nothing is more delightful than to treat trifles in such a way that you do not seem to be trifling at all" (p. 4). But what is it that should be taken seriously? What is not folly? Is wiseness found only in negative criticisms of society? The "serious ideas" referred to seem to indicate much more. If *The Praise of Folly* leads to "serious ideas" that are not folly and if Thomas More is as far as one can get from folly, do the "serious ideas" of *The Praise of Folly* tie in with the serious ideas of More? Or, as always imagined, could there be all the diffe ence between More's outlook and what *The Praise of Folly* is about?

If *The Praise of Folly* and More represent the same thing, *The Praise of Folly* should represent More's unitary both/and outlook. But how could this be the case? Readers have seen the message of the work – if there is a message – in one-dimensional terms. Dominic Baker-Smith is not alone in holding that *The Praise of Folly* and *Utopia* espouse, in common, a transcendent Platonism.[19] Michael A. Screech's *Erasmus: Ecstasy and the Praise of Folly* encapsulates and develops the view, widespread, that the third and last section of the treatise sets forth a Platonist and beatific vision (a "mad ecstatic union") that finally resolves multitudes of "Lucianesque" paradoxes, jests, ironies and obliquities. "Disregarding detail or emphasis, the general drift of what Folly was saying must have been clear to anyone who had read Pseudo-Dionysius, say, or,

18 CWM 15, xxiii. By 1515, *The Praise of Folly* had already been printed more than seven times (ASD IV-3, 44). Resulting from the attacks of theologians, Erasmus included in the 1514 edition interpolations that ratchet up criticism of scholastic methodology. On the gathering storm and the lengthy debates with critics of his *New Testament* (1516), see Rummel, *Erasmus and His Catholic Critics*.

19 See Baker-Smith, "Uses of Plato by Erasmus and More," 90 and *More's Utopia*, 53–4. According to Kaiser, the conclusion expounds a "quasi-Platonic dualism between spirit and matter which stands more explicitly at the heart of the *Enchiridion*" (*Praisers of Folly*, 89). Bené argues that the Platonist opposition between body and spirit, found (he believes) in *The Praise of Folly*, was inspired by Augustine. See *Erasme et Saint Augustin*, 428 passim. Clarence Miller shows a more complex and inconsistent use of Plato. See his *The Praise of Folly*, xv–xvii.

Bernard, Aquinas, Hugo of St. Victor, Bonaventure, or, indeed, almost any of the medieval mystics."[20] Walter Gordon, in his *Humanist Play and Belief*, sees a transformation from darkness to light, mortal to immortal and mystical, matter to spirit, ludic to faith. Folly represents "the fi - tional nature of human affairs. [21]

What I will demonstrate, to the contrary, is that *The Praise of Folly* is about More's two-dimensional – and profoundly Stoic, as detailed by Erasmus – personality. Human nature and human affairs are anything but "fictional." ruth is unitarily both/and.

In developing his Stoic both/and frame of thought, as epitomized in his mind by Thomas More, Erasmus uses the methodology employed by More – see Part III above – in his rendering of Lucian. This is evident in that, going beyond anything he had previously written, he brings out the both/and by setting forth false polarities. Just as *Cynicus* opposes abstract values to worldly ones, so too does Folly (and, later, Hythloday in Book I of *Utopia*). Just as *Menippus* opposes worldly values to abstract ones, so too does another side of Folly (and, later, "More" in Book I of *Utopia*). And just as More makes clear, with *Philopseudes*, that *Cynicus* does not see positive worldly values, as well as false ones, and *Menippus* does not see positive abstract values, as well as false ones, and that truth is unitarily about positive abstract and positive worldly values, so too does the author of *The Praise of Folly* – through Folly – show that there are two positive types of value and two negative types of value and that the positive abstract type and the positive worldly type form a unitary both/and (a both/and that frames in its own way, we will see, Book II of *Utopia*). While More had with *Philopseudes* merely sketched out the negative and positive abstract positions and the negative and positive worldly positions, Folly develops these alternate positions at length – presenting multitudes of dead ends.

Clearly, the Folly that depicts false worldly values is not More, as represented by Erasmus, and just as clearly the Folly that depicts false abstract values is also not More, as represented by Erasmus. So in these regards Erasmus' statement that More is as far as can be gotten from

20 Screech, *Erasmus*, 13 and 142. Thinking in post-modern (non-historical) terms, Haarberg concludes, against Screech, that the ending is merely "a joke at the expense of the entire endeavor." See *Parody and "The Praise of Folly,"* 243. Geraldine Thompson, like most discussants, holds that the concluding section is deeply serious, not ironical. But what is the nature of this seriousness? See her *Under Pretext of Praise*, 70.

21 Gordon, *Humanist Play and Belief*, 157–64 and 159. Boyle contends, similarly, that Folly sees worldly affairs as "illusions." See "Folly Plus," 437

folly is correct. The true worldly values and the true abstract values represented by Folly the person say something very diffe ent. These are the "serious ideas" Erasmus talks about in the preface and they correlate with More's personality. More's personality, as described by Erasmus, is two-dimensional, and so too is the truth represented by Folly.

But why would Erasmus use a methodology that leads into the both/and by showing polar, either/or, thinking? Without doubt he saw the rhetorical possibilities, but what inspired him above all was his deep knowledge of More's real-life transit from either/or thinking to a unitary both/and mindset. And he saw that the contrast between either/or and both/and thinking was still indelibly imprinted on More's mind, as had been evident in his setting forth the polar views of *Cynicus* and *Menippus* before working out the solution with *Philopseudes*. At the time they were working on Lucian, only three years earlier, Erasmus would have well recognized how seismic the sudden change from the one outlook to the other had been for More and that this was worked out in his rendering of Lucian. Living with More in London, he would have seen yet again that More was very consciously playing out in his personality and life the unitary both/and against this either/or backdrop, that for most of his life More had not been a person who represented simultaneously both a "Democritus" and "a man for all seasons." In short, *The Praise of Folly* presents a universalized picture while at the same time graphically describing the quandaries of More's former mindset and setting forth the solution More had arrived at – as a direct result of reading *De taedio Iesu* and the *Enchiridion*. Erasmus saw that More's transformation from either/or to both/and thinking entailed a lesson for individuals in all walks of life – and this is precisely what *The Praise of Folly* so brilliantly works out, employing all the author's rhetorical skills.

2 Is Reality Abstract or Worldly? Or Both?

Abstract Values against (False) Worldly Values

Hardly noticed by the secondary literature, the abstract and Democritean side of More's personality, as depicted by Erasmus, is paralleled by discussions of Democritus within *The Praise of Folly* itself.[22] More

22 Clarence Miller, like others, notices no significant elationship between the Democritean More and Democritus within the work itself. See *The Praise of Folly*, 2n5, 41n5. Zatta relates Folly, as she sees Folly, to Democritus in "Democritus and Folly."

than this, Democritus' outlook represents one of two sides of Folly – the abstract and all-seeing Folly, rather than the worldly Folly. Also evident is a correlation with More's rendering of *Cynicus* (and of Hythloday in Book I *Utopia*).

Some abstract values, wise Folly shows, are valid and their proponents admirable. Critiques of worldly affairs based on these values are exceedingly accurate. The philosopher Democritus was a master at discerning the varieties and foibles of human behaviour.

> What good would it do to talk about the common people, the mere mob, for there is no question that they all belong to me [i.e., my assessments].[23] Wherever you look they abound in so many forms of folly, and they think up so many new ones from day to day, that a thousand Democritus's would not be enough to laugh at them – though we would need one more Democritus to laugh at the thousand ... Good lord, what a theater, how manifold the feverish fretting of fools! ... One man is head over heels in love with a wench and the less she responds, the more helplessly he loves her. Another marries the dowry, not the wife ... One man can think of no greater happiness than sleeping and loafing ... Another skims over all the oceans in search of a trifling (and uncertain) profit, entrusting his life, which no amount of money can buy back, to the wind and the waves. Another would seek riches in warfare ... Nor is there any shortage of men who hope to gain the same end by making love to rich old ladies. (76–7)[24]

Other things Democritus and "the gods above" see are unrestrained ambition and pride, adulation of wicked tyrants, glory achieved in baseness, cheating, risks taken for the tiniest profit, interminable lawsuits, pretence, jealousy, plotting, and warring (77–8).

> In brief, if you could look down from the moon, as Menippus once did, and see the innumerable broils of mortals,[25] you would think you were looking at a great cloud of flies or gnats quarreling among themselves, warring, plotting, plundering, playing, frisking, being born, declining, dying. It is downright incredible what tumults, what tragedies can be

23 The common people belong to Folly not because she herself is here a fool but because she grasps and laughs at, from high above, the foolishness of the world. Her very ability to criticize and evaluate worldliness shows that she is here representing abstract truths.

24 ASD IV-3, 134–6/189–213.

25 Lucian, *Icaromenippus* 15.

> stirred up by such a tiny creature, so frail and short-lived. Sometimes even a slight blast of war or plague seizes, scatters, and destroys many thousands at one swoop. (78)[26]

Earlier in the treatise, discussing the role of fables, flatter , money, and vainglory, Folly had brought Democritus into the picture to illustrate, by his laughter, that such foolishness was responsible for even the creation of states and civil and religious institutions.

> Add to these absurdities the conferral of titles and surnames, add the divine honors paid to some puny mortal, add the public ceremonies elevating the most wicked tyrants to the rank of gods: these things are foolish indeed – one Democritus would not be enough to make fun of them. Who denies it? Nevertheless, from this source flow all those exploits of brave heroes which have been praised to the skies in the writings of so many eloquent men. Such foolishness as this creates states, it constitutes empires, civil offices religion, counsels, judgments – nor is human life as a whole anything but a kind of fool's game. (41)[27]

Elsewhere we learn, in support of wise Folly and, in effect, Democritus, that wisdom makes men neglected, inglorious, and despised, whereas (worldly) fools are rolling in attention and prestige; everything can be bought with money (116–17). Real learning, like spirituality, goes begging because this requires great effort while happiness takes no effort (72). "To lack all wisdom is so very agreeable that mortals will pray to be delivered from anything rather than from (worldly) folly" (66). The more braggadocio, the more ignorance (68–9). In religion, similarly, true spirituality takes effort while performing religious ceremonies is easy. Businessmen, soldiers, and judges imagine that dropping a coin into the collection plate means "their acts of perjury, lust, drunkenness, quarreling, murder, deception, dishonesty, betrayal are paid off like a mortgage, and paid off in such a way that they can start off once more on a whole new round of sinful pleasures" (65). Reminding us of Lucian's *Philopseudes*, Folly says that many delight in hearing or describing miracles or monstrous lies. The more lacking in truth, the more credence (62–3). And – this is not unrelated to More's criticism of books on saint's lives – people seek all sorts of worldly favours from the intercession of saints, attributing more powers to them and to Mary than to Christ (65).

---

26 ASD IV-3, 138/232–7.
27 ASD IV-3, 102/548–55. Cf. Augustine on how states have been created, above, 59.

Immediately before turning to the other side of her personality – ridiculing those who pretend to be wise (79–115), and supporting worldly values – wise Folly again brings in Democritus:

> But I myself would be most foolish and a very fitting target for the long and loud laughter of Democritus if I should go on to enumerate the forms of folly and madness among the common people. (78)[28]

As shown above, some of Erasmus' contemporaries were tying Democritus to divinity and even highest Christianity. In line with these trends, towards the end of the work the place of the true wiseman, exemplified by Democritus, slides into that of the pious person (132–8).[29] Related to her description of Democritus, Folly describes a stark polarity between the outlook of pious persons, a few of whom have had a slight foretaste of the afterlife, and the vast run of mortals. Of course the Christian knows something Democritus didn't, that St Paul defined faith as "the substance of things to be hoped for and the evidence of things not seen" (90).[30]

Worldly Values against (False) Abstract Values

A diffe ence between Folly and Democritus is that Folly, like Thomas More, has a second and opposite side to her personality. The worldly and "man for all seasons" side of More's personality, as described by Erasmus, is paralleled by a Folly that revels at entering into the game of life. Far from being only rigid and looking at the worldly scene from only an abstract perspective, More could adapt completely to all the variables of life, and so too could the worldly side of Folly. While above were shown, through Democritus, the worldly values Folly ridicules, there is much about worldly values that Folly admires and finds indispensable – comparable to More's rendering of *Menippus* (and "More" in Book I *Utopia*). And from this worldly standpoint there is much about abstract values that she disdains. Since the worldly values Folly

28 ASD IV-3, 138/238–9.

29 The *Enchiridion* advises laughter, "like Democritus," at those who ponder at length their pedigrees and fail to realize that true nobility is to be reborn in Christ (H 93/14–17). The translator leaves out the word "Democritus" (CWE 66, 88).

30 Democritus, as Tychiades points out in *Philopseudes* (193), believed that souls do not exist after death (above, 126).

admires, those built on the irrevocableness of human nature, are best seen from the vantage point of the abstract values she scorns, epitomized by the caricatured, one-dimensional, Stoic wiseman, I will begin with the latter.

1. *The Abstract Values (Worldly) Folly Rejects*

The worldly side of Folly finds nothing positive about the wiseman depicted by the Stoics, most especially "that dyed-in-the-wool Stoic, Seneca." This wiseman is "a marble statue of a man, utterly unfeeling and quite impervious to all human emotion,"a wiseman such as would be at home "in Plato's *Republic*, or in the realm of Platonic ideas, or in the gardens of Tantulus [i.e., nowhere]" (45).[31] For one thing, Seneca and other Stoics consider emotional perturbations diseases (45).[32] Imagine a Stoic wiseman dropped down from heaven, pontificating on the evil passions of worldly leaders and all the shenanigans that go on in the world. "Just as nothing is more foolish than misplaced wisdom, so too, is nothing more imprudent than perverse prudence" (44). "Bring a wiseman to a party: he will disrupt it either by his gloomy silence or his tedious cavils. Invite him to a dance: you would think it was a camel dancing" (39). "What state has ever accepted the laws of Plato or Aristotle or the teachings of Socrates?" (40).[33] Even the great Athenian orator Demosthenes was inept in worldly matters, "as cowardly in a battle as he was wise in a speech" (36). Alienated from the world, observing all the world's deceits and evils from a watchtower (46), the wiseman would do better in "some deserted spot where he can enjoy his wisdom all by himself" (39). As Solomon said, "the heart of a wiseman resides with sorrow" (120). Is it any wonder that wisemen "have been the most likely to commit suicide"? (47).

---

31 Cf. Seneca, *Ep.* 85.2–16. Although Seneca's wiseman considers emotions false judgments and "stands erect under any load" (*Ep.* 71.26–7), he feels bodily pain and infirmit , loss of friends and children, the ruin of his country from warfare, and the like, "for we do not claim for him the hardness of stone or of steel" (*Const.* 10.4). In fact, Seneca (*Ep.* 63.14), like Cicero (*Letters to Atticus* 12.15, *Tusc.* 3.76), could on occasion feel extreme emotion. Epictetus denies that the wiseman should be unfeeling like a statue (*Disc.* 3.2.4), and Gellius emphasizes the point, with regard to physical pain, in his rendering of Epictetus, *Noctes Atticae* [*Attic Nights*] 12.5.

32 Cf. Seneca, *Ep.* 75.8–14, 85.10, and Cicero, *Tusc.* 3.23, 4.31, *Fin.* 3.35, *Ac.* 1.38.

33 Seneca shows that wiseman must (as such) be involved in worldly affairs and how this is possible, in *De otio* and *De tranquillitate animi*. See above, 32–7.

Again and yet again Folly comes back to the (caricatured) Stoic wiseman:

> Who would not flee in horror from such a man, as he would a monster or a ghost – a man who is completely deaf to all human emotion, no more moved by love or pity than a chunk of flint or a mountain crag,[34] who never misses anything, who never makes a mistake, who sees everything as if he had "x-ray vision," measures everything "with plumb line and T square," never forgives anything, who is uniquely self-satisfied, who thinks he alone is rich, he alone is healthy, regal, free,[35] in brief, he thinks that he alone is all things (but he is also alone in thinking so), who cares nothing about friendship,[36] who makes friends with no one, who would not hesitate to tell the gods themselves to go hang,[37] who can find nothing in all human life that he does not condemn[38] and ridicule as madness? Yet just such a creature as this is that perfect wiseman of theirs. (45–6)[39]

In Part VIII, I will demonstrate that the traits of the Stoic wiseman, as here described, have much in common with the description of wiseman Hythloday in Book I of *Utopia*.

Importantly, Folly's attack on the Stoic wiseman is not built from a serious consideration of Stoic philosophy. The author was an authority on Stoicism, two-dimensional, both/and Stoicism, but Folly's view of the wiseman is one-dimensional and supports fifteenth-century humanist views. Nor did Folly have to go to Peripatetics or Platonists or Sceptics or scholastics or various literary figu es to find material for this attack. Cicero himself, a person who could consider Stoics "perhaps the only true philosophers," in *Tusculan Disputations* (4.53), provided the groundwork. His *Paradoxa Stoicorum* (46 BCE), printed in 1465, is a

34 Cf. Cicero, *Par.* 33. Laelius' criticism of Stoic hardness in Cicero's *De amicitia* relates to that of Folly. "When the soul is deprived of emotion, what diffe ence is there – I do not say between man and the beasts of the field, but between man and the trunk of a tree or a stone? Nor are we to listen to those men who maintain that virtue is hard and unyielding and is, as it were, something made of iron" (48). *Tusculan Disputations* discusses Stoic thinking on the emotions in detail.

35 Cf. the Stoic Cato's conclusion, *Fin.* 3.75, *Par.*, and *CN* 1068B.

36 The Stoics believed in friendship but only among the wise. See DL 7.124, *Fin.* 3.70–1, and Graver, *Stoicism and Emotion*, 178–85.

37 Cf. *Par.* 34, *CN* 1076A, *Ep.* 92.3 ("In short, to give you the principle in brief compass, the wiseman's soul ought to be such as would be proper for a god").

38 Cf. *Par.* 27. It may be noted that Seneca advises others *not* to say: "What a great man! He has learned to despise all things" (*Ep.* 68.8).

39 ASD IV-3, 106/637–46.

parody of the Stoic wiseman, as is his witty description of the outlook of the Stoic Cato in his legal defence of Lucius Murena (*Pro Murena*) (63 BCE).[40] Stoic philosophy was easy to make fun of because the Stoics themselves were well known for their paradoxes, set forth, it appears, as a way of drawing neophytes into discussion of much larger, deeply philosophical, issues.[41] As Cicero points out, in his preface to *Paradoxa Stoicorum*, Stoic paradoxes seem ridiculous, entirely opposed to common sense and universal opinion. *Paradoxa Stoicorum* discusses six paradoxes: that the *honestum* is the sole good, that virtue alone is sufficien for happiness, that all bad deeds are equal, that every fool (non-sage) is a madman, that only the sage is free and that every fool (non-sage) is a slave, and that the sage alone is rich.[42]

Cicero's facetious criticism of the Stoic Cato's outlook, in *Pro Murena*, is even closer to Folly than *Paradoxa Stoicorum* in its striking encapsulation of the alleged faults of Stoics.[43] Consider the following excerpt:[44]

> Here are examples of Zeno's maxims and precepts: the wiseman is never moved by favor, never forgives anyone's misdeed; only the fool or the trifler feels pity; a real man does not yield to entreaty or appeasement; only the wiseman is handsome however misshapen, rich however needy, a king however much a slave.[45] We who are not wise are by their account runaways, exiles, enemies or even madmen. All misdeeds are equal; every misdemeanor is a heinous crime.[46] The casual killing of a cock is no less a crime than strangling one's father.[47] The wiseman never "supposes" anything, never regrets anything, is never wrong, never changes his mind.[48] (*Mur*. 61)

---

40 See *In Catilinam 1–4. Pro Murena. Pro Sulla. Pro Flacco*, 186–301.

41 Early Stoics had tended to argue in a terse and compressed manner. In *Tusculan Disputations*, Cicero words issues in the Stoic manner before developing, using all relevant intellectual and language tools, the questions raised (3.13, 4.9).

42 Plutarch denigrates at length Stoic thinking on the Stoic wiseman, but his criticisms were far too learned for Folly's purposes. See *CN*, esp. 1060–76, and *SR*.

43 In *De finibus* Cicero explicitly states that he was only jesting, faced with a jury rather than scholars, when he criticized Stoicism in his speech in defence of Murena (4.74).

44 On the setting of the speech and Cicero's purposes see Christopher P. Craig, "Cato's Stoicism and the Understanding of Cicero's Speech for Murena."

45 Cf. Plutarch's criticism, *CN* 1060B.

46 Cf. Plutarch's criticism, *SR* 1038C.

47 See *Par*. 24–5.

48 Cf. Seneca on intention and the "reservations" that allow the wiseman to never fail: *Ben*. 4.4–5, *Tr*. 12.2–3, 13.3.

Contemporary intellectuals also spew out, Folly contends, abstractions that are wrong-headed and at odds with worldly realities and true worldly values. Grammarians, poets, rhetoricians, authors, lawyers, logicians, sophists, philosophers, and theologians have more in common than they think, for they are all governed by pride, self-interest, deceit, and false reasoning (cf. 78–98). Most of all, however, the fault lies in scholastic logical methodologies and the moral failings brought about by these methodologies and related assumptions. Philosophers know nothing but "claim that they can see ideas, universals, separate forms, prime matter, quiddities, ecceities" (86). Theologians protect themselves from truth "by rows of magistral definitions, conclusions, corollaries, explicit and implicit propositions ... distinctions ... new terms ... monstrous jargon" (87–8).[49] They arrogantly discuss propositions such as "Whether God could have taken on the nature of a woman, of the devil, of an ass, of a cucumber, of a piece of flint" (88). Then follows Folly's notorious criticisms of friars and monks (98–106), popes, cardinals, bishops, and priests (110–15). At one point she exclaims, to give just one example: "As if the church had any more deadly enemies than impious popes, who allow Christ to fade away in silence, who bind him with mercenary laws, who defile him with forced interpretations, who murder him with the pestilent wickedness of their lives" (113).

2. *The Worldly Values Folly Admires*

Opposite the false wisdom and lack of morality of persons considered learned and wise and superior to the humdrum of commoners and worldly affairs, Folly focuses on the unyieldingness of natural instinct and praises ignorance – vis-à-vis, again, the satirized Stoic wiseman.

The Stoics equate reason with wisdom and emotion with folly,[50] but Jupiter established that there is a pound of feeling for every ounce of thought, that anger is the fountainhead of life, and that passionate desire spreads "all the way down to the genitals" (28). Equally false, the Stoics hold that what is not reason is insanity[51] and that reason equates

49 In his commentary on *The Praise of Folly*, a standard appendage beginning in 1515, Girardus Listrius compares the methodologies of modern theologians to the astronomers who "invented eccentric circles and epicycles in the orbits because they could not find the cause of the varied motions." See Gavin and alsh, "*The Praise of Folly* in Context," 200–1.

50 Cf. *Tusc.* 3.19 and 4.12.

51 Cf. *Tusc.* 3.8–11, 4.54, *Par.* 4, *Luc.* 2.136; Seneca, *Ep.* 94.17, *De ira* 2.4–5; DL 7.124; and Horace, *Sermones* 2.3.221 in *The Complete Odes and Satires.*

with happiness and unreason with misery (57, 71).[52] In fact, there is a type of madness that is very desirable and not at all miserable. "It occurs whenever a certain pleasant mental distraction relieves the heart from its anxieties and cares and at the same time soothes it with the balm of manifold pleasures" (58). The wiseman distinguishes between his happiness and the misery of the ignorant person, but being deceived and ignorant is what it means to be a human ("Imo hoc est hominem esse") (49).[53] This is the way humans are constituted. "Nothing is miserable merely because it follows its own nature [Nihil autem miserum quod in suo genere constat]" (50).[54] All humans are born with faults, but philosophers, "severe wisemen," are incapable, unlike foolish persons, of even friendship (32). The bond of marriage is sustained by foolishness. Think of all the divorces that would ensue did not couples laugh things off and pretend things are not as they are (33). How can one be a father or have sex without foolishness? The "iron clad principles" of the Stoics are here worthless (18). Happiness depends not on getting rid of deceptions but on being deceived (71). In the Golden Age, people "lived their lives completely under the guidance of natural impulses [Solo naturae ductu instinctuque vivebat]" (51).[55] Those men are happiest "who have nothing whatever to do with any branch of learning and follow nature as their only guide [solamque naturam ducem sequi]" (52).[56] "How much more attractive is the life of flies and little birds, who live for the moment purely by natural instinct [ex tempore soloque naturae sensu degentium], as long as they can avoid the snares of men" (53).[57] Bees follow nature alone and yet what architect has ever produced comparable buildings, what philosopher established a comparable republic? (52).[58] Only man has tried to go beyond the limits of nature (53). Only man has aspired to the life of the gods and waged war against nature.

> Therefore, just as among mortals those men who seek wisdom are furthest from happiness – indeed, they are fools twice over because, forgetting the human condition to which they were born, they aspire to the life of the immortal gods and (like the giants) wage war against Nature with

52 Cf. *Par.* 19, *Fin.* 3.26; Seneca, *Ep.* 92.2, *Vit. Beat.* 6.2.
53 ASD IV-3, 110/707.
54 ASD IV-3, 110/709–10.
55 ASD IV-3, 110/728.
56 ASD IV-3, 112/755–7.
57 ASD IV-3, 112/771–2.
58 Cf. Seneca, *Ep.* 121.22. Regarding discussion of bees in the ancient world, see Whitfield, " irgil and the Bees."

> the engines of learning [et gigantum exemplo disciplinarum machinis naturae bellum inferunt] – so too, the least miserable among men are those who come closest to the level of intelligence (that is, the folly) of brute animals and never undertake anything beyond human nature. (54)[59]

Erasmus, we now know, was completely serious in having Folly criticize scholars for "forgetting the human condition to which they were born." This focus relates directly to the deepest experiences of his life and the very reason for his attachment to Stoicism – notwithstanding Folly's unending criticism of the Stoic wiseman, seen as one-dimensional. *De taedio Iesu*, his edition of *De officiis*, and the *Enchiridion* all testify, I have shown in *The Stoic Origins of Erasmus' Philosophy of Christ*, to a pervasive determination to show that Christianity cannot be separated from natural instinct, character traits, and particular worldly situations.[60]

Two Realities, Not Just One

Note one thing regarding the above: there are no contradictions. One side of Folly shows what is right about abstract values and what is wrong about worldly values (comparing to More's rendering of *Cynicus*), and another side shows what is right about worldly values and what is wrong about abstract values (comparing to More's rendering of *Menippus*). What abstract values oppose are false worldly values. What worldly values oppose are false abstract values. But the abstract values condemned (exemplified by the Stoic wiseman and scholastics) are not the same as those praised (exemplified by Democritus and pious persons), and the worldly values rejected (pretence, false adulation, cheating, etc.) are not the same as the worldly values admired (based on natural instinct). Folly does not contradict herself in showing what is right about some abstract values and what is wrong about other abstract values. Nor does she contradict herself in showing what is right about some worldly values and what is wrong with other worldly values. What emerges is that there is a valid type of abstract value and a valid type of worldly value. Otherwise stated, there are two opposite types of value, and both types can be valid. Neither type is foolish, as such. At odds with many interpretations, there is no "deliberate ambiguity," no "irony" (if defined as a "deliberate contrast between apparent and

59 ASD IV-3, 112–13/789–94.

60 On warring with nature like the giants, see also *De taedio Iesu*, LB 5 1272A–B and the *Enchiridion*, H 70/30–71/1, CWE 66, 68. See also above, 87n6.

intended meaning"), no "inconsistency," no "leaving interpretation up to the reader."

As with Thomas More's personality (not to mention his *Philopseudes*), there is a valid abstract, Democritean, type of value and there is a valid worldly, natural instinct, and "man for all seasons" type of value. The diffe ence with Folly is that she leads into the two opposite but valid types of value by subterfuge, contrasting valid abstract values with false worldly values and valid worldly values with false abstract values (in line with More's *Cynicus* and *Menippus*).

Nor does the text reveal, any more than with the author's description of Thomas More, disaccord – however radically diffe ent they are – between valid worldly values and valid abstract values, or vice versa. Nowhere is it shown that values based on natural instinct are at odds with Democritean-type values. Unseen, abstract, rigid, non-worldly values and bending worldly values are opposite types, but they do not, as such, conflict. Conflict arises only where there is a perversion of one of the two types.

In short, there is a system to the way Folly deals with issues, modelled on More's rendering of Lucian. This system allowed rhetorical amplifications but in itself was eminently logical and represented a deeply rationalized and set outlook. The only fundamental irony in the work is with Folly herself. Folly presents herself as the personific - tion of foolishness, but what she reveals throughout is that she and she alone is truly wise. She and she alone sees what is true and what is false about abstract precepts and she and she alone sees what is true and what is false about worldliness. Folly as "folly" is something that exists everywhere, we are shown, yet Folly the person – Moria, the person named after Thomas Morus – is the wisest of the wise in that she sees through all these examples of folly.

Folly's referrals to life as a stage play and her analysis of Plato's myth of the cave reveal even more clearly the theses the author is developing – and the misreadings.

Life Is a Stage Play

> If someone should try to strip away the costumes and makeup from the actors performing a play on the stage and to display them to the spectators in their own natural appearance, wouldn't he ruin the whole play? Wouldn't all the spectators be right to throw rocks at such a madman and drive him out of the theater? ... This deception, this disguise, is the very thing that holds the attention of the spectators. Now the whole of life of mortal men, what is it but a sort of play, in which various persons make

> their entrances in various costumes, and each one plays his own part until the director gives him his cue to leave the stage? ... True, all these images are unreal, but this play cannot be performed in any other way. (43–4)[61]

Criticized here, as so often, is the wiseman's (alleged) belief that reality is found not in the world but *only* in the realm of ideas. The wiseman sees worldliness through a single, non-worldly, lens. Geared to hard and abstract truth, he desires that the play of life not be a play (49). But this is impossible. "This play cannot be performed in any other way." The wiseman does not want to focus on the "unreal [adumbrata]" found in the varieties of human behaviour, common assumptions, and worldly affairs generally, but on the "real," as in Plato's "ideas,"[62] or Stoic "reason." In fact, however, the worldly stage is entirely real. It simply represents a diffe ent type of reality. Take away self-love, for example, and the actors will be hissed off the stage (35).[63] If actors were represented as in the world of ideas, without costumes, the play would be ruined. "The whole of life of mortal men, what is it but a sort of play?" (restated 120). Lacking the play, life would cease. The worldly spectacle is "unreal," from a Platonist perspective, "but this play cannot be performed in any other way." A little later we are told that philosophers, most notably Stoic wisemen, think being deceived and ignorant is a miserable way to live – happiness depending, in their view, on reason (as inherent to *honestum*) – but "One thing is sure: such it is to be a man" (49).

Notice that Folly is not – at odds with the either/or assumptions of readers – pitting worldliness and the worldly stage against all abstract and unseen values. She does not show or imply that worldly values unavoidably contradict absolute values. Nothing is said that would detract from the admirable abstract values and insights which Folly herself has described, with the help of Democritus. Nor, most certainly, is this emphasis on worldly realities opposed to the unseen realities adhered to (see further below) by pious persons, not to mention St Paul and Christ. Nor does she state here that Stoic "reason" or Plato's

61 ASD IV-3, 104/591–4, 598–601, 602–3. On life as a play see Curtius, *European Literature and the Latin Middle Ages*, 138–44. Cf. Lucian, *Icaromenippus* 17 (*Lucian*, vol. 2, 297–9), *Menippus* (see above, 139); Epictetus, *Ench.* 17, *Disc.* 1.24.20, 1.25.7–11, and the commentary by Dobbin, *Epictetus: Discourses, Book I*, 204–9.

62 Cf. *Parmenides* 129a–35e, also *Symposium*, *Phaedo*, *Republic*, *Sophist*, *Statesman*, and *Philebus* in *Complete Works*.

63 Self-love is inherent to the self-preservation instinct. See Long, "Hierocles on *Oikeiosis* and Self-Perception," 254.

"ideas" are entirely wrong. What she states is only that the unbending abstractions referred to are inapplicable, as such, to worldly affairs and that human life is inseparable from the complexities of personality and social situation.

In insisting on the necessity of worldliness, Folly is not setting forth an ironical or rhetorical thesis – something for debate and amusement. She argues the thesis using rhetorical tools, but the thesis itself is not rhetorical. Nor does she change her mind in the course of discussion, rejecting what she has said about the necessity of worldliness. Readers have imagined that worldly values and abstract values, the former "unreal [adumbrata]" and the latter real, can't both be valid, but the text does not indicate a necessary conflict. The assumption that there is a conflict has seemed obvious because readers have been looking at the work in rhetorical terms alone.[64] Folly uses her language skills to drive home the issues, but the issues themselves are not, as such, rhetorical. Neither here nor elsewhere is the treatise built from a rhetorical platform.

Plato's Myth of the Cave Becomes a Stoic Myth

> Num quid interesse censetis inter eos, qui in specu illo Platonico variarum rerum umbras et simulacra demirantur, modo nihil desiderent neque minus sibi placeant, et sapientem illum, qui specum egressus veras res aspicit.[65]

> Surely you don't believe that there is any diffe ence between those who sit in Plato's cave gazing in wonder at the images and likenesses of various things – as long as they desire nothing more and are no less pleased – and that wiseman who left the cave and sees things as they really are? (72–3)

In Plato's myth (*Rep.*, 514a–520a), what is "real" – the "form" or "idea" of the good – is outside the cave and what is unreal is inside the cave. There is every diffe ence between the outlook of that person who manages to get outside the cave and the outlook of the masses inside – a postulate at centre court in the Neoplatonism streaming out from Florence, represented most particularly by Marsilio Ficino's writings and

64 Marsh, for example, imagines that Folly's stage-play metaphor is simply a rhetorical statement built from manuals of rhetoric, Lucian, and opposition to philosophy. See *Lucian and the Latins*, 174.

65 ASD IV-3, 132/127–30.

translations of Plato's works (see above, 69). But Folly takes exception to this thesis. She doubts there is any diffe ence between those within the cave, who see only "the images and likenesses of various things," and the wiseman imagined by Plato, who gets outside the cave and sees things "as they really are" (also 133).

On what basis does Folly place those within the cave on the same level as Plato's wiseman? Folly does not claim to be a philosopher and yet she denies an argument set forth by one of the greatest philosophers who has ever lived. Is she joking, merely playing with words, "ironically" setting forth an opposite stance, hoping to arouse a debate *in utramque partem*?[66] Does the text exemplify, that is, a rhetorical game? Plato opposed real to unreal, and Folly, it is commonly imagined, is playfully turning Plato on his head, setting unreal against real.[67] In fact, the text reveals something quite diffe ent.

Note first of all that Folly doesn't say that the wiseman's view is wrong and the perceptions of those within the cave are correct. Her contention is that there appears to be no diffe ence between the two outlooks.

Never grasped and of overriding importance is that Folly's explanation for why there is no diffe ence between those within the cave and the wiseman outside relates far more directly to Stoicism than to Plato.[68] Look carefully at her wording. There is no diffe ence, "as long as they [those within the cave] desire nothing more and are no less pleased [than the wiseman outside]." As the author certainly recognized, Plato's wiseman is not known for being "pleased" with himself. On the other hand, being "pleased" and happy with oneself directly ties with Stoic discussions of their wiseman. Plato's wiseman affo ds only the larger talking point. What Folly is really saying is that those within the cave are as pleased with themselves as the *Stoic wiseman* is pleased

66 Kahn sees the entire work as a debate *in utramque partem*, "the dialogic text par excellence." It is up to the reader to choose between the higher and lower folly. See "*Stultitia* and *Diatribe*," 365.

67 According to Miller, Folly "contemptuously dismisses the wiseman" and uses Platonic ideas "with the same inconsistent nonchalance" as other philosophers (*The Praise of Folly*, xvi). He finds that Folly epresents "diametrically opposite attitudes" towards the myth in that later in the treatise she uses it to support the invisible truths glimpsed by a few pious persons (ASD IV-3, 19). Regarding the later usage, see below, 200.

68 Baker-Smith argues that Plato's cave analogy, seen as a (one-dimensional) "ascent" to truth, is fundamental to Erasmus' *Enchiridion* and *The Praise of Folly* and that the Utopian state, as represented by Hythloday, is More's version of the myth. See his "*Civitas philosophica*."

with himself. She well knows that the Stoic wiseman is always pleased with himself and happy precisely because he desires nothing more than reason and virtue (and all other components of the *honestum*) and at all times protects himself from mistakes or failures with "reservation" clauses.[69] *Tusculan Disputations* 5.54, for example, contrasts the contentment of the wiseman with the lack of contentment of the fool: "For just as folly, although it has secured its coveted object, yet never thinks it has obtained enough; so wisdom is always contented with its present lot and is never self-repentant."Early on in the treatise, Folly is very explicit, alleging that Stoics drive others away from pleasure so they can better enjoy it themselves (19). Throughout the treatise she attempts to dethrone this one-dimensional and seemingly arrogant outlook.

Worldly fools exemplify, in an opposite context, key traits the Stoic wiseman prides himself on. If worldly fools are oblivious to everything outside themselves – as exemplified by the wiseman in Plato's cave myth – and yet, like the Stoic wiseman, are pleased and happy, how can there be any serious diffe ence between them and the wiseman (whether Platonist or Stoic)? The worldly fool is as pleased and happy with his life as the wiseman is with his. And there is as much to be said for the happiness and outlook of the worldly fool as for the happiness and outlook of the Stoic wiseman. Like the Stoic wiseman, the worldly fool "desires nothing more" than to hold rigidly to his view of reality and, also like the Stoic wiseman, finds complete happiness in never allowing anything to breach his mindset. The Stoic wiseman is entirely self-centred, and so too is the worldly fool. The wiseman desires nothing more than reason and virtue, and the worldly fool desires nothing more than acceptance of things as they are. The wiseman is in a cocoon, and so too is the worldly fool, which is not to deny the wiseman's view, whether Platonist or Stoic, but to insist that there is equal justification for the standpoint of worldly fools.

Folly does not ask the reader to replace one type of value with another type but to focus on what the two contrary outlooks have in common. "Surely you don't believe that there is any diffe ence" doesn't imply that one type of value is right and the other wrong. What is asked is that readers make comparisons. Isn't the outlook of those unwise as justifiable as the outlook of the wise? Both groups live in self-centred and circumscribed worlds, albeit they hold radically diffe ent suppositions. And they are both happy, albeit their happiness has completely diffe ent

69 Cf. Seneca, *Tr.* 11.6–11, 12.2–3, 13.3, 14.1, *Ben.* 4.45; Marcus Aurelius, *Med.* 5.20, 6.50, 9.29.

foundations. The Stoic wiseman associates happiness with holding unflinchingly to reason, while the worldly fool associates happiness with doing whatever, in his view, comes naturally. The Stoic wiseman associates truth with mental firmness and the happiness bound up with this, and the worldly fool associates truth with variability and the happiness found in instant gratification. Wisemen see everything in terms of hard reality, as exists in Plato's "ideas," while worldly fools see everything as bendable, in terms of immediate desires, self-interest and the like. So what's the diffe ence between the worldly fool and the wiseman? The fool is as undeviating in his mindset as the wiseman and just as happy.

Folly goes on to say that "there is either no diffe ence" between the two positions or that the lot of (worldly) fools is preferable (73) – which is not saying there is only worldly reality. The fool enjoys happiness, and the company of most other humans, while the wiseman idealized by Stoics and the Greeks is seldom or never found (73).[70] Worldly fools find happiness not in unseen truth, which is hard to come by, but in immediate impressions. Versus Plato's myth: "Nothing could be further from the truth than the notion that man's happiness resides in things as they actually are [the "ideas" or "forms" represented by Plato's wiseman and the "reason" represented by the Stoic wiseman]. It depends on opinions" (71).[71] Worldly fools are impressed by mere appearance and not reality. In accepting the hurly-burly of life and doing whatever comes naturally, i.e., without reflection, they easily arrive at happiness. "The human mind is so constituted that it is far more taken with appearances than reality. If anyone wants clear and obvious evidence of this fact, he should go to church during sermons: if the preacher is explaining his subject seriously, they all doze, yawn, and are sick of it. But if that screacher – I beg your pardon, I meant to say preacher – tells some old wives' tale, as they often do, the whole congregation sits up and listens with open mouths" (71). "What diffe ence does it make to his happiness?" if a person has ridiculous opinions, if he thinks, for example, that rotten fish tastes wonderful, of if someone thinks his

70 Even Stoics had doubts about the actual existence of their wiseman. See Cicero, *ND* 3.70, *Luc.* 2.145; Seneca, *Const.* 7.1, and Plutarch, *CN* 1076B ("This sage does not exist, however, and has not existed anywhere on earth"). Even the Stoic Epictetus, criticizing those who claim to be Stoics, doubts that there has ever been a true Stoic, "a man who though sick is happy, though in danger is happy, though dying is happy, though condemned to exile is happy, though in disrepute is happy" (*Disc.* 2.19.24).

71 "Nimium enim desipiunt qui in rebus ipsis felicitatem hominis sitam esse existimant. Ex opinionibus ea pendet" (ASD IV-3, 130/96–8).

ugly wife is gorgeous, and the like (72)? A person named after Folly – i.e., Thomas More, "a clever jokester" – gave his bride imitation gems and she enjoyed them as much as if they were real.[72] And what difference is there from the wiseman? The wiseman also sees reality in one-dimensional terms and is very consciously proud and happy. The self-satisfaction of the worldling and the wiseman being equal, the lot of the worldling might seem preferable, as he is surrounded by those like himself, whereas the wiseman, if he can be found, lives alone.

The myth does not reveal, Folly demonstrates, what Plato thinks it reveals. Although Folly doesn't reject abstract truth as such or even Plato's "ideas" as such, she emphatically rejects Plato's one-dimensional interpretation of the cave myth. In fact, the myth reveals not just one truth but two truths, two radically diffe ent types of truth represented by two opposite types of people. The worldly truth represented by those within the cave is as indispensable as invisible truth. Reality is not represented by invisible ideas alone. What Folly insists on is not (either/or) the falsity of invisible truths but the reality of worldliness and the fact that invisible truths do not, in themselves, account for these worldly truths. There are two sides to what is real. The wiseman sees things in terms of an invisible and unbending reality, but life cannot go on without what this wiseman sees as "unreality," the practices and outlook of those within the cave employing very diffe ent skills. Folly's corrected, two-dimensional version of the cave myth brings to the fore, yet again, the unyieldingness of natural instinct and the undeniableness of worldly values. Life is a play inseparable from worldly involvements. There is as much to be said for worldly reality as there is for invisible reality.

Knowing, as we do now (see my *The Stoic Origins of Erasmus' Philosophy of Christ*), that Erasmus like no one in a thousand years had come to see that Stoicism is two-dimensional, and unitarily so, is it not obvious that he is here very consciously turning Plato's myth into a two-dimensional Stoic myth? In Stoicism abstract truths and things indiffe ent (*adiaphora*, or, with late Stoicism things useful, *utile*) are two radically diffe ent types of value that exist side by side and are parts of one thing: *honestum*. I have shown that in *De taedio Iesu* Erasmus simply moved emotion from the cognitive realm (where it was a false judgment) to the

72 More's Utopians were to ridicule those who are "captivated by jewels and gemstones, and think themselves divinely happy if they get a good specimen" (C168/13–15). "Why should a counterfeit give any less pleasure, if, when you look at it, your eyes cannot distinguish it from a genuine gem?" (C168/20–2).

realm of things indiffe ent (including natural instinct, *oikeiosis*). In Platonism, in contrast, there is only one true reality, the unseen "forms."

3 Truth Is "Truer Than Truth Itself" (The Stoic Unitary Both/And)

Early on, Folly shows that truth is unitarily both/and, that abstract and worldly realities are not two separate things but comprise one truth. Truth is "truer than truth itself."

> Another point – by all the gods in heaven! Should I say it or keep still? But why keep still, since it is truer than truth itself? [Cur autem sileam, cum sit vero verius?] ... Be present, then, you daughters of Jove, for a bit, while I show that no one can reach the heights of wisdom and the very inner sanctum, as the wise themselves say, of happiness except with the guidance of [worldly] Folly. (45)[73]

Truth is something truer, something larger, than abstract truth, that which is considered "truth itself." Abstract values exist, but they constitute only one aspect of truth. Truth includes "unreal" worldly realities as well as "real" unseeable realities. Those who wish to "reach the heights of wisdom" can do so only with the help of worldly values – only, that is, as a human. Truth in this life is inseparable from worldly happenings. The worldly fool, unlike the (caricatured) one-dimensional Stoic wiseman, accepts the realities of life, individual oddities and desires, the particularities of worldly situations, the conniving of princes, the nonsense everywhere admired by commoners and lords alike (so insistently focused on by Lucian), the ever so convenient compromising of ideals. The worldly fool is admirable precisely because he recognizes that he is part of this drama, takes his surroundings very seriously, and is totally involved. In short, what is "truer than truth itself" is that truth is not just one-dimensional, not something that consists of only hard, rational, and abstract pronouncements. Bodily and external factors, emotions and all the variables of life, comprise an indispensable part of truth – and, thus, "the very inner sanctum of happiness." The orthodox

73 ASD IV-3, 106/620–4. On "vero verius" see Adage 3802 (IV.ix.2). ASD II-8, 179–80/15–24.

Stoic wiseman holds that happiness is found in *honestum* alone, but this is not the case.[74]

Adapting to worldly conditions is a precondition of wisdom – but does not contradict the need for abstract truth. Those wisemen who separate themselves from all this worldly hubbub are in fact lacking in the very thing they claim, true wisdom. Nor can abstractions be imposed, as such, on worldly affairs. Becoming genuinely wise and genuinely Christian is impossible lacking a both/and mindset. There is an unbending type of value but also a bending type, and both are required. Thinking of Horace, Folly advises us to mingle folly with our deliberations. "'It is delightful to be foolish at the proper time and place'" (118).[75] The wise, so-called, will begin to learn true wisdom only when they begin to recognize the limitations imposed by man's nature – and the actuality, relevance, and indispensability of that nature. In short, the play of life described by Folly is about two types of reality, their radically diffe ent natures and the relationship between them. Wisdom – and the happiness it represents – begins (cf. Antiochus, in *Fin.* 5) with the acceptance of worldly conditions.

Even emotion is part and parcel of what it means to be human and what it means to see worldly values as indispensable parts of wisdom. Folly doesn't deny that emotion can be very negative. The problem is that the wiseman sees only this. Dropped down from heaven, he correctly berates worldlings for holding up as a god a person who is "controlled by his passions like an animal" (44). But what about valid emotions? Seeing emotions as bereft of reason, the Stoic wiseman considers emotions nothing but diseases.[76] That "dyed-in-the-wool Stoic Seneca" insists on this (45).[77] But what about love,[78] pity, friendship, and all the tragedies of life, such as sickness, poverty, betrayals, disgrace,

74 Cicero sometimes finds the Stoic view that happiness esides only in *honestum* too restrictive, as in Book 5 of *Tusculan Disputations*. On More's referral to *Tusc.* 5.51 in connection with happiness and Cicero's view, see above, 110–17. In Book 4 of *De finibus*, reflecting Antiochus, Cicero contends that the Stoics "again abandon nature" in refusing to allow that the primary objects of nature have anything to do with happiness (4.43).

75 Horace, *Carmina* 4.12.27 and 28. Horace (65–8 BCE) makes considerable use pro and con of Stoicism in his poetry, and Erasmus sprinkles the work with oddities from his writings. On Horace's use of Stoicism, see Colish, *The Stoic Tradition from Antiquity to the Early Middle Ages*, vol. 1, 160–94.

76 Cf. the *Enchiridion* (44, H 44/25–45).

77 See above, 167.

78 Cf. Plutarch's criticism of Stoics, *CN* 1072F–1073B.

death, and sadness? (45–7). Wouldn't the Stoic wiseman be considered a raving lunatic were he to tell someone suffering the death of a parent that he should laugh instead because this life is really a sort of death? (44).[79] Emotion, like all natural instincts (and character traits), can be very positive. Emotion can help humans advance towards the canons of the faith as well as carry out positive worldly actions. Although the wiseman considers emotions antithetical to reason (i.e., false judgments), "actually the emotions not only function as guides to those who are hastening to the haven of wisdom, but also, in the whole range of virtuous action, operate like spurs or goads, as it were, encouraging the performance of good deeds" (45).[80] Although this statement is Peripatetic, the only recognizable use of Peripatetic thought in the entire work, the frame of thought remains Stoic.[81] Here, as in *De taedio Iesu* and the *Enchiridion*, Erasmus expands – going far beyond late Hellenistic trends – the second side of the both/and. Emotions are natural (not false judgments of reason) and as such things indiffe ent – as defined by Stoics. As things indiffe ent, emotions can be dealt with either positively or negatively – as either, in Stoic terms, "preferred indiffe ents" or "dispreferred indiffe ents."

"Truer than truth itself" was by no means a thesis just dreamed up by Folly for the occasion. Though diffe ent words are used, *De taedio Iesu* and the *Enchiridion* are all about, I have shown, truth that is "truer than truth itself." Truth is not one-dimensional but two-dimensional (*honestum/indifferens*), and worldly values are essential aspects of truth. Nothing demonstrates more conclusively that Christianity is about something "truer than truth itself," Erasmus came to believe, than Christ himself. *De taedio Iesu* had been about proving – against a thousand years of theology – that Christ was incapable of separating himself and did not want to separate himself from natural instincts

79 The Stoics had discussed at length methods and steps to be taken in helping those suffering, f om things like the death of a loved one, to mitigate or overcome their emotions (cf. *Tusc.* 4.58–62, 3.77 resp.; Seneca, *Ep.* 64.8, 90.20–1). In referring to life as a sort of death, Folly is again relating Plato's thinking to the unbending side of the Stoic wiseman. In *Phaedo* Socrates famously defines philosophy as a meditation on death (64A), a freeing of the soul from the body, and Folly later refers to this definition as the "Platonist" view (133). The *Enchiridion* (44) had also tied, momentarily, Socrates' contention with the outlook of the Stoic wiseman.

80 ASD IV-3, 106/628–30.

81 On the Peripatetic view see *Tusc.* 4.43–6 and Seneca, *De ira* 1.9.2, 1.17.1, 3.3.1. For Aristotle's view see *Nicomachean Ethics* 1116b24–1117a5 and *Magna Moralia* 1185b29–32, in *Complete Works*. At one point Folly disdainfully refers to Aristotle as "the god of our master-doctors" (121).

and worldly realities, notwithstanding that he was the wisdom of the Father. More than any human who has ever lived, Erasmus had argued, Christ experienced to the full his (inescapable) natural instincts. More than any human, he knew that he had to play the game of life. *The Praise of Folly* comes back to this: "Though he was the wisdom of the Father," he became somehow foolish "when he took on human nature" (130). The *Enchiridion*, building on Stoicism, centres on this bifocal truth, as it applies to ordinary humans. Christian faith takes unbending Stoic truths (*honestum*, oneness with the universe and god) one step further. On the bending side, we are shown in great detail what it means for the Christian to hold that all things are indiffe ent. What it means is that one must study and uncover with the greatest care every detail of one's nature, inborn and existing. At centre court here are natural instincts and, even more complex, particular natural and habitual characteristics – as well as external circumstances. Spirituality can take place only within this context. Spirituality begins with "a third world" (or "soul"), everything between spirit (*honestum*) and flesh (*turpe*), the world of *indifferentia*, and comprises a mindset that deals with these bending worldly values holding unitarily to unseen unbending values. Folly sees this unitary both/and outlook as a truth that is "truer than truth itself."

The difficult of the Stoic enterprise, not minimized by Erasmus in the *Enchiridion*, is encapsulated by Epictetus:

> [Material things] must be used carefully, because their use is not a matter of indiffe ence, and at the same time with steadfastness and peace of mind, because the material is indiffe ent ... It is, indeed, difficul to unite and combine these two things – the carefulness of the man who is devoted to material things and the steadfastness of the man who disregards them, but it is not impossible. Otherwise happiness were impossible. (*Disc.* 2.5.7–9)[82]

Compare *The Praise of Folly*. Using shock treatment, Folly demonstrates, in her own way, why the road to this combining is so difficult Neither the (caricatured) Stoic wiseman on the one hand nor the worldly fool on the other grasps that life and truth are two-dimensional. The wiseman retains peace of mind as he holds unbendingly to abstract and

82 Cf. Epictetus, *Enchiridion*, 13. Plutarch, for one, argued that the Stoics contradict themselves in that holding to two types of value amounts to having two diffe ent ends (*CN* 1070F–1071E). Stoics vigorously denied such arguments (cf. *Fin.* 3.22).

unseen principles but fails to recognize the reality of material things. The worldly fool is oblivious to invisible truth but is totally involved in material things. Only within this setting does it become clear that there is a type of abstract truth that allows and deals with material realities and there is a type of materiality that requires abstract truth. However much Folly has built up the content of *indifferentia*, the Stoic unitary both/and frame of thought remains.

It also becomes evident that Folly has described a unitary both/and outlook that Thomas More himself, as depicted by Erasmus in the introduction, matchlessly epitomizes.

Deciding between True and False Worldly Values: The Methodology of *De officiis* Book 3 and More's *Philopseudes*

Particularly enlightening are Folly's distinctions between true and false prudence and true and false flatter . Here again readers have gone astray in assuming that Folly's base thinking is rhetorical and represents a conglomeration of ironical and contradictory theses, a supposition embedded in the belief that there is no firm foundation to Erasmus' writings or mindset or life, that he vacillated from one viewpoint to another, at ease, as a rhetorician, with inconsistency – and that all this is magnified by *The Praise of Folly*. In fact, prudence and flattery are for Folly philosophic concepts. Her brilliant employment of rhetoric is secondary.

True Prudence Is Both Flexible and Inflexible – Unitarily

Folly begins by looking at prudence in either/or terms. Wisemen, those who "insist that the play should not be a play" (44), imagine that prudence consists of abstract and rigid principles that need to be imposed on worldly affairs [83] Folly adamantly denies this, in favour of "the play of life." "True prudence recognizes human limitations and does not strive to leap beyond them; it is willing to run with the herd, to overlook faults tolerantly or to share them in a friendly

83 In fact, of course, as the fifth-century Greek anthologist Stobaeus brings out, Stoic prudence is unitarily both/and. "In their [Stoics'] opinion the doctrine that the prudent man does everything well is a consequence of his accomplishing everything in accordance with right reason and in accordance with virtue, which is expertise concerned with the whole of life" (LS 61G). Prudence (*phronēsis*) is, in Stoicism, states Graver, "the cardinal virtue of good sense; that is, the disposition to act properly in any and all circumstances" (*Stoicism and Emotion*, 117).

spirit" (44).[84] But all worldly prudence is not, she reveals, "true" worldly prudence. The fact that "true prudence," in contrast with the "perverse prudence" of the wiseman, "recognizes human limitations and does not strive to leap beyond them" does not entail that all prudence that "recognizes human limitations and does not strive to leap beyond them" is valid. Acknowledgment that human nature and the human condition are indispensable components of prudence is only a first step. There is an invalid type of worldly prudence as well as a valid type. Some actions considered prudent only appear to be such. Nor is the diffe ence between true worldly prudence and misconceived and false worldly prudence in any way ambiguous. The valid type of prudence is not valid in and of itself but requires something else, oneness with abstract values.

Prudence that is only apparent and therefore false is evident where humans simply do whatever it takes, measured by immediate pleasure and profit, to achieve goals (108). Such persons are prudent in that they are expert in the tools of perceived self-interest. Guided by gut instinct and habit, they often display highly developed methods of cunning and deceit. From their perspective, abstract values seem irrelevant and, were they to be applied, counter-productive or even positively detrimental.

> If anyone thinks that happiness consists in gaining the favor of great rulers and living on familiar terms with those bejeweled and golden gods, what could be less helpful than wisdom? Indeed, among such men what could be more harmful? If money is the object, how much profit would a merchant make if, as wisdom dictates, he had scruples about perjuring himself, if he were ashamed when someone caught him lying, if he cared in the least about all those fine points laid down by wisemen about theft and usury? (116–17)[85]

---

84 Assessing the discussion of prudence in either/or terms, Clarence Miller believes that Folly is simply "mocking" the wiseman, which illustrates "that peculiar blend of contempt and compassion with which Folly seems to view the miseries of mankind" (ASD IV-3, 32). According to Geraldine Thompson, Folly, like her author, cannot decide between what is prudent and what is wise or, otherwise stated, between "one prudence that is wise and one not wise but only expedient." "Deception and accommodation are shabby terms." Here as elsewhere in the work Thompson finds only speculation and paradox. See *Under Pretext of Praise*, 72–4 and 64–5 resp.

85 ASD IV-3, 178/872–7.

Note the assumption here that abstract values exist, notwithstanding the perception that they are harmful in worldly affairs

True prudence is something else. Immediately after concluding (in either/or fashion) that the fool is more prudent than the wise in that he is not modest or hesitant in worldly affairs, but jumps into the middle of things, Folly shows that there are two ways of evaluating the prudence of worldly fools, only one of which is valid. Which has the better judgment, she asks, a king exhibiting apparent prudence or a king exhibiting true (both/and) prudence?

> But if mortals prefer to take prudence as consisting in [worldly] good judgment, listen (I beg you) and hear how far the men who boast of this quality actually are from possessing it. First, it is clear that all human affairs, like the Sileni of Alcibiades [objects which look entirely diffe ent on the inside than the outside], have two aspects quite diffe ent from each other ... Doesn't everyone admit that a king is both rich and powerful? But suppose he possesses none of the goods of the mind [animi bonis]; suppose nothing is ever enough for him: then clearly he is the poorest of the poor. Then say that his mind is subject to many vices: then he is the basest sort of slave. (43)[86]

Appearance is one thing, reality another. The king appears to have everything, but this is not the case. He imagines, along with others, that his riches and power, worldly savvy, and worldly decisions prove that he is an extremely prudent person, but his prudence is only apparent. Unlike the wiseman, he does deal with worldly variables, but true worldly expertise, true prudence, requires more than this. What the king lacks are goods of the mind, unseen truths.[87] Notwithstanding, that is, Folly's incessant criticisms of the Stoic wiseman, she shows that there are abstract values and that true prudence is inseparable from these values.

More than merely a failure to hold to unseen truths, false prudence is both self-destructive and socially destructive.[88] If kings and courtiers "had an ounce of good sense, what could be more wretched and repellent than the life they lead?" (107). Consider all the burdens of office the fact that their decisions affect the entire commonwealth,

---

86 ASD IV-3, 104/577–80, 587–9.

87 On blindness to incorporeal things, as contrasted with what can be seen, see Seneca, *De brevitate vitae* 7.1–2.

88 The sixth paradox in *Paradoxa Stoicorum* shows, similarly, that wickedness is destructive even to its practitioners (discussed *Par.* 33–41).

economically and morally, the ever-present inducements to evil, the dangers from plots against them, and, not least, the final judgment of God. "If truly wise," truly prudent, such a person would not be able to eat or sleep with enjoyment (107). While true prudence is effective in worldly affairs, false prudence is not. False prudence takes away from one's worldly happiness and the worldly happiness of others. Abstract truths are not simply rules, precepts, principles, or tenets that need to be obeyed. They comprise the sine qua non of all effective worldly acts. And since ineffective worldly acts do not reflect the both/and, one's eternal life is also in jeopardy.

As with *De officiis*[89] and More's rendering of Lucian's *Philopseudes*, false prudence no more represents the *utile* than the *honestum*. Although they are opposite types, abstract values and worldly values are inseparable. It is never the case that something can be an effective or valid worldly value and yet be at odds with valid abstract values. True prudence arises out of actual worldly issues, not rigid or abstract rules, and deals with them effectivel , but it would not be true prudence and would not be truly effective were it at odds with the principles of the faith. Conversely, where true unseen values are in place, there is also true worldly prudence. What goes on in the world is for the most part only apparent prudence, not true prudence. The prudent practitioner of Christianity always holds to a both/and frame of mind, whereas the false practitioner sees no connection between worldly and non-worldly or, if a connection is seen, judges the relationship in either/or terms (as had Thomas More before late 1504).

Again, prudence that "recognizes human limitations and does not strive to leap beyond them" is not incompatible with abstract values. Not only are the two radically diffe ent types of value not incompatible, they require each other. While true prudence is not compatible with the one-dimensional prudence of the Stoic wiseman caricatured by Folly, it cannot be separated from the abstract values of Democritus and, most of all, Christianity. Rigid abstract values exist and are indispensable, but unlike the abstractions espoused by the (caricatured) Stoic wiseman, they do not micromanage the variables found in human nature and human affairs. The tenets of Christianity are few and simple, as are Stoic tenets, and contrast with the multitudes of "distinctions" made by scholastics (cf. 85–99), but these tenets do not impose on human affairs a one-dimensional view of prudence. The Stoic wiseman (as caricatured) believes, wrongly, that rigid and abstract conceptions of prudence can

89 On the diffe ence between true and false prudence in *De officiis* see 2.33, 3.71, 95, 117.

be applied as is to the worldly stage, while those on the stage imagine, just as wrongly, that abstract truths are not applicable. There is a right type of abstract value and a right type of worldly value but they would not be such were they not conjoined. "True prudence" is flexible, in accordance with human nature, individual personalities, and particular situations, but it is at the same time inflexible

Philosophical Flattery

Flattery also, Folly demonstrates, exemplifies the two types of worldliness. Here too there is no ambivalence or rhetorical vacillation, at odds with modern views. One modern view, for example, is that Erasmus, "like More, loathed flatte ers, but was not above invoking fla - tery himself if he thought it could do some good."[90] The assumption here is that in loathing flatte ers Erasmus loathed all flattery and that where he himself employed flattery he was contradicting his ideals. More perceptive readers have seen that Erasmus sometimes sees fla - tery as positive and beneficial, and yet they do not imagine that the meaning he gives to the word *flattery* and his employment of flatter in his writings as in his life could rest on a very solid philosophical foundation.

Plato had formally separated flattery and rhetoric from philosophy in *Gorgias* (455a, 527c), and Folly alludes to Plato's distinction where she states that medicine is a subdivision of flattery just like rhetoric (*Gorgias* 463a–65c) (52). But Folly has an answer. She does not doubt the power of flattery to move "that enormous and powerful monster, the mob," as exemplified by ancient history (39–41), but there is all the diffe ence between positive and negative flatter , and this diffe ence is not explained by common sense or rhetoric but by a certain philosophical frame of mind. *Flattery* is a term much discussed by rhetoricians in that the aim is persuasion, but there is a method, built from Stoicism, for determining whether flattery is true or false.[91] False flattery is one-dimensional, true flattery two-dimensional and both/and. One prominent example of false flattery is what goes on in the courts of

90 Guy, *Thomas More*, 67.

91 Quintilian recognized in his *Institutes* that rhetoric can be perverted to bad ends and emphasized the need for morality, "the good man" (*The Orator's Education*, vol 1, book 2, ch. 16, 1–11). See Winterbottom, "Quintilian and the *Vir Bonus*." Unlike Erasmus, Quintilian sets forth no method by which true and false rhetoric can be gauged.

kings. Wisemen, in their dealings with princes, "turn black into white, blow hot and cold in one breath, profess to believe one thing in their speech but conceal quite another in their hearts" (56). Kings, for their part, won't listen to anyone who isn't fawning and, in turn, they are not averse to spouting out a few words of flattery while reducing, under a pretext of justice, the wealth of their subjects (108).

Flattery that promotes war is extraordinarily harmful and common. Such flattery supports something that is both "so inhuman it befits beasts, not men" ("insane," "noxious," and "unjust") and "so impious that it is utterly foreign to Christ" (114).[92] "Learned flatte ers," not the least being theologians trained in scholastic methodologies, are adept at deceitfully hiding Christ's precepts from themselves and from others:

> Nor is there any lack of learned flatte ers who call this patent madness by the names zeal, piety, fortitude, having devised a way to allow someone to unsheathe cold steel and thrust it into his brother's guts without any offense against that highest duty of charity which, according to Christ's precept, he owes to his fellow Christian. (114)[93]

Such flattery reverses the meaning of Christ's teachings, in the case at hand his absolute prohibition of war – according to Erasmus' interpretation of the New Testament (124–6). And exemplifying what happens when the *utile* is not tied with the *honestum*, it promotes activities that are self-defeating and contrary to the best interests of society, as war "reduces all human affairs, laws, religion, and peace, to utter chaos" (114, cf. 35). As I have demonstrated elsewhere, Erasmus' many writings on war – particularly notable are *Dulce bellum inexpertis* (1515), *Querela pacis* (1517), and *De bello Turcico* (1530) – develop in great detail this both/and way of thinking and talking about war.[94]

Although the flattery Folly advocates is based on a philosophical way of thinking and not on rhetoric, it can surely be abetted, she shows, by expertise in communication. True flattery encourages men indirectly and decorously not to engage in war, and what could be more apropos here than rhetorical skills? The way one words things has everything to do with getting people to realize what is in their worldly and their heavenly interest. Such flatter , for example, "advises and teaches

92 On war as madness even worse than found among beasts see Seneca, *Ep.* 95.31–2.

93 ASD IV-3, 174/821–5.

94 See Dealy, *Stoic Origins*, 320–5 and "The Dynamics of Erasmus' Thought on War."

princes under the cover of an encomium, without giving offense" (71).[95] Statements of advice that would cost the wiseman his life are accepted with pleasure when offe ed by the (both/and) fool (55–6). Such flattery does not resort to abstruse and rigid one-dimensional lectures but sees issues from the standpoint of two polar but inseparable types of value. Regarding the unbending side, note one thing: No matter how inoffensive their words and no matter how their words are made relevant to particular situations, Christian flatte ers will always hold rigidly to Christ's precepts. Regarding war, for example, they will never allow that Christ did not prohibit all war. At no time will they reverse – as do scholastic theologians, with their many "just war" distinctions – the meaning of Christ's words. Folly was not here countering scholastic logic with thin rhetorical talk (or rhetorical debate *in utramque partem*), the prevailing view. She was replacing one type of philosophical thinking with another. True flattery is unitarily both/and

Thomas More's Prudence, Flattery, and Decorum

Compare Folly's characterization of herself with Erasmus' description in the preface of Thomas More as a heavenly based Democritus, ridiculing from the standpoint of highest truth all the nonsense that goes on in the world, and simultaneously being a worldly "man for all seasons."

Like More, Folly accepts people on equal terms, with all their diversity and foolery – unlike all the other gods:

> I, Folly, am the only one who embraces everyone equally with such ready and easy generosity. I do not care for vows, nor do I grow angry and demand expiatory gifts if some point of ceremony is overlooked. (74)[96]

What we see here is simply a personalizing of earlier theses. Contrasting with the (caricatured) Stoic wiseman, the (worldly) fool considers

95 According to Erasmus, the purpose of his *Panegyric of Philip* (1504) was not fla - tery as such but flattery with a higher purpose *Ep.* 180, Allen 1, 398–403). In the 1508 adage "Polypi mentem obtine [Adopt the outlook of the polyp]," similarly, Erasmus agrees that we must adapt to the customs of a country, but adds, "Let no one think that by this adage we are taught a disgusting type of flatter , which assents to everything in everybody, or an improper changeability in behavior."We must follow the path of St Paul, who had "a higher purpose" to his prudence and flatter , to wit that he might "become all things to all men, that he might win all for Christ." Adage I i 93. LB 2.63C, E, CWE 31, 134 and 135.

96 ASD IV-3, 132/154–6.

nothing human foreign to him (46).[97] "It is perverse not to adapt yourself to the prevailing circumstances." "True prudence recognizes human limitations and does not strive to leap beyond them; it is willing to run with the herd, to overlook faults tolerantly or to share them in a friendly spirit" (44).

True prudence and true flattery are no more found in the prudence and flattery of ordinary humans, which deceitfully and conveniently take advantage of others, than in the unbending prudence of the wiseman, which holds human limitations in contempt. True prudence and flattery are practised only by persons who hold to unseen truths (truths which, in contrast with Folly's wiseman, do not deny worldly variability) as they interact with multiple personalities and situations. Lacking in evil intentions, both/and prudence and flattery build on the particular needs of recipients. They make people feel better about themselves at the same time as they correct them. To this end, expertise in rhetoric – not something learned from Stoics – can be a powerful tool.

> Nowadays flattery is thought of as disreputable, but only by people who are more concerned about words than about things themselves. They judge that flattery is inconsistent with good faith [i.e., the precepts of the faith] ... But this flattery of mine proceeds from a kind disposition and a certain frankness [Verum haec mea ab ingenii benignitate candoreque quodam proficiscitur] ... This kind of flattery gives a lift to those whose spirits are low, consoles those who mourn, stimulates the apathetic, rouses the dull, cheers the sick, tames the fie ce, unites lovers and keeps them united. It entices children to learn their lessons, it cheers up old people, it advises and teaches princes under cover of an encomium, without giving offense ... Not to mention that this flattery plays a large part in that eloquence everyone praises ... In sum, it is the honey and spice of all human intercourse. (70–1)[98]

Later (see below) Folly associates St Paul, known for his unbending faith in unseen truths, with this same openminded frankness ("animi candorem") towards others (122) – which accords with her conception of Christ. "Though Christ was the wisdom of the Father," he became involved with mankind and the healing of mankind when he took on human nature (130).

"Christ requires the fulfillment of his own precept, namely charity" (John 15:12). Charity is a precept, but a precept that is by definition

97 Terence, *Heautontimorumenos* 77, quoted in *De officiis*, 1.30, and by Seneca, *Ep.* 95.53.
98 ASD IV-3, 130/77–95.

bending (100, cf. 111, 114). Represented by prudence, flatter , and decorum, charity responds to nature and natural instinct and the varieties of personalities and situations. Similarly, decorum, closely related to prudence, is in Stoic philosophy (as distinct from Folly's depiction of Stoics) a concept that is unbending, inseparable from *honestum* (*Off.* 1.93), and yet by definition bending. Early on Folly states that decorum "is the guiding principle not only in art but also in all the actions of life" (34).[99] Compare *De officiis* 1.126: "Decorum can be seen in every deed, in every word, and even in every bodily movement or state, and the latter depend on beauty, order and embellishment that is suited to action ... and include a concern to win the approval of those with and among whom we live."[100]

Clearly, all the above relates directly to Erasmus' description of Thomas More as both a Democritus and "a man for all seasons." Just as More accepts his own natural instincts, character traits, and particular situations, so too does he accept all the variability and foibles found in other humans. He could play the game of life with anyone at any time and enjoy doing so. Like Folly, he does not approach others with harsh, abstract rules. He does not wreck their happiness by being dour and negative. He does not make demands from the standpoint of "real" truth, unlike the arrogant one-dimensional prudence of the (caricatured) Stoic wiseman mocked by Folly. He treats everyone equally, entering into their lives in an extremely agreeable, affable, and constructive manner. He is entirely open to the particularities of other humans, their personalities, experiences, situations, and opinions. In short, he enters upon the stage and plays the game – his performance enhanced, undoubtedly, by superlative rhetorical skills.

There is, however, all the diffe ence between More and other worldly fools, even those with rhetorical skills. Unlike others, he adheres with all firmness to unseen truth, the truth represented by Democritus – and most fully by the axioms of the Christian faith. Although he is

99 "Est enim non artis modo, verumetiam omnis actionis caput, decere quod agas" (ASD IV-3. 96/443–4).

100 *De officiis* discusses decorum at 1.93–141. According to Sherman, "Cicero offers [in *De officiis*] a philosophical defense of decorum that is unparalleled in the ancient world" (*Stoic Warriors*, 52). See also Dyck, *A Commentary on Cicero, De Officiis*, esp. 241–58, and Erasmus' Adage 3402 (IV.v.2), ASD II-7, 244/270–81. Decorum is, of course, a major theme in rhetoric also. See Quintilian, *Institutes* 11.3.177, Cicero, *De oratore* 1.32, *Orator* 70–2. For the ancient rhetoricians, states Patterson, "decorum was the most important of all criteria." See *Hermogenes and the Renaissance*, 3.

an unrivalled master of prudence, flatter , and decorum, it is not the one-dimensional worldly types but the two-dimensional types. Lacking this two-dimensional, Stoic/Christian, unitary both/and, mindset he would be little diffe ent from those he interacts with. Compare the *Enchiridion*: "Adapt yourself to everyone exteriorly [with gentleness, affabilit , friendliness, agreeableness], provided that interiorly your resolution remains unshaken."[101]

Prudence, Flattery, and Decorum in *Utopia* and *Richard III*

In Book I of *Utopia*, Hythloday acknowledges only evil flatter , decorum, and prudence, while persona "More" in Book I shows that flatter , decorum, and prudence can have positive consequences. Hythloday represents, in effect, the Democritean side of Folly and More's personality, whereas character "More" represents the "the man for all seasons" side of Folly and More. While "More" does not clearly reveal the both/and frame of mind that allows positive flatter , decorum, and prudence, the author's Utopians, in Book II, correct (I will demonstrate in Parts VI and VII) this deficienc . They demonstrate in detail how prudential and decorous decisions are made, within a unique social/political context, and the inseparability of these decisions from the unbending principles that govern their society.

The extremely harsh methods of engaging in war employed by the Utopians were not a joke or a contradiction, contrary to the assumptions of scholars. They were methods, worked out in situation after situation, of holding to the principles of their society while appropriately confronting and triumphing over the equally harsh methods of cunning and deceit employed, without a both/and frame of mind, by their evil opponents (Part VII below). Similarly, Morton is the hero of *Richard III* notwithstanding Morton's deep involvement in prudential cunning, deceit, and flatter . Like Richard, Morton was a master at cunning, deceit, and flatter , but, unlike Richard, his prudence had a heavenly dimension as well as a worldly (Part VIII below). Many things are allowed on the worldly scene if one's motivations are not at odds with the precepts of the faith. In Stoicism, it may be remembered, even

101 CWE 66, 104, H 110/29–30. See also 190n95 above. Accommodation to the needs of others was to become a core emphasis of Erasmus. Remer, like many, sees Erasmus' referrals to decorum and accommodation entirely in terms of rhetoric. See *Humanism and the Rhetoric of Toleration*, ch. 1.

cannibalism *could* be allowed, all the doctrinal particulars having been worked out.[102]

In *The Praise of Folly*, as many years earlier in his *Enchiridion*, Erasmus allows great latitude wherever the both/and is firmly in place. There exists extreme variety among humans as a result of natural instincts, particular character traits, and life situations, but this does not entail, he demonstrates, that one person is, by these factors alone, more at odds with the dogmas of the faith than another.[103] What matters is only the degree to which one appropriately responds to the challenges at hand, the extent to which, that is, one employs a two-dimensional mindset. The Utopians were to systematically develop this mindset, I will demonstrate in Parts VI and VII, within a New World social/political setting.

4 Highest Piety Is Unitarily Two-Dimensional

In believing that *The Praise of Folly* is simply a brilliant rhetorical parade of vacillating and contradictory positions, readers have focused for meaning on the conclusion, which they consider to be unquestionably about Platonist and Christian transcendence. They have concluded that Erasmus' outlook in the work was clearly otherworldly and one-dimensional. In proof they point to Folly's great admiration for the frenzied madness, complete happiness, and worldly disdain now and then experienced by pious persons.

In fact, even in this final section Folly's outlook is two-dimensional, unitarily both/and. Let's analyse the evidence:

(1) Note first that what is referred to in the final pages is not the present but the future, what happens with eternal life (136). The ecstasy and "madness" that pious persons now and then experience is only "a meditation," "a foreshadowing," "a faint taste," of future happiness (137, 138).[104]

---

102 DL 7.121. As if taking his cue from this Stoic contention, Erasmus avers in *Dulce bellum inexpertis* that cannibalism carried out by necessity alone might have been excusable, but now we kill with machines and without humanity. Adage 3001 (IV.i.1). ASD II-7, 18/165–9, CWE 35, 406.

103 As Inwood notes, "There was never a monolithic ideal of life for the Stoics ... accordingly, the particularities of each agent's character had to have been given considerable weight in selection of the morally correct action." See "Rules and Reasoning in Stoic Ethics," 126 and my discussion of Erasmus' employment of the four-personae theory of Panaetius/Cicero in *Stoic Origins*, 122–6, 337.

104 See also *Ep.* 337 (to Dorp, 1515). Allen 2, 103/489–91, CWE 71, 19.

(2) Ecstasy does not contradict worldly values, as such. What invisible truth opposes is only false worldly values, the values most humans adhere to. Repeatedly, Folly contrasts the outlook of "the ordinary run of men" (134) with that of the pious. Ordinary mortals see the precepts of Christianity as foolishness and think only corporal things exist (134). Pious persons, few in number (133), are contemptuous of false worldly practices, everything that takes place through mere habit and perverse self-interest, things like evil passions, seeing religiosity in ceremonies alone, developing prudential skills that merely support a desire for wealth and power, etc.

(3) Pious persons are not one-dimensional mystics. Their feet are still firmly planted in the world. Where Folly maintains that pious persons conflict with the vast run of mortals "in their whole life style" (133), flee the perceptions of ordinary men "in absolutely every activity of life" (136), and "war unceasingly" against their own shortcomings (135), she is not saying that pious persons escape from the realities of living. She is saying that the pious, in contrast to run-of-the-mill Christians, employ in "every activity of life" attitudes and practices that reflect their piety. Earlier, Folly imagines "some odious wiseman" standing up and singing out "the true state of affairs: 'You will not die badly if you live well ... if you change your whole way of life'" (67).

(4) Folly has already demonstrated, over and over, that there are two types of *worldly* outlook and practice, one type in accord with the axioms of the faith, one type not. Pious persons employ the former type.

(5) Nor is it the least bit surprising that, notwithstanding their worldly side, pious persons hold that "the world takes second place" (134), consider what is visible "far less valuable than what cannot be seen" (135), or, even more extreme, "are completely taken up with the contemplation of invisible things" (134). Faith in eternal life is central to Christianity. Not unrelated, the Stoics hold that *honestum* is far more valuable than anything that can be seen.

(6) Holding firm to invisible truth throughout all the happenings of life, whatever their nature and whether good or ill, is part and parcel of the author's Stoic/Christian outlook. In emphasizing the otherworldliness of the pious, Erasmus is merely restating the mindset, illustrated throughout much of the *Enchiridion*, that should accompany the Christian layman. Christians should hold uncompromisingly to the supernal tenets of the faith, much as Stoics hold to *honestum*, as they deal with all the variables of existence, things indiffe ent – natural instinct, character traits, and particular external situations.

(7) Holding to unseen truth not only does not inhibit involvements of the pious in worldly affairs but also makes them masterful practitioners. Just

as, in Book 3 of *De officiis*, the *utile* and the *honestum* are shown to be one and the same, so too in Christianity are the useful and the pious one and the same. Worldly outlooks and practices that are in accord (albeit representing a diffe ent type of value) with the tenets of the faith *work* in the world. Attitudes and behaviour that are not in accord are counterproductive and self-defeating. In short, the more one holds to the invisible values the better one carries out worldly affairs. This being the case, worldly realities will often be dealt with in unusual ways (as the Utopians were later to illustrate).

(8) Compare the meaning of statements found in many important later writings, such as *Dulce bellum inexpertis* (War is sweet to those who know it not) (1515). There is no contradiction where Erasmus states, on the one hand, that "our one aim in life is to take flight from life," and on the other hand, not far away, that "the end and aim of the faith of the Gospel is conduct."[105] Taking flight from life, holding to one type of value, allows one to engage in life, holding to another type of value, in the best possible ways. What should be seen in such examples is not carelessness or rhetorical licence or contradiction but a particular philosophical mindset. Christianity is simultaneously about flight from life and the practice of life – as in Stoicism. Look again at my quote of Epictetus above, 183.

Finally, how could pious persons not be worldly when even St Paul and Christ himself stressed, according to Folly, their human nature and involvements in human affairs? The insane contemplativeness of the pious person represents hard truth but not the whole of truth. St Paul held to invisible truth but he also considered himself, Folly shows, a worldly fool, "just as if it were shameful to be outdone in folly" (2 Cor. 11:23) (122). In considering himself a fool, Paul represents, we are shown, the view expressed in Ecclesiastes 10:3: "As the fool walks along the street, he thinks that, since he himself is stupid, everyone else is also foolish."

> What about this: Holy Scripture even attributes to the fool a spirit of openminded generosity, while the wiseman thinks no one is as good as he is ... Isn't it a mark of a certain openminded frankness to take everyone as your equal and, though no one does not have a grand notion of himself, nevertheless to share your praises with everyone else? (122)[106]

105 Adage 3001 (IV.i.1). ASD II-7, 43/943–4, 40/834–5 resp, cf. CWE 35, 438 and 433 resp. Christians don't, as with Augustine, simply use the world as pilgrims, like captives and strangers (*City of God*, 19.16–17). Christianity is by its very nature two-dimensional, unitarily both/and.

106 "Quid quod animi quoque candorem divinae literae stulto tribuunt, cum sapiens interim neminem sui similem putet." "An non istud eximii cuiusdam candoris est, omnes aequare tibi ipsi cumque nemo non magnifice de se sentiat, omnibus tamen tuas communicare laudes?" (ASD IV-3, 182/963–4, 966–8).

Even Christ became a fool and openly acknowledged such to the Father (128). Christ is not here held to be a fool in that he holds to unseen truths but in that he is at one and the same time totally involved in humanness:

> Do not [states Folly] all these witnesses cry out with one voice that all mortals are fools, even the pious? And that even Christ, though he was the wisdom of the Father, became somehow foolish in order to relieve the folly of mortals when he took on human nature and appeared in the form of a man? Just as he became sin in order to heal sins. (130)[107]

On the one hand Christ was "the wisdom of the Father," that which is perfect, but on the other hand he "took on human nature." From the standpoint of that which is perfect, in a one-dimensional sense, becoming a man represents highest imperfection and thus foolishness. But from another standpoint, that of human nature, Christ was of course anything but foolish. Pious persons also were bound by their human nature, the text shows, and, as Christians, followers of Christ, it could not be otherwise.

All of which relates directly, we can see, to Erasmus' "Democritus"/"man for all seasons" – Stoic – representation of Thomas More's personality and outlook.

I have shown that in *De taedio Iesu* Erasmus had demonstrated in detail precisely what this so-called foolishness of Christ consisted of. Erasmus did not think in that work that he needed to spend time getting people to believe that Christ was the wisdom of the Father. What he found imperative to think out, in debating Colet, was the nature of Christ's humanness. Christ had no way of escaping his human nature. Building on Stoic natural instinct (*oikeiosis*), Erasmus shows why Christ in being human did not suffer in his Passion mere "pre-emotion" – as theologians had argued for a thousand years – but full-fledged emotion. His natural instincts were our natural instincts and his emotions (building from and correcting Stoic sources) were our emotions. Even in the state of innocence Christ possessed all the natural instincts, including the emotion of fear. By many routes we are shown that Christ's fear of death incomparably exceeded anything ever experienced by another human in that, unlke others, he had no way to mitigate his fear. Against "Colet's" one-dimensional understanding of Stoicism Erasmus shows that Christ was not a martyr. Martyrdom would have

107 ASD IV-3, 188/106–10.

made Christ something other than human. The fact that Christ was not a martyr does not detract but adds exponentially to what his life was all about.

In 1515, in his response to Martin Dorp's criticism, Erasmus defended the idea that Christ was foolish, i.e., worldly, in the following way:

> Nor is there any risk that someone at this point may suppose that the apostles or Christ were foolish in the ordinary sense, but that in them too there was an element of weakness, something attributable to our natural affe - tions, which when compared with that pure and eternal wisdom might seem less than wise. But this same folly of theirs overcomes all the wisdom of the world.[108]

In being entirely human, with all our "natural affections," the apostles and Christ overcame all the *false* worldly values and *false* wisdom of ordinary humans, but they did not overcome their natural instincts and worldly involvements. The game of life can be played in no other way (43–4, 120).

"A Third World"

In this final section we can see, yet again, the Stoic distinctions between that which is *honestum* (the good, virtue, reason, oneness with God) on the one hand, that which is base (*turpe*) on the other, and, in between, things that are indiffe ent. In *De taedio Iesu* and, especially, the *Enchiridion*, Erasmus radicalizes, I have shown in *Stoic Origins*, the thinking of Origen on these categories. While Origen had contended that indifferents are not independent but always attached to either flesh (Stoic baseness) or spirit (Stoic *honestum*), Erasmus saw indiffe ents as Stoics saw them and transferred the meaning to the very heart of Christianity. For Stoics, indiffe ents comprise the "material" of life,[109] and Erasmus follows suit, referring to the material of life as "soul." The "soul" comprises "a third world" between flesh and spirit. It is "the life-giving element" and (at odds with Origen) profoundly substantive. Comprising things such as natural instinct, character traits, ceremonies, and

108 *Ep.* 337. Allen 2, 103/476–80, CWE 71, 19.

109 Compare the words of the Stoic Cato in *De finibus*. The primary objects of nature "fall under the judgment of the wise person, and form so to speak the subject matter and the given material of wisdom [estque illa subiecta quasi materia sapientiae]" (3.61). Compare Chrysippus as reported by Plutarch, *CN* 1071AB, 1069E; Epictetus, *Disc.* 2.51; and below, 255–6.

the multitudes of worldly situations that confront humans, the "soul" is through and through indiffe ent. Christianity is about developing things that are indiffe ent (and as such not evil) as one holds to spirit.[110] The three Stoic categories are represented in the final section of *The Praise of Folly* as follows:

1. Flesh (cf. Stoic *turpe*). Here one finds "the ordinary run of mortals," those who exhibit false passions and are consumed by the desire for wealth and the like (134). Such persons can't imagine life without the capital sins of lust, passion for food and sleep, anger, pride, and envy (135). They see religiosity purely in terms of ceremonies, such as fasting (135). Their mental energies are concentrated on the lower senses, such as touch, sight, smell, and taste (134). Lacking belief or even interest in things unseen, they consider pious persons insane. Among these worldlings are those at the opposite end of the social spectrum, scholastic theologians and other so-called wisemen, those who wage war with nature (54). Immediately preceding the final section is found a lengthy and particularly harsh ridiculing of these theologians and the way they distort biblical teachings (124–7). Within the final section itself, scholastics and other would-be wise persons are compared to the biblical condemnations of scribes, pharisees, and doctors of law (Matt. 23:13–27, Luke 11:42–3) (129).

2. Spirit, invisible truth (cf. Stoic *honestum*, conceptualized as oneness with god). Pious persons, opposite the "flesh" (as *turpe*), have experienced "a faint taste" of this reality, ultimate happiness, as it actually is – in heaven.

3. "Soul" (cf. Stoic indiffe ents, as expanded by Erasmus). Here again, natural instinct provides an essential part of "the third world." Christ took the greatest delight in simple people, his "sheep," women and children, as well as lilies and sparrows, "all leading their lives according to the dictates of nature" (130, cf. 51–3). Children, old people, women, and simpleminded persons are always nearest the altar "out of natural inclination" (132). Lacking the pretentiousness of those who consider themselves wise, such persons are willing to beg forgiveness (131). According to Paul, "Whoever seems wise among you, let him become a [worldly, in Folly's estimation] fool, that he may be wise" (1 Cor. 3:18) (128). As shown above, Paul entered into human affairs "with a spirit of openminded generosity" (122), and even Christ became foolish, and admitted such, when he took on human nature (130).

110 See Dealy, *Stoic Origins*, 121 ("augent materiam segetemque virtutis"), 126–41, and 267–75.

True wisdom is impossible lacking a foundation in human nature and worldly affairs – things ind ffe ent.

Spirituality occurs *only* when humans deal with "soul" – the realm of things indiffe ent, the material of life – as they hold unbendingly to spirit. Bendable values – natural instincts, emotions, and the varieties and multitudes of worldly situations humans find themselves in – are not something separate from Christianity but inherent to Christianity. In radically changing their life style, pious persons begin with nature and the actualities (as against perceived actualities) of worldly situations. In short, they live and think in both/and terms. Christianity is all about holding to spirit as one develops at one and the same time particulars found in the "third world." Spirituality that bypasses the "third world" is not spirituality.

In short, Folly does not take back, at the conclusion, anything said about the essentiality of worldliness. In emphasizing the experiences of a few pious persons, she is just expanding on the adherence to hard and invisible truth – much as Stoics insist on the oneness of *honestum* with the universe and god – that accompanies true worldliness. Folly again brings in Plato's myth of the cave (133, 136), here giving the palm not to worldly values but to the few pious persons mentioned; however, the worldly values referred to, as a contrast, are false worldly values, not true worldly values (133–4). The myth here represents, that is, the spirit/flesh either/or, not the spirit/soul both/and. There is no vacillation or contradiction.

Kathekon and *Katorthoma*

In his conclusion Erasmus also returns to the Stoic diffe entiation between "right action" (*katorthoma*) and "appropriate action" (*kathekon, officium*), which he had so deeply absorbed at least ten years earlier, as evident in his editing of *De officiis* (published in 1501), and had systematically worked out in the *Enchiridion* (1503). A central thesis of Stoics is that "appropriate action" (*kathekon, officium*) is common to both the virtuous and the non-virtuous but "right action" (*katorthoma*) applies only to the virtuous (the wise). "Appropriate action" takes place in the realm of things indiffe ent. "Right action" requires the addition of a higher type of value. The diffe ence between "perfect" and "imperfect" appropriate actions is the moral character of their agents.[111]

111 "Intermediate appropriate actions," Long and Sedley note, "are neither good nor bad, when considered in abstraction from their agents, but in reference to these they are either 'perfect' or 'imperfect,' right actions or wrong ones." See LS 367.

One illustration, set forth by Folly in the conclusion, concerns love of parents. Before quoting her I will bring in on this subject a Stoic source and then the *Enchiridion*.

1. The sceptical philosopher Sextus Empiricus (second century CE) describes the Stoic way of thinking about parents as follows:

> [The Stoics say] The virtuous man's function is not [just] to look after his parents and honour them in other respects but to do this on the basis of prudence. For just as the care of health is common to the doctor and the layman, but caring for health in the medical way is peculiar to the expert, so too the honouring of parents is common to the virtuous and the not virtuous man, but to do this on the basis of prudence [one with *honestum*] is peculiar to the wiseman.[112]

2. Without mentioning the author's source or the words used by Stoics, the *Enchiridion* illustrates over and over the diffe ence between an "appropriate action" and a "right action." As a beginning illustration, he describes the attitude towards parents and the like that should exist:

> You respect your parents; you love your brother; you love your children, you cherish your friend. It is not so much a virtue to do such things as it is unnaturally wicked not to do them. Why would you, a Christian, not do what even pagans do by natural instinct, or even what brute animals do? Whatever comes from nature cannot be ascribed to merit. But if you find yourself in a situation in which you must either neglect your duties to your father, triumph over your affection for your children, disregard the devotion owed to a friend, or offend God, what will you do? (52

3. Discussing the mentality of pious persons at the conclusion of *The Praise of Folly*, Erasmus again focuses on parents and kinfolk:

> There are some intermediate feelings [affectus medii], which are in a sense natural [quasique naturales], such as patriotism, or love of children, parents, friends. Ordinary men have regard for these, but the pious strive

112 Sextus Empiricus, *Against the Professors* 11.200–1, LS 59G. Discussing duties towards one's parents, brothers, children, friends, and guests, Seneca states, similarly, that "The same act may be either shameful or honorable; the purpose and the manner make all the diffe ence" (*Ep.* 95/37–46 at 43). Cf. *Fin.* 3.32, 5.67–9, and DL 7.108. See also Gill's discussion of Epictetus, *The Structured Self*, 384–5; Graver, *Stoicism and Emotion*, 177; and Vogt, *Law, Reason, and the Cosmic City*, 189–93, 202, and 209.

> to root out even these from their minds, except insofar as they can be assimilated to that highest part of the mind, so that a father is no longer loved simply as a father (for what did he beget except the body? – though even that too is owing to God, the father of all), but as a good man whose personality projects a shining image of that highest mind of all, to which alone they [the pious] give the name "highest good" and apart from which they teach that nothing is to be loved or sought. (135)[113]

Pious persons don't simply love their kinfolk; they love them in a certain way. "Intermediate" feelings or instincts, in themselves neither flesh nor spirit, are natural, part of the material of life. But pious persons know that spirituality requires, at one and the same time, something more, the "highest good." Natural feelings are not, it needs emphasizing, overcome by the highest good. The diffe ence, in the example, is that one no longer loves a father "simply as a father." Pious persons try never to allow that natural feelings, however real, are all there is. Here, as in the author's reinterpretation of St Paul and Origen in terms of Stoicism, intermediate things (including feelings) are substantive as well as indiffe ent. Things indiffe ent don't vacillate (either/or) between flesh and spirit but are inherent to the human condition and to Christian spirituality – one side of a both/and frame of mind.[114]

"*By the same rule*," Folly continues, "*they measure all the other duties of life*" (135; italics mine).

Immediately following is found another illustration of the distinction between an appropriate action and a right action. Here the focus, so

113 ASD IV-3, 191/202–9. Regarding Erasmus' referral here to "the highest good" rather than, as in Stoicism, "the only good," note *Off.* 3.11 and More's referral to *Tusc.* 5.51, discussed above, 110–17. In his 1515 *Commentary*, Gerardus Listrius states here that Erasmus took the tripartite division of man from St Paul as interpreted by Origen (LB 4, col. 502, n. 5). One wonders if he recognized Erasmus' radical reinterpretation of Origen's division in *De taedio Iesu* and the *Enchiridion*.

114 Misunderstanding Erasmus' meaning, Nelson imagines that Erasmus is here replacing "Roman theory" and the *vita active* with Ficino's Platonism. See "Greek *Nonsense* in More's Utopia," 31–2. Screech recognizes the importance of Erasmus' discussions of indiffe ents (*adiaphora*) in explicating Folly's statement about parents, but believes – failing to grasp the Stoic and Erasmian meaning – that the theme was common and that "The Stoic associations of these ideas often encouraged Renaissance moralists to assume that these 'intermediate', 'indiffe ent', things become good when treated with 'indiffe ence', that is negligently" (97). He also imagines – directly at odds with the distinction Erasmus is so at pains to make – that *adiaphora* relate to the flesh and contrast either/or with spirituality (98). See *Ecstasy and "The Praise of Folly,"* 96–112, and below, 204n120.

central to the *Enchiridion*, relates to ceremonies and the like. Again, I will begin with a Stoic source, followed by the *Enchiridion*.

1. A centrepiece of the Stoic Cato's argument in Cicero's *De finibus*, analysed by Erasmus in his edition of *De officiis*,[115] is the following:

> Now although we say that what is moral [honestum] is the only good, it is still consistent to perform appropriate actions despite the fact that we regard them as neither good nor evil [but intermediate]. This is because reasonableness is found in this area, such that a rational explanation could be given of the action, and so of an action reasonably performed. (3.58)
>
> It is evident that even those who are wise act in the sphere of these intermediates [rebus mediis], and so judge such action to be appropriate action [officium] And, since their judgement is flawless, appropriate action will belong to the sphere of the intermediates. The same conclusion can be reached by the following argument: We observe that something exists which we call right action [recte factum] and that this is an appropriate act perfectly performed. So there will also be such a thing as an imperfect appropriate action. If to restore a trust as a matter of principle is a right action, to restore a trust must be counted as an appropriate action. The addition of the qualification "on principle" makes it a right action. The mere restitution in itself is counted an appropriate action. (3.59)[116]

2. I have shown that the *Enchiridion* transposes the foregoing way of thinking to the very essence of Christianity.

> But if your eye is not sound and you look elsewhere than towards Christ, even if you have acted with propriety, your actions will be unfruitful or even harmful. For it is a fault to perform a good action in an improper way. (61)[117]

Importantly, this statement is followed by a discussion of the three (Stoic) categories of *turpia*, *honesta*, and things in-between, *media*.

3. At the conclusion of *The Praise of Folly*, Folly places "ceremonies" – a central theme of the *Enchiridion*, directly related to Erasmus' youthful

115 See Dealy, *Stoic Origins*, Part II.2.

116 The translations make use of the wordings of both Annas, *On Moral Ends*, and Rackham (Loeb edition).

117 "Quod si nequam erit oculus tuus et alio quam ad Christum spectaris, etiam si qua recta feceris, infrugifera fuerint aut etiam perniciosa. Vitium enim est rem bonam non bene agere" (H 63/24–7).

sufferings and why he had been so affected by Stoicism – within this two-dimensional, appropriate action/right action frame of thought:

> Even in the sacraments, they say, and in religious observances, a bodily and a spiritual dimension can be found. Thus in fasting, they do not think it amounts to much to abstain from flesh and food – ordinary people think this is all that fasting is ... So too in the eucharist, although the ceremonies with which it is administered are not to be scorned, still in themselves they are not very profitable and may even be harmful, unless what is spiritual is also present, namely, what is re-enacted by these visible signs. (135)[118]

Both fools and wise, pagan and Christian, formally Christian and truly Christian, carry out "appropriate actions," but these actions do not in themselves have anything to do with spirituality. Spirituality – right action – entails that they be carried out with a certain mindset. Not only ceremonies but all the actions of life require this higher motivation – or they are not spiritual.

Geraldine Thompson considers the last quotation representative of that which Erasmus refers to a few years later as "the philosophy of Christ" – a phrase which has distinguished for moderns his religious thought.[119] But what has not been seen is the Stoic-based way of thinking within which this extract is embedded – worked out in Erasmus' edition of *De officiis* and *De taedio Iesu* and throughout *The Enchiridion* and, as evidenced by all the above, *The Praise of Folly*. "The philosophy of Christ" models and builds on the philosophy of Stoicism – and Erasmus saw Thomas More as reflecting "the philosophy of Christ" in his entire way of thinking and living.[120]

---

118 "Aiunt autem et in sacramentis atque ipsis pietatis officiis corpus et spiritu inueniri. Velut in ieiunio non magni ducunt, si quis tantum a carnibus coenaque abstineat, id quod vulgus absolutum esse ieiunium existimat ... Similiter et in Synaxi, tametsi non est aspernandum, inquiunt, quod ceremoniis geritur, tamen id per se aut parum est conducibile aut etiam perniciosum, nisi id quod est spiritale accesserit, nempe hoc quod signis illis visibilibus repraesentatur" (ASD IV-3, 192/212–15, 217–20).

119 Geraldine Thompson, *Under Pretext of Praise*, 81–2.

120 Attempting to support a preconceived idea, that the meaning of the work is found in the one-dimensional ecstasy of the pious, Screech imagines that "the philosophy of Christ" should be seen in terms of Socrates' definition of philosophy in *Phaedo*, as a meditation on death (*Ecstasy and "The Praise of Folly,"* 75–83, esp. 82). See my discussion of the actual context within which Erasmus refers, in the *Enchiridion*, to Socrates' definition in *Phaedo*, *Stoic Origins*, 301–5. Screech makes no mention of natural instincts or even the Stoic wiseman (!) and refers to Stoicism, in passing, only three or four times.

5 Why Is Folly Silent Regarding the Foundation of Her Thinking?

From cover to cover, *The Praise of Folly* is clearly a Stoic work. But why would Folly berate and lampoon the Stoic wiseman while silently passing over the Stoic foundation? Folly ridicules the wiseman from the standpoint of nature but fails to point out that the base sources and inspiration for her view of nature are Stoic; that her focus on natural instinct was inspired and built from Stoic *oikeiosis*. She makes fun of Stoic belief that emotion is a judgment of reason but fails to mention that her view of emotion was prompted by Stoic *oikeiosis* and worked out without a touch of humour in *De taedio Iesu* and the *Enchiridion*. Not least, she relocates emotion, as do *De taedio Iesu* and the *Enchiridion*, within one of three fundamental Stoic categories, that of *indifferentia*. And it was within this Stoic frame that her author had already shown that Christ himself, contrary to all previous theological thought, had suffe ed ineradicable fear.[121]

Even more striking, Folly lampoons the wiseman for being one-dimensional, abstract, rigid, utterly lacking in decorum, and divorced from the variables and actualities of worldly living, but does not notice that the unitary both/and outlook she lays out, in opposition, is precisely that of the Stoic wiseman – correctly understood. She attacks head on "that dyed-in-the-wool Stoic Seneca" (45) for considering emotion a disease, but fails to acknowledge the source of her alternative view, built on the two-dimensional, both/and, way of thinking of Seneca and other Stoics. Unlike other humans, the Stoic wiseman excels at worldly decorum. The following statements encapsulate a theme worked out by Seneca in multiple volumes:

> Virtue is divided into two parts – into contemplation of truth and conduct. And right conduct both practices and reveals virtue. (*Ep.* 94.45)
>
> Philosophy is both theoretic and practical; it contemplates and at the same time acts. (*Ep.* 95.10)[122]

---

121 See Dealy, *Stoic Origins*.

122 Mitsis argues that for Seneca *decreta* (or *dogmata*) and *praecepta* – the one requiring deduction from principles, the other induction from particulars – are mutually dependent and mutually strengthening, "inescapable features of our linguistic and conceptual framework." See "Seneca on Reason, Rules, and Moral Development," 312. Erasmus produced two editions of Seneca's works, one in 1515, to which he contributed little more than the introduction, and a second in 1529.

Multitudes of citations are brought in, but the sources upon which everything is built go unmentioned. Folly knows what the reader does not know but needs to learn, that truth is two-dimensional, unitarily both/and, *honestum/indifferens*. And there is good reason why she is so convinced of this view of truth and so determined, by many routes, to lay out the evidence: Her author had already worked out the mindset of "my Stoics" at length, in major works – impelled by deeply personal youthful problems.

Scholars have failed to grasp the meaning of *The Praise of Folly* for reasons closely related to their misunderstandings of *De taedio Iesu* and the *Enchiridion*.[123] What is not seen is the way Folly's author uses sources and the consistent, non-rhetorical, philosophy he is determined to set before the reader. I have shown that in *De taedio Iesu* and the *Enchiridion* Erasmus radically rewrites in Stoic terms Origen, Gellius, "Colet," Bonaventure, and Socrates (as well as authors who figu e less prominently, such as Augustine and St Bernard). In like manner, *The Praise of Folly* silently and radically rewrites in Stoic two-dimensional terms the contemporary one-dimensional picture of the Stoic wiseman.

In short, it is not surprising that contemporaries as well as moderns have failed to see the Stoic wellsprings, failed to see that the wiseman Folly ridicules was only a ploy – a ploy set in place by a person who, at the time, was far and away the world's greatest expert on Stoicism.

The question remains, however: Why does the author conceal the Stoic sources and larger Stoic outlook that governs the work? Note first that Stoic-framed thinking was second nature, indelibly imprinted – in resolving his early existential sufferings – on his view of himself, life, and Christianity. Over many years he had worked out complex issues in Stoicism, made revisions, and applied the resulting product to Christianity. In *De taedio Iesu* he had demonstrated in detail that the Stoic wiseman is in actuality subject to irrevocable natural instincts, including emotion – and that, notwithstanding, this does nothing to the wiseman's unitary *honestum/indifferens* frame of mind. His *Enchiridion* works out over and over, in real-world situations, the workings in Christian terms of this unitary both/and way of thinking – the thinking More was to develop in *honestum/utile* terms, modelling *De officiis*, in his

123 In a long (1515) letter to Martin Dorp in defence of *The Praise of Folly*, Erasmus states that his aim was the same as that in the *Enchiridion* and other writings (*Ep.* 337. Allen 2, 93/86–92, CWE 71, 9), but readers, then as now, have not believed him. Goldhill, for example, thinks Erasmus was speaking "disingenuously" (*Who Needs Greek?* 51).

translations and introduction to Lucian. In short, Erasmus may have conceived the work as he thought of More while travelling by horseback over the Alps from Italy to London, but it was built on concepts that had long formed the very matrix of his mind. Explaining any of this background would have defeated his purposes.

As for Folly's humorous ridiculing of the Stoic wiseman, Cicero himself had provided a model.[124] As shown earlier (168–9), his *Paradoxa Stoicorum* (46 BCE) is a short parody of the wiseman, as is his witty description of the outlook of the Stoic Cato in his legal defence of Lucius Murena (63 BCE). The wiseman presented in *Paradoxa Stoicorum* has nothing in common with the assumptions and practices of ordinary folk. Only the wiseman is noble, good, happy, virtuous, rich – lacking even a penny, subject to no authority, unconquerable, immune to emotion. Contemptuous of what goes on in the world of affairs, the wiseman considers everyone else foolish and insane, not free but slaves, and sees all sins as equal. Printed in 1465, along with *De officiis*, *Paradoxa Stoicorum* went through more editions before 1500 than even *De officiis*. Virtually all fourteenth- and fifteenth-century humanists subscribed to the view of the Stoic wiseman represented in *Paradoxa Stoicorum*.[125] Lacking understanding and interest in the serious works on Stoicism, which Erasmus had so deeply absorbed, contemporary humanists and others could take note of, ridicule, and feel superior to the message of *Paradoxa Stoicorum*. Folly plays on this.

How little fun would *The Praise of Folly* have been had Erasmus determined to expound Stoicism philosophically! And who would have understood, or even listened? Like the *Enchiridion*, *The Praise of Folly* was written for laymen and literate persons. Many humanists and educated persons would have well understood Folly's criticism of the Stoic wiseman, but not one would have grasped the larger, both/and mental stance of that wiseman; not one would have seen or appreciated Stoic thought on human nature. Nor did contemporary scholastic philosophers and theologians have any serious interest in or knowledge of Stoicism. Not least, referrals to the true nature of Stoicism would have distracted readers from the Christian message. In the interest of holding the audience, the author limits even the depth to which the work goes into his Stoic/Christian outlook. The both/and frame is developed, but not the steps to spirituality so carefully worked out in the

124 Bietenholz is not alone in believing that Folly's criticism of the Stoic wiseman is Epicurean. See his *Encounters with a Radical Erasmus*, 140.

125 See Dealy, *Stoic Origins*, Part I.

Enchiridion. As a rhetorician, and a rhetorician of unequalled abilities, Erasmus had well considered his purposes. Folly is the consummate rhetorician, supremely able "to teach, to delight, and to move [docere, delectare, movere]," as Cicero might word it, the intended audience.[126] But this rhetoric is not – any more than in Cicero's books on philosophy – freestanding. Rather than overtly work out the basis of his thought, Erasmus plays on people's imaginations, questioning their opinions, pulling them towards larger conceptions, showing them that truth is not just about rigid abstractions but derives from human nature as well and is unitarily both/and.[127] Along the way he describes multitudes of false values, abstract as well as worldly – and celebrates More's personality and the Stoic/Christian, unitary both/and, conversion of late 1504 that had allowed this personality to emerge.

126 *Brutus* 185. Alternately worded, the goal of the orator is "to prove, to please and to sway or persuade [probare, delectare, flecte e]" (*Or.* 69, cf. *De or.* 2.115). At the beginning of *De officiis* Cicero refers to his ability as an orator "to speak with propriety, clearness, and elegance [proprium, apte, distincte, ornate dicere]" in expounding philosophy (1.2).

127 During Erasmus' lifetime there were thirty-six Latin editions as well as translations into French, German, and Czech. An English translation appeared in 1549.

PART VI

Utopian Philosophy, 1516: Epicureanism within a Stoic *Honestum* / *Utile* Frame

There is a pattern of thought in the Utopian discussion of pleasure philosophy in Book II, and this pattern equates, exactly, with that found in More's *Lucian*, Erasmus' description of More's personality, and *The Praise of Folly*. As in each of these cases, the philosophy section is initially framed by two seemingly opposite types of value, Stoic *honestum* and Epicurean *voluptas*, the one unbending the other bending, the one abstract the other worldly. Here too the author's goal is to show – logically and systematically – how two contrary types of value actually require each other. Although readers have always imagined that the author is forcing together what can't be forced together,[1] in that the ancients had shown over and over that *honestum* and *voluptas* are

1 Illustrating Thomas More's alleged "two minds," Logan holds that even Utopian discussions of moral philosophy, "the cornerstone of the Utopian edifice," eflect conflicting goals and "dubious a guments." See his introduction to the Cambridge *Utopia*, xxxii, xxxiii; 2016 edition, xxix; and *The Meaning of More's "Utopia,"* 219. According to Wegemer, More "cleverly dramatized," in seeking the "dialectical engagement" of his readers, a reconciliation of the two opposite philosophies. See *Young Thomas More*, 28n27. Recently Wegemer has argued that, like many ancient writers, More saw the need for virtue, not pleasure, and that his discussion of pleasure is filled with twists and turns, Lucianic i ony, humour, exaggerations, and contradictions, reflecting Mo e's desire "to encourage reflection and stud ." See "Thomas More's 'Rule' of Pleasure before, after, and in *Utopia*." In his summary and assessment of the literature on *Utopia*, Grace plays on Epicurean thought on pleasure while taking no notice of relationships to Stoicism. See "*Utopia*." Employing his literature-inspired "New Historicism" or "Cultural Poetics" approach, Greenblatt assumes that *Utopia* is all about Epicureanism and that the discordant theses therein show that More wanted "to turn Epicureanism from the philosophy of a privileged few to the principle of a just society." See "Utopian Pleasure," 317; also his *The Swerve*, 227–33.

incompatible, More shows what the ancients were never able to show, that *honestum* and *voluptas* actually require each other. Deeply knowledgeable of the intricacies of Epicurean and Stoic thought, he works out unitary both/and solutions with all determination and care, in situation after situation – building from a frame of thought that is fundamentally Stoic. Just as in his *Lucian* and *The Praise of Folly*, there are both valid and invalid renderings of abstract truth and there are both valid and invalid renderings of worldly truth. Valid abstract truth and valid worldly truths are never such considered by themselves.

Opening up Thomas More's mind and his astonishing intellectual ability requires a meticulous working out of the text. What will be shown is that there is a very carefully developed and logical rationale behind every statement made in the philosophy section. At no time does the author vacillate between incompatible ideas. At no time does he simply contrive or fabricate a solution. At no time is the basis of his thinking rhetorical. He systematically develops, with all cogency and rigour, a particular way of thinking.

1 Moral Philosophy

Embedded between accounts of Utopian enthusiasm for literature, their utter lack of interest in scholastic-type thinking, their experiential frame of mind (Cambridge edition 154/27–158/8),[2] and accounts of Utopian devotion to study, their desire to master Greek learning, their interest in printing and the books Hythloday left with them (180/1–184/7), is found the rather lengthy (158/9–178/18) discussion of Utopian philosophy. The discussion begins as follows. (Here and throughout Part VI the numbering is mine.)

> (1) In matters of moral philosophy, they carry on the same arguments as we do. They inquire into the goods of the mind and goods of the body and external goods. They ask whether the name of "good" can be applied to all three, or whether it refers only to goods of the mind. (2) They discuss virtue and pleasure, but their chief concern is what to think of human happiness, and whether it consists of one thing or of more. (3) In this matter they seem to lean more than they should to the school that espouses

2 In Parts VI and VIII, I use the Cambridge edition unless otherwise noted. In Part VII, I use the Yale edition unless otherwise noted.

pleasure as the object by which to define either the whole or the chief part of human happiness.[3] (159)

(1) The moral philosophy debates carried on by the Utopians are like the debates carried on by Renaissance humanists, debates that focus in particular on Cicero's discussions of the ancient philosophies. The Stoics had contended that the name of "good" applies only to goods of the mind, that *honestum* "can justly be commended in and for itself, apart from any profit or reward" (*Fin.* 2.45). The Peripatetics held, in contrast, that there are bodily and external goods as well as mental, although mental goods are incomparably the highest. Carneades (d. 129 BCE) and later Antiochus (d. 69 BCE) had argued that the debate was in fact over mere words, not reality, that what the Peripatetics regarded as goods the Stoics considered advantages (*commoda*) (*Tusc.* 5.119–20, *Fin.* 5.73–4).

(2) All the ancient philosophies – whether Platonist, Aristotelian, Epicurean, or Stoic – were eudaemonist, so the Utopian focus is in this regard just a continuation. Whether happiness consists of one thing or more relates directly to conceptions of the good. In holding that virtue (*honestum*) is the only good, Stoics contended that the wiseman is always and invariably happy no matter what bodily or external vicissitudes befall him. Pain and death are not evils (*Fin.* 3.26–9). Peripatetics and others, such as Antiochus, denied this. They held that the things Stoics called "preferable" and Peripatetics called "goods" made a person happier (*Fin.* 5.88) – and, this being the case, happiness is not one thing.

(3) What is problematic, lacking further explanation, is the assertion that the Utopians "seem to lean more than they should" on that school of philosophy (Epicureanism) that contends that all or most happiness is found in pleasure (as distinct from the Stoic belief that all happiness is found in virtue).

3 "In ea philosophiae parte qua de moribus agitur eadem illis disputantur quae nobis. De bonis animi quaerunt et corporis et externis, tum utrum boni nomen omnibus his an solis animi dotibus conveniat. De virtute disserunt ac voluptate, sed omnium prima est ac princeps controversia quanam in re, una pluribusve, sitam hominis felicitatem putent. At hac in re propensiores aequo videntur in factionem voluptatis assertricem ut qua vel totam vel potissimam felicitatis humanae partem definiant" (158/9–16). I have used the Yale translation of point (3) because the Cambridge incorrectly indicates that the Utopians rather than the Epicureans "conclude" that all or most happiness is found in pleasure.

(a) Hythloday is the narrator, and yet he is described in Book I as a rigid idealist, a person clearly uninterested in pleasure philosophy.

(b) On the other hand, the author would have known from Martin Waldseemüller's 1504 account that Vespucci in his voyages to the New World saw Indian life as "entirely given over to pleasure" and considered Indians "Epicureans."[4] Hythloday allegedly accompanied Vespucci on the last three of his four voyages (45).

(c) How did the Utopians envision pleasure? Renaissance humanists had only gradually come to appreciate the true meaning of Epicurean pleasure philosophy, what Epicurus meant in seeing pleasure as the highest good and pain the highest evil. Epicurus "rejects pleasures to secure other greater pleasures, or else he endures pains to avoid worse pains" (*Fin.* 1.33). "So when we say that pleasure is the goal we do not mean the pleasure of the profligate or the pleasures of consumption ... but rather the lack of pain in the body and disturbance in the soul. For it is not drinking bouts and continuous partying and enjoying boys and women, or consuming fish and the other dainties of an extravagant table, which produce the pleasant life, but sober calculation which searches out the reasons for every choice and avoidance and drives out the opinions which are the source of the greatest turmoil for men's souls" (DL 10.131–2). All this Epicurus contrasts with Stoics, persons who "stroll about prating meaninglessly about the good"[5] – a point of view worked out by the humanist Lorenzo Valla many years before the Utopians in his *On Pleasure*.[6]

(d) The Utopian focus on pleasure is unusual, but does this mean that the Stoic emphasis on virtue has been entirely rejected? Is happiness found in pleasure philosophy alone?

(e) The "seem to lean more than they should" on pleasure appears to be said facetiously.[7]

(f) Considering ancient views, wouldn't Utopian adherence to pleasure philosophy necessarily entail the rejection of Stoic virtue?

---

4 See Waldseemüller, *Quattuor navigationes*, 97.

5 Quoted by Plutarch, *A Pleasant Life*, in *Moralia* 14.1091B. Plutarch considers Epicurus' philosophy a joke in that "he does away with providence but says he has left us with piety." See *Against Colotes*, in *Moralia* 14.1111B.

6 See Valla's *De voluptate* (1431–49), in later editions titled *De vero falsoque bono*. *De vero falsoque bono* has been translated as *On Pleasure/De voluptate*.

7 Seeing nothing of either Epicureanism or Stoicism and believing that the Utopians are governed by "reason alone," Skinner ("Thomas More's *Utopia* and the Virtue of True Nobility") sees "too much inclined" to pleasure as referring to the fact that the Utopians lack Christian revelation. See Part I above, 16n56.

Or was the author unconcerned about logic? Hardly anyone in the ancient world had thought it possible to combine these two philosophies. Cicero notes that Calliphon (third century BCE) in some obscure way saw a combination of *honestas* and *voluptas* and that some say Carneades defended this view, but Cicero concludes, in line with Chrysippus, that since the essence of morality is scorn of pleasure and since virtue links humans with god, combining morality and pleasure would be like combining a human with a beast. Such a combination is inconceivable, a contradiction in terms (*Luc.* 138–9).[8] Seneca sees the matter similarly. Epicurus' claim that what makes one happy is not virtue itself but the pleasure that results from virtue is absurd (*Ep.* 85.18); the honourable – one with god – can have nothing to do with that not honourable (*Vit. Beat.* 15.1–7). Even Antiochus rejects the Epicurean view (*Fin.* 5.21–2).

2 Stoic Corrections of Epicureans: Religious Absolutes

The actual place of pleasure philosophy within Utopian thought is not what the ancients or previous humanists would have expected – and not what modern readers have seen. Stoicism, the traditional enemy of pleasure, is present and given critical prominence. The focus, that is to say, is on Stoic as well as Epicurean thought. More than this, Stoicism corrects Epicureanism. Nor is Stoicism confused with Epicureanism. There is no hesitating or vacillating back and forth. Stoic rigidity and harshness, whatever its shortcomings, is greatly admired and found indispensable. Epicureanism, we are shown, must learn to trust in and make use of the absolutes, or type of absolutes, set forth by Stoics. There is a logic to the author's reasoning. He does not force together – rhetorically – two contradictory theses.

While some of the Utopian philosophical absolutes are directly religious, others, discussed in chapter 3 below, involve belief and adherence to moral precepts. Not of little significance, it will be found, the Utopians apply their absolutes not just to philosophical issues but to all the situations and institutions found in Utopia – whether political, social, or economic. Unseen by previous researchers, these absolutes are part and parcel of everything the Utopians

8 Cf. *Fin.* 2.36–8, *Off.* 3.119.

find admirable and indispensable in their own society – and lacking in other societies.[9]

Consider, for a beginning, the following.

A Serious and Strict Religion

> And what is more surprising, they seek support for this comfortable [Epicurean-based] opinion from their religion, which is serious and strict, indeed almost stern and forbidding. (159–61)

> Et quo magis mireris, ab religione quoque (quae gravis et severa est fereque tristis et rigida) petunt tamen sententiae tam delicatae patrocinium. (158/16–160/2)

While their pleasure thinking is "delicata," a soft doctrine, their religion in great contrast is serious and strict, almost harsh and rigid: "gravis et severa," even "tristis et rigida." The strictness and hardness clearly refer to Stoicism and, most especially, the outlook of the Stoic wiseman. Stoics had always been looked at in this way. Frequently the same words had been used, as where Cicero describes Marcus Cato as stern and severe, "gravitas" and "severitas" (*Mur.* 66). A page later in *Utopia* the second phrase is repeated: Stoics are "tristis ac rigidus" (162/19). Much later, criticizing the care of fools, reference is made to persons (Stoics) who are solemn and severe, "severus ac tristis" (192/29) – one word is found in the first phrase above, the other in the second

But what in actuality is the relationship between pleasure philosophy and religion? Scholars have repeatedly held that the Utopians have reason but lack religion, at least true religion,[10] but is this the case? In the

9 Missing the importance for the Utopians of religious and moral absolutes, Skinner holds that for the Utopians "nothing about religion is certain and everything ought to be tolerated." See "Thomas More's *Utopia* and the Virtue of True Nobility," 237.

10 See Surtz, Yale *Utopia*, 463. With regard to the above passage, Surtz allows that "The religion here meant is not natural – that is, such knowledge of God's existence and nature as can be gained by reason – but supernatural – that is, truths about the Creator involving some kind of divine revelation" (443 on Y160/24). And yet, seeing nothing of Stoicism, he concludes that "there is no clue as to how or when or through whom the divine revelation has been made. The qualities which More uses to describe the Utopian religion may be those which he would like to see, in some measure, in a simplified, pur fied, and eformed Catholicism." A page later, recognizing Epicurean belief in the indiffe ence of the gods, Surtz sees Platonic agreement with the Utopian referral to religious principles and happiness (444 on Y160/29; C158/16–159/6, 159–61). This outlook, with its failure to recognize Stoicism, is supported by the editors of the Cambridge *Utopia*, as at 161n62 (2016 edition 69n69).

present context we see that reason, Epicurean-based reason, requires the support of unbending religious doctrines. Although it appears that these two types of truth are utterly diffe ent, one soft and the other hard, one a worldly philosophy and the other an abstract religion, somehow the reason found in (Epicurean) philosophy requires religious absolutes that are not derived from this (Epicurean) way of reasoning. Why should this be the case? Why is it that the Utopians don't find religion in Epicurean philosophy alone, unencumbered by the hard principles related to an alien philosophy, i.e., Stoicism? The humanist Lorenzo Valla saw religion and even Christianity in Epicurean terms – and from this standpoint systematically criticized Stoic harshness.[11] Why don't the Utopians follow this path? The sentences which immediately follow help clarify their thinking.

Happiness Has an Absolute Side

> For they never discuss happiness without joining to the rational arguments of philosophy certain principles drawn from religion. Without these religious principles, they think that reason by itself is weak and defective in its efforts to investigate t ue happiness. (161)[12]

Thought about happiness requires two types of value: (1) philosophical reasoning that is built from the Epicurean methodology and (2) religious principles that are in their strictness, rigidity, absoluteness, and nature related to Stoic *honestum* (one with nature, abstract reason, God). Clearly, the Utopians are here somehow combining Epicurean and Stoic philosophies. For Epicurus, happiness results from finding those solutions to life that in the long run eliminate the most physical and mental pain. Pleasure is the only good and pain is the only evil. The Stoic conception of virtue plays no role in these calculations.[13] Stoics, in contrast, see happiness as residing in virtue alone. The wiseman is always happy because no matter what befalls him in life, even torture on the rack, his virtue remains intact. The Utopians support pleasure philosophy but believe that it is weak and defective unless it recognizes that highest

---

11 See 212n6 above.

12 "Neque enim de felicitate disceptant umquam quin principia quaedam ex religione deprompta cum philosophia quae rationibus utitur coniungant, sine quibus ad verae felicitatis investigationem mancam atque imbecillam per se rationem putant" (160/2–6).

13 In his *The Praise of Pleasure*, Surtz holds that for the Utopians "virtue is subordinate to pleasure" (19) – an often repreated view.

pleasure – highest happiness – is non-existent lacking Stoic-type religious principles. The Utopians don't just hold to religious principles, they make them, as noted in a marginal (the marginals have been attributed to Peter Giles or Erasmus), "principles of philosophy" – that is, principles inseparable from the pleasure philosophy way of reasoning. Pleasure philosophers must recognize that highest happiness requires a faith in something that is outside the realm of worldly pleasure/pain reasoning. Otherwise said, Epicurean *voluptas* is "weak and defective" lacking Stoic *honestum*. Happiness requires not just pleasure philosophy reasoning but Stoic-type absolutes.

But why are the Utopians so determined to show that happiness requires both religion and reason, and that the two be joined? Aren't they contradicting themselves?[14] What is the source of this outlook? What can be seen is that those scholars who have contrasted "pagan" Utopian reason with religion and faith are certainly far from the mark. Happiness requires hard Stoic-type religious principles.

Actually, hardness as such is nothing new in *Utopia*. Hythloday, the reporter of Utopia, is shown in Book I to be hard and severe in that he lives as he pleases ("nunca sic vivo ut volo," 50/28), unconcerned about family or friends, uninvolved in the messiness of worldly affairs (*otium* not *negotium*, 52/17).[15] So too, it appears, is the common-life foundation of Utopian society a hard and unbending principle (247). But again, how does this hardness tie in with pleasure philosophy, a philosophy that is not hard but eminently bendable? Is the contention that happiness comprises two seemingly opposed concepts simply a rhetorical construct – at odds with all logic?

Immortality of the Soul and Divine Providence: Versus Epicurus

Hythloday continues as follows:

> (1) The religious principles they invoke are of this nature: that the soul is immortal, and by God's beneficence born for happiness; and that after this life, rewards are appointed for our virtues and good deeds, punishments

14 Wegemer holds that the above quote shows that even the Utopians recognize that combining pleasure and virtue is "philosophically untenable." See *Thomas More on Statesmanship*, 144.

15 Cf. the one-dimensional wisemen described in *Paradoxa Stoicorum*, who defines freedom as "the power to live as you will [potestas vivendi ut velis]" (5.33). In *De officiis*, however, Cicero contrasts those philosophers who live "just as they please," divorced from politics, with the two-dimensional mindset statecraft requires (1.70, 72, cf. 1.19).

for our sins.[16] (2) Though these are indeed religious principles, they think that reason leads us to believe and accept them. (161)[17]

The first thing to notice is that belief in the immortality of the soul and in divine providence, including the dispensing of rewards and punishments, is entirely opposed to Epicurean pleasure philosophy. Epicurus had wanted to rid humans of all such concerns or anxieties. The gods exist, but they are unconcerned with humans and human affairs, and the soul perishes with the body. These doctrines were not mere add-ons but fundamental to the attainment of pleasure and happiness. In his *Principal Doctrines*, which More could have read in Diogenes Laertius' *Lives of the Philosophers*, Epicurus states that "Death is nothing to us; for the body, when it has been resolved into its elements, has no feeling and that which has no feeling is nothing to us."[18] Lucretius' book-length poem, *On the Nature of Things* (*De rerum natura*) (Poggio Bracciolini had discovered a manuscript in 1418), graphically describes the Epicurean outlook. Early man, filled with anxiety and fear, not understanding the causes of thunder, lightning, astrological phenomena, and the like, attributed everything to the gods. In fact, however, the gods are far removed from our senses, the standard of all truth, and thus have nothing in common with us. The world – look at all its faults – could not possibly have been made for man. Why, moreover, would immortal and blessed beings want to do things for humans? It is the movement of atoms which explains what we see and who we essentially are.[19]

In the ancient world, Stoic views on immortality of the soul and, especially, providence were continually contrasted with the Epicurean outlook. This contrast is made to stand out in many of Cicero's philosophical works – works Thomas More was certainly acquainted with. *De officiis* notes that Stoics, in contrast to Epicureans, believe God is continually directing his world (*Off.* 3.102).[20] Plutarch states that the Stoics "make no end of fuss crying woe and shame upon Epicurus for violating

16 Cf. C218/13–16, 222/27–224/6, 238/33–4.

17 "Ea principia sunt huiusmodi: animam esse immortalem ac dei beneficentia ad felicitatem natam; virtutibus ac benefactis nostris praemia post hanc vitam, flagitiis destinata supplicia. Haec tametsi religionis sint, ratione tamen censent ad ea credenda et concedenda perduci" (160/7–11).

18 DL 10.139–54 at 139; cf. *Fin.* 1.40–1.

19 Lucretius, *De rerum natura* 5.1161–1226, 5.146–99.

20 According to Chrysippus, Zeus directs everything, and humans must conform to his will (DL 7.87–9). Plutarch states that Chrysippus would discuss no ethical issue without first eferring to Zeus, Destiny, Providence, and the single power that holds the universe together (*SR* 1035B–C).

the preconception of the gods because he does away with providence, for they say that God is preconceived and conceived to be not only immortal and blessed but also humane and protective and beneficent" (*CN* 1075).[21] In Cicero's *The Nature of the Gods*, the Stoic Balbus affirm that from the beginning all the parts of the universe were ordered by the providence of the gods, and this ordering continues, extending to each of us – though not to the smallest matters (*ND* 2.75, 164, 167). The universe is by no means the outcome of the random movement of atoms (*ND* 2.115). The Epicurean Velleius complains against Balbus that the Stoics have "implanted in our heads the notion of an eternal lord whom we are to fear day and night; for who would not stand in awe of a god who is a prying busybody, who foresees and reflects upon and observes all things, believing that everything is his business?" (*ND* 1.54).[22] Although much Stoic thought seems to have concluded that souls survive as part of the world-soul a long time after death, but not for ever (*Tusc.* 1.77), emerging in Cicero's time was the notion that individuals could obtain immortality on the basis of patriotic achievements (*ND* 1.39, 2.62). Building on this theme, Cicero declares in the *Dream of Scipio* that the souls of illustrious and righteous persons pass at death directly to heaven (*Rep.* 6.106).[23]

Clearly, the Utopian religious principles have nothing to do with Epicureanism and everything to do with Stoicism. But how closely do these principles align, other than background, with later fifteenth- and early sixteenth-century preoccupations with immortality and providence?[24] A marginal to the above quote of the Utopians reads as follows: "The immortality of the soul, about which nowadays no small number even of Christians have their doubts" (161). Averroists had long denied the soul's immortality, and nominalists, such as Gabriel Biel (d. 1495), held that the immortality of the soul could not be philosophically established. By far the most original and controversial contemporary denier was Pietro Pomponazzi, a humanistically trained Aristotelian. Pomponazzi argued at length and with acuity, culminating in *On the Immortality of the Soul* (1516), that the soul's immortality could not be proven

21 Cf. Seneca's criticism of Epicurus, *Ben.* 4.19.

22 "Nothing disquieted Epicurus more profoundly than the notion that supernatural beings control phenomena or that they can affect human affairs" (LS 41). This n - withstanding that Epicureans, like Stoics, believed "that there are gods, because we have implanted, or rather innate, conceptions of them. For what all men by nature agree about must necessarily be true" (*ND* 1.44). Cf. *Tusc.* 1.30, *Leg.* 1.24.

23 In this regard Cicero ties together the deaths of Cato and Socrates (*Tusc.* 1.74).

24 On these preoccupations see Kristeller, *Renaissance Thought and Its Sources*, 181–96 and Blum, "The Immortality of the Soul."

by philosophy because the concept was based not on the principles of nature but on divine creation of the soul. Only faith and revelation could uphold the soul's immortality. In opposition to such views, Cajetan, Master General of the Dominicans from 1508 to 1518, contended along with Albertists and other Thomists that philosophical arguments could clearly establish the soul's immortality. The humanist Marsilio Ficino argued for the soul's immortality from a radically diffe ent, Neoplatonist, standpoint in his massive *Platonic Theology: On the Immortality of Souls* (1476).[25] Concerned about the problem, those attending the Lateran Council of 1513 made immortality of the soul officia church doctrine.

Although Utopian thinking ties with those who argued for the immortality of the soul, Utopian reasoning has a diffe ent foundation. Note first that the Utopians are not in any obvious way taking into consideration Aristotelian- or Platonist-based views. Most importantly, consider the actual meaning of (2) above: "Though these [immortality of the soul and divine providence] are indeed religious principles, they think that reason leads us to believe and accept them." We need to remember here that, for the Utopians, reason is "weak and defective" (above, 215) without the religious principles (i.e., principles accepted on faith). Stated otherwise, reason is strong and viable only when religious principles, principles not based on reason, are an inseparable part of reason. It follows that the reason referred to in (2) is a reason *already* reformed and inseparable from absolutes such as belief in providence and the immortality of the soul. Since Utopian religious principles are *preconditions* of true reason, only when the principles are in place can reason determine the believability of the principles. In short, it is only *after* the Utopians have tied the religious absolutes with reason that they can prove by reason the truth of these absolutes.

In Stoicism, we may note, a strict and severe adherence to religious principles is found in reason. In his *Hymn to Zeus*, Cleanthes holds that Zeus "directs the universal reason running through all things" (LS 326). Chrysippus "says that divine power resides in reason, and in the soul and mind of the universe" (*ND* 1.39). "Right reason" "pervades all things, and is identical with this Zeus, lord and ruler of all that is" (DL 7.88). "This perfect reason is called virtue and is identical to rectitude [*honestum*]" (Sen. *Ep*. 76.10, LS 395).[26]

25 See especially the thirteenth and fourteenth books of Ficino's *Platonic Theology*.

26 "And the virtue of the happy man and his good flow of l fe are just this: always doing everything on the basis of the concordance of each man's guardian spirit with the will of the administrator of the whole ..." (DL 7.88, trans. LS 395).

Scholars have long held, building on R.W. Chambers' classic 1935 biography,[27] that the Utopians have only reason to guide them and that the author's purpose was only to show what pagans without (supernatural) revelation could accomplish – as compared with the shortcomings of Christian Europe. In his monumental and vastly influential notes to the Yale edition, Edward Surtz contends, seeing Utopian reason in terms of Thomas Aquinas' thinking, that "Utopia represents the highest form of commonwealth that can be created by the reason of the philosopher" and "The diffe ence between a religion revealed by God [i.e., Christianity] and a hedonistic philosophy reached by reason [reason that may even posit the existence and nature of God] is the diffe ence between holiness and human prudence" (Y463, cf. 538).[28] The Utopians were not holy? In direct contradiction of Surtz, Hythloday considers Utopian institutions not just extremely prudent but extremely holy, "prudentissima atque sanctissima" (C100/23–4). The problem here may be two diffe ent definitions of "holy." Utopian religious principles may not be well described as "revealed," but what in fact was their standing in Utopian thought? Were they simply the outcome of a linear employment of reason, "human prudence"? In fact, as has been shown, their religious principles were not built from reason. They preceded reason.[29]

Not seen by readers has been the role of Stoicism in Utopia and therewith the fact that the "religious principles" referred to are Stoic-based. These principles do not relate to Aquinas or Cajetan, much less the Neoplatonism of Ficino.[30] Here and throughout the discussion of Utopian philosophy, these Stoic religious principles and the reasoning tied

27 Chambers, *Thomas More*, 128, 227.

28 Surtz is commenting on Y179/12–15 (C178/11–13), but even here the contrast is not between reason and the holy. The question is only whether something can be found "more holy [sanctius]" than Utopian virtue/pleasure philosophy. Marius believes, like Surtz, that Utopian naturalism contrasts entirely with the "supernaturalism that Thomas More upheld all his life and died to vindicate" (*Thomas More*, 173).

29 In fact Surtz himself shows, in commenting earlier on their religious principles, that the Utopian view was "supernatural," although he has no idea where this could have come from other than Catholicism. The Cambridge editors have a very similar outlook. See above, 214n10.

30 Baker-Smith believes the Utopians were reflecting in their view of the soul Ficino's Neoplatonist argument that "The whole effort of our soul is to become God." See *More's Utopia*, 173. Nor does Plato's depiction in *Phaedo* of a soul in the prison house of the body (82E; cf. Cicero on *Phaedo*, *Tusc*. 1.24f, 58, 75, 118) in any way resonate with the Utopian view. Scholars have so easily looked for and found connections with Plato because they assume that the Utopian state was somehow mimicking Plato's *Republic* and because Hythloday is, avowedly, a Platonist.

therewith top the reasoning found in Epicurean pleasure philosophy. What will be shown below is that everything the Utopians say in their discussion of pleasure philosophy represents religion and, if you will, "holiness" to the highest degree. In line with their philosophy, we will find that Utopian practices and institutions all depend on these abstract and absolute principles. Belief in immortality and divine rewards and punishments are in fact only examples ("Ea principia sunt huiusmodi") of this importation of religious principles into reason. Other examples include, we will find, "no advantages at the expense of others," "utter loathing of war," "no private property," and "no exchange of money."

And yet, it will be shown below, the religious principles found in Utopian reason make up only one aspect of this reason. As in Stoicism, reason is unitarily *honestum/utile*. The Utopians are as prudent as they are holy and as holy as they are prudent. The author makes a point of inserting pleasure into philosophy, but he is at pains to show that the reason found in bending Epicurean-type pleasure calculations (the *utile*) is inseparable from the reason found in unbending Stoic-type truths (the *honestum*). However indispensable, the role of pleasure calculations is limited. Compare the author's treatment of Lucian in late 1505 and early 1506. He recognized that Lucian did not believe in immortality or even abstract truth, but he greatly admired Lucian's ridiculing of "superstition," which he interpreted as "deceit," and used Lucian's outlook to set forth a Stoic-based *honestum/utile* understanding of Christianity.

Lacking Absolutes, the Lesbian (or Lydian) Rule

A fundamental reason why the Utopians are so certain that reason is "weak and defective" without absolutes and why true reason "leads us to believe and accept" religious principles (and other absolutes) is that by themselves Epicurean-type pleasure calculations inevitably lead, the Utopians argue, to evil – which they demonstrate over and over.

> And they add unhesitatingly that if these [religious] beliefs were rejected, no one would be so stupid as not to feel that he should seek pleasure, regardless of right and wrong. His only care would be to keep a lesser pleasure [voluptas] from standing in the way of a greater one, and to avoid pleasures that are inevitably followed by pain. (161)[31]

31 "quibus e medio sublatis sine ulla cunctatione pronuntiant neminem esse tam stupidum qui non sentiat petendam sibi per fas ac nefas voluptatem. Hoc tantum caveret ne minor voluptas obstet maiori, aut eam persequatur quam invicem retaliet dolor" (160/11–13).

The Epicurean claim that pleasure (in the highest meaning of the term) left to its own devices would result in moral behaviour is entirely wrong. It is not true that what is truly virtuous can be learned from the Epicurean pleasure calculus. It is not true that conscience and fear of being caught are sufficien to curtail injustice in that bad conscience and fear are not pleasurable (DL 10.131–2). To someone lacking belief in the soul's immortality and rewards and punishments in heaven, considerations of right or wrong make no sense. Acting righteously (if anything like this could even be imagined) would be just plain "stupid." A choice has to be made: either abstract principles or evil. In this context also, faith must come *before* the pleasure principle is put into effect and must be part and parcel of the pleasure principle.

Discussing "the good hope of immortality" in Book 1 of *Tusculan Disputations*, Cicero states: "Take this feeling away and who would be such a madman as to pass his life continually in toil and peril?" (1.33). In *The Nature of the Gods*, a debate between an Epicurean, a Stoic, and an Academic, Cicero ends the work by declaring that he thinks the Stoic came nearest the truth. Even near the beginning he makes his sentiments clear: Morality would seem to require religion. If worship of the gods is mere pretence, there can be no virtue, and "all sense of the holy and of religious obligation is also lost. Once these disappear, our lives become fraught with disturbance and great chaos. If reverence for the gods is removed trust and the social bond between men and the uniquely pre-eminent virtue of justice will disappear" (*ND* 1.3–4).[32] This is a theme that the Stoic emphasizes, against the Epicurean, in the second book (*ND* 2.153). It is a perennial Stoic theme.[33]

In Book I the idealist Hythloday is determined to show that in fact "More's" decorous approach – pleasure philosophy is a type of decorum (Parts VII and VIII below work this out) – is or leads to nothing but evil. Approaching the end of Book I, Hythloday contends as follows:

> Most of his [Christ's] teachings are far more alien from the common customs of mankind than my discourse was. But preachers, like the crafty fellows they are, have found that people would rather not change their lives to fit Christ's rule [normam], and so, following your ["More's"] advice, I suppose, they have adjusted his teaching to the way people live, as if it were a leaden yardstick [plumbeam regulam]. (99)

---

32 Cf. Seneca: "What diffe ence is there between denying the gods and dishonoring them?" (*Ep.* 123.15).

33 Cf. Epictetus, *Disc.* 2, ch. 20: "Against Epicurus and Academics."

According to Hythloday, that is, "More's" decorous reasoning, his "indirect" approach, leads to nothing but the bending of Christ's precepts to make them fit, ever so conveniently, the way people actually live – rather than how they should live. However ignored, Christ's teachings constitute an absolute standard that should be held to "everywhere," but "More's" "indirect approach" would "dissemble" these teachings. Seeing nothing viable in worldly "prudence," Hythloday accepts only two possible positions: either common opinion – which he interprets as equivalent to the (evil) leaden yardstick – or unbending truth.

Historically, the leaden rule (*plumbeam regulam*) referred to was a fle - ible mason's rule used on the island of Lesbos and in Lydia that could be bent to fit the irregular curves of a moulding. Erasmus gives a precise definition of the "leaden ule" in his adage *Lesbia regula*:

> [We speak of the Lesbian rule] when things are done the wrong way round, when theory is accommodated to fact and not fact to theory, when law is suited to conduct, not conduct corrected by law ... Aristotle mentions this adage in his *Ethics*, book 5: "For the rule of what is indefinite is also indefinite, like the leaden rule used in Lesbian architecture; the rule changes to fit the shape of the stone and does not emain a rule."[34]

Of course Erasmus places this criticism within a Christian context. Humans do not admit, much less hold to, nature or Christ's precepts, simple and understandable by all, because all their thoughts and actions are governed – as in the world observed by Hythloday – by the Lesbian rule. As stated, for example, in his *Paraclesis* (1516): "We drag heavenly doctrines down to the level of our own life as if it were a Lydian [or Lesbian] rule."[35] Even in his early work, *Enchiridion militis christiani* (1503), the presence of the Lesbian rule is very evident. "Would it not be preposterous to try to fit the rule to the stone rather than the stone to the rule? Would it not be even more absurd if instead of trying to adapt men's morals to Christ one should adapt Christ to men's lives?"[36] Nothing of Erasmus' social thinking can be understood lacking constant attention to the view of human psychology and human behaviour represented by the Lesbian rule – whether the phrase is used or

34 *Adagia* I v 93, ASD II-1, 563, CWE 31, 465. The referral is to *Nicomachean Ethics* 5.10.7, 1137b.

35 *Paraclesis* LB 5.141E, trans. Olin in *Christian Humanism and the Reformation*, 100.

36 *Enchiridion* H 91.1–2, CWE 66, 86.

not. As his dialogue *Julius Excluded from Heaven* (1514) puts it: Because Christ's teachings are not easy and thus "seem intolerable to those who are not guided by the spirit of Christ, they take refuge in empty words and vain ritual, and they invent a false body of Christ to go with the false head of Christ."[37] All so conveniently, and perversely "natural," humans perfectly calibrate their thinking and acts in terms of this Lesbian rule. As he shows over and over in his books on war, so-called Christians everywhere invent rationalizations to cover non-Christian and non-natural desires and actions.[38]

In their pleasure philosophy, as throughout Book II, the Utopians show how – at odds with Hythloday's criticism of "More" in Book I – the Lesbian rule is overcome. There are two types of decorum. Abstract beliefs and principles are in no instance separate from truly decorous (and pleasurable) worldly practices.[39]

A Reformulation of Both Epicureanism and Stoicism

The Utopians eliminate the Lesbian rule by carefully redesigning not only Epicurean pleasure philosophy but Stoicism as well. Consider what immediately follows the above (221) "regardless of right or wrong" statement:

> They think you would have to be actually crazy to pursue harsh and painful virtue, give up the pleasures [suavitatem] of life, and suffer pain from which you can expect no advantage [fructum]. For if there is no reward after death, you have no compensation for having passed your entire existence without pleasure [insuaviter], that is, miserably. (163)[40]

37 *Opuscula*, 120.1114–16, CWE 27, 194.

38 Cf. *Dulce bellum inexpertis*, ASD II-7, 32/601–2, CWE 35, 423.

39 Not seeing the Utopian two-dimensional mindset – much less the side of Cicero's thought that is made up of hard religious principles and his belief that society becomes totally disordered without such – Wegemer believes the Utopians contradict themselves and are cruel in holding (*Utopia* 161, above, and *Utopia* 223–5) "that 'reason' [pleasure philosophy] is insufficient to guide a fe to virtue, peace, and happiness." See *Young Thomas More*, 153.

40 "Nam virtutem asperam ac difficilem sequi ac non abig e modo suavitatem vitae sed dolorem etiam sponte perpeti cuius nullum exspectes fructum (quis enim potest esse fructus si post mortem nihil assequeris quum hanc vitam totam insuaviter, hoc est misere, traduxeris?), id vero dementissimum ferunt" (160/14–162/5).

Lacking belief in immortality and rewards and punishments in heaven, as do Epicureans, one would be "crazy" not to pursue rational self-interest even if evil (as Cicero holds, above, 222), and the Stoic wiseman would be "crazy," lacking belief in immortality and rewards and punishments in heaven, to insist on hard and painful virtue rather than pleasure. There has to be an otherworldly "advantage" to hard virtue, or worldly pleasure should be the goal. Since pleasure in the afterlife is incomparably advantageous ("unending joy," 167), suffering in this world on behalf of Christian principles, where needed, has its place. The marginal quite precisely sums up the meaning: "Not every pleasure is desirable, neither is pain to be sought, except for the sake of [Christian] virtue [Ut non quaevis expetenda voluptas, ita nec dolor adfectandus nisi virtutis causa]."

Epicurean pleasure philosophy strays in that there is no way to distinguish right from wrong, and Stoicism strays in holding to a virtue that is unable to truly appreciate or experience the pleasures of life and in lacking a firm belief in a Christian (as distinct from Stoic) hereafter and the incomparable pleasure this will bring. Epicurean pleasure philosophy corrected and Stoic philosophy corrected coalesce – as do worldly advantage and heavenly advantage. It is "crazy" to talk about pleasure calculations without absolutes, and it is "crazy" to talk about Stoic hardness without pleasure calculations. Virtue is not one-dimensional but two-dimensional, unitarily both/and.

What needs to be seen is that the author was very consciously reworking the content and dynamic relationship between the two sides of the Stoic unitary both/and frame of thought. Cicero in *De officiis* had transferred the Stoic wiseman's *katorthoma/kathekon* mindset to the everyday world and had judged worldly things – following the Stoic Panaetius – not in terms of "things indiffe ent" and how this indifference should be dealt with but in terms of the *utile*, diffe entiating expedient actions from inexpedient in terms of whether or not *honestum* is present.[41] Although Stoics had given increasing attention to the second side of the *honestum/indifferens* both/and, Cicero's focus on the *utile* makes the second side even more prominent. Thomas More goes much further in making pleasure a central feature of that which is *utile* or advantageous. *Honestum* is not, by itself, the sole good. That which is "good" comprises a dynamic relationship between *honestum*

41 On employment of the term *utile* in Stoicism and especially Panaetius' usage, see above, 10n24.

and pleasure (*voluptas*). Happiness is not found in *honestum* alone but in the inseparable combination of *honestum* and pleasure, a combining in which the scope of each has been limited. Utopian moral philosophy is no more about pleasure than *honestum* and no more about *honestum* than pleasure. While the Stoics had held unbendingly to *honestum* while at the same time – and by the very definition of *honestum* – deciding between *indifferentia*, the Utopians make unbending *honestum* and bending pleasure equal in stature. Although the Stoics developed elaborate rules for dealing with worldly events, they always held that *honestum* is the only good. With the Utopians this is no longer the case. While Peripatetics had in ancient times argued that *honestum* is only the highest good, not the only good, and that bodily and external goods add to the highest good, the Utopians see the good as comprising at one and the same time both pleasure calculations and the *honestum*. Pleasure is not simply a low-level good outside of the good that is *honestum*, comparing to Peripatetic bodily and external goods. Pleasure calculations and the *honestum* form an integral whole in which the scope of each has been limited. The good has two distinct but inseparable sides. In short, *honestum* is no longer something that has an all-inclusive status. It is part of a new entity. The *utile* (and the pleasure found therein) has now become an inherent part of "the good."

In thinking about the source of More's interest in making pleasure an inherent aspect of the *utile* our mind goes back to Erasmus' youthful fi -ation, in dealing with his inability to conquer certain bodily and mental proclivities, on Stoic ineradicable natural instincts (*oikeiosis*). Erasmus' writings led More, I have shown (above, Part II), to see his problems with sex and worldly involvements in a related manner. More's deep interest in pleasure philosophy appears to be a conscious response to what he sees as an instinctual trait in himself. Not of little relevance here is Erasmus' depiction of More's personality in his introduction to *The Praise of Folly* (above, Part IV):

(a) Contrasting, in effect, with the rigidity and moroseness of Stoics we are here shown a convivial More – built from instinct, it may seem.

(b) Contrasting, in effect, with the pliable pleasure philosophy of the Epicureans, we are shown a More who is abstract and unbendingly hard.

(c) More unites in his personality and outlook, Erasmus shows, two seemingly contradictory standpoints. And yet they are not contradictory once one grasps the Stoic-based unitary both/and frame of More's mind – brilliantly worked out by Erasmus in the body of *The Praise of Folly*.

Clearly, More works out this same outlook in his discussions of Utopian philosophy.

3 Stoic Corrections of Epicureans: Moral Absolutes

Honestum, as glimpsed above, is a *sine qua non* of pleasure. Just as the Utopians make a point of the fact that they never discuss pleasure without joining to it certain hard religious principles, so too they never discuss pleasure without joining to that discussion certain hard moral principles – Stoic-type moral principles. Actually, moral principles and religious principles are for the Utopians simply diffe ent aspects of the same thing, *honestum*. Moral principles are every bit as absolute as religious principles. As with the Stoics, *honestum* is about the workings of God, virtue, nature, and reason. Throughout, the Utopians set forth the moral principles that at all times correct Epicurean pleasure calculations.

Can Pleasure Be "Honest"?

In the margin directly across from the sentence where we are first told that the Utopians favour pleasure philosophy is found a strange statement:

> The Utopians consider honest pleasure the measure of happiness. (159)

> Utopiani felicitatem honesta voluptate metiuntur. (158/14–16)

Does this referral to "honest pleasure" have a serious meaning? Or is this an example of the easy-going rhetorical blending of thoughts that many have found in the book? Note first the word "honest" (*honesta*). This is not an Epicurean word but a word at the heart – as the author well understood – of everything Stoicism stands for. The Stoic wiseman, unbending and the embodiment of perfection, is a person who lives by the *honestum*.[42] Virtue, including the four cardinal virtues (prudence, justice, temperance, and fortitude), is inherent to *honestum*, as is reason itself. "Haec ratio perfecta virtus vocatur eademque honestum est" (*Ep*. 76.10). It is this same reason and this same virtue that God himself uses (*ND* 2.30f).[43]

42 Dyck points out that, prior to the arrival of Stoicism, the ideals *honestum/honestas/honestus* were "rarely used and of vague significance in the Roman political voca - ulary." See *A Commentary on Cicero, De Officiis*, 31.

43 Cf. *ND* 2.79, 3.38; *Leg*. 1.25.

Although the marginals are considered the work of Giles or Erasmus, the marginal referred to is no fluke. The text backs up and expands it very shortly thereafter, following the discussion of the religious principles always present in Utopian philosophy:

> To be sure, they think happiness is found, not in every kind of pleasure, but only in good and honest pleasure. (163)

> Nunc vero non in omni voluptate felicitatem sed in bona atque honesta sitam putant. (162/6–7)

How should this passage be interpreted? Most scholars have simply passed over it. Edward Surtz comments but sees it primarily in non-philosophic terms: the Utopians want pleasure to be good and decent and not the contrary. If there is a subtle connection with Stoicism, this connection, he believes, is benign in that the Stoic Seneca sometimes (in early letters) had nice things to say about Epicureanism.[44] A deliberate, consistent, and logical tying together of contradictory philosophies is not imagined or considered – much less that the thinking represented was long standing and deeply engrained in the author's psyche.[45]

If above it was shown that happiness requires religious principles as well as pleasure philosophy reasoning, now it is shown that happiness also requires Stoic moral philosophy as well as pleasure philosophy. Happiness consists not just of pleasure but of *bona atque honesta* pleasure. While in Epicureanism pleasure is the highest good (*Fin.* 1.29) and in Stoicism *honestum* is the only good, with the Utopians the two types of good are combined. "Honesta" holds here a position very comparable to the religious principles. Pleasure is not true or viable pleasure unless it comprises at the same time the *honestum*.[46]

Note the assertion that happiness is found "not in every kind of pleasure." Epicurus did not seek licentiousness or luxury or any other

---

44 Yale *Utopia*, 446.

45 McCutcheon argues that the discussion of "good and honest pleasure" is a rhetorical paradox. See "More's *Utopia* and Cicero's *Paradoxa Stoicorum*," esp. 14–19. Prévost sees the union of Stoic virtue and Epicurean pleasure as an eclectic synthesis of "pleasure and virtuous action" that had much to do in its framing with theses in Aristotle's *Nicomachean Ethics*. See *L'Utopie de Thomas More*, 684–8.

46 In *De vita beata* Seneca allows pleasure with the proviso, argued at some length, that virtue go first and bear the standa d. "We shall have pleasure but we shall be the master and control her. At times we shall yield to her entreaty, never to her constraint" (*Vit. beat.* 14.1). Thomas More may have been building on Seneca's argument.

type of debauchery but, rather, the pleasure that results from the removal of pain. He and his adherents searched for pleasures that, all things considered and in the long run, are most pleasurable and pains that, all things considered and in the long run, are the least pain. But the Utopians give "not in every kind of pleasure" a second and higher, absolutist, meaning, a meaning never given by Epicureans. And the Utopians consistently tie this second meaning to the first[47] Acceptance of Stoic *honestum* is a requirement of true pleasure and the happiness found therewith. In recognizing the existence and necessity of Stoic *honestum*, the Utopians obviously reject the Epicurean view of pleasure. Pleasure philosophy by itself is not sufficient What is required is *honesta voluptas*. The *honesta* referred to by the Utopians signifies a nonfle - ible absolute that pleasure must conform to. But what is going on here? Does this make any sense? Once again, is there any true rationale to their way of viewing things? On what grounds can the Utopians accept *honestum* and yet not reject, as did Stoics, Epicureanism?

In Epicureanism it is pleasure that governs virtue and not the other way around: *Honestum* did not determine or modify pleasure. To the contrary, virtue had meaning only in terms of *voluptas*. Pleasure determined the value of virtue. *Voluptas* is utilitarian while Stoic *honestum* is abstract and rigid. Seeing these polarities and understanding that Stoic *honestum* had no need of pleasure, Epicureans even made fun of Stoic *honestum* (*Fin*. 1.61) – as does in their wake Lorenzo Valla.[48] Yes, the Epicureans talked about virtue, but the virtues were not chosen for their own sakes, in total contrast to Stoic virtues, but for the purpose of pleasure.[49] It was only in this context that Epicureans considered a life of pleasure a life of virtue (*Fin*. 1.57). Pleasure determined what was virtuous and what wasn't, not abstract reason. As Epicurus explicitly states, the virtues are merely "natural adjuncts" of the pleasant life (DL 10.132). Virtue has no independent role. Plutarch quotes Epicurus as follows: "I summon you to constant pleasures, and not to [Stoic-type] virtues, which provide [only] empty, pointless, and disturbing expectations of rewards."[50] Athenaeus, the Christian father, quotes Epicurus as saying: "One must honor the noble, and the virtues and things like that, *if* they produce pleasure. But if they do not, one must bid them goodbye." "I spit upon the honorable and on those who vainly admire

---

47 Cf. 160/11–14, 166/4–7, 176/33–5.

48 See 212n6 above.

49 DL 10.138; *Fin*. 1.42, 47–54. The Cambridge editors believe this is the Utopian view (167n68; 2016 edition, 72n76).

50 *Reply to Colotes*, *Moralia* 14.1117A *The Epicurus Reader*, 78.

it, whenever it produces no pleasure."[51] In *De finibus*, the Epicurean Torquatus shows that the greatest heroes of history held to "honour" because doing so gave them all sorts of self-interested advantages (1.35), a theme that was to be built on by Valla (*On Pleasure*, 2.3.3).[52]

All of which was of course anathema to everything Stoicism stood for. The Stoic Cleanthes imagined in derision a painting where pleasure is the queen and the virtues are her slaves (*Fin.* 2.69). For Stoics the virtues are not adjuncts of anything. Pleasure is irrelevant to the achievement of virtue (*Tusc.* 3.41–2). The standard of judgment cannot be placed, Cicero contends, entirely in the senses (*Luc.* 142). Man is made for higher ends than pleasure (*Fin.* 2.111). The highest good is the soul, not the body (*Fin.* 3.50). As regards pleasure versus *honestum*, Chrysippus didn't have to do much cogitating. The idea that virtue can be driven by pleasure is nothing but a sham, something worthy of the mob: all human fellowship depends on disinterested virtue. (*Luc.* 140, *Off.* 1.105–6).

Importantly, the word *honestum* or its cognates are used on quite a few occasions, and significant occasions, in *Utopia*. In no instance does the usage reflect the Epicurean way of talking about pleasure.[53] Take, for example, where in Book I "More" advises Hythloday, with his generous and truly philosophic spirit ("animo tuo tam generoso, tam vere philosopho") to look out for the public interest even at the cost of personal advantage by persuading the king to follow just and noble courses ("recta atque honesta") (52/5, 9). Or where Hythloday imagines, against this advice, the little or negative effect he would have were he to advise the king that certain actions were dishonourable ("inhonesta") (90/17). In Book II, Utopian official can't be drawn from an honourable path ("ab honesto") (196/22–3). Since butchers (slaves) "kill animals only out of necessity," their work is more useful and honest ("utiliores et honestiores") than hunting per se, which the Utopians disallow (170/22–3). "Solemnly and seriously [serio ac severe]" a prospective wife is shown naked to the suitor by a "gravis et honesta matrona" (188/14–17). Care is taken to assign children "to a grave and honorable householder [ut gravi atque honesto patrifamilias mancipetur]"

51 Athenaeus (d. c. 230 CE), *Deipnosophists* 12, 546ef and 547a; *The Epicurus Reader*, 78 and 103.

52 Logan believes this is the Utopian view. See his introduction to the 2016 Cambridge *Utopia* (xxix–xxx) and, at length, his *The Meaning of More's Utopia*.

53 For all the locations of *honestum* or its cognates in *Utopia*, see Bolchazy, ed., *A Concordance to the Utopia of St. Thomas More and A Frequency Word List*, 120, 140.

(124/27). No one dines at home willingly, even though not forbidden, since this is not considered honourable ("honestum") (140/14). Under the eyes of all, the Utopians work at their trades or take leisure that is "non inhonesti" (144/28). Belief in the presence of their forefathers keeps them from carrying out any secret dishonourable deed ("ab inhonesto secreto") (226/22). The elders introduce proper subjects of conversation, "honestos sermones" (143/21). Let wool working be restored, Hythloday exclaims, as an honest trade, "honestum negotium" (67/8–9). Comparable to Stoics of old, the Utopians don't hold life so dear as not to give it up when honour ("honestas") requires it (213/17).

In line with the *voluptas/honestum* both/and described above, the final paragraph of the philosophy section does not refer to pleasure alone but also to virtue, and not just to virtue alone but to "virtue and pleasure." Summarizing what has preceded, Hythloday states the following:

> This is the way they think about virtue and pleasure [virtute ac voluptate]. Human reason, they think, can attain to no truer conclusions than these, unless a revelation from heaven should inspire men with holier notions. (179, 178/11–13)

Both the Senses and *Recta Ratio*

So, again, if the Utopians have a deep understanding and appreciation of Stoic hardness, how is it that they can unite this hardness with pleasure philosophy? A little beyond the "good and honest pleasure" statement (163), "our senses," as discussed by Epicureans, and "right reason" are explicitly tied together:

> (1) By pleasure they understand every state or movement of body or mind in which we find delight according to the behests of nature. (2) They are right in including man's natural inclinations. By following the senses as well as right reason [recta ratio] we may discover what is pleasant by nature: (3) it is a delight that does not injure others, (4) does not preclude a greater pleasure, (5) and is not followed by pain. (167)[54]

54 "Voluptatem appellant omnem corporis animive motum statumque in quo versari natura duce delectet. Appetitionem naturae non temere addunt. Nam ut quicquid natura iucundum est, ad quod neque per iniuriam tenditur nec iucundius aliud amittitur nec labor succedit, non sensus modo sed recta quoque ratio persequitur" (166/8–12). The translation is dependent on the Yale edition (167/7–14) as well as the Cambridge.

(1) Although the referral to "body and mind" may seem unclear in that Epicureans focused (according to Stoics) on the senses, the referral to nature fits with Epicureans – as it does in diffe ent ways with Stoicism. In his *Principal Doctrines* Epicurus states: "If you do not on every separate occasion refer each of your actions to the end prescribed by nature, but instead of this in the act of choice or avoidance swerve aside to some other end, your acts will not be consistent with your theories" (DL 10.148).

(2) In their own ways both Epicureans and Stoics talk about natural inclinations. But what is emphatically not Epicurean is the referral to right reason (*recta ratio*). The assertion that what is pleasant by nature is discovered by following "the senses as well as right reason" explicitly ties together Stoicism and Epicureanism. What can be seen here is another and even more definitive way of referring to "good and honest pleasure." Pleasure is found not in following the senses alone but in at one and the same time following *recta ratio*.[55] Pleasure can be found only where *recta ratio* and natural inclinations of the senses are seen as one thing. The senses and right reason are the tools, working together, by which what is pleasant by nature can be discovered. Pleasure is both/and for the *Utopians* in that true pleasure is made to depend on hard and unbending truths, *recta ratio*. *Recta ratio* is both/and in that it does not reject but wholeheartedly accepts pleasure calculations.

Significantl , particular activities or things that are pleasant by nature have to be "discovered." In each case analysis is required, employing *voluptas/recta ratio* calculations.

(3) Although particulars have to be worked out, "pleasant by nature" is, for one thing, something that "does not injure others" – a Stoic theme song.[56] While the Utopians see "pleasant by nature" as a "delight [iucundum]" that does not injure others, Stoics had insisted over and over on "advantage [commoda]" that does not injure others (see below, 253–4). The word "delight [iucundum]" replaces the Stoic word "advantage [commodum]." In short, the author sees pleasure as simply

55 Seneca advises in a late letter following "a straight course and attain[ing] a goal where the words pleasant and honorable have the same meaning!" "The pleasures take one down hill, but one must work upwards toward that which is rough and hard to climb [i.e., *honestum*]" (*Ep.* 123.12, 14). Could these statements have infl enced More?

56 Logan cannot understand "how they conclude that true pleasure must satisfy this condition ['does not injure others']" and states in a note that many of the diffic ties in this section are brought about by "the contamination" of Utopian Epicureanism by Stoicism (*The Meaning of More's Utopia*, 155). His attempt, over and over, to relate the Utopian view to Valla's pleasure philosophy is untenable.

another and more important type of advantage. While the Epicureans show that it is self-interest that keeps one's personal pleasure from injuring others, the Utopians hold that it is only the *recta ratio* side of their pleasure philosophy that makes it possible not to injure others.[57]

(4 and 5) These statements express the essence of the Epicurean method, but even here the Stoic-based Utopian modification is firmly in place. That which "does not preclude a greater pleasure and is not followed by pain" can be discovered only by reasoning based on the combining of the senses and right reason. Elsewhere, the author doubles down on the inherency of *honestum* to Utopian pleasure/pain calculations. Near the end of the philosophy discussion, for example, the following statements are made:

> (a) But in all these pleasures, they observe this rule, that the lesser shall not interfere with the greater, (b) and that no pleasure shall carry pain with it as a consequence. (c) If a pleasure is dishonorable [inhonesta], they think it will inevitably lead to pain. (177, 176/33–5)

While points (a) and (b) follow very closely Epicurus' definition of pleasure,[58] point [c] has no place in that definition. The Stoics would not have agreed with points [a] and [b] and the Epicureans would not have agreed with point [c]. The *honestum* is not produced by pleasure thinking, but pleasure thinking cannot be valid or productive without it. A pleasure that is not *honestum* is not a true or acceptable pleasure in that it inevitably leads to pain. Just as the *utile* is not such separate from *honestum* so too is pleasure (now an aspect of *utile*) not a pleasure separate from *honestum*.

(5) tells us that the task of the pleasure calculus/*honestum* both/and is to discover things that are "not followed by pain," and yet, we discover, pain may be required in holding to *honestum*. Consider the marginal across from the "good and honest pleasure" statement (163).

> Not every pleasure is desirable, neither is pain to be sought, except for the sake of virtue. (Marg. 163)

> Ut non quaevis expetenda voluptas, ita nec dolor adfectandus nisi virtutis causa. (Marg. 162)

---

57 Compare Seneca: "Self-command is the greatest command of all. Let her teach me what a hallowed thing is the justice which ever regards another's good and seeks nothing for itself except its own employment" (*Ep.* 113.31).

58 Cf. *Fin.* 1.33, *Tusc.* 5.95, DL 10.129.

Honestum (and its virtue), we remember, is an absolute and not arrived at by employing pleasure calculations. Pleasure calculations bend in terms of *honestum*, but *honestum*, as such, does not bend in terms of pleasure calculations – notwithstanding that pleasure calculations (the *utile*) and *honestum* at all times require each other. And yet the pain (and not the pleasure) sometimes necessitated by holding to *honestum* still has, we can see, a pleasure philosophy goal – unsurpassed pleasure in the hereafter (even here bound up, it would seem, with *honestum*). This is clearly the meaning where the Utopians conclude, "after carefully considering and weighing the matter, that all our actions, including even the virtues exercised within them, look toward pleasure as their happiness and final goal" (167) [59]

Pleasures against Nature

Not pleasant by nature, and thus not true pleasure, are things that injure others, preclude greater pleasure, and are followed by pain. Like true pleasures, false external pleasures (167–73) are discovered by following both the senses and right reason.[60]

Note first Epicurus' teaching that false pleasures are found where individuals – against nature – are not frugal, are not self-sufficient and are governed by vain and unnecessary desires.

> And we believe that self-sufficienc is a great good, not in order that we might make do with few things under all circumstances, but so that if we do not have a lot we can make do with few, being genuinely convinced that those who least need extravagance enjoy it most; and that everything natural is easy to obtain and whatever is groundless is hard to obtain; and that simple flavors provide a pleasure equal to that of an extravagant life-style when all pain from want is removed. And barley cakes and water provide the highest pleasure when someone in want takes them. (DL 10.130–1, trans. *Epicurus Reader*, 30)
>
> By the neither natural nor necessary he means desires for crowns and the erection of statues in one's honor. (DL 10.149)

59 Not grasping the Utopian unitary both/and way of thinking, the editors of the Cambridge *Utopia* (167n68; 2016, 72n76) state that the passage quoted represents Epicurus' contention that "we choose the virtues too on account of pleasure and not for their own sake" (DL 10.138). As shown above, in so many contexts, for the Utopians pleasure is not such unless virtues are choosen for their own sake.

60 I am preparing a separate publication on the bodily and mental pleasures (as distinct from external pleasures) discussed at 173–85. See the summary below, 267–8.

Not of little importance, both Cicero and Seneca greatly admired Epicurus' teachings on living simply and in accord with nature. "No one," states Cicero, "has said more about plain living than Epicurus" (*Tusc.* 5.89). He praises Epicurus' teaching that "nature herself teaches us daily how few, how small her needs are, how cheaply satisfied" (*Tusc.* 5.103). Against the cost and splendour of banquets, for example, Epicurus points to the value of simple living and the joy found in simple foods and appetite rather than repletion (*Tusc.* 5.97–101). What can't be repeated too often, states Seneca, is Epicurus' belief that "Real wealth is poverty adjusted to the law of nature" (*Ep.* 27.9, 4.10). And he applauds Epicurus for striving to live according to nature rather than opinion and for stating that "He who needs riches least, enjoys riches most" (*Ep.* 16.7, 14.17).

But what neither Cicero nor Seneca allows is the overall context in which Epicurus placed these teachings. In his conception of pleasure, states Cicero, "Epicurus has severed the highest good from virtue" (*Tusc.* 3.47). As Seneca words it, "Those who rate pleasure as the supreme ideal hold that the good is a matter of the senses; but we Stoics maintain that it is a matter of the understanding, and we assign it to the mind" (*Ep.* 124.2). Nothing is *bonum* unless it is *honestum* (*Ep.* 120.3).

Here as elsewhere the Utopians are determined to show that pleasure philosophy and Stoicism do not necessarily contradict each other. They show that Stoic-type unbending truths are in fact inherent to pleasure and that false pleasures arise not only from what pleasure calculations demonstrate but also from not seeing that these calculations must at all times include unbending truths. False pleasures are such because they do not reflect eality, the oneness of the senses and "right reason."

> A person's taste [iudicium] may be depraved by disease or by custom, but that doesn't change the nature of pleasure or of anything else. (173)
>
> All pleasures which are against nature, and which men agree to call "delightful" only by the emptiest of fictions (as if one could change the real nature of things just by changing their names), do not, they have decided, really make for happiness; in fact, they say such pleasures often preclude happiness. And the reason is that once they have taken over someone's mind, they leave no room for true and genuine delights, and they completely fill the mind with a false notion of pleasu e. For there are a great many things which have no genuine sweetness in them but are for the most part actually bitter – yet which, through the perverse enticement of evil desires, are not only considered very great pleasures but are even included among the primary reasons for living. (167)

False pleasures reflect, that is, the diffe ence between appearance and reality, word and thing, deceit and truth.[61] Owing to the "perverse habits" of mortals (173), false pleasures are so common outside Utopia that true pleasures are hardly glimpsed.

Examples of false pleasure (167–71) are found – building on fifteenth-century humanist outlooks[62] – with those who flatter themselves regarding their nobility and ancestry and demand that others give them special respect and admire the fine clothes they wear. In fact they are not better than other people but worse, and they perform useless functions. Even the clothes they pride themselves on are less useful than the coarse thread found in the clothes of ordinary persons. They are enthralled by jewels and gemstones, the silliest pleasures of all ("stultissima voluptas") (168/13 marg.), and take great pains to find those that are genuine, but "why should a counterfeit give any less pleasure, if, when you look at it, your eyes cannot distinguish it from a genuine gem?" (169).[63] Nor can there be true pleasure in uselessly piling up money.[64] The hunting and hawking of these great people – the howling of their dogs, the relishing of slaughter, the blindness to cruelty – are sick pleasures in the extreme. (The Utopians assign hunting to their butchers, whose work is "more useful and honest [utiliores et honestiores]" 170/22, since they kill only out of necessity.)

The arrival of the Anemolian ambassadors graphically and hilariously depicts, in the discussion of Utopian social life, what happened when the citizens of Utopia were on one occasion confronted with the false pleasures endemic in other societies. Bedecked in silk, gold, and gems, a hundred followers in their train, the ambassadors imagined that their appearance vied with the gods, but the reaction of the Utopians was not what they expected and "a sight to see."

---

61 Compare Seneca: "Evil things have sometimes offe ed the appearance of what is honorable, and that which is best has been manifested through its opposite" (*Ep.* 120.8). For Erasmus, the covering up of reality with fine wo ds is the fountainhead from which spring "practically all the world's evils." See *The Education of the Christian Prince* (1516), CWE 27, 259; ASD IV-1, 188.

62 See Rabil, ed. and trans., *Knowledge, Goodness, and Power.*

63 And we may remember (above, 179) that a person named after Folly – i.e., Thomas More, "a clever jokester" – gave his bride imitation gems, and she enjoyed them as much as if they were real (*The Praise of Folly*, 72).

64 Compare Seneca: Choose liberty and abandon slavery to gold and silver (*Ep.* 104.34; cf. 110.14–18). For Erasmus, true honour is not piling up wealth by fair means or foul but, as in Stoicism, "the spontaneous consequence of virtue and right action." See *The Education of the Christian Prince*, CWE 27, 213; ASD IV-1, 144.

> The onlookers considered this splendid pomp a mark of disgrace. They therefore bowed to all the humblest of the party as lords, and took the ambassadors, because of their golden chains, to be slaves, passing them by without any reverence at all. You might have seen children, who had themselves thrown away their pearls and gems, nudge their mothers when they saw the ambassadors' jeweled caps and say, "Look at that big lout, mother, who's still wearing pearls and jewels as if he were a little boy!" But the mother, in all seriousness, would say, "Quiet, son, I think he is one of the ambassadors' fools." (153)

In short, what matters is not what the mass of humans living outside Utopia think. What matters is reality, the nature of nature. Those things commonly taken for pleasure are perversions of nature. The mass of humans may feel happy, but in fact they are not. Their thinking (and behaviour) is not in accord with nature and, as such, cannot result in true happiness.

The Two-Dimensional Frame Is Stoic, Not Epicurean

Of great consequence, Epicureanism is one-dimensional while Stoicism, as Thomas More understood so well – evident in his *Lucian* and Erasmus' *Praise of Folly* – is two-dimensional. The Utopians do far more than simply show how Epicurean pleasure calculations and Stoic virtue coalesce. They are intent on developing the Stoic unitary *honestum/utile* way of thinking (224–7 above). They demonstrate throughout the philosophy section (and, we may discover, throughout Book II) that there are two types of value and that, once negative understandings of each have been discarded, they unite. What More does in the philosophy section is place Epicurean pleasure calculations on the *utile* side of the Stoic *honestum/utile* both/and. Although the *utile* side had been expanded in late classical times and Erasmus had leapt far beyond these earlier developments in placing emotion on the *utile* side – making emotion inhere in Stoic natural instinct (*oikeiosis*) rather than Stoic reason (*ratio*), and therewith a thing "indiffe ent" – More goes even further, in making pleasure a core aspect of the *utile*. Of course, building up the *utile* side often meant that something was being taken away from the *honestum* side. When Erasmus took emotion from the hard side and made it a thing indiffe ent ("exciting inclination and aversion," DL 7.104), he was taking away an element of the hard side – while not at all denying hardness itself. In excerpting from the hard side the denial that pleasure is a natural objective (DL 7.85–6, 93) and placing it on the bending side,

More was in like manner lessening the scope of the hard side (though not its hardness) while widening the scope of the bending side.

In short, what the Utopians do to the Epicurean way of thinking is far more radical than what they do to the Stoic frame of thought. They impose on Epicurean pleasure calculations a second type of value, while Stoicism already comprised two types of value. And while the unbending type of value imposed on Epicureanism was completely alien to what this philosophy had stood for and was closely modelled on Stoicism, there were, on the other hand, parallels between the bending side of the Stoic mindset and the Epicurean way of thinking. The Stoics distinguish on the bending side between preferred indiffe ents and dispreferred indiffe ents or, as in the more lay approach of *De officiis*, between things that are expedient and those that are not, and the Utopians simply incorporate into the expedient (or *utile*) side the Epicurean distinctions between that which is pleasurable and that which is not pleasurable – or less pleasurable. Pleasure calculations, properly carried out, are eminently expedient.

Consider in this context the *recta ratio* (right reason) to which the Utopians refer (167, above, 231–3). Thomas More well knew that *recta ratio* encompasses in classical Stoicism not just one type of value but two. As Stobaeus reports, "the doctrine that the wiseman does everything well is a consequence of his accomplishing everything in accordance with right reason and in accordance with virtue, which is expertise concerned with the whole of life" (LS 61G). That person (the Stoic wiseman) who carries out a right act (*katorthoma*) by that very fact carries out appropriate acts (*kathekonta*) (*Fin.* 3.59). Elsewhere we are told that Stoic "right reason" "pervades all things, and is identical with this Zeus, lord and ruler of all that is" and that Diogenes (d. c. 152 BCE) "expressly declares the end to be to act with good reason in the selection of what is natural" (DL 7.88).[65] More also knew that where Epicureans talk about the "senses" they are thinking in one-dimensional, worldly, terms. His Utopians, accordingly, place the "senses" (above, 231) on the bending side of the two-dimensional Stoic frame. Epicurean employment of reason in deciding between what gives the most pleasure and what the

65 Dyck notes, regarding *De legibus* 1.23, "the odd step of reasoning from *ratio* to *recta ratio* (the former applying to human beings generally, the latter to sages and gods)." "Where the function of law is to command *recte facere* (#19), law is defined as *recta ratio* (##23, 33, 41, 2.10), *recta* are correct responses to sensory inputs (#31), and the *rectum* is a synonym for the *honestum* (#37; 3.2)." See Dyck, *A Commentary on Cicero, De Legibus*, 125 and 154.

least can be compared to Stoic employment of reason in "the selection of what is natural" and in deciding between preferred indiffe ents and dispreferred indiffe ents – but there is nothing in the Epicurean way of thinking that can be compared with Stoic right actions (*katorthomata, recta facta*). There is all the diffe ence between an appropriate act (*kathekon*) and a right act (*katorthoma*). Deeply influenced by the Stoic frame of thought, the Utopians see in *recta ratio* no separation from valid worldly acts. To "discover" (167) that which is pleasant by nature, the Utopians believe we must hold rigidly to *recta ratio*. But differing from traditional Stoicism, where the wiseman makes choices among *indifferentia* as one aspect of his hold on *recta ratio*, with the Utopians (building on *De officiis*) *recta ratio* (or *honestum*) and *voluptas* (or *utile*) are at all times simply two inseparable and equally indispensable types of value.[66]

4 Stoic *Utile* Expanded

At one with Erasmus' unitarily two-dimensional depiction of Thomas More's personality, worked out – supported by Christ himself – by Folly in *The Praise of Folly*, the Utopians show that holding to unbending absolutes does not entail harshness towards others or even oneself. Stoics had applied rigidity too broadly. Although Stoic harshness had of course been criticized in ancient times – by Peripatetics, Academics, and Antiocheans in particular – the Utopians realign and move far beyond earlier discussions in placing pleasure (as does Folly)[67] on the expediency side of the Stoic wiseman's both/and outlook. One aspect of this was their insistence that the wiseman remove misery and install joy in those around him – and also in himself.

We Must Remove Misery and Install Joy

> (1) The most hard-faced [tristis ac rigidus] eulogist of virtue and the grimmest enemy of pleasure, while he invites you to toil and sleepless nights and mortification, (2) still admonishes you to relieve the poverty

66 More was likely also holding in mind the Stoic Seneca (c. 4 BCE–65 CE) who distinguishes in late letters between *decreta* – dogmas that are unchanging, absolute, and universal, requiring unflinching belief *Ep.* 95.10, 57) – and *praecepta*, which are rules of advice and exhortation (*Ep.* 94.1, 31). Neither *decreta* nor *praecepta* are functionally separable. *Decreta* require *praecepta* and *praecepta* require *decreta* (*Ep.* 94.48–50; 95.34, 41, 60). See above, 11 and n25.

67 Miller trans. 19, 55–6, 58.

> and distress of others as best you can. It is especially praiseworthy, they think, when we provide for the comfort and welfare of our fellow creatures. Nothing is more humane (and humanity is the virtue most proper to human beings) (3) than to relieve the misery of others, remove all sadness [tristitia] from their lives, and restore them to enjoyment [iucunditati], that is, pleasure [voluptati]. (163–4)[68]

Note the Stoic context. The Utopians recognize that Stoics, however sad and rigid, see the need to provide for the well-being of other humans (*Fin.* 3.62–71). But the Utopians are intent on taking this much further, not only removing misery from others but restoring them "to enjoyment, that is, pleasure."

(1) If in criticizing Epicureans we saw a very positive side to the Stoic mind, here we see emerging a negative aspect. Contemptuous of pleasure, the Stoic follows virtue wherever it leads and at whatever cost to the emotions. He is "tristis ac rigidus," sad, harsh, solemn, rigid, cold, stern. For him pain is not an evil. Happiness is found in virtue alone, irrespective of surroundings (*Fin.* 5.83). As *Tusculan Disputations* words it, Stoic virtue "keeps beneath its own level all the issues that can fall to man's lot, and looking down upon them despises the chances of mortal life, and free of all reproach thinks that nothing concerns it besides itself" (5.4).[69] And we may see here a correlation with the down side of Hythloday's character as portrayed in Book I of *Utopia*. Hythloday is proud of the fact that he lives as he pleases, without obligations to family or the powers that be (51) – comparable to the Cynic in More's *Lucian* and negative abstract folly in *The Praise of Folly*.[70] In Stoicism the unwise can comprehend many things, but only the wiseman *knows* anything (*Luc.* 144–5). Seeing only the *honestum* as good, Zeno claimed in a series of paradoxes that only the wiseman is a king or wealthy. All

---

68 "Neque enim quisquam umquam fuit tam tristis ac rigidus assecla virtutis et osor voluptatis qui ita labores, vigilias et squalores indicat tibi, ut non idem aliorum inopiam atque incommoda levare te pro tua virili iubeat, et id laudandum humanitatis nomine censeat hominem homini saluti ac solacio esse, si humanum est maxime (qua virtute nulla est homini magis propria) aliorum mitigare molestiam et, sublata tristitia, vitae iucunditati, hoc est voluptati, reddere" (162/18–164/1).

69 Cf. *Off.* 1.69–73. Exercising the divine element within themselves, devotees of learning, states Antiochus in *De finibus*, "are so far from making pleasure their aim, that they actually endure care, anxiety and loss of sleep" (5.57).

70 At odds with Hythloday, the Stoic wiseman is interested in increasing his resources "and acquiring advantages for one's self and one's family" *as well as* "rising superior to these very things" (*Off.* 1.17).

other humans are exiles, slaves, and madmen.[71] The wiseman is devoid even of the four primary passions – sorrow, fear, lust, and delight (*hedone*) – as these do not inhere in nature. Even the passions of pity and mercy do not move him.[72] Personal grief, as at the death of one's child or wife, must be borne with great moderation.[73]

(2) Remarkable is the fact that Thomas More not only deftly outlines the harshness that critics had so often lambasted but brings out another and more complicated aspect of the picture. The Stoic may hold rigidly to virtue, but that same virtue requires him to deal – per a series of rules – with other humans and the everyday world. Although modern scholars as well as ancient debate precisely how Stoics were able to get from their initial contention that the newborn has an instinct for self-preservation to the argument that this self-preservation instinct eventually leads to a concern for others and humanity at large,[74] this development was in fact a fundamental Stoic teaching. Cicero gives a rather lengthy discussion of Stoic *humanitas* in Book 3 of *De finibus*. The Stoic Cato here emphasizes that we are born for society and social intercourse (3.62–71).[75] The instinctual love of parents for their offspring and offspring for their parents (*oikeiosis*), common to all animals, has broad ramifications and effects. The feelings which humans have for other individuals, for society, for their state, for all mankind, and for the universe are rooted in this basic instinct. How can we expect the gods to cherish us if we don't cherish each other? We should try to benefit as many people as we can. Even the virtue of justice, giving to each his due, derives from this source (*Fin.* 5.65). Epictetus (c. 60–c. 120 CE) avers that Zeus "has so constituted the nature of the rational animal man, that he can attain nothing of his own proper goods unless he contributes something to the common interest" (*Disc.* 1.19.13).

(3) But whatever the correctness of Stoic ideology regarding humanity, how, the Utopians ask, can sad (in their view) and rigid Stoics

71 *Paradoxa Stoicorum, Fin.* 3.75–6, *Luc.* 136.

72 *Fin.* 3.35, *Ac.* 38, *Luc.* 135, *Mur.* 61. Cf. *The Praise of Folly* 45–6 (above, 168 and 181–2). Long and Sedley point out that hostile ancient sources focused on lack of pity, but "it should also be noted that the wise man could be sociable, generous, affectionate cheerful and gentle" (LS 420).

73 *Tusc.* 1.111, 3.77, 83 passim.

74 See Engberg-Pedersen, "Discovering the Good"; Striker, "Following Nature," 230; Gill, *The Structured Self in Hellenistic and Roman Thought*, 359–70; and Schofield, "Two Stoic Approaches to Justice."

75 Cf. *Off.* 1.149. Seneca's statement at *Ep.* 5.4 reminds us of Thomas More as a "man for all seasons": "the first thing which philosophy undertakes to give is fellow-fee - ing with all men; in other words, sympathy and sociability."

remove the sadness of others? How can the "grimmest enemy of pleasure" restore pleasure to others? Stoics need to expand their otherness concerns. Importantly, it is only at this point that pleasure philosophy is brought in. Pleasure philosophy here augments and goes beyond Stoic teaching, it does not replace it. The Utopians admonish Stoics not only to look out for the comfort and welfare of fellow humans, but to remove their misery and sadness and restore them to joy and pleasure. While the Stoics talk rather abstractly about humanity and focus on physical well-being, pleasure philosophy focuses on mental states and the need to provide humans with a feeling of joy and pleasure (happiness). As Seneca notes, Epicurus emphasized emotion and feeling and rebuked Stoics for holding to a supreme good that did not include these responses to life (*Ep.* 9.1). Epicurus could feel great joy and tenderness with friends and sought out the company of other humans. Epicurus even allowed women in his Garden. Because of these benevolent feelings, rather than abstract rules, he would never give up a friend.[76] He felt pity for others, such as servants.[77] He could grieve with others and for others. At the death of friends, Plutarch states, the Epicurean would weep copiously.[78] What needs to be noticed at this point is that even Cicero, ever the opponent of Epicurean theory and the person often impressed by the logic of the Stoic system, could severely criticize Stoics for the same shortcomings. In *How to Be a Friend* he contends that, lacking emotion, there is no diffe ence between a man and a beast or a stone (48).[79] "Nor are we to listen to those men [Stoics] who maintain that virtue is hard and unyielding and is, as it were, something made of iron; whereas, in many relations of life, and especially in friendship, it is so pliable and elastic that it expands, so to speak, with a friend's prosperity and contracts with his adversity" (48). And yet love and friendship spring from nature, not Epicurean pleasure and expediency (32, 51–2). Here again the Utopian advocating of Epicureanism must be seen not as a rejection of Stoicism but as an attempt to develop and expand the expediency side of Stoicism.

In fact, even Book I of *Utopia* shows us a great deal about the negatives (as well as positives) of Stoicism – without once mentioning or

76 *Fin.* 1.67, DL 10.117, 120. Although Aristotle's discussion of friendship is dispassionate and detailed, it focuses on friendship between equals and lacks the Epicurean (or even Stoic) concern with going out to others. See *Nichomachean Ethics* 9 (in *Complete Works*).

77 DL 10.118, 149, *Fin.* 1.70.

78 Plutarch, *A Pleasant Life*, in *Moralia* 1101A.

79 Cf., regarding friendship, Folly's criticism of abstract folly (*The Praise of Folly*, 32, 45–6).

even implying Epicurean pleasure philosophy. The context there was not moral philosophy as such but individual crimes and social dysfunctions. In approving and illustrating equity, Hythloday criticizes "the Stoic decree that all crimes are equal" (69).[80] This "Stoical decree" is another way of referring to the lawyer's "strict justice," a type of "justice" which not only is lacking in conceptual truth but is entirely inexpedient in that it cannot deal with type of offence and degree of offence. Utopian thinking opposed to this type of Stoic rigidity and in accord with Epicurean softness and feeling is exemplified in many other contexts, such as in the pity (going beyond even Epicureans here) that the Utopians feel for even the animal victims of hunting and butchering (171). But perhaps nothing in the volume better illustrates what Utopians find lacking in Stoic attitudes towards their fellow humans and what is right about Epicureanism than what they have to say about fools and how in actual practice (as not in mere words) they treat fools:

> They are very fond of fools, and think it contemptible to insult them. There is no prohibition against enjoying their foolishness, and they even regard this as beneficial to the fools. If anyone is so solemn and severe [severus ac tristis] that the foolish behavior and comic patter of a clown do not amuse him, they don't entrust him with the care of such a person, for fear that one who gets not only no use from a fool but not even any amusement – a fool's only gift – will not treat him kindly. (193)[81]

The Utopians enter into the fool's world – just as had Folly a few years before in *The Praise of Folly*. They thoroughly enjoy and appreciate the gifts of the fool. Their personal amusement and enjoyment benefit not only themselves but the fool. Stoics, on the other hand, *severus ac tristis*, are not only unable to benefit either themselves or the fool but may actually harm the fool. Their virtue comes at the expense of fools and lesser folks. The appreciation of fools – found in the courts of kings (and even in More's household)[82] – takes the Utopians a step beyond even

80 *Par.* 3, *Fin.* 4.21, 75–7, *Mur.* 61. See Annas on the larger Stoic meaning, below, Part VIII, 312n3.

81 "Moriones in deliciis habentur, quos ut adfecisse contumelia magno in probro est, ita voluptatem ab stultitia capere non vetant. Siquidem id morionibus ipsis maximo esse bono censent. Cuius qui tam severus ac tristis est ut nullum neque factum neque dictum rideat, ei tutandum non credunt, veriti ne non satis indulgenter curetur ab eo, cui non modo nulli usui sed ne oblectamento quidem (qua sola dote valet) futurus esset" (192/26–32).

82 Cambridge *Utopia*, 193n97. Fools were not found in ancient courts.

the purview of the Epicureans. The Utopians give joy and pleasure not merely to ordinary persons but even to the outcasts or odd members of society.

What stands out here is what Erasmus says about the second side of More's personality in his Introduction to *The Praise of Folly*. More could play the game of life with anyone and enjoy it. He was a "man for all seasons." *The Praise of Folly* shows that wise Folly and, most important of all, Christ himself could play to perfection this worldly "all seasons" role. And yet, as with the Utopians, there was a hard and unbending side to the mindset of Thomas More and Folly – and of course Christ.

We Must Ourselves Feel Joy and Pleasure

The Utopians agree with Epicureans in holding not only that we must lead others to joy and pleasure but that we ourselves must be joyous. In truth, the latter step must precede the former. We can do nothing truly helpful for others unless we ourselves have been reformed:

> Well, then, why [if nothing is more humane than to restore others to pleasure] doesn't nature equally invite all of us to do the same thing for ourselves? Either a joyful life (that is, one of pleasure) is a good thing, or it isn't. If it isn't, then you should not help anyone to it – indeed, you ought to take it away from everyone you can, as being harmful and deadly to them. But if you are allowed, indeed obliged, to help others to such a life, why not first of all yourself, to whom you owe no less favor than to anyone else? For when nature prompts you to be kind to your neighbors, she does not mean that you should be cruel and merciless to yourself. (165)[83]

Before advancing the pleasure of others, we must "first of all" see our own life in terms of pleasure. A sad (*tristis*) Stoic cannot remove the sadness (*tristitia*) of others. The "grimmest enemy of pleasure" cannot restore pleasure to others. Helping one's neighbours is not possible unless it comes about as a result of the search for personal pleasure. Pain,

---

83 "Quidni natura quemque instiget ut sibimet idem praestet? Nam aut mala est vita iucunda, id est voluptuaria, quod si est non solum neminem ad eam debes adiutare sed omnibus utpote noxiam ac mortiferam quantum potes adimere; aut si conciliare aliis eam ut bonam non licet modo sed etiam debes, cur non tibi in primis ipsi? cui non minus propitium esse te quam aliis decet. Neque enim quum te natura moneat uti in alios bonus sis, eadem te rursus iubet in temet saevum atque inclementem esse" (164/1–8).

unlike in Stoicism, is the great enemy. Searching for the least amount of pain and the greatest amount of pleasure for oneself will lead one to profit from the pleasure of others and to help others achieve greater pleasure.

Think here of More's life-altering January 1505 decision after seeing himself for years in extremely negative and harsh terms – far from joy. Think of his joy while working with Erasmus a few months later (above, 97–8). Think of the joy expressed in his work on *Lucian* (above Part III, Ch. 1). Think of Erasmus' description of More's personality in his introduction to *The Praise of Folly* as – on one side – joyful and willing to enter in and play the game of life with anyone (above Part IV). Think of the positive side of worldly folly in *The Praise of Folly* itself (above Part V).

Asceticism Is Crazy "Unless" ...

The penultimate paragraph of the philosophy section takes direct issue with the Stoic wiseman's harshness towards himself. And yet even here (cf. above, 233–4) the Utopians insist that pain *should* be sought if it is for the sake of virtue (*honestum*).

> (1) Moreover, they think it is crazy for a man to despise beauty of form, to impair his strength, to grind his agility down to torpor, to exhaust his body with fasts, to ruin his health and to scorn all other natural delights, (2) unless by so doing he can more zealously serve the welfare of others or the common good. (3) Then indeed he may expect a greater reward [voluptatem] from God. (4) But otherwise to inflict pain on oneself without doing anyone any good – simply to gain the empty and shadowy appearance of virtue, or to be able to bear with less distress adversities that may never come – this they consider to be absolutely crazy, (5) the token of a mind cruel to itself as well as most ungrateful to Nature – as if, to avoid being in her debt, it is rejecting all her gifts. (179)[84]

84 "At certe formae decus contemnere, vires deterere, agilitatem in pigritiam vertere, corpus exhaurire ieiuniis, sanitati iniuriam facere et cetera naturae blandimenta respuere, nisi quis haec sua commoda negligat dum aliorum publicave ardentius procurat, cuius laboris vice maiorem a deo voluptatem exspectet: alioquin ob inanem virtutis umbram nullius bono semet adflige e vel quo adversa ferre minus moleste possit, numquam fortasse ventura – hoc vero putant esse dementissimum, animique et in se crudelis et erga naturam ingratissimi, cui tamquam debere quicquam dedignetur, omnibus eius beneficiis enuntiat" (178/1–10).

(1) The Utopians admire bodily beauty, strength, agility, food, health, and other "natural delights" and reject, as such, harshness towards oneself that diminishes any of these natural delights. We remember here that Thomas More had himself scorned "natural delights" before late 1504 and his readings of Erasmus' writings.[85] And More was deeply cognizant of Erasmus' conviction that fasting was for him ruinous of health (and mind) and impossible to hold to. In developing their thinking here, the Utopians employ both Epicurean and Stoic thought.

Many sources see Epicurean pleasure calculations as beginning and ending with the senses. One ancient source quotes Epicurus as saying, in *On the Goal*, that "I at least do not even know what I should conceive the good to be, if I eliminate the pleasures of taste, and eliminate the pleasures of sex, and eliminate the pleasures of listening, and eliminate the pleasant motions caused in our vision by a visible form."[86] Elsewhere we read that Epicureans believed that the standard of value should not be birth or position or rank but beauty and age and figu e.[87] Categorizing things in terms of whether they are "natural and necessary" or "natural but not necessary" or "neither natural nor necessary," beauty, age, and figu e are said to be natural but not necessary.[88]

And yet on both sides of the statements above quoted we find ties to Stoicism. The Utopians cherish the beauty, strength, and agility which humans receive from nature – things "preferred" in Stoicism (*Fin.* 3.51).[89] They believe that nature made the pleasures of sound, sight, and smell the particular province of man (177).[90] Man's ability to

85 In line with the Utopian belief that scorning natural delights is "crazy" (above, 245), Epicurus had held that reason "forbids attention to vexations, withdraws the soul from morose reflections, blunts its keenness in dwelling upon w etchedness" (*Tusc.* 3.33).

86 Athenaeus, *Deipnosophists* 12, 546ef. See *The Epicurus Reader*, 78.

87 Note that the Utopians live temperately (comparing to Epicurus), and as a result, "Nowhere are people's bodies more vigorous or less susceptible to disease" (179).

88 *Tusc.* 5.94. Cf. *Principal Doctrines*, DL 10.149.

89 According to an Antiochean, by nature humans try to get rid of bodily defects and for the same reason see beauty, form, health, strength of body, and freedom from pain or weakness or disease as desirable for their own sakes and not just utility (*Fin.* 5.47). In this regard, we may note Renaissance focus on the human body, as evident for example in Michelangelo's statue of David, 1504.

90 Epicureans had discussed at some length the physics of such things as hearing, voice, smell, colour, vision, and taste – but not the relationships to pleasure. See DL 10.52–3, 68–9; Sextus Empiricus, *Against the Ethicists* 7.207–9; Lucretius, *De rerum natura* 4.522–721.

distinguish dissonant sounds is unique, as is also his ability to observe – at one with Stoicism – the beauty of the heavens (177).[91]

(2) And yet (1) is not always admirable. Harshness towards oneself is entirely justifiable, necessary, and laudable if by so doing one can better serve others or the common good. What is being referred to here is a yardstick, the *honestum*. For Stoics, of course, pain is not an evil. This meant that pain was something perfectly allowable for the person carrying out virtue, which could include working for the good of others. Were the statement Epicurean it would be pleasure, if not short-term then long-term, that would impel one to serve others or, more broadly stated, the common good. But this is not the case. As shown earlier, the Utopians explicitly recognize that serving others and humanity is obligatory for Stoics, however much the Stoic thesis needs development.

(3) God rewards, gives heavenly "pleasure," for actually serving others and the common good, not for harm to oneself per se. If serving others entails harm to oneself, then this harm is admirable and rewarded by God – and *voluptas* can be expected in heaven. But inflicting pain on oneself without a larger reason wins no points. Although Stoic virtue has for the Utopians in no way come into being as a result of the search for pleasure, true pleasure – and most of all pleasure in heaven – is inseparable from this virtue. Stating the matter in terms of the pleasure calculus, one rationally endures Stoic pain if the result is greater pleasure than would otherwise be the case.

While Stoics don't have sufficien concern with human advantage and pleasure, going so far as to harm their own bodies (as did young Erasmus and young More), Epicureans don't see that pleasure must always acquiesce to the *honestum* and don't see – in seeking to free humans from anxiety by eliminating concern about the gods or God – that pleasure must be expanded to include heavenly pleasure. Virtue is larger than either Stoics or Epicureans allow.

(4) (a) As long as Stoics inflict pain on themselves by holding to that which is merely "the empty and shadowy appearance of virtue" (the virtue young Erasmus and young More mistakenly sought) they will never find joy. (b) Another defect is that Stoics hold to their virtue, and inflict pain on themselves, for "adversities that may never come." Epicurus, in direct contrast, thought it "folly to dwell upon an evil which has still to come or maybe will not come at all" (*Tusc.* 3.32). In Stoic

91 Cicero states in *De officiis* that Nature and Reason are manifested in the fact that "no other animal has a sense of beauty, loveliness, harmony in the visible world" (1.14). Cf. *ND* 2.18, 2.75, 2.98ff, *Tusc.* 5.71, and Seneca, *Ot.* 5.3.

thought every statement relating to a future issue or event is made "with reservation."[92] This reservation clause inheres in the very nature of the wiseman. Always perfect, always virtuous, never mistaken, he could never be proven wrong by future happenings or happenings outside his control (*Fin.* 3.75). Whatever comes, the wiseman cannot be defeated. However much he may focus on the present, he always has an escape route, guaranteeing that his virtue will always remain intact. For the Utopians, however, this stance meant that the Stoic would never be able to fully join the world of affairs, a world of heartache and jo .

A problem with (4) is that it may seem to go against not only a central tenet of Stoicism but a central thesis of Erasmus' *Enchiridion*. Throughout, Erasmus is set on "arming" Christians for whatever challenges or adversities may come, to this end giving example after example of possible future pitfalls. Probably More is not denying Erasmus' thesis but simply pushing to the forefront the need to see immediate pleasures blossom and holding that this may be impossible if all one does is think in negative (as distinct from positive) terms about what could happen in the future.[93]

(5) The "gifts" of nature comprise not just abstract virtue (as popularly the Stoic view was understood) but the pleasures of life.

Unitary (Stoic-Framed) *Voluptas/Honestum* Words: Happiness, Virtue, the Supreme Good, Nature, Reason

De officiis 3 is all about the diffe ence between false and true *utilia* and between false and true *honesta* – and therewith showing how it is that things truly useful and truly honourable are inseparable. More's *Lucian* and Erasmus' *Praise of Folly* work out in their own ways these distinctions, and so too do the Utopians in their philosophy. It is not possible to talk about a *utile* that is worked out in terms of pleasure calculations without talking about the *honestum*, and it is not possible to talk about the *honestum* without taking into consideration pleasure calculations. In all cases the combination is made possible by the rejection of Epicurean disdain for abstract rules and non-worldly concerns

92 Cf. *Tr.* 11.6–11, 12.2–3, 13.3, 14.1, *Ben.* 4.45; Marcus Aurelius, *Med.* 5.20, 6.50, 9.29.

93 Note that reservation clauses did not entail that the wiseman does not focus on the present but only that, whatever happens, he has a way out. This is probably how we should interpret an early letter of Seneca where he states, regarding hope and fear, that "the chief cause of both these ills is that we do not adapt ourselves to the present, but send our thoughts a long way ahead" (*Ep.* 5.8).

and by the expansion of Stoic worldliness – all within a Stoic-derived frame. Within this context, happiness, virtue, the supreme good, nature, and reason are throughout (as in *The Praise of Folly*) unitary both/and concepts.

As one example, let us expand the "good and honest pleasure" statement discussed earlier (228):

> (1) To be sure, they think happiness is found not in every kind of pleasure but only in good and honest [bona atque honesta] pleasure. (2) Virtue itself, they say, draws our nature to pleasure of this sort as to the supreme good. (3) There is an opposed school which attributes happiness to virtue alone.[94] (4) They [the Utopians] define virtue as living according to nature; and God, they say, created us to that end. (5) When an individual obeys the dictates of reason in choosing one thing and avoiding another he is following nature. (163)[95]

Analysis reveals the following:

(1) If "the chief concern" of the Utopians "is what to think of human happiness, and whether it consists of one thing or more" (159), we now have the answer. Happiness is not, as with the Stoic wiseman, something dependent solely on holding to the *honestum* – no matter what happens in life. Happiness now comprises two fundamental but inseparable components: *honestum* and *voluptas*, "honest pleasure." Neither component can be defined by itself. The Utopians are happy because they recognize what the worldly pleasure calculations of Epicurus lacked and what the otherworldly focus of the Stoics lacked and have greatly benefited from the resulting unitary both/and product. Indeed they are supremely happy (241–7) because – it will be discovered – the structure of their commonwealth is through and through built from the mindset found in their philosophy. While Cicero in *De*

94 I have here changed the Cambridge reading of (3). To say that the opposed school holds that "virtue is itself happiness" misses the point being made. The Utopians do not deny that happiness is found in virtue. What they argue is that the role and place of virtue should be expanded. The Cambridge editors actually give my reading in 162n27.

95 "Nunc vero non in omni voluptate felicitatem sed in bona atque honesta sitam putant; ad eam enim velut ad summum bonum naturam nostram ab ipsa virtute pertrahi, cui soli adversa factio felicitatem tribuit. Nempe virtutem definiunt s - cundum naturam vivere, ad id siquidem a deo institutos esse nos. Eum vero naturae ductum sequi quisquis in appetendis fugiendisque rebus obtemperat rationi" (162/6–12).

officis distinguishes expedient things from inexpedient things in terms of whether there is agreement with *honestum*, as do the Utopians, the Utopians hold in addition that the *utile* (one aspect being *voluptas*) is not only inseparable from the *honestum* but equal in status with the *honestum*. The issue is not one-way but two-way.

(2) Virtue "draws our nature to pleasure of this sort as to the supreme good [summum bonum]" means that (a) virtue, like happiness, is two-dimensional in that it is all about "honest pleasure" and that (b) the virtue found in "the supreme good" is likewise two-dimensional in that "the supreme good" is about "honest pleasure." While the virtue of the Stoic wiseman comprises one thing, *honestum*, and it is from this vantage point that he distinguishes between things that are indifferent, Utopian pleasure calculations do not deal with "indiffe ents." The pleasure calculations involved in working out the *utile* are not a subsidiary of virtue but one of two equally important and inseparable aspects of virtue.

(3) While the Stoics see happiness residing in virtue alone – irrespective of outcomes (*Par*. 2, LS 63) – the Utopians argue that one would be crazy to pursue virtue alone, virtue that is "asperam ac difficilem and has no end other than virtue itself (162/1). The happiness of the Utopians depends on a virtue that is at once both broader and narrower than Stoic virtue, broader in that it is always tied with pleasure and narrower in that its expanse has been limited by pleasure. In stating that "there is an opposed school which attributes happiness to virtue alone," readers have wrongly imagined that what is being contrasted is the traditional opposition of Stoicism to Epicureanism and vice versa.[96] In fact the Utopians are staking out their own view – a view that had been partially foreshadowed, it may be noted, by Cicero's broadening of happiness in *Tusculan Disputations* 5 (see above, 110–17) and in *De finibus* 4. Although Zeno placed all the ingredients of happiness in virtue alone, no matter what happens in life, and Epicurus placed all the constituents of happiness in pleasure alone, the Utopians are not looking at the issue in either/or terms. They are not choosing the Epicurean view of happiness over the Stoic. The happiness they see is found in virtue that comprises not one thing but two things. Nor is pleasure simply an adjunct of virtue. *Voluptas* and *honestum* are two fundamental components of virtue.

(4) In defining virtue as living according to nature and believing that we were created by God for this purpose, the Utopians are mimicking a

96 The Cambridge editors see no diffe ence between the Utopian definition of virtue and the Stoic (163n65).

Stoic theme. As the marginal here states: "This is like Stoic doctrine."[97] Virtue, the Stoics contend, "is nothing else than nature perfected and developed to its highest point; therefore there is a likeness between man and God" (*Leg.* 1.25). Unlike the Epicureans, the Utopians see nature as not one-dimensional but two-dimensional. Unlike the Stoics, the Utopians see pleasure as inherent to the *utile* and therewith an inherent part of both nature and virtue.

(5) How precisely should we interpret the Utopian belief that an individual is following nature when he "obeys the dictates of reason in choosing one thing and avoiding another"? The Cambridge editors see the "reason" referred to here and in what follows as equating with Stoic "right reason" (*recta ratio*), which they define as a faculty that holds to the natural law and is thus able – as allegedly interpreted in the Middle Ages and Renaissance – "to distinguish right and wrong with instinctive clarity" (163n66). Clearly this is not the interpretation of Thomas More's Utopians.[98] It is true that Stoics contrast mere opinion with the law of nature implanted in humans "by a kind of natural instinct" (*Inv.* 2.161), but the wiseman's reason is not one-dimensional but two-dimensional. A statesman, we learn in *De legibus*, employs the right reason inhering in natural law to deal, prudently, with fluctuating worldly issues (1.18–19, cf. Cicero, *Rep.* 3.33). As *De finibus* puts it, "The chief good [summum bonum] consists in applying to the conduct of life a knowledge of the working of natural causes, choosing what is in accordance with nature and rejecting what is contrary to it" (3.31).[99] In short, the Stoics do not impose on the world one-dimensional views that they have grasped with "instinctive clarity," nor do the Utopians. Like Stoics the Utopians see a direct tie between following nature and employing reason in choosing between worldly issues. Like Epicureans the Utopians see a direct tie between following nature and the employment of reason in choosing between worldly pleasure and pain by analysing comparative advantages and disadvantages (DL 10.34, 130). The diffe ence from the Utopians is that they, unlike Epicurus,

97 Cf. DL 7.87: Zeno was the first to designate as the end "'l fe in agreement with nature' (or living agreeable to nature), which is the same as a virtuous life, virtue being the goal towards which nature guides us."

98 Combine what follows with my discussions of *recta ratio* above, 231–2 and 238–9.

99 Regarding "natural causes," a philosopher quoted by Gellius states, at odds with the standard thesis, that Stoics considered the "sensation" of pleasure (as well as pain) one of the first principles of natu e (*Noctes Atticae* 12.5.8). Note Antiochus' comment in Book 5 of *De finibus*: "If we add pleasure to the roll of nature's primary elements, then we have simply added one more bodily advantage. We have not altered [as he defines it] the basic st ucture of the supreme good" (5.45).

see reason in two-dimensional terms. A diffe ence from both Stoics and Epicureans is that the Utopians follow nature in calculating by means of reason "good and honest pleasure" and avoiding pleasure that is not good and honest. Nature comprises two fundamental but inseparable components, *voluptas* (inherent to the *utile*) and *honestum*. Pleasure calculations (deciding between *utilia*) are not an offshoot of *honestum* any more than is *honestum* an offshoot of pleasu e calculations.

5 Stoic Justice Expanded

The Utopians hold not only to Stoic *honestum* but to specific parts of *honestum*, the four cardinal virtues: wisdom, justice, courage, and temperance. Their focus on justice is particularly important for what it can tell us not only about their philosophy but, potentially, about the meaning of their institutions. Hythloday insists in Book I (101–7) that true justice can be found only in the common life, but what needs to be analysed is the kind of justice the Utopians actually envision, as evidenced by their philosophy. Is it Platonist, as Hythloday imagines, or Stoic?

> (1) [Nature, who prescribes pleasure and joy and makes no one her sole concern,] repeatedly warns you not to seek your own advantage [commodis] in ways that cause misfortune [incommoda] to others. (2) Consequently, they think that one should abide not only (a) by private agreements but (b) by those public laws which control the distribution of vital goods, (c) that is to say, the material of pleasure [materia voluptatis]. (3) Any such laws, when properly promulgated by a good king, or ratified by the common consent of a people free of tyranny and deception, should be observed. (4) So long as they are observed, to pursue your own interests [commodum] is prudent; (5) to pursue the public interest as well is pious; (6) but to pursue your own pleasure [voluptatem] by depriving others of theirs is unjust. (165)[100]

100 "eadem [natura] te nimirum iubet etiam atque etiam observare, ne sic tuis commodis obsecundes ut aliorum procures incommoda. Servanda igitur censent non inita solum inter privatos pacta sed publicas etiam leges quas aut bonus princeps iuste promulgavit aut populus nec oppressus tyrannide nec dolo circumscriptus, de partiendis vitae commodis, hoc est materia voluptatis, communi consensu sanxit. His inoffensis legibus, tuum cura e commodum prudentiae est: publicum praeterea, pietatis. Sed alienam voluptatem praereptum ire dum consequare tuam, ea vero iniuria est" (164/15–24). The translation of (2c) is mine. Cambridge reads: "such as are the very substance of pleasure."

(1) No Profiting at the Expense of Others

Note, first, that if we didn't know the larger pleasure-philosophy context, the contention that one should not seek advantage (*commoda*) at the expense (*incommoda*) of others and that this is written in nature would seem entirely Stoic. This thesis is anything but a minor appendage of Stoicism, and Cicero emphasizes the point in all three books of *De officiis*.[101] Unlike the Peripatetics and others, who hold that something may be *utile* (expedient) but not *honestum* (morally right) and *honestum* but not *utile*, the Stoics hold (and this is why Cicero follows "their system and doctrines," 3.20) that what is *honestum* is always *utile* and what is truly *utile* is always *honestum*, one consequence being that all human friendship and social harmony depend on not letting advantage (*commodum*) disadvantage (*incommodum*) others (3.21). Humans have a common humanity. Preferring the common advantage to one's own is something inherent in nature and divinity. Profiting at the expense of others, even foreigners, is more contrary to nature, more inexpedient, than is poverty or pain or anything else affecting one's person or property. It would take away everything that makes humans human. Making money by trickery or craft is not expedient, for it destroys the very basis of civilization, "the law of nature," "a bond of fellowship uniting all men." Even loss of children, kin, or friends should be valued less than an act of injustice against another human. Selfish pleasure, riches, or even life itself should be considered as nothing when weighed against the good of the commonweal. Justice entails "rendering to each his due," and this is impossible where one's own advantage disadvantages others.[102] At the level of governmental affairs, Cicero justifies his opposition to Caesar's ambitions by reference to this very precept. The *gloria* Caesar seeks is at the expense of Rome.[103] Greatness in Rome has not been about the acquisition of pleasures and "doing whatever will be" for personal advantage – usurping *honestum* and the cardinal virtues located therein (*Fin*. 2.117).

Epicureans, Stoics held, cannot find pleasure for themselves without ultimately disadvantaging others, including even their friends. This is the case because Epicureans do not consider justice and the other virtues desirable in themselves but desirable for the pleasure they yield.[104] They deny, complains Epictetus, that there is a natural community of

---

101 *Off*. 1.31, 43, 2.83–5, 3.21–32; cf. *Fin*. 3.62–70. See below, 323n23.

102 *Off*. 1.15, *Fin*. 5.63–5, *ND* 3.38, *Leg*. 1.19, *Rep*. 3.24.

103 *Off*. 1.26, 2.24f.

104 DL 10.138, *Fin*. 1.47–50, 2.117, *Off*. 3.118.

men, rational beings (*Disc.* 2.20.6–7). Against Epicurus' utility-based reasons for wanting friends – his belief that "the justice of nature is a pledge of reciprocal usefulness"[105] – Stoics held that true friendships exemplify the exercise of virtue. The point of friendship, as Seneca and other Stoics emphasize, is not to use a friend but to attend to this friend even in extreme situations, such as in sickness or imprisonment (*Ep.* 9.1).

Here again Stoicism frames Utopian pleasure philosophy. Although Epicurus held that it is not advantageous to cause misfortune to others, the Utopians don't buy – any more than do Stoics – his reasoning. They don't believe (supported by "nature") that pleasure calculus by itself, something concerned only with what is useful, can ultimately result in anything other than the Lesbian rule.

That the Utopians are very deliberately placing *voluptas* within a Stoic frame is reinforced by (6). In (6) *voluptas* is inserted into the position held by *commoda* in (1): "to pursue your own pleasure [voluptatem] [i.e. advantage] by depriving others of theirs is unjust." Other than this interchanging of Stoic and Epicurean words, there is no diffe ence between (1) and (6).[106]

(2) Laws and "the Material of Pleasure"

The fact that the Utopians hold to "private agreements" and to "public laws which control the distribution of vital goods" relates directly to nature's, so to speak, "no advantage at expense" command (and thus

105 *Principal Doctrines* 31, DL 10.150; *Fin.* 1.66.

106 An expert on Utopia in faraway New Spain, Vasco de Quiroga, made the Utopian "no advantage at the expense of others" precept a core feature of the two Utopian-inspired communities for Indians which he began building around 1531. Against scholastics such as Jason Maynus (late fifteenth century), he establishes in a highly technical legal discussion a *Regula ubi commodum*, the purpose of which was to make it impossible for the owner of a Native to advantage himself at the expense of the Native. No matter the conditions under which a Native (or other free person) sells himself into slavery, whether from the deceit or trickery of a buyer or the ignorance or fraud or complicity on the part of the person sold, what matters is only that the person enslaved has the option of returning, at any time, the price he was paid for giving up his freedom and being immediately set free. Were this option available, the intentions of those originally involved in the transaction (evil or not) and the behaviour of the owner after the sale would be irrelevant. See my "Vasco de Quiroga's *Regula Ubi Commodum*, the Utopian Roots." Compare actual Utopian practices: When (for example) they lose their goods through fraud, "their anger [in contrast to practices of their enemies and in Europe] goes no further than cutting off trade elations with that nation till restitution is made" (C203).

honestum and the virtue that is justice). Regarding private agreements (2a), Cicero tells us in *De finibus* that Epicurus "assigns more authority to the senses than the law allows to us when we sit as judges in private suits" (2.36). The fact that private agreements can be adjudicated in court prevents one party advantaging itself at the expense of another (*Off.* 2.83, 85). Regarding public laws (2b), consider the following statement from *De officiis*: "But this principle [no advantage at expense] is established not by Nature's laws alone, that is, by the common rules of equity [iure gentium],[107] but also by the statutes of particular communities, in accordance with which in individual states the public interests are maintained" (*Off.* 3.23). Note, however, that the Utopians focus not merely on public laws as such but public laws "which control the distribution of vital goods." Cicero would not at all have agreed (see *Off.* 2.73) that a controlled (common-life) distribution of vital goods is a valid public law or represents *honestum*. The Utopians were in this regard closer to Pythagoras, the founders of Stoicism, and Plato than to the outlook of later Stoics and Cicero.[108] Cicero saw any threat to private property as a failure to render each his due.[109]

The material of pleasure (*materia voluptatis*) (2c) is found in the vital goods distributed in the controlled (common-life) manner made possible by public laws (2b).[110] Not of little significance, the *materia voluptatis* replaces – very consciously – the *materia virtutis* referred to by Stoics. The Stoic Chrysippus held, states Plutarch, that getting the "things selected," i.e., the primary things according to nature, is not the end but rather "virtues matter."[111] As *De finibus* words it, for Stoics the primary

107 Cf. *Off.* 3.69 and Atkins on the diffe ence here between *ius genitum* ("law of nations"), *ius civile* ("civil law"), and natural law. See *Cicero on Politics and the Limits of Reason*, 218–24.

108 It appears that the ideal of the early Stoics was to equalize property as much as possible. See Dawson, *Cities of the Gods*, 190 and Schofield, *The Stoic Idea of the City*.

109 Private ownership is not established by nature but by long occupancy, war, or law (*Off.* 1.21). Although she makes no mention of Stoicism, Eden encapsulates the differences, small and large, between the thinking on private property of Pythagoras, Plato, Aristotle, and Cicero. Cicero distinguishes ownership of material property from the commonality of intellectual property. See *Friends Hold All Things in Common*, 78–108. Erasmus opens the 1515 edition of his Adages with a discussion of the ancient proverb "Among friends all things are common," which he attributes to Pythagoras (CWE 31, 29–30). On relationships to *Utopia* see Baker-Smith, "Reading *Utopia*," 152–4, 157. On Pythagoras in the Renaissance, see above, 154n22.

110 See the discussion of how vital goods are actually distributed in Utopia, at C137–45.

111 *CN* 1071AB, 1069E. Cf. *Disc.* 2.51.

things of nature "form so to speak the subject-matter, the given material with which wisdom deals [quasi materia sapientiae]" (3.61). In a long and important letter to William Croy in 1519, criticizing Croy's one-dimensional view of Stoicism, Erasmus states that worldly goods and benefits "must be turned into opportunities and materials for virtue [in materiam organumque virtutis]."[112] Thinking in like manner, the Utopians see the "vital goods" distributed in accord with their (common-life) laws as "materials of pleasure" ("good and honest pleasure").

Here as elsewhere the Utopians are developing the meaning of both *advantage* and *pleasure* – neither of which is at the expense of others. Interchanging the words *advantage* and *pleasure*, the vital goods distributed can be indistinguishably advantageous and pleasurable.

(3) Epicurean Justice Disallowed

Not Epicurean, certainly, is the admonition to observe laws "properly promulgated by a good king, or ratified by the common consent of a people free of tyranny and deception" – which reminds us of King Utopus (111) and the election of leaders, such as governors (121–5) A theme song of Epicurus' *Principal Doctrines* is that justice is not and has never been anything per se. Justice consists only of contracts which people have originated in order not to be harmed or to harm. Injustice is bad not per se but only because of fear that one will be discovered and punished by authorities (DL 10.151). Stoics and those who speak of natural law, rather than facts, are only mouthing words. What is just is what is useful and what is useful may differ from one individual to another or one social setting to another and can change in reaction to a particular situation or over time (DL 10.139–54).[113] Lorenzo Valla, the brilliant fifteenth-century humanist, supported all of these variables in his *On Pleasure*.[114]

Erasmus read Valla at a young age and so too, undoubtedly, did his friend More. But the Epicurean view of law and justice was not that of the Utopians. Utopian thinking here accords with Cicero, who held in his *Laws* that if it is only fear of punishment that keeps men from crime and there is no such thing as justice per se (as with Epicurus), then the

112 *Ep.* 959. Allen 3, 569/28–30, CWE 6, 345/36–8. The "materials for virtue" are discussed at length in *De taedio Iesu* and the *Enchiridion*. See above, 198–9.

113 Cf. Plutarch, *A Pleasant Life*, 1104b. Porphyry (d. c. 305 CE) reported that the Epicureans "established a rational calculation of utility" with regard to laws, terrifying those not able to use reason with threats of penalties (LS, 22M.3).

114 See above, note 6.

only thing that would matter is individual shrewdness and prudence (1.40–1).[115] The Utopian attitude outside the philosophy section is the same. Not believing in rewards and punishments in an afterlife, "Who can doubt that a man who has nothing to fear but the law, and no hope of life beyond the grave, will do anything he can to evade his country's laws by craft or to break them by violence, in order to gratify his own personal greed?" (225, cf. 237–41).[116]

(4) *Honestum/Utile-Voluptas* Communism

A major issue comes into focus with (4), the contention that it is "prudent" to pursue one's own interests "so long as they [the laws referred to in 2] are observed [as in 3]." Prudence is allowable and viable only if the laws are in place, and one of these laws is "the common life" precept. What can be seen here again are the workings of the *honestum/utile* mindset. On one side is the "common-life" precept and on the other the allowing of persons to follow their interests, as long as these interests do not violate the precept.

Not only, that is, does the "no advantage at expense" precept disallow, it allows. The Utopians make a point of seeing personal advantage as a positive goal. They focus not just on what the "no advantage at expense" precept takes away but on the freedom it gives – and they see the "common-life" precept in this context.

Contrast the Conclusion to Book I

Compare and contrast all the above (252–7) with the opinions on personal advantage and the common life of Hythloday and "More" expressed at the conclusion to Book I. Utopian communism, as found in their philosophy, is not that of either Hythloday or "More" (in responding to Hythloday's view of communism). Hythloday and "More" (in responding) see a Platonist-type communism, whereas the Utopians envision in their philosophy a Stoic-type communism.

---

115 Excoriating Epicurus for holding that one should not be a slave to laws and should avoid public life, provided there be no fear of punishment, Plutarch (though not a Stoic) holds that Epicurus and his disciple Metrodorus would abolish human life. See *Against Colotes*, *Moralia* 14.1127d.

116 Neither here nor elsewhere in his discussion of *Utopia* in *Renaissance Self-Fashioning* does Greenblatt see (employing his "New Historicism") any serious relationships to ancient thought: not Plato, not Aristotle, not Epicurus, not Stoics, not Cicero (53 passim).

Hythloday's View

Hythloday holds that laws may be made, but where there is private property the advantage of one person *always* ends up disadvantaging another person:

> While you try to cure one part, you aggravate the wound in other parts. Suppressing the disease in one place causes it to break out in another, since you cannot give something to one person without taking it away from someone else (103–5).
>
> Quin dum unius partis curae studes, aliarum vulnus exasperaveris, ita mutuo nascitur ex alterius medela alterius morbus, quando nihil sic adici cuiquam potest ut non idem adimatur alii. (102/27–104/2)[117]

But what is the obverse of this statement? Is Hythloday implying (x) that in a communistic society, as not elsewhere, all advantage is equal, that the advantage of one person is in some undefined way the advantage of another person? Or could he be assuming (y) that you *can* in a communistic society, unlike elsewhere, "give something to one person without taking it away from someone else"? Should the latter be the case, note that the advantages individuals are "given" appear to be dictated by the government, top down. This being true, Hythloday would seem to be thinking, with his admiration of Plato, of a state that reflects a rationally balanced and holistic arrangement of the soul.[118]

Whichever interpretation is correct ("x" or "y"),[119] Hythloday entirely rejects, in effect, the thinking of Cicero and the Stoics, the massively argued belief that in fact as well as in theory it is possible where there is private property to advantage one person without disadvantaging another – and that this can be witnessed in everyday affairs and even in the way Rome was built, notwithstanding egregious examples of advantage at the expense of others and often at the highest levels of government.

---

117 Although Plato repeatedly talks about sick people making laws where what is needed is a physician (statesman), as at *Rep.* 4.425e–426a, he makes no statement equivalent to Hythloday's.

118 In his *Republic* Plato talks about "the 'equality' that unequals deserve to get," but, this being difficult, "one can simply distribute equal aw ds by lot" (6.757).

119 Note Hythloday's observation that with the Utopians "virtue has its reward [virtuti pretium sit] yet everything is shared equally" (101) and later, in his peroration to Utopia, that, "distribution of goods [rerum distributio]" having replaced private business, "every man zealously pursues the public business" (241).

"More's" View

Interpreting Hythloday's statement in terms of "x," "More" contends in response that Hythloday is eulogizing a society where advantage is the same for everyone and that this would be disastrous in that everyone would be on the same level. "More's" reasoning is as follows:

> "But I don't see it that way," I said. "It seems to me that people cannot possibly live well where all things are in common [ubi omnia sint communia]. (1) How can there be plenty of commodities where every man stops working? The hope of gain does not spur him on, and by relying on others he will become lazy. (2) If men are impelled by need, and yet no man can legally protect what he has obtained, what can follow but continual bloodshed and turmoil, (3) especially when respect for magistrates and their authority has been lost? I for one cannot even conceive of authority existing among men who are not distinguished from one another in any respect." (105)

Criticisms 1 and 2 are clearly scholastic and based on Aristotle.[120]

More problematic is Criticism 3, in that holding "all things in common" is seen as entailing not only economic equality but social and political equality. Unable to find scholastic sources for this postulate, Edward Surtz long ago contended that it was "unfair."[121] And yet there most certainly is a reason why the author has "More" hold, versus Hythloday, that in a communistic state everyone would be on the same level politically as well as economically. If Hythloday is saying that advantage is one and the same everywhere when private property is eliminated ("x" above), "More's" belief that all authority is being ruled out is not unreasonable – notwithstanding scholastic views.Add to this the author's knowledge of the political and social equality envisioned in late medieval communistic uprisings, not least being England's Peasant Revolt in 1381,[122] and contemporary humanist interest in the

120 Regarding point 1 see Aristotle *Pol.* II.3, 1261b 33–8 and Aquinas *ST* II-II, q. 66 a.3. Regarding point 2 see *Pol.* II. 4 and 5, and *ST* II-II, q. 66 a.3. Erasmus emphasizes in his *Dulce bellum inexpertis* (1515) that it was from Aristotle (and the scholastics), *not* Christ, that "we have learned that no commonwealth in which all things are common can flourish" (ASD II-7, 28/506–7, CWE 35, 419)

121 Yale *Utopia*, 382. Aquinas held that even in a state of nature there would have been mastership between man and man (*ST* I, 96, 4).

122 See Froissart, *Froissart's Chronicles*, 211–30.

Golden Age, an age entirely egalitarian, without magistrates, discussed at length (especially by Cynics and Stoics) in ancient literature – and often related, from various angles, to Indigenous life in the recently discovered New World.[123]

The Utopian View Is Stoic-Based and Not That of either Hythloday or "More"

The Utopians support, in the philosophy section, a common-life distribution of the essentials of life, if approved by the people, and yet, of crucial importance, their conception of the common life (above, 252–7) does not support the one-dimensional assumptions in Book I of either Hythloday or "More" (in responding to Hythloday's view). With (4) – as with (1), (2), and (3) – the frame of thought is Stoic. In common-life settings as in private property settings, that is, it is "prudent" – the "no advantage at expense" injunction in place – to pursue one's own advantage. In both instances the Stoic two-dimensional mindset governs.

Regarding the need in Stoic thought to seek personal advantage, *De officiis* could not be more clear:

> And yet we are not required to sacrifice our own interests and surrender to others what we need for ourselves, but each one should consider his own interests, as far as he may without injury to his neighbor's. "When a man enters the foot-race," says Chrysippus [c. 279–206 BCE, third head of the Stoic school] with his usual aptness, "it is his duty to put forth all his strength and strive with all his might to win; but he ought never with his foot to trip, or with his hand to foul a competitor. Thus in the stadium of life, it is not unfair for anyone to seek to obtain what is needful for his own advantage, but he has no right to wrest it from his neighbor. (*Off.* 3.42)
>
> Lacking any conflict with nature's laws, it is granted that everybody may prefer to secure for himself rather than for his neighbor what is essential for the conduct of life. (3.22)[124]

123 See Lovejoy and Boas, *A Documentary History of Primitivism and Related Ideas*, vol. 1; Levin *The Myth of the Golden Age in the Renaissance*; and Cohn, *The Pursuit of the Millennium*. In the second edition of More's and Erasmus' *Lucian* (1514), Erasmus added pieces that deal directly with the Golden Age. See CWM 3, 58. Guillaume Budé mentions the Golden Age in his introductory letter to *Utopia* (15).

124 Brennan discusses passages such as these in *De officiis* (and there are many) at length in *The Stoic Life*. See especially 206–14.

The Utopians see nature as one with the common-life "distribution of vital goods" precept and in this context (just as where private property is a precept) think everyone should seek advantage – as long as the precept is held to.

Contrast the Utopian View with Hythloday's View

In demonstrating over and over in Book I that the legal setups found in known societies are entirely unworkable in that the greed of those of noble birth and/or wealth always trumps the common good, Hythloday shows, in effect, that the Stoic and Ciceronian "no advantage at expense" precept is a sham, ultimately unworkable – just words. Yet in fact the Utopians hold up, in discussing their philosophy, the Stoic "no advantage at expense" precept and focus on what it allows as well as disallows. In neither case, it is important to note, is their thinking that of Plato or Aristotle or Epicurus or any other non-Stoic ancient philosopher.

The Utopians find the Stoic *honestum/utile* outlook directly applicable to a communistic way of life – notwithstanding that this same *honestum/utile* outlook applies to the world of private property, the world so disdained by Hythloday. Although Hythloday graphically describes the evils of private property and contemporary society and insists that it is never possible in this setting to advantage one person without disadvantaging another – a theme which reaches a climax in his peroration at the conclusion of Book II[125] – the Utopians transfer the Stoic and Ciceronian *honestum/utile* frame of mind, deeply embedded in the world of private property and Roman culture, directly to the common life.

Utopian reasoning in the philosophy section is eminently rational, anything but specious. Why personal advantage can be sought in Utopia but hardly ever comes at the expense of others, unlike societies elsewhere, is explained by the iron grip of the Utopians on certain

125 In his peroration Hythloday surmises – after decrying and illustrating the "justice" elsewhere that allows those noble and wealthy to take advantage of everyone (243–5) – that the whole world would have come to adopt the laws of the Utopian commonwealth were it not for pride, a monster which "measures prosperity not by her own advantages but by others' disadvantages" (Y243/33–5) ("Haec non suis commodis prosperitatem, sed ex alienis metitur incommodes," C246/6–7). Further below we will find that Hythloday is himse f guilty of pride in that he refuses to recognize the Utopian *honestum/utile* way of thinking and acting (327–30).

unbending values, many not found elsewhere, and the fact that their bending values are always in accord with these unbending values – as evidenced throughout their pleasure philosophy. Among the unbending values not found elsewhere are laws that "control the distribution of vital goods" – which replace private property laws. It is within this sanitized context that they find it "prudent" to seek one's own advantage. Where disadvantaging others has lost much of its raison d'être, in that struggles for the vital goods that contribute to "the material of pleasure" have been eliminated, a person can concentrate on things that are truly advantageous. In short, the Utopians eliminate private property *and yet* see justice, giving each his due, entirely in Stoic and Ciceronian *honestum/utile* terms.[126] The two-dimensional frame of mind that governs a common-life world is the same frame of mind that governs the world of private property, the diffe ence being only the content of the absolutes (common-life rather than private property).

In Part VIII below it will be shown that Hythloday sees all worldly happenings in terms of the Lesbian rule (advantaging oneself at the expense of others) and eulogizes in contrast Utopia, yet fails to understand anything about the Utopian outlook, no matter the subject. Pigheadedness and pride keep him from seeing that the Utopians throughout work out in their own terms the Stoic *honestum/utile* way of thinking and acting.

---

126 In his long introductory letter (7–19), Budé ties the ancient meaning of "giving each his due" and "real equity" with "the norm of truth" and "the rule, established by Christ, founder of our human condition" (11). But how exactly did he see the relationship between the ancient meanings and Christ's "rule"? Griffin an Atkins state that "The fundamental Stoic definition of justice was giving each his due." See their edition of Cicero's *On Duties*, 19. Cf. *Off.* 1.15, 42, 59; *Fin.* 5.67; *Leg.* 1.19; ND 3.38. In context Budé is contrasting contemporary civil law and papal and royal decrees with true justice, as described in Roman law and in Christ's "Pathagorean rule of mutual charity and community property." Regarding Christ's "Pathagorean rule," see Acts 2:44–5 and the first adage in Erasmus' 1508 *Adages*, above, 154n22. Significantl , Budé does not mention Plato. Regarding Roman law, note Budé's important and influential analysis of Justinian's *Digest, Annotationes in XXIV Pandectarum libros*. Book I, Title 1 of Justinian's *Institutes* (535 CE) begins as follows: "Justice is the set and constant purpose which gives to every man his due" (cf. *Digest* 1.1.10). See Moyle's translation of the *Institutes*. In summarizing the many publications of Budé, Marie-Madeleine de la Garanderie concludes that the crucial question for him was "when and how to insert ancient culture into the intellectual and spiritual life of the Christian" – which relates, we can see, to More's concern in *Utopia*. See "Guillaume Budé" by Jean Clouet, in *Contemporaries of Erasmus*, vol. 1, 212–17 at 217.

Contrast the Utopian View with "More's" View

"More" rejects in Book I the communism advocated by Hythloday and adjudged by contemporaries in one-dimensional terms (105), but what he does not bring out at this point is that in Utopian philosophy the common life is framed by Stoicism – not the equality found among Indigenous people or peasant revolts or the Golden Age. Authority is not done away with, resulting in continual bloodshed and turmoil, because both private agreements and public laws – laws that have been established by a good king "or ratified by the common consent of a people free of tyranny and deception" – are in Utopian common-life thinking, as in Stoicism, entirely valid and necessary and reflect highest truth. The diffe ence with Stoicism is not the framework but the type of laws, including laws that control the distribution of goods. "More" also rejects in Book I (105) a communism that would make the lives of all individuals the same, but here too he does not point out that this is not the Utopian view, that in Utopian philosophy each individual is advised, as in Roman thought, to pursue his own advantage once the absolutes are in place.

Look once again at the Utopian *honestum/utile* frame of mind. On the one side are laws, laws – notably the common-life precept – that have been developed free of tyranny and fraud and that are one with the virtue of justice, giving each his due, and thus one with *honestum* and its reason and divinity. On the *utile* side, the "prudent" (and pleasurable) thing is to pursue one's own "interests" as long as these interests are not – and this is the rub – at odds with the precepts. Utopian communism, as described in the philosophy section, is not one-dimensional but unitarily two-dimensional – in accord with the frame of their entire outlook.

6 Corollaries

A. Not Rhetoric but Philosophy

The pleasure philosophy section details how the Utopians think, how they go about solving problems, how it is that two polar types of value can unite. Specificall , we learn how it is that Epicurean philosophy and Stoic philosophy are not, correctly understood, contradictory – unrecognized by earlier philosophical thinking. What unites these two schools of philosophy is the Stoic *honestum/utile* frame of thought – on each side slightly reformulated. *Voluptas* is simply an augmentation of the traditional way of conceptualizing and representing *utile*.

Unseen by previous readers, there is a very carefully developed and logical rationale behind every statement made in the philosophy section. Every issue is systematically worked out in terms of a pre-existing way of thinking. At no time does the author vacillate between incompatible ideas. At no time does he simply contrive or fabricate a solution. At no time does he subordinate virtue to pleasure. At no time does he engage in rhetorical twists and turns, ambiguity, paradox, absurdity, "double coding," jeu d'esprit, irony, satire, humour, exaggeration, or contradiction. The philosophy set forth is real and in the author's mind entirely relevant to the world that surrounds him – the European world.

Where the Stoic unitary two-dimensional mindset is not in place the Utopians find nothing but evil, often covered by a veneer of righteousness – the Lesbian rule. Seeing little more than the Lesbian rule when he surveys the world of private property, the Platonist Hythloday contends in Book I that only a communistic revolution can change things, but the Utopians show in their philosophical thinking that the common-life principle is best explained by the Stoic two-dimensional way of thinking, not Platonism.

B. Not Platonist Institutions but Stoic

To what degree does the discussion of Utopian philosophy tie with actual institutions and social practices found in Utopia? Do these institutions and practices exemplify at all times the uniting of two opposite types of value? Do they describe, in a non-Christian context, "advantageous" and therewith "pleasurable" solutions to worldly and spiritual well-being once the absolutes are in place and firmly held to? Evidence of a non-Platonist Stoic *honestum/utile* mindset is not hard to find. Take religion. In their philosophy the Utopians work out at length the two-dimensional nature of religion (see above, esp. 213–24), and we find the same frame of thought embedded in actual practices (*Utopia* 219–41). Utopians are allowed to choose their beliefs, which in fact vary greatly, as long as certain absolutes are in place, not least being belief that the soul does not perish with the body and belief that the universe is not ruled by blind chance (225). However diffe ent or faulty individual beliefs, it is the "consensus of all nations" that a single "divine majesty" is above all these varied forms of worship

(219).[127] Without these precepts there is no possibility of virtue (237).[128] Nor, another absolute, can one disadvantage with one's beliefs other humans. Persons can proselytize (seek their own advantage) only if this is done "quietly, modestly, rationally and without insulting [disadvantaging] others" (223). Utopian priests observably hold to unbending divine truths at the same time as they treat harsh worldly affairs with a decorum and mercy that accords with these truths (233).

Nor is there reason to doubt that the "common-life" discussions of Utopian officials occupations, and social relations, as at 121–55 and 185–201, reflect the same *honestum/utile* mindset. Note even the conclusion to Book II. Immediately after referring to "their methods of waging war, their religious practices, as well as other customs," "More" states that "their communal living and their moneyless economy" is "the basis of their whole system [maximum totius institutionis fundamentum]" (247). How could things that emanate from the base not reflect that base? If the extensive discussions of Utopian philosophy, warfare (Part VII below), and religion are all built from a Stoic two-dimensional frame and if the author's reasoning is as logic-based as we have seen that it is, specific common-life aspects of Utopian life must have been built from the same frame.

Many "common-life" practices indicate that Thomas More very consciously set out to rewrite Plato in Stoic terms. Note, for example, that Plato's approach in the *Republic* is throughout prescriptive, while Thomas More is much more interested in causation from the ground up. Plato thus wants to make it unlawful for the guardians to touch or handle gold or silver or wear it as jewellery, so that they will not seem like hostile masters but allies of those they rule (*Rep.* 3.417a), whereas

127 Cf. the Stoic Balbus, ND 2.52: "Though there is a range of opinions regarding their nature," all persons, no matter where, "have an innate conviction that gods exist, for it is, so to say, engraved in their hearts." This is true even if many men, as a result of corrupt natures, have faulty views of the gods (*Tusc.* 1.30).

It may appear that More's emphasis on the consensus of the faithful, as against individual convictions (such as those held by adherents of Luther), was deeply influenced by the Stoics. Cf. Mo e's 1515 letter to Dorp, where he refers to "that living gospel of faith which has been infused into the heart of the faithful throughout the whole Church" – even before it was written down by anyone (CWM 89, lxxv–lxxxiii). According to Hitchcock, "More's notion of divine truth being written in the hearts of men was saved from subjectivism by an equally strong theory of consensus, a theory which was perhaps the most extreme statement of the position in the entire history of the Church." See "Thomas More and the *Sensus Fidelium*," 150.

128 Cf. ND 1.3–4, quoted above, 222.

More shows us *why it is* that in Utopia even children hold gold, silver, and jewellery in contempt (147–55). While air, water, and earth are "gifts" of Mother Nature (149; cf. 177 on natural and automatic gifts of Mother Nature), Nature has hidden vain and unhelpful things like gold and silver. Not without reason, therefore, Utopian chamber pots are made of gold and silver and children mistake jewellery-laden foreign ambassadors for slaves. Clearly, the Nature referred to here is not Platonist. Plato describes what he considers basic and legitimate human needs (cf. *Rep.* 2.369b–372d),[129] but Stoics talk incessantly (see Parts V and VI above) about what it means to "live according to Nature."[130]

Closely related, the Utopians again and again distinguish practices that are useful (and natural) from those that are "useless."[131] They choose, for example, not only useful trades ("utiles artes," 133) but for governor the man "whom they judge most useful" ("maxime utilis," 122). Note also the combining at times of the useful and the pleasurable, as in Utopian philosophy: Nothing, for example, is "more useful or more pleasant to the citizens [sive ad usum civium sive ad voluptatem commodius]" than their gardens (119). After every evening meal, diners are cheered up by music and the burning of incense, for "no kind of pleasure is forbidden, provided harm [disadvantaging others] does not come of it" (143). And once the equality of distribution mandate has been met (165, above, 254–6), citizens (in accord with Stoic doctrine) can advantage themselves: "After the halls have been served with their quotas of food, nothing prevents an individual from taking home food from the marketplace" (141).

Lacking evidence to the contrary, we conclude that Utopian institutions and practices are throughout not one-dimensional but two-dimensional, unitarily both/and – built like More's *Lucian*, Erasmus' *Praise of Folly*, and Utopian pleasure philosophy from two polar types of value. In accord with one type of value, the Utopians hold to absolutes, including the denial of private property and money, while, in accord with another type of value, they simultaneously work out (possible because and only because the absolutes are in place) truly advantageous, decorous, useful, and pleasurable solutions to the particular problems that surround them.

---

129 On Plato's notion of "nature" in *Republic* see Nicholas P. White, *A Companion to Plato's Republic*, 86.

130 Although disallowing Epicurus' overall outlook, Stoics praised his advocating of simple living in accord with nature (see above, 234–5).

131 Thomas I. White has pointed to the many places in Utopia where the focus is on practices or goals that are "useful," in "Festivitas, Utilitas, et Opes," 137–9.

So, again, what can be said about the great Hythloday's eulogizing of Plato? The evidence pointed to above shows that he failed to see how the Utopian state was actually constructed, that it was not, as with Plato's guardians in the *Republic*, a communism that reflects a rationally balanced and holistic arrangement of the soul.

C. A Detailed Rejection of Plato's Way of Thinking

Regarding Plato and Utopian pleasure philosophy, there is something else – not taken account of above. No discussion in the entire book is more grounded in rigorous and multifaceted analyses of ancient sources than More's silent criticism and rewriting of Plato's complex discussions of "mixed" and "unmixed" pleasures and health in *Gorgias*, *Republic*, and *Philebus* (173–7 [172/16–176/25]) – a subject that requires extensive documentation and a separate publication. The goal of the Utopians here is not just to correct Plato on a few points but to tear down the entire edifice of his thought

Briefl , the Utopians reject Plato's contrast of illness/medicine with the pain/pleasure that is bound up with hunger/eating. Unlike the mixed pleasure that is hunger/eating (the constant battle between emptiness and satiation), illness/medicine reflects for Socrates the opposition of disease and health, injustice and justice (harmony of the soul), bad and good. Health is not a pleasure and illness is not a pain. Although Socrates recognizes the existence of unmixed pleasures (pleasures that are not mixed with pain, such as smell), health per se does not represent even unmixed pleasures. Health represents the good.

But the Utopians show that illness is in fact pain and as such bad while medicine is in fact pleasure producing and as such good. Life is not described by two separate spheres of thought but one. The fact that medicine and surgery cure the pain of illness, and not merely the illness, means that medicine and surgery do the same things as eating or scratching. In fact, illness/medicine is an inferior type of mixed pleasure. It is inferior to hunger/eating because eating when hungry is a gift of Mother Nature and as such comes about naturally and automatically (cf. Stoic *oikeiosis*).

Regarding mixed pleasures, More places much greater emphasis on physiological excess than Plato, even giving his own examples: accumulation in the bowels and the buildup of sexual forces. And unlike Plato he never allows that physiological excess (any more than physiological deficiency) can be transformed into perverse and unrestrained pleasures. At every step he gives a physiological and necessarian twist at odds with Plato's account.

Pleasure, in this context, is for the Utopians a two-dimensional concept. Health, for them the highest bodily pleasure, differs radically from mixed pleasures in that health is stable and tranquil. And yet mixed pleasures and health require each other. Beyond both Epicurus and Socrates, health is for the Utopians something profoundly felt, deeply experiential – building, it may seem, on the Stoic Panaetius, who had denied that health is merely a preferred indiffe ent.

Contrast More's rigorous analyses and criticism with previous humanist treatment of Plato. Marsilio Ficino (1433–99), who translated from the Greek all of Plato's works, saw in Plato a spiritualist, mystical, and Neoplatonist message.

D. Even the Debate between Hythloday and "More" in Book I Is Stoic-Based

Part VIII below will demonstrate that the debate between Hythloday and "More" is actually resolved – comparing to Seneca's *De tranquillitate animi*, above (32–7). Platonist Hythloday eulogizes the Utopians but fails to grasp (as the author expected readers to see) the obvious, that his exemplifications of Utopian thinking are not Platonist but Stoic, unitarily two-dimensional. "More" represents the author's view in that he, unlike Hythloday, knows implicitly that his "indirect approach" is inseparable from unbending truths – and that the Utopians everywhere illustrate the point.

PART VII

Utopian Warfare: A Unitary Two-Dimensional Mindset

1 Super Machiavellians?

A cornerstone of many interpretations of *Utopia* has long been the discussions of warfare. Readers have responded to these accounts in various ways – none of which relate to the mind uncovered in Parts II–VI. Believing that *Utopia* is about an ideal society, a "utopia," many readers either have not commented on the warring stratagems of the Utopians or have found them lacking in seriousness.[1] J.H. Hexter in his *More's Utopia* (1952), which has become a classic, simply ignored Utopian views on warfare.[2] Not wanting the author to be seen in a negative light, those writing from a Catholic perspective have concentrated on the debate in Book I between Hythloday and "More." Brushing aside the thinking and practices of the Utopians regarding war in Book II, they have concluded that the Utopian state was not More's ultimate ideal but merely the maximum which human reason, unaided by divine revelation, can ever achieve. In *Thomas More* (1935), R.W. Chambers took the argument a step further in

1 Avineri shows that many nineteenth-century and early twentieth-century writers on *Utopia* seldom say anything at all about the discussions of war. He names Georg Thomas Rudhart (1829), Karl Grün (1846), Karl Marx and Friedrich Engels (various dates), Frederic Seebohm (1867), Karl Kautsky (1888), G.R. Potter (1925), Karl Vorländer (1926), Emile Dermenghem (1927), Edmond Privat (1935), and A.L. Morton (1952). See his analysis of the secondary literature up to 1962 in "War and Slavery in More's Utopia."

2 Hexter also skirted questions regarding Utopian philosophy and religion: "a reconstruction of More's own opinions based on these sections has shaky foundations" (*More's Utopia*, 56). Donner had claimed that *Utopia* could only be interpreted subjectively. "With characteristic optimism More left it to his readers to decide which parts of his book were seriouly intended and which were spoken 'in sport.'" See his *Introduction to Utopia*, 17.

contending that, even with only reason to guide them, the Utopians do better than English and European Christians.[3] Edward Surtz was to build on this thesis in his editing of the Yale edition of *Utopia* (1965).

Readers who have taken Utopian warfare seriously have almost all believed or argued that expediency here overrules principle and that the Utopians are Machiavellians or even super-Machiavellians. According to Shlomo Avineri, the first parallel between Machiavelli and More was drawn by the Russian Populist Yury Zhukovsky in 1861.[4] In post-Versailles Germany (i.e., after 1919), many scholars saw Utopian warfare as the epitome of evil cunning and craft, *Realpolitik*, and often tied this outlook with anti-British sentiments. One of these scholars was Henry Oncken, who argued in 1922, in *Die Utopia des Thomas Morus und das Machtproblem in der Staatslehre*, as summarized by Avineri, that

> More's teaching tends, in spite of himself, to be morally even more objectionable and reprehensible than Machiavelli's: for whereas Machiavelli only emancipates politics from ethics and religion, More constructs a code of rational absolutist ethics which enables him to argue that a war which is being waged by the Utopians is by necessity a just war, as "Utopia" is, by definition, *the* ideal state ...[5]

In his *Die Dämonie der Macht* (1940), Gerhard Ritter saw ties between Utopian warfare and Hitler's Third Reich, with which he sympathized. After the war he greatly revised the book, and it was translated as *The Corrupting Influence of Power* (1952). Explicitly tying his views with Ritter's, Giuseppe Di Scipio has concluded (1983) that "in order to arrive at the ideal state of Utopia the realities of power and the means to achieve it are very Machiavellian, notwithstanding the Christian Humanism of its author."[6]

---

3 Chambers, *Thomas More*, 128.

4 Avineri, "War and Slavery in More's *Utopia*," 271n1.

5 Avineri, "War and Slavery in More's *Utopia*," 273. Similar views were expressed by Ernst Troeltsch (1923), Oscar Bendemann (1929), and Michael Freund (1930). Avineri supports (1962) the Machiavellian view (286–90).

6 Di Scipio, "*De Re Militari* in Machiavelli's *Prince* and More's *Utopia*," 19. One important exception to these earlier views was Adams' *The Better Part of Valor*. Believing that the Utopians were born with "godlike reason" (135) and that they are "rational and uncorrupted men" (152) who demonstrate "rational humanitarianism" (153, 227), he sees Utopian warfare as merely a "satire" on contemporary European practices (140, 146, 150 passim). Hexter appears to be building on Adams where he states in his introduction to the Yale *Utopia* (1965) that "What distinguishes the treatment of war in *Utopia* from medieval treatments of the problem is the way in which More has inextricably woven together an invective against war and a powerful satirical assault on Europe's warrior class" (li).

In *The Meaning of More's Utopia* (1983), George M. Logan contends that Utopian warfare on other nations is necessitated by their pleasure philosophy, their "hedonic calculus." "Doubtless" the Utopians "regret self-interest," "But clearly they regard such actions as sometimes necessary to preserve their state and, as Machiavelli, another city-state theorist, says ..." (236).[7] More seems even to "insist," claims Logan, on the discrepancies between Utopian practices and Erasmian ideals (238). And he finds no diffe ence between Utopian methods of warfare and the cunning and deceit that go on in the meeting of the French privy council described so graphically by Hythloday in Book I. "As much as possible, the Utopians implement the ideal of universal brotherhood. But when the implementation of this ideal conflicts with securing the welfare of Utopians, it must be sacrificed (236). More's concern is the "real interests of Utopians, not humanity at large" (236).[8]

Seeing *Utopia* in rhetorical terms, Arthur Kinney finds a veritable "epidemic" of inconsistencies in Utopia in his *Humanist Poetics: Thought, Rhetoric, and Fiction in Sixteenth-Century England* (1986) (62). "They desire peace, yet they have no hesitation in annexing territory not their own; they claim selflessness yet remain imperialistic" (63). Just as Erasmus' Folly "invites us to a game only to involve us, to turn up our own portraits on her face of cards" (63), Hythloday's view turns out to be dystopian as well as utopian. Dystopian are Utopian offensive and defensive warfare, their "intimidation and violence" (74), creation of disturbances, hiring of mercenaries, offering rewards for capturing or killing enemy leaders, and the ease with which they themselves kill. What explains all this? It's up to "us," "the readers," to discover meaning through our active "participation." Thomas More deliberately set forth paradoxes, irresolvable contradictions, and, this being the case, the work ultimately "depends on us" for its meanings (66).

---

7 Prévost holds in his edition of *L'Utopie de Thomas More* that the Utopian ideal compares with the monastic ideal (as represented by Cluny) (171), but in worldly affairs the ideal can never be completely held to, since compromise is always necessary, and in their wars the Utopians break with the ideal (706, 712). As both More and Machiavelli saw, there is all the diffe ence between speculation and political reality (191, 710). Mansfield has ecently repreated the argument: Utopian discussions of war and slavery show that humanistic ideals can't be applied to practice. See "Erasmus and More," 154.

8 Believing that the Utopians embody a contradiction in being "both warlike and peaceable," Wootton (1999) sees a "double coding." Unlike Erasmus, More saw "that there is no guarantee that there is a single reference point [Christ] that enables us to resolve disputes over politics. This is the fundamental problem that More explores in *Utopia*." See the Introduction to his *Thomas More's "Utopia,"* 26 and 27.

Comparing *Utopia* and Machiavelli's *The Prince* from a rhetorical standpoint (1988), John F. Tinkler finds, like others, that Utopian warfare is "practical without being honorable." Although the Utopian state is a product of the *demonstrativum* literary genus, the goal of which is *honestas* (moral goodness), their warfare is an exception. Like that in *The Prince*, Utopian warfare is a product of the *deliberativum* literary genus, the goal of which is *utilitas*.[9]

In his *Young Thomas More and the Arts of Liberty* (2011), Gerard B. Wegemer finds, again and again, nothing but contradictions in Utopian depictions of warfare. In their warfare, as throughout the book, "Raphael [Hythloday] tells us one thing but shows us another" (185).[10] Notwithstanding Hythloday's tirade in Book I against those who, against the law of God, support killing, in Book II his Utopians support capital punishment and take pride in their desire to exterminate the Zapoletans (145). What we find with the Utopians are "Machiavellian tactics, especially in imperialist wars designed to destroy trust and augment fear, that are anything but simple and virtuous" (185). Their justifications of war and societal focus on war bring to mind "an imperial Rome with warring Sparta's aspirations" (157). "Utopus is the antithesis of Cicero's princeps, and Utopia is a case study in disguised tyranny beneath a rhetoric of peace and *respublica*" (158).

But is it really possible, notwithstanding prevailing views, to separate the war discussions from the meaning of the book as a whole – or even from the meaning of the Utopian state as a whole? If the author's purpose in writing *Utopia* was to represent the way of thinking that had consumed him since late 1504, how could the war discussions be at odds with other discussions in the work? Part VI above, for example, has detailed the care with which More worked out the unitary two-dimensional nature of Utopian philosophy. In short, if the Utopians were Machiavellian, as is unanimously believed, everything I have shown regarding the working of the author's mind since late 1504 will have to be radically revised. What does deeper analysis of Utopian warfare actually show?

9 Tinkler, "Praise and Advice," 205 and 204 resp. See also the rhetorical interpretations of McCutcheon, "War Games in Utopia," and Müllenbrock, "Krieg in Morus' Utopia."

10 In his introduction to his translation of *Utopia*, Miller talks about Hythloday's "bipolarity" (x). We both believe and disbelieve him (xix).

2 "Utter Loathing of War" and Yet a Thoroughly Militarized State

The section on military affairs (*De re militari*) (Y199/36–217/5)[11] is located between the philosophy section and the religion section (which concludes the discourse on Utopia). The first two sentences are of utmost significance

> (1) War, as an activity fit only for beasts and yet practiced by no kind of beast so constantly as by man, they regard with utter loathing. Against the usage of almost all nations they count nothing so inglorious as glory sought in war. (2) Nevertheless men and women alike assiduously exercise themselves in military training on fixed days lest they should be unfit for war when need requires. (Y199/38–201/4)[12]

While the first sentence seems pacifistic, the second seems militaristic. At minimum, are not the two sentences in tension or conflict? At maximum, are they not inherently or inevitably contradictory?

Not by chance, surely, the sentences which conclude the discourse on Utopia (and also conclude the section on religion) sound very similar.

> (1) After this prayer [expressing longing for God over against material concerns] has been said, they prostrate themselves on the ground again. Then shortly they rise and go away to dinner. (2) The rest of the day they pass in games [chess-like, training them in military strategy] and in exercises of military training. (Y237/33–6)[13]

On the one side we see unexcelled spirituality and faith; on the other great mental and physical preparations for war. Their physical training includes swimming under arms, archery, and the use of battle-axes (213/36–215/2) as well as training in how to fight in a disciplined

---

11 In my discussion of warfare, I use the Yale edition of *Utopia* rather than, as in Parts VI and VIII (below), the Cambridge.

12 "Bellum utopte rem plane beluinam, nec ulli tamen beluarum formae in tam assiduo, atque homini est usu, summopere abominantur, contraque morem gentium ferme omnium nihil aeque ducunt inglorium, atque petitam e bello gloriam. eoque licet assidue militari sese disciplina exerceant, neque id uiri modo, sed foeminae quoque, statis diebus, ne ad bellum sint, quum exigat usus, inhabiles" (198/30–200/4)

13 "Hac prece dicta rursus in terram proni, pauloque post erecti, discedunt pransum, & quod superest diei, ludis & exercitio militaris disciplinae percurrunt" (236/28–31). On the games see 129/19–29 (128/13–28), discussed below, 277–82.

manner (211/22–3). But again, isn't there an inherent or inevitable conflict between this alleged spirituality and their extreme militarism? Most readers have certainly thought so.

Note also that the author places the section on military affairs immediately before the religion section. Is there not a conflict even here – on the one side lengthy workings out of military practices and on the other side lengthy discussions of religion, including priests who, "with hands outstretched to heaven," do everything in their power to halt or contain wars? "Merely to see and to appeal to them suffice to save one's life; to touch their flowing garments protects one's remaining goods from every harm arising from war" (231/14–17).

Yet it is the justifications of war and the methods of war that follow that have most influenced readers – scholars as well as laymen. Most of the space in the military section is taken up with detailing the reasonings of the Utopians where they undertake wars and their unequalled cunning and deceit in warfare. Readers learn how the Utopians take over land from other peoples, "according to their rights"; how they undertake wars on behalf of their friends; how they purchase victory in war by dispersing vast amounts of money; how they stir up enemies against each other with bribes; how they callously use mercenaries, giving no heed to loss of life; how they reward citizens of enemy states who kill their king. Should the Utopians themselves ultimately have to go to war, they exhibit not only unsurpassed cunning but unbending determination and great ferocity. If necessary they will fight and die to the last man.

Militarism is not, moreover, a theme restricted to the section entitled *De re militari*. It is a theme inherent to the building of that state. While the last sentence of the Discourse is a strong statement on military training (237/34–6), as shown above, even the early pages of the Discourse bring out the militaristic nature of that state. Utopus and his soldiers used force to conquer the land (113/3), and in deciding where to locate the capital city, Amaurotum, they chose a natural setting at one with their strategic and defensive needs. As one consequence, the tower on the rock in the mouth of the bay holds a garrison (111/20–2). A connected stratagem was to destroy enemy fleets by shifting landmarks (111/28–30). Utopus on occasion even improved the defences affo ded by the natural setting, most notably using his own soldiers as well as the natives to completely separate the island from the mainland (reminding us of England) by digging a fifteen-mile-wide channel (113/8–18). The fortress-like construction of Amaurotum is carefully pointed out. The city has "a high and broad wall with towers and battlements at frequent intervals" and "a moat, dry but deep and wide and made impassable by thorn hedges" (119/34–7). The river which affords drinking water is connected to the city "by outworks, lest in case of hostile attack the water might be cut off and diverted or polluted" (119/26–30). Leaving aside setting and architecture, the most powerful statement of "just cause" for war is not found in the military section but much earlier, within a section entitled "Social Relations" (137/17–22). Even earlier in the Discourse is found a description of the war games Utopians practise in preparation for war (129/19–29). Using money to defeat enemy states is a major theme in the military section, yet this subject too is first discussed much earlier (149/39–151/13) [14]

Hythloday's Loathing of War

Hythloday in Book I, like the Utopians in Book II, loathes war: "Almost all monarchs prefer to occupy themselves in the pursuits of war – with which I neither have nor desire any acquaintance – rather than in the honorable activities of peace" (57/26–8). "You never have war unless you choose it, and you ought to take far more account of peace than of war" (65/32–4). And against pervasive English and European laws and practices that support strict justice, he holds up God's commandment, "Thou shalt not kill" (73/22). Seething with anger, he pits his philosophic concern with peace against the Lesbian rule (accommodating precept to desires rather than desires to precept)[15] warmongering and warfare found everywhere in Europe. Unconcerned with Christ's teachings, leaders seek their personal glory and wealth at the physical and mental expense of their people; stir up wars with evil pretexts; use evil deceit and dissimulation in the practice of war; seek with unsurpassed cunning to expand their kingdoms; fail to see true self-interest; evince little or no concern with administering the kingdom that they already have; and let the horrors of war fall on those least guilty, on both sides. Over and over Hythloday pillories such evils. One example is his picture of what goes on at the court of the French king.

> In a most secret meeting, a circle of his [the French king's] most astute councilors over which he personally presides is setting its wits to work to consider by what crafty machinations he may keep his hold on Milan

14 It may also be noted that Henry VIII is lauded as "invincible" in the first paragraph of Book I (47/8) and that Vespucci, we learn a little later, left Hythloday behind in a fort (51/11).

15 On Erasmus' definition of the Lesbian ule, as well as Hythloday's referral to this rule, see above Part VI, 223–4, and below, 330–1.

> [quibus artibus ac machinamentis Mediolanum retineat, 86/26–7] and bring back into his power the Naples which has been eluding his grasp; then overwhelm Venice and subjugate the whole of Italy; next bring under his sway Flanders, Brabant, and, finall , the whole of Burgundy – and other nations, too, whose territory he has already conceived the idea of usurping.
>
> At this meeting, one [councillor] advises that a treaty should be made with the Venetians to last just as long as the king will find it convenient, that he should communicate his intentions to them, and that he should even deposit in their keeping part of the booty, which, when all has gone according to his mind, he may reclaim ... Another thinks that a settlement should be made with the King of Aragon and that, as a guarantee of peace, someone else's kingdom of Navarre should be ceded him! ... They agree that negotiations for peace should be undertaken [with England] ... that the English should be called friends but suspected as enemies. The Scots therefore must be posted in readiness, prepared for any opportunity to be let loose on the English if they make the slightest movement. (Y87/27–89/2, 6–9, 13–14, 15–18)
>
> One [councillor] advises crying up the value of money when he [the king] has to pay any and crying down its value below the just rate when he has to receive any ... Another suggests a make-believe war under pretext ... and then ... to throw dust in his simple people's eyes ... Another councilor reminds him of certain old and moth-eaten laws ... an outward mask of justice! ... double profit ... There will be no cause of his so patently unjust in which one of them [his judges] will not ... find some loophole whereby the law can be perverted ... no amount of gold is enough for the ruler who has to keep an army. (Y91/32–93/39)

Readers have heretofore seen little diffe ence between the European outlook and practices *criticized by Hythloday in Book I* and the Utopian outlook and practices *praised by Hythloday in Book II*. Aren't these assessments correct? Often the Utopian practices are seen as far worse even than European. Erasmus argues over and over that so-called Christians "fight against Turks with the spirit of Turks," and readers up until now have found no reason to believe that the Utopians are not doing the same.[16] Responding to Hythloday's eulogy of Utopian communism in Book I, "More" sets forth the traditional belief that communism – as described by Hythloday – would result in discord, anarchy, use of force, and bloodshed (107/10–12).[17] Isn't this proven, at least in part, by what occurs in Utopian warfare?

---

16 See Erasmus' *Utilissima consultatio de bello Turcis inferendo* (1530), ASD V-3, 38/213, cf. CWE 64, 220. Cf. *Dulce bellum inexpertis* (1515), ASD II-7, 38/792, CWE 35, 431.

17 See Part VI above, 259–60.

But let us take a closer look at what actually goes on in Utopia, beginning with the war games they continually play. Do these games support the accepted modern views or do they show something else – a profound unitary two-dimensional mindset?

War Games

Following a prayer in which they ask for the harshest possible death should they be kept away from God "by the most prosperous of earthly careers," and after they again prostrate themselves on the ground, the Utopians "rise and go away to dinner. The rest of the day they pass in games and in exercises of military training" (237/33–6). These statements, as mentioned above (273), conclude the Discourse on Utopia and are made long after the lengthy discussions of military affairs. The section on military affairs (*De re militari*) begins similarly to the way the Discourse ends, as also mentioned above (273), with the assertion that the Utopians "utterly loathe" war and glory in war and yet assiduously and continually train for war. But even long before the section on military affairs, this thesis, which readers have found so contradictory, had been set forth at greater length in a description of the war games the Utopians play – after supper in the common halls or the gardens, depending on the time of year.

What needs to be carefully looked at are the components of these war games and what this says about the Utopian mindset. Why do the Utopians see themselves as representing "virtuous" outlooks and practices and contrast this with the "vices" of their opponents?

> They do play two games not unlike chess. The first is a battle of numbers in which one number plunders another. The second is a game in which the vices fight a pitched battle with the virtues. In the latter is exhibited very cleverly, to begin with, both the strife of the vices with one another and their concerted opposition to the virtues; then, what vices are opposed to what virtues, by what forces they assail them openly, by what stratagems they attack them indirectly, by what safeguards the virtues check the power of the vices, by what arts they frustrate their designs; and, finall , by what means the one side gains the victory. (Y129/19–29)

> caeterum duos habent in usu ludos, latrunculorum ludo non dissimiles. Alterum numerorum pugnam, in qua numerus numerum praedatur. Alterum in quo collata acie cum uirtutibus uitia confligunt. Quo in ludo perquam scite ostenditur & uitiorum inter se dissidium, & aduersus uirtutes concordia. item quae uitia, quibus se uirtutibus opponant, quibus uiribus aperte oppugnent, quibus machinamentis ab obliquo adoriantur,

quo praesidio, uirtutes uitiorum uires infringant, quibus artibus eorum conatur eludant, quibus denique modis alterutra pars uictoriae compos fiat. (Y128/18–27

(1) Note first that there are two games, and both are "battles." The first game, described in one sentence, is simply strife between numbers. The point of the game, it seems, is to instil in Utopians the idea that winning – leaving aside right or wrong – requires certain rules and skills. Learning these rules and skills is a serious matter best accomplished in the form of a game, a game played over and over. Major focus is given to the second game, a game which works out stratagems of the vices and stratagems of the virtues. Physical force is clearly important, but the overall focus is on stratagems, whether for evil or good, that do not require the direct use of physical force. Note the words used: "perquam scite [very cleverly]," "machinamentis [contrivances, stratagems]," "ab obliquo [indirectly]," "artibus [arts]." The Utopians want to become experts in stratagems by first understanding the stratagems employed so masterfully by their evil opponents and then incorporating what they learn into their own way of thinking. Unlike their enemies, who simply follow ever so conveniently and expertly immediate self-interest in their dissimulations, the Utopians are determined to incorporate what they learn about these deceitful practices into their virtuous outlook. Indeed it appears that the stratagems practised by the virtues require much greater effort than the stratagems practised by the vices, in that the vices by their very nature engage in stratagems, whereas the virtues have to consciously and carefully study, conceptualize, and practise stratagems. The Utopians don't just want to consider vices in general, they want to understand specific vices and to determine precisely what virtues are compromised by particular vices. Therewith they constantly study how to defend the virtues and how by arts (*artibus*) to frustrate the "concerted opposition" of the vices.[18] In short, the Utopians believe that the only way they can overcome those who employ deceit, stratagem, cleverness, and indirection against them is to become expert in deceit, stratagem, cleverness, and indirection.[19]

---

18 Incomprehensible is Philip Abbott's contention that "the 'battle against the virtues game' is so keyed to moralizing the rules of society that any element of contingency is absent." See "Utopians at Play," in *Remapping the Humanities: Identity, Community, Memory, (Post)Modernity*, ed. M. Garrett, H. Gottfried, and S. VanBurkleo (Detroit, 2008), 19–36 at 28.

19 Note Erasmus' contention, in rather diffe ent contexts, that one needs to "cut the enemy's throat with his own sword." See below, 310n68. Entirely untenable is Adams' claim in *The Better Part of Valor* that Utopian strategizing is a satirical attack

(2) Let's further break down the second game. (a) Note the "strife of the vices with one another." This situation relates not only to the opponents of the Utopians fighting with each other but also, we can see, to the contentions between European states as evidenced by what goes on in the councils of kings, described in Book I, and the many evil actors described by More in *Richard III* (1513–18). From cover to cover *Richard III* is a magisterial account of how the vices fight the vices. In the Ricardian world (1483–5), masters of evil cunning and deceit fight against masters of evil cunning and deceit. Every action is carried out with "machinamentis." It's all a masquerade, evil deceiving evil. As pointed out earlier, the most emphasized and repeated word in *Richard III* is *pretext* – and related words (67). The main diffe ence from the Utopian games, as such, is that in the Richardian world the fight of vices with vices is directly related to actual political and battlefield situations. Below we will see that the Utopians apply their game thinking to multitudes of actual (purportedly) situations. (b) Note that the vices attack the virtues both "openly [aperte]," with physical force, and "indirectly [ab obliquo]," with "machinamentis." The Utopians are students of both methods. (c) For their part, the goal of the virtues is not only to break the strength of the vices with their defences, "praesidio," but to frustrate the vices with "artibus." (d) Note finally Utopian recognition that battles are unforgiving and that the virtues don't necessarily win. Only "one side gains the victory." As stated elsewhere, "the fortunes of war are always incalculable" (209/24–5).

(3) Importantly, the Utopians here contradict in effect Hythloday's argument against "More" in Book I. Hythloday *opposes* "More" precisely because "More" advocates fighting evil by means of "the indirect approach [obliquo ductu]" (98/30). He holds not only that the indirect approach would be in practice entirely ineffective but that it is impossible to employ the indirect approach without oneself becoming corrupted or even a party to the evil one would correct. And yet in their war games the Utopians are determined to fight the vices by means of the indirect approach – and indeed by masterful uses of this approach. The vices attack the virtues "ab obliquo" and the Utopians are determined to attack the vices employing the same method. So if the Utopian state is thought to represent Hythloday's argument in Book I against "More," as is everywhere believed, we again have a problem, for the overriding point of the paragraph on war games is to show that the

---

on the lack of stratagem employed in European warfare ("chivalry") (228). Book I of Utopia shows at length that European leaders are masters of evil stratagem, a thesis that ties with discussions of the opponents of the Utopians in Book II.

Utopians take great pains to become expert in the indirect approach. In Book I, Hythloday holds that the common life practised by the Utopians will make talk about the indirect approach irrelevant, but this is emphatically not the case.

(4) And yet what is it that separates the virtues from the vices? Isn't talk about Utopian virtue nonsense, a joke, just words? If they are learning from their enemies how to carry out war, and in all sorts of deceitful ways, isn't their so-called virtue actually vice? If the Utopians are possibly the world's greatest experts in "machinamentis," as may appear from my analyses of actual practices further below, aren't they themselves engaging therewith in the vices? On what grounds do the Utopians think or assume that their outlook is virtuous and contrast the outlook of their enemies? If they are actually virtuous, the meaning of their actions cannot have the same meaning as the actions of their enemies. Supporting the accepted view, Gerard Wegemer states that the two games "constitute an integral part in teaching the Machiavellian tactics which the Utopians proudly use in their foreign wars" – which illustrates "their dehumanizing way of life."[20]

In fact there is not the slightest problem with Utopian expertise in "machinamentis." The absolutes in place, including the "utter loathing of war" which later begins the military section, the Utopians can engage with true freedom and with true creativity in "machinamentis." The Utopians *are* virtuous, and this is anything but a mere assertion. Their enemies hold either no abstract values or false abstract values and, this being the case, are wholly incapable of distinguishing between positive and negative indirect approaches. In holding to their "utter loathing of war" absolute – along with their other absolutes – the Utopians, in contrast, cannot hold to a false indirect approach, nor can they practise false types of decorum, as such approaches would conflict with this absolute. There are two types of decorum and two ways of practising the indirect approach, but Hythloday, unlike his Utopians, recognizes only one of these, evil decorum, and does not recognize therewith that positive decorum requires the absolutes. It is only their "utter loathing of war" and their other positive abstract values that make the positive indirect approach possible. Since the enemies of the Utopians don't have valid abstract principles, they cannot see or employ valid decorous values. The indirect approach is *always* evilly self-serving, lacking valid abstract principles. In short, the key that separates virtuous stratagems from evil is purpose and the consequences of purpose. Unlike their opponents, the Utopians hold to a unitary non-worldly/worldly

20 Wegemer, *Thomas More on Statesmanship*, 142.

understanding of truth. What can be seen here is a pacifism, if we want to use the word, a pacifism that holds to the "utter loathing of war" absolute at the same time as it practises an indirect approach that does not conflict with the absolute.[21] Whether their indirect approach does or does not look like the indirect approach of their enemies, it always has a diffe ent meaning.

(5) Compare with their war games the Utopian two-dimensional, *honestum/utile*, discussion of pleasure philosophy (above Part VI), where *honestum* is shown to accept what is valuable about pleasure (the *utile*) while controlling pleasure. Remember also Hythloday's own alternative to strict justice referred to above (275 and below, 312), where he brings up Christ's denial of killing (a positive abstract value) at the same time as he advocates (contradicting his thesis against "More") decorum and merciful approaches. The latter would be impossible were one to hold to the strict justice ideal (negative abstract value). With the strict justice principle, only evil, self-serving, decorum would be possible.

(6) Compare also the Utopian two-dimensional outlook in their war games with the role of Morton in More's *Richard III* (1513–18). Here, as in Book I of *Utopia* (59–61, 81–5; see below, 327–9), Morton entirely contradicts, in effect, Hythloday's insistence that ideals cannot be implemented and Hythloday's self-righteous determination to live as he pleases ("nunc sic vivo ut volo," *Utopia* 56/1). Throughout *Richard III*, More plays on the fact that Richard (1483–5) was a consummate master of dissimulation (pretext, deceit, and trickery) – as were those surrounding him and competing with him, the vices fighting as in Utopia the vices – but what he also shows is that the virtuous Morton (who had served Henry VI and Edward IV) had ultimately triumphed through craft, flatter , and pretext that was equally brilliant. And yet there was all the diffe ence between Richard and Morton. Morton was never motivated, in More's view, by a self-serving indirect approach but by Christain ideals, and Morton's actions had what More saw as very positive results, the installation of the first Tudor, Henry VII. And, of course, More well recognized that Morton then combined worldly and otherworldly positions: Lord Chancellor of England 1487–1500, Archbishop of Canterbury 1486–1500, Cardinal 1493–1500.[22]

---

21 Not of little significance, Utopian pac fism cor elates with with the two-dimensional pacifism worked out over and over by Erasmus in his books on wa . See Dealy, *Stoic Origins*, 320–5.

22 Moderns have repeatedly assumed that the means used by Morton to accomplish his ends were evil, whatever his goal may have been, and indeed Morton may himself have seen his tactics as less than Christian (see the conclusion to

The Utopians, similar to the situation confronted by Morton, face in real life as in their war games opponents who engage in warfare with unsurpassed cunning, stratagem, pretence, indirection, and savagery, entirely lacking in honour or principles, but the righteous Utopians ultimately triumph by perfecting the cunning and harsh methods of their opponents. The crucial diffe ence between the Utopians and their opponents is that the Utopians hold unbendingly to absolute precepts. The flexible worldly methods they decide on in accord with one type of value are never in contradiction, we will discover, with their unflinc - ing hold on another type of value – their non-worldly precepts. Their enemies, in contrast, lacking any higher principles, practise only the Lesbian rule.

Actual Warfare

At one with the author's outlook and writings since late 1504, the purpose of the lengthy illustrations of Utopian thought and practice regarding actual warfare is to work out the unitary principles/decorum way of thinking practised in their war games. The methods employed by the Utopians when confronted with actual war situations reveal in each instance, I will demonstrate, the following:

(1) The Utopians at all times regard war "with utter loathing" and "count nothing so inglorious as glory sought in war." These assertions are always at play not only in their war games but also in their many and varied dealings with actual warfare. They are not odd comments but absolutes, unbending principles – made with total seriousness and with complete truthfulness. And there is good reason why the Utopians espouse and hold to this unbending "utter loathing of war" state of mind. As Hythloday argues in Book I, there is "nothing in the world that fortune can bestow can be put on a par with a human life" and,

---

Kendall, ed., *History of King Richard III*, More's English version, 109–10 [cf. CWM 2, 90/22–91/17]). But one cannot conclude that the author of *Richard III* saw the issue in this way. Everything we know about More's mindset after late 1504, including everything we know about the Utopian state, would indicate that he wholeheartedly believed in Christian (unitary both/and) dissimulation. More well knew that Morton was not a humanist, not a philosopher, and did not think in unitary both/and terms, but he had as a child personally experienced Morton's indirect approach and Christian ideals as a page at Morton's court, circa 1489–91 (see page 48 above) – and had without doubt learned from Morton himself details regarding the contrasting outlook of Richard III.

even more importantly, "God has forbidden us to kill anyone" (C69).[23] Of great significance, potentially, compare Utopian "utter loathing of war" and Hythloday's belief that "God has forbidden us to kill anyone" with Erasmus' contention in book after book that Christians must hold with unbending tenacity to what he sees – rejecting accepted views – as Christ's absolute rejection of war.[24]

As shown in Part VI, Stoic *honestum* is the platform from which the Utopians see all their absolutes. *Honestum* is one with nature, reason, and God. It is the only good, that which "can justly be commended in and for itself, apart from any profit or reward" (*Fin.* 2.45). In no instance do Utopians, either in theory or practice, make exceptions to "the utter loathing of war" absolute – or their many other absolutes. Other absolutes include (a) a religion that is serious and strict, almost stern and forbidding, comprising belief in one supreme power, divine providence, immortality of the soul, and punishment of vices and rewarding of virtue in the afterlife, (b) belief that nature does not allow one's own advantage at the expense of others, and (c) the denial of private property and money. In no instance do they whittle away at their absolutes. In no instance do they bend them to make them fit contrary worldly realities. Nor do they at any time find scholastic "conditions" under which one is not required to hold – or even that one would be wrong to hold – such absolutes.

(2) And yet the "utter loathing of war" absolute is never something separate from worldly values. As in Stoicism, that person who holds to the *honestum* will of necessity work out the *utile*. In every instance there are two valid types of value at play, unbending and bending, abstract and relative, non-worldly and worldly, and they are inseparable. Were they separable, neither would be valid. As with the discussion of Polylerite practices in Book I (75–9) – to which Hythloday adds the equity and mercy found in Christ's teachings (73)[25] – the Utopians' thinking and practices exhibit at all times not just absolute truths but decorum and expedience. In short, the issues are never either/or, never Utopian ideals opposite Machiavellian practices. In all cases, however varied, the Utopian response is unitarily two-dimensional.

23 In his introductory letter the ever so perceptive Guillaume Budé appears to equate the "utter loathing" absolute with the second of three "divine principles" of the Utopians: "a fixed and unwavering dedication to peace and tranquillity [pacis ac tra - quillitatis amorem constantem ac pertinacem]" (C12/27, Y10/7–8). The first divine principle is equality of all things and the third is contempt for gold and silver.

24 See Dealy, *Stoic Origins*, 320–5.

25 See my discussion in Part VIII below, 312.

Looking at the frame of Utopian thought in greater detail, we see that there are (as in their philosophy) not one but two types of unbending principles at play and not one but two types of worldly expedience at play. Regarding the principles, the Utopians could have held (counterfactually) that killing and warfare is something very honourable (as does the English lawyer in Book I, 61) or they could hold, as they do, an utter loathing of war. Similarly, they could have seen and practised (counterfactually) worldly decorum and expedience in terms of the Lesbian rule (as is the case everywhere in Europe, Hythloday shows) or they could see expedience as they do in positive, non-Lesbian-rule, terms. Were the "utter loathing of war" absolute (or other absolutes) not in play, positive and valid decorum and expedience would be impossible; worldly affairs would be governed by the Lesbian rule (73/33–6, 101/33–6).[26] Stated otherwise, what makes Utopian stratagems not only expedient but righteous is their unbending hold on their "utter loathing of war" absolute. No expedient action is valid if it in any way is at variance with the absolute. Were this unitary both/and mindset not in play, there would be no diffe ence between Utopian motivations in warfare and the Lesbian rule motivations that govern the warfare of their enemies – or warfare in the Old World.

In no instance do the Utopians contradict themselves. In no instance does the author set forth an argument that is rhetorical in the sense that it can be interpreted in various ways. In no instance does a discussion of Utopian warfare – theory or practice – lack logic. In no instance does the author present Utopian practices of warfare that are separable from their unbending abstract values. It is their opponents and the Europeans who are lacking in principles and thus Machiavellian, not the Utopians. In all cases their reasonings are unitarily two-dimensional, at one and the same time non-worldly and worldly.

Note one thing, however: The Utopians never seek or find "perfect" solutions. They never see problems in absolutist terms. They seek only the best possible solutions, all circumstances taken into consideration. In this sense, the Utopians are not "utopians." They make situations as little bad as possible, exactly what "More" had asked for (following Cicero) in his debate with Hythloday (101/1–2).

In what follows my goal will be only to demonstrate how the Utopians think. Though correlations with various aspects of Erasmus' writings on war can be made regarding virtually every issue, I will show little of this here. What will become evident, however, once again, is the

26 On the relation to Erasmus' thought on war, versus scholastics, see below, 331n33.

extent to which the Utopian way of thinking builds on Erasmus – and behind him the Stoics.

3 Righteous Cunning, Stratagem, and Ferocity

> If they overcome and crush the enemy by stratagem and cunning, they feel great pride and celebrate a public triumph over the victory and put up a trophy as for a strenuous exploit. (Y203/18–21)
>
> arte doloque uictos, oppressos hostes impendio gloriantur, triumphumque ob eam rem publicitus agunt, & uelut re strennue gesta, tropheum erigunt. (Y202/15–17)
>
> It is not easy to say whether they are more cunning in laying ambushes or more cautious in avoiding them. (Y213/17–18)
>
> If they feel themselves to be inferior in number or in position ... [they] evade the enemy by some stratagem [stratagemate] ... (Y213/ 21–6)

These statements and others found in the section on military affairs illustrate the performance of the Utopians in actual warfare. Having studied and practised in their games the stratagem and cunning employed by their enemies, they take great pride in overcoming their enemies by perfecting the tools of their enemies, such as in laying ambushes. If they win by these methods, they set up a trophy just as if they had won by physical force.[27]

But what about their "utter loathing" of war? Isn't there a contradiction here? And what about their contempt for glory and most especially glory begotten from war? "Against the usage of almost all nations they count nothing so inglorious as glory sought in war [contraque morem gentium ferme omnium nihil aeque ducunt inglorium, atque petitam e bello gloriam]" (201/1–2). Clearly they themselves glory ("gloriantur") in their triumphs. So what diffe ence can there in fact be between the "virtues" the Utopians talk about in their games and the vices? Doesn't their behaviour in warfare just prove that there is no diffe ence – that what they call "virtue" is some type of joke? What virtue can there be in the stratagem and cunning ("arte doloque") with which they carry out war and then glory in their successes? Is the author playing games with our mind – as so many readers have believed?

27 Commenting on *De officiis* 1.80, Dyck notes that "Panaetius had argued that in warfare it is not strength of body but mental powers that are decisive" (*A Commentary on Cicero, De Officiis*, 34).

Problematic also has been the relationship between Utopian stratagem and cunning in warfare and practices in Europe. In his *The Better Part of Valor: More, Erasmus, Colet, and Vives, on Humanism, War, and Peace, 1496–1535* (1962) Robert P. Adams contends that the Utopians are actually ridiculing the "chivalry" practised in Europe.[28] The Utopians use rational stratagem and cunning while European warfare, according to Adams, reflects the irrational bloodletting and glory seeking found in chivalry. "Instead of feeling delight at the idea of the kind of head-on pitched battle customary in medieval romances, the Utopians think such behavior stupid and 'beastly' (subhuman); they prefer to use their wits to triumph, if possible, through some crafty and life-saving stratagem" (228). Edward Surtz sees the matter similarly: "The Utopian views expressed here on warfare are the reverse of the contemporary chivalric ethic, which regarded stratagem as contemptible as blood-letting honorific. [29] The Cambridge editors also follow Adams on this point.[30] What sounds warlike on the part of the Utopians was merely, Adams argues, satire, "witty realpolitik" (152). The Utopians are "utopian" and thus epitomize a rational and pacifistic outlook which entails that their stratagem and cunning in warfare are not meant seriously. Unlike Adams, more recent studies hold both that the Utopians were deadly serious and that their warfare diffe ed very little from that of their opponents in the New World. But again, is this understanding supportable?

In fact, much of *Utopia* is about the brilliant but evil stratagem and cunning actually practised by contemporary Europeans – anything but a counterpoint to the irrational chivalry found in medieval romances.[31] Over and over *Utopia* shows us that stratagem and cunning are the accepted and admired way of life and thought in Europe; that European cunning is the opposite of Utopian cunning. In Book I Hythloday focuses directly on the extreme stratagem and conniving found in the courts of kings.[32] His lengthy analysis of European practices (see above, 275–6), contains statements such as the following:

28 See also 270n6 and 278n19 above.

29 Surtz, Yale *Utopia*, 501.

30 Cambridge *Utopia*, 201n103.

31 Harari shows that even in the age of chivalry "a small investment of resources" employing "unconventional and covert" military methods produced a "disproportionate strategic or political impact." See *Special Operations in the Age of Chivalry, 1100–1500*, 1. While knights may have often held to the honour code of chivalry, ordinary soldiers engaged in bribery, deceit, surprise, assassination, and treason – though not, unlike the Utopians, psychological warfare.

32 While Erasmus focused on the ways in which, blind to the unitary both/and demands of Christianity, individuals ever so conveniently hide from themselves and

> Come now, suppose I were at the court of the French king and sitting in his privy council. In a most secret meeting, a circle of his most astute councilors over which he personally presides is setting its wits to work to consider by what crafty machinations [quibus artibus ac machinamentis] he may keep his hold on Milan and bring back into his power the Naples which has been eluding his grasp; then ... (Y87/26–32)

These councillors have no concern for the economic and social well-being of their own country, much less the lives of their soldiers. What matters is only conquest. All is governed by conniving and trumped-up charges. In his peroration to the work, discussing the "conspiracy of the rich," Hythloday even employs the same words used in Book I. These European evildoers carry out their schemes, "machinamenta" (240/26), with "malis artibus" (240/23). Without question Hythloday sees the Utopian outlook on war as the opposite of the European outlook on war. But do actual Utopian practices support Hythloday's view or do they not?

What the European conniving described by Hythloday forcefully reminds us of is More's *Richard III*, begun around 1513 – three years before *Utopia* was published. In this work we are graphically shown that the world of Richard III is a "green world"[33] governed only by pretext and dissimulation (see above, 62–5). Outwardly friendly, Richard would "kiss whom he thought to kill ... He spared no man's death whose life withstood his purpose."[34] *Richard III* is said to be "the first work in Western literature with a dissembling hypocrite as the major protagonist."[35] Not just Richard but almost everyone portrayed in this work is a dissembler, the Duke of Buckingham for example. Even

---

others the reality of who they are and the actualities of the situation at hand, More was fixated – not un elated to his early attachments to Morton and an unforgiving political and legal environment – on what he saw (exemplified by Richa d III) as the very conscious and elaborate deceit of key players in society. His concern was to be worked out in very personal ways. In 1522, long before his martyrdom (1535), his son-in-law William Roper had been amazed and overjoyed at seeing the king walking with More, holding his arm around his neck for about an hour at More's home, but More assessed the event diffe ently: "I believe he [Henry] doth as singularly favor me as any subject within this realm. Howbeit, son Roper, I may tell thee I have no cause to be proud thereof, for if my head could win him a castle in France (for then was there war between us) it should not fail to go." See Roper, *The Life of Sir Thomas More*, 208.

33 Kendall, ed., *History of King Richard III*, English version, 109 (cf. CWM 2, 92).

34 Kendall, ed., *History of King Richard III*, 35.

35 Marius, *Thomas More*, 119.

the great Cardinal Morton, at whose house More lived as a young lad, is a dissembler – though for noble ends. Everywhere in this "green world" life swims in deceit, one thing pretended while another meant. Everything is trickery, evil expedience, flatter , personal dominion, tyranny, contrived reasoning, feigned friendship, secrecy, and, not least, desire for war rather than peace.[36]

Throughout *Utopia*, both the enemies of the Utopians and the Europeans accomplish their evil purposes by means of indirection, deceit, and cunning. The words used by the Utopians to describe the vices fighting the virtues in their games, "quibus machinamentis ab obliquo adoriantur" (128/24/5), equate with the words Hythloday uses in describing evil European practices, "quibus artibus ac machinamentis Mediolanum retineat" (86/26–7).

Very similar words are used by the Utopians in describing their own outlook and practices, as for example where they study in their games "quibus artibus eorum conatur eludant" (128/26) and where in actual warfare they win by "arte doloque" (202/15, above, 285). So is there or is there not a diffe ence between the "virtues" Utopians pride themselves on and the "vices" of their enemies?

Two Types of Glory

As worked out at length in their philosophy, Utopian thinking is throughout a rejection of Lesbian rule practices – the bending of truth or ideals or abstractions to make them fit immediate desires (perceived self-interest). Unlike their enemies and unlike Europeans, the Utopians have overcome the Lesbian rule. Throughout the discussion of warfare we are shown that they practise cunning and deceit from a unitary both/and, *honestum/utile*, standpoint. They never carry out actions only in terms of that which seems *utile*, which always ends up as evil expertise and evil decorum. Consider, first, the statement that immediately precedes the quote that begins chapter 3 (285):

> They not only regret but blush at a victory that has cost much bloodshed, thinking it folly to purchase wares, however precious, too dear. (Y203/16–18) ["If they overcome and crush the enemy by stratagem and cunning [arte doloque], they feel great pride [gloriantur] and celebrate a public triumph over the victory and put up a trophy as for a strenuous exploit." (Y203/18–21).]

36 Shore's wife, described with sympathy, is one exception to this picture.

Unlike their enemies, the Utopians are devoid of interest in glory from killing and bloodshed. The pride or glory that they take in defeating an enemy by cunning and stratagem is thus not based on European conceptions of glory. Unlike Europeans, their cunning and stratagem have no evil ulterior motives. They hold the absolutes high. Not at all contradicted is the assertion at the beginning of the military section that they have an "utter loathing" of war. They have no interest at all in evilly advantaging themselves at the expense of others. They conceive and carry out truly decorous stratagems at the same time as they hold unbendingly to their absolutes – and because they hold to these absolutes. Nothing decorous or useful occurs that is not one with their precepts. When these unitary both/and, *honestum/utile*, stratagems work, they feel immense pride.

In holding firm their absolutes, decorous reasoning shows the Utopians that it is inexpedient for themselves as well as others to bring about any more bloodshed, any more lives lost, than absolutely necessary. Nor do they glory in warfare as such. Unlike their enemies and Europeans, they do not carry on wars without regard to the economic cost and well-being of their own country – and do everything possible to limit harm even to the country conquered (cf. 201/35–8, 203/6–9). The Utopians don't expect that they can limit the costs of war absolutely, but they are determined – using both/and tools – to limit the cost as much as possible. Not a touch of evil self-interest is involved. In short, the cunning and stratagem practised by the Utopians against their enemies contrast entirely with the European practices described by Hythloday in Book I. Though cunning and stratagem govern both Utopians and Europeans, the purpose, meaning, and way they are carried out are entirely diffe ent. The Utopians are dead serious about employing stratagem and cunning, but they know, unlike their enemies, that stratagem and cunning can be and must be carried out in two-dimensional unitary both/and terms. Seen in *honestum/utile* terms, the stratagem and cunning employed by the Utopians are entirely compatible, it may be noted, with "the indirect approach [oblique ductu]" advocated by "More" against Hythloday in Book I (98/30). The problem with both European leaders and the enemies of the Utopians is that they don't have any absolutes and therefore can and do use stratagem and cunning only for evil ends.

Consider now the sentence that immediately follows my beginning quote, where it is stated that the Utopians take great pride ("gloriantur") in crushing the enemy by stratagem "and celebrate a public triumph over the victory and put up a trophy as for a strenuous exploit":

> They boast themselves as having acted with valor and heroism [cum uirtute] whenever their victory is such as no animal except man could have won, that is, by strength of intellect. (Y203/21–4)

Most wild beasts, it is then explained,

> are superior [superantur] to us in brawn and fie ceness, but they are all inferior in cleverness and calculation. (Y203/26–7)

The Utopians here glory not in bloodshed but in conquest through ingenuity, cleverness, and smartness.[37] The contrast is between what is animal-like and what is human-like. And yet the contrast is not an either/or matter but a matter of degree. Their enemies are superior ("superantur") in brawn and fie ceness but inferior in cleverness and calculation. Nor is it implied that non-Utopians don't have diffe ent degrees of intellect and are not at lesser and greater distances from animals. Further below it will be shown that no people are closer to animals than the Zapoletans. While non-Utopian leaders are often masters of ingenuity and cleverness, the problem is only that they use these abilities for false ends. At all times they advantage themselves at the expense of others. But to the extent that humans, such as the Utopians, are able to use "cleverness and calculation" not merely to discover their true self-interest but to implement this true self-interest, they leave bestiality behind and become more and more – degree is always involved – peculiarly human. The thoughts, feelings, and assumptions of the Utopians are not found among their enemies – or among Europeans.

When in the conclusion to the book the author refers to "their method of waging war" (245/19–20) as one of the things "very absurdly established" (245/18) in Utopia, he is speaking – facetiously – in terms of common opinion, evil decorum, the Lesbian rule. What he is saying is the opposite, as shown above – and will be demonstrated over and over in what follows.

Purchasing Victory

Money is central to Utopian "stratagem and cunning" in fighting wars. The various ways in which they use money in these wars are even illustrated at considerable length. Money?! Isn't this usage clearly a contradiction? After all, "no exchange of Money" is a very prominent absolute on which that state is built. Long before the section on military affairs

---

37 See 285n27 above.

but some pages after the discussion of war games are found discussions of the crucial role of money in warfare.

> [The Utopians are] well aware that by large sums of money even their enemies themselves may be bought and sold or set to fight one another either by treachery or by open warfare. (Y149/39–151/13)
>
> [A marginal reinforces the meaning:] It is better to avoid war by money or diplomacy [arte] than to wage it with much sacrifice of human blood. (149/36–8)

Sometimes they use money to pay off enemies rather than fight them, and at other times they get enemies to fight each other "either by treachery or by open warfare." In their chess-like games (129/17–29), similarly, the Utopians sometimes "set [their enemies] to fight one another" and at other times show how the vices assail, not other vices, as in the present instance, but the virtues "indirectly" or by "open warfare." What the Utopians have obviously learned from the vices found in the non-Utopian world is that money governs – and that if they are to survive they must deal with this reality, not just in general but in multitudes of situations (see below).

Here again the context of the quotation shows us what it is that separates Utopians from their enemies – and, therewith, from evil. Following the quotation is the important and rather considerable discussion of how the Utopians acquire ideas and feelings so diffe ent from other people (151/18–159/6). So little do they value the gold and silver from which money is made that they make bedpans and the like from these materials (153/6–7) and they stigmatize evildoers by having them wear pearls and gems (155/14–16). Preceding the quotation is a discussion of the great monetary wealth of the Utopians and of how this has come about notwithstanding that the Utopians make no use of this wealth within their own society. Since on the one hand there is an enormous surplus of goods in Utopia and on the other hand foreign countries have great needs, the Utopians export goods to them. But since Utopia is almost entirely self-sufficient foreign countries can repay only in gold and silver, the result being that the Utopians are owners of huge amounts of these metals. Having no need for money themselves, they generously leave much of it out on credit. They call it in only if there should be a case of extreme necessity in foreign affairs, most particularly "when they must wage war."

> The Utopians never claim payment of most of the money. They think it hardly fair to take away a thing useful to other people when it is useless to

> themselves. But if circumstances require that they should lend some part of it to another nation, then they call in their debts – or when they must wage war. It is for that single purpose that they keep all the treasure they possess at home: to be their bulwark in extreme peril or in sudden emergency. (Y149/29–36)

In short, the Utopians hold on the first side of their unitary both/and, *honestum/utile*, mindset a "no money" absolute, while on the second side decorous reasoning guides their handling of money. The diffe - ence between the ways they handle money within the Utopian state and outside that state is explained by the decorous side. The hard side remains firm. What is decorous with regard to money within Utopia is not what is decorous with regard to money outside Utopia. But in neither case is this decorum evil. Using money within Utopia would be evil and indecorous while not using money outside Utopia would also be wrong and indecorous. The absolute, "no exchange of money," doesn't require that Utopians never hold money or that they can't use money outside Utopia. In using money to carry out wars, they in fact hold at all times to an "utter loathing" of money just as they hold to an "utter loathing" of war. They keep their money at home for the "single purpose" of loaning it to another nation or fighting wars. Money plays no role within their society. They have, in other words, no ulterior or Lesbian rule motives.

Their matchless understanding of the power of money in non-Utopian societies allows the Utopians to deeply grasp the psychology of humans who live in these societies and to act. Only the Utopians have a double vision. Non-Utopians cannot grasp Utopian thinking because they are totally absorbed in their one-dimensional Lesbian rule lifestyles. All this being the case, the Utopians of all people are brilliantly prepared to deal with the governance of money elsewhere. They of all people are experts at handling precisely and appropriately real situations. They of all people are able to come to grips with imperfection. Whether handling problems outside Utopia or inside Utopia, the Utopians are not "utopians." What they have that others don't is an outlook, a methodology. They know how to deal with an imperfect world. Utopian society is filled with problems, and the solutions they work out are in no way "perfect." Even within Utopia, slavery, for example, may now and then be the only solution to a person's misdeeds (147/8–12). What makes the Utopians superior to all other peoples is that they know how to make the best of problems, whether within their own society or outside it. We should not be surprised if, outside Utopia, war is sometimes necessary, and that great mental effort ("stratagem") is put into this endeavour.

Utopian usage of money and therewith "stratagem" are just other aspects of decorous reasoning, "adapted to their way of life rather than to ours" (151/15). No evil falls on Utopian shoulders. The absolutes are always in place. Here as elsewhere the Utopians make the best of bad situations. Imperfection is for them the human condition. There is not a touch of inconsistency in Utopian attitudes and behaviour. Far from falling away from their unitary both/and outlook, they work out and implement this outlook whatever situation arises. The factors that allow them to understand and deal with their own society are one and the same factors that allow them to understand and deal with alien countries.

Methods Employed in Actual Warfare

In the military section, much later, we are shown at considerable length and in a variety of ways how the Utopians get their enemies to fight each other – and for what purposes. One method (203/36–205/18) is to secretly set up placards promising huge rewards to anyone who will kill the enemy king[38] and somewhat lesser rewards to anyone who will kill or bring to them the named individuals most responsible for the hostile measures taken against them. The result is that these enemies don't trust each other and are in a state of panic and often betrayed. Note, however, that everything is proportionate and geared towards preventing unnecessary loss of life. The reward is doubled, for example, for the person who brings one of the guilty persons alive to them. Most importantly (205/22–32), in having those most responsible killed, the Utopians save great number of persons from having to die in battle, both on their own side and on the enemy side – because of "the madness of kings." "They are as sorry for the throng and mass of the enemy as for their own citizens."

If these procedures do not work (205/33–9), the Utopians "foster strife by leading a brother of the king or one of the noblemen to hope that he may obtain the throne" and then "involve the neighbors of their enemies by reviving some forgotten claims to dominion such as kings have always at their disposal" – and supply the neighbours with money. All of which closely corresponds with Hythloday's discussion

38 More had approved, in his declamation in reply to Lucian (1506), the right to kill a tyrant. See CWM 3.1, 109, 123, 127. Cicero holds that where tyrants ("fie ce and savage monsters in human form") are killed, the *honestum* is the *utile* (*Off.* 3.19, 3.32). Unlike all other situations, here advantage at the expense of others is necessary and even a requirement of the *honestum/utile* mindset (3.26).

of what goes on in the councils of European kings in Book I and with the "green world" depicted in *Richard III*. Here again the Utopians are carrying out with their stratagems only what is absolutely necessary to control a situation, nothing more and nothing less. What changes is not their mindset but only the situation. They hold firm their "utter loathing" absolute at the same time as they work out decorous solutions.

When necessary, the Utopians hire the Zapoletans to fight for them. Readers have found the Utopian attitude towards these mercenaries to be the epitome of callousness, cynicism, and self-righteousness, and even genocidal in that a large proportion of the Zapoletans sent to battle usually die, and yet the Utopians expressly don't care and even imagine that in allowing this they are doing the human race a service.

> The Utopians do not care in the least how many Zapoletans [their mercenaries] they lose [in battle], thinking that they would be the greatest benefactors to the human race if they could relieve the world of all the dregs of this abominable and impious people. (Y209/11–15)

But here again what needs to be grasped is the Utopian *honestum/utile* mindset. Nowhere in this discussion do the Utopians lose their "utter loathing" of war and nowhere here do they lose their determination, therewith, to think out and practise truly decorous solutions. Entirely at opposite poles from the Utopians, the Zapoletans hold to no precepts, fight without regard to necessity, and practise from birth only evil decorum. Throughout, the Utopians are in fact shown to absolutely abhor killing and bloodshed, whereas the Zapoletans are born for killing and bloodshed. The Zapoletans are as close to being animals as is possible for humans. Living five hundred miles to the east, the Zapoletans are a ferocious, barbarous, totally unrefined, and totally unethical people. "They are born for warfare and zealously seek an opportunity for figh - ing" (207/18–19). "The only trade they know in life is that by which they seek their death" (207/22–3). Nothing governs in their lives but money (their name means "busy sellers"). As mercenaries, they will change sides for only a penny more in daily pay (207/39). "Forgetting both kinship and friendship," they fight on both sides and "run one another through with the utmost ferocity" (207/34–5). Since the Utopians "hire at sky-high rates of pay" (149/36–7; cf. 209/4–6), the Zapoletans are most eager to serve them. In everything they do, they have no gauge other than money.

In total contrast, the Utopians not only give money no place in their society but do everything possible to distance themselves from any type of killing and bloodshed. In their religious sacrifices they slay no animal. "They do not believe that the divine clemency delights in bloodshed and slaughter, seeing that it has imparted life to animate creatures that they might enjoy life" (235/9–12). When it is necessary for subsistence to slay animals, they leave this, we learn early on, to slaves ("servos"). "They do not allow their citizens to accustom themselves to the butchering of animals, by the practice of which they think that mercy, the finest feeling of our human nature, is gradually killed off" (139/16–21). Later, in the philosophy section, the point is emphasized.

> Or what sweetness can there be, and not rather disgust, in hearing the barking and howling of dogs? ... if you are attracted by the hope of slaughter and the expectation of a creature being mangled under your eyes, it ought rather to inspire pity when you behold a weak, fugitive, timid, and innocent little hare torn to pieces by a strong, fie ce, and cruel dog. In consequence the Utopians have imposed the whole activity of hunting, as unworthy of free men, upon their butchers – a craft, as I explained before, they exercise through their slaves. They regard hunting as the meanest part of the butcher's trade and its other functions as more useful and more honorable, seeing that they do much more positive good and kill animals only from necessity, whereas the hunter seeks nothing but pleasure from the killing and mangling of a poor animal. Even in the case of brute beasts, this desire of looking on bloodshed, in their estimation, either arises from a cruel disposition or degenerates finally into cruelty through the constant practice of such brutal pleasure. (Y171/13–33)

The Utopians see the Zapoletans as infinitely lower on the scale than even their slave butchers. Lacking a trace of religion or godliness or divinity, they kill not from necessity but as a way of life. They lack principles and they lack, therewith, any understanding of true decorum. In contrast, the Utopians place harm where it most belongs, with those who start wars and those mercenaries who live and thrive on warfare. They let those suffer and die who most deserve to suffer and die; not as in Europe where the innocent pay, with most of the suffering and deaths caused by kings and by mercenaries.

And Yet the Utopians Will Fight to the Death

Sometimes, however, the Utopians find direct involvement in warfare a necessity. What is striking is the unexcelled ferocity and determination of the Utopians in fighting, once they have committed themselves. Some may imagine, considering the ingenuity with which they avoid warfare and let the weight of warfare fall on others, not to mention their loathing of war, that they would either refuse to go into battle, or at least be squeamish and wimpish about the prospect, or be the world's worst fighters. Most readers have found it obvious that pacifism ("utter loathing" of war) and militarism are by definition mutually exclusive. The Utopian reality does not align with any of these assumptions. The Utopians can be every bit as ferocious and determined, when necessity demands this, as even the almost non-human Zapoletans.

> When personal service is inevitable, they [the Utopians] are as courageous in fighting as they were ingenious in avoiding it as long as they might. They are not fie ce in the first onslaught, but their strength increases by degrees through their slow and hard resistance. Their spirit is so stubborn that they would rather be cut to pieces than give way. (Y211/13–18)

The larger context is shown in the page preceding the quotation. The use of force by the Utopians themselves is only the very last step (209/16–18). They add "a contingent of their own citizens" only after they have (a) used intellectual cunning and stratagem to work to the greatest degree possible psychological and material havoc on enemy leaders, (b) employed mercenaries (mostly Zapoletan), (c) added "forces of the people for whom they are fighting," and (d) added "auxiliary squadrons of all their friends." Let us not forget, moreover, that the cases discussed are only cases of extreme necessity. If there is no extreme necessity, there is no war.[39] And if the previous steps taken by the Utopians are adequate (a–d), they do not involve themselves. Every step is based on degree and decorum. In war as in other matters, Utopian method and practice is a direct and demonstrably proportionate dealing with empirical reality.

The unbending mental strength of the Utopians reminds us immediately of the Stoics of old and their determination to fight to the death rather than bend the precepts by which they live (cf. *Off.* 3.114).[40]

39 Utopian judgments of "extreme necessity" are accurate because the Utopians have no ulterior motives and they can see clearly what situations are a threat to their entire unitary both/and system and way of thinking – unlike Europeans, who see extreme necessity in terms of the Lesbian rule and the logic-based "conditions" of scholastics. Unlike Utopian reasons for carrying out war, Socrates describes the luxurious city and its desire for ever more goods (*Rep.* 373e).

40 Erasmus holds that Christians must hold unbendingly to the "rule of Christ" (*Ench.* 86) and "the standards of Christ" (*Ench.* 88). Brahmans, Cynics, and Stoics hold with grim tenacity to their beliefs, no matter the protests of the world, and so too must Christians hold to the dogmas (*decreta*) taught by Christ (*Ench.* 93). Cicero refers to Brahmans who throw themselves into the flames without uttering a wo d (*Tusc.* 5.77, cf. 2.52).

Contrasting with soldiers, who tend to begin at peak energy and then, especially if things are not going well, gradually or precipitously lose strength and spirit,[41] the Utopians begin with as little harm as possible to themselves and others but rise unflinchingly to whatever the situation demands (cf. *Off.* 1.81). If necessary they will fight to the last man, at peak strength and ferocity, with unbending spiritual determination. Again, their souls are governed by completely diffe ent rules from non-Utopians. Their outlook and spirit cannot be conquered.

What underpins their unexcelled mental strength in warfare? Besides the confidence that comes from their military training (211/22–3) is the fact that they don't have to worry about the livelihoods of anyone (211/18–21). Support also comes from the fact that wives are encouraged "by expressions of praise" to accompany their husbands (211/1) and that children and relatives also come along.[42] Relatives who return without a fighter are severely chastised.[43] No one has to fight in foreign wars against his will, but if their own country is invaded, they mix the timorous with the bolder or "put them here and there to man the walls where they cannot run away" (209/32–3) – and thus, here as elsewhere, "make a virtue of extreme necessity" (209/36).

Supporting the unbending spirit of Utopian soldiers are not just the social institutions and practices that surround them but, indispensably, the way they have been educated to think since childhood.

> Their good and sound opinions, in which they have been trained from childhood both by teaching and by the good institutions of their country, give them additional courage. So (1) they do not hold their life so cheap as recklessly to throw it away and (2) not so immoderately dear as greedily and shamefully to hold fast to it when honor bids them give it up. (Y211/23–8)[44]

In short, they hold fast to unchanging truths and do not hesitate to give up their lives if honour necessitates this, and yet they do not

41 Contemporaries contrasted, especially in Italy, the performance of mercenaries with citizen soldiers. See 305n57 below.

42 The author may well be taking note here of Plato's *Republic*, where "women must be taught music, gymnastic, and military exercises equally with men" (5.452), and children go along on military expeditions (4.466).

43 Praise and dispraise are, of course, important humanist tools.

44 "Postremo rectae opiniones (quibus & doctrina & bonis reipublicae institutis imbuti a pueris sunt) virtutem addunt: qua neque tam vilem habent vitam, ut temere prodigant, neque tam improbe charam, ut quum honestas ponendam suadeat, avare turpiterque retineant" (210/18–22).

unnecessarily throw their lives away – all this like the Stoics of old.[45] Here as elsewhere they respond to events appropriately and decorously. Did not the absolutes tower gloriously above them, however, they would have no ability to even see that which is truly decorous and appropriate – would have no ability to see, for example, when it is necessary to give up their lives and when it is not.

Many more examples of Utopian practices in warfare could be brought up here, but let us simply note that even in victory their outlook is unitarily both/and. If the enemy is routed, for example, they try to take prisoners rather than kill them (211/39–213/1). Non-combatants are left unharmed, while anyone who recommended surrender of a town is given the property of those leaders who prevented surrender – who are put to death (215/17–21). The Utopians seek no "gain" from the war, and, unlike Europeans, they see to it that the cost of war is borne proportionate to the responsibility for the war. What they seek, here as elsewhere, is only the best possible resolution of a problem.[46] This attitude and behaviour are possible only because they "utterly loathe" war at the same time as they carry out decorous practices that entirely accord with their precepts. If contemporary and traditional opinion held, as interpreted by "More" in Book I (responding to Hythloday), that the common life inevitably leads to discord, anarchy, and bloodshed (107/10–12),[47] we see here again demonstrated the converse – in the most trying of all human social and individual circumstances. But the solutions the Utopians work out are not in fact the one-dimensional solutions Hythloday imagines in Book I.

45 Taking the side of the Stoics against Epicurus, Cicero concludes that "It is enough for duty if the wise man is brave in endurance; I do not require him to rejoice [in being tortured]" (*Tusc.* 2.18, cf. 4.37). Seneca shows that the wiseman tries not to be a martyr and is a master at finding deco ous and prudent solutions to worldly situations. Martyrdom is only a last recourse – when the precepts by which he lives are threatened (*Tr.* 11.1–6, 14.10, 16.3). Though not recognizing the Senecan tie, Guy describes More's martyrdom in very similar terms. See *Thomas More*, 190–7.

46 "When they lose their goods anywhere through fraud, but without personal violence," for example, "their anger goes no further [in contrast to the practices of their enemies and Europeans] than abstention from trade with that nation until satisfaction is made" (201/35–8). Cf. above, 254n106. In wars between Greeks, as distinguished from "natural enemies," Socrates rejects pillaging, killing or enslavement, and punishment of those not directly responsible, and advises a conclusion that is mutually acceptable to both sides (*Rep.* 5.470c–471c). But there seems to have been very little, if anything, of the *Republic* in Utopian warfare. On the framing of warfare in the *Republic* see Leon H. Craig, *The War Lover*; Kochin, "War, Class, and Justice in Plato's Republic"; and Frank, "Wages of War."

47 See Part VI, 259–60.

Justifications of War

Utopian justifications of war are systematically worked out with the same unitary both/and logic that governs their methods of fighting wars discussed above. See Y137/7–22, 197/18–199/35, 201/4–203/15, 203/28–35, 217/1–5. In no instance, analysis shows, is there a breakdown in their logic. Throughout, we are shown, and this has not been understood, the diffe ence between Utopian "just war" thinking and the "just war" logicizing of scholastics worked out in large tomes. While scholastic thinking actually abets, the Utopians believe, the Lesbian rule motives so rampant in the everyday world, the Utopians show that they alone are qualified to make truly decorous judgments, judgments based on nature and circumscribed by absolute principles. For space reasons, I will not go through these arguments here.

Non-Worldly/Worldly Priests

The section on religion immediately follows the section on war and concludes the discourse on Utopia. Why is it that the section on religion follows the section on warfare? Is the author trying to correct Utopian thinking on warfare by contrasting military practices with abstract priestly views or simply spinning out odd or off-the-cuff "utopian" ideas unrelated to what was said about warfare? Or, unseen by readers, could there be a fundamental relationship between the two sections? Most relevant here are the discussions of priestly attitudes and behaviour regarding war.

> They [priests] are not more esteemed among their own people than among foreign nations. This can easily be seen from a fact which, I think, is its cause. (a) When the armies are fighting in battle, the priests are to be found separate but not very far off, settled on their knees, dressed in their sacred vestments. With hands outstretched to heaven, they pray first of all for peace, next for a victory to their own side – but without much bloodshed on either side. (b) When their side is winning, they run among the combatants and restrain the fury of their own men against the routed enemy. Merely to see and to appeal to them suffice to save one's life; to touch their flowing garments protects one's remaining goods from every harm arising from war.
>
> This conduct has brought them such veneration among all nations everywhere and has given them so real a majesty [tantum verae maiestatis] that they have saved their own citizens from the enemy as often as they have protected the enemy from their own men ... Never had there

> been any nation so savage, cruel, and barbarous that it had not regarded their persons as sacred and inviolable. (Y231/5–21; 27–8)

As powerfully and movingly represented by the quotation, Utopian priests (a) utterly loathe war and yet (b) are at the same time masters of decorum – worked out in their merciful worldly behaviour.

(a) By their very lives priests epitomize everything highest truth stands for. Peace is for them an unbending absolute. Representing highest religiosity and truth, the hands of Utopian priests are "outstretched to heaven." Before praying for anything else, they pray for peace. They keep the absolute in their minds at all times. They see war as lacking even a trace of glory. As far as possible, they are above nationalism. As representatives of God, they do not allow that God's teachings have anything to do with supporting war, not even the necessary wars carried out by their own side in extreme situations. Amid all the horrors of war they rigidly hold to truth. There is no bending of abstract truth, as with scholastics and others, to make it fit human desires or human practices (the Lesbian rule).

(b) And yet their behaviour also bespeaks Christian mercy and charity, the second side of their both/and mindset. Actively involved, they do everything possible to restrain atrocities by the winning side, whether this be their own side or the enemy's. Their mercy is unbounded: "Merely to see and to appeal to them suffice to save one's life; to touch their flowing garments protects one's remaining goods from every harm arising from war." All in contrast to European priests, so incessantly criticized by More's friend Erasmus in his many books on war, their behaviour is entirely decorous. European priests were nationalistic, often supported wars, and sometimes even took part in fighting wars.[48] Yet Utopian priests are not mere mystics or contemplatives. Their pacifism is two-dimensional. They hold high their abhorrence of killing, an unchanging absolute, at the same time as they do everything possible to mitigate the effects of war. They are actively "involved" with evil, even the harsh realities of warfare, but they do not themselves partake of these evils. In short, they represent more perfectly than anyone the unitary both/and model. An Erasmian sounding marginal keeps the European contrast in focus: "O priests far more holy than ours!"

48 Erasmus was horrified by the spect e of Pope Julius II (1503–13) even commanding his own army. See *Dialogus Julius exclusus e coelis* (c. 1513, pub. 1517), *Erasmus Opuscula* pp. 65–124, CWE 27, 155–97.

In the midst of mankind's most difficul and terror-filled circumstances, that of war, their priests are venerated by all sides. And there is good reason for this. All men are necessarily affected by their unbending/bending mindset, even their enemies – and no matter how barbarous or lacking in humanity these enemies. Truth works. Christianity works. Goodness and good example is a powerful force.[49] Contrasting with the false majesty so pervasive among priests in Europe, Utopian priests have true majesty ("tantum verae maiestatis").

Note one thing, however: the mindset of priests differs not at all from the mindset of ordinary Utopians. In both cases their outlook is unitarily both/and, *honestum/utile*. Ordinary Utopians want nothing from war and in fact gain nothing from war. Their only goal is to halt the harm and rectify actual damages. In their decisions to go to war and in their manner of waging war, ordinary Utopians also represent, like the priests, highest truth – an embryo Christian truth. Their priests have merely a higher-level function. If Utopian priests don't practise cunning in warfare, it is not because those Utopians who do aren't exhibiting highest truth but merely that priests have diffe ent responsibilities. The both/and mindset espoused by priests is the same both/and espoused by non-priest Utopians. What separates the virtue of priests from that of non-priests is only societal place and function. Priests are God's representatives and therewith "the very best among the good" (229/31–2).

4 Beyond Machiavelli, a Seamless Mindset: Embryonic Soldiers of Christ

No aspect of Utopian attitudes and practices has been more abhorred, ridiculed, and found contradictory than their warfare, yet the Utopian way of thinking here does not differ from their way of thinking about philosophy or, it appears, anything else that goes on in Utopia. The Utopian mind is essentially seamless. Readers haven't understood Utopian warfare for the same reasons they haven't understood the meaning and

49 Good example plays an important role even among those Utopians that are not priests. Allies of the Utopians, for example, are so impressed by the incorruptibility of Utopians that they obtain their officials om them (197/1–17). Vasco de Quiroga, who built two communities for Indians based on *Utopia* (beginning in the 1530s), saw good example as a fundamental Utopian and Erasmian concept. See my *The Politics of an Erasmian Lawyer, Vasco de Quiroga.*

functioning of all other happenings in Utopia – as also everything we now know about More's mindset after late 1504.

Far from indicating a breakdown of Utopian ideals, the portrayals of warfare pinpoint the nature and actual workings of the Utopian mind – how the Utopians solve even the most trying and difficul of problems. These discussions no more support Hythloday's Platonist understanding of Utopian thought and communism than they do the traditional belief, noted by "More," that communism inevitably breaks down, leading to discord, anarchy, and bloodshed (Y107/10–12). Utopian communism is two-dimensional, not as everywhere believed one-dimensional (above, 252–63). The discussions of warfare play out yet again the Stoic-based Democritus/"man for all seasons" mindset seen by Erasmus in Thomas More.

What brings forth the "utter loathing of war" absolute (in addition to their other absolutes) and makes it so necessary is the emergence of a new experiential reality, not problems internal to Utopia but external. In matters of war, the Utopians must deal with peoples who know nothing of the Utopian way of thinking and living, countries where attitudes and customs are entirely at odds with the Utopian outlook and the practices and institutions that have evolved from this outlook. In holding to *honestum* and therewith their "utter loathing of war" absolute, the Utopians guarantee that even in these most trying of circumstances their minds and hearts will always be clean and that they will always work out the *utile* in terms of this absolute. It is not merely that they seek out decorous practices (*utilia*) that are one with a rigid "utter loathing of war"; holding to this unitary both/and mindset forces them to think creatively, not bound, like their enemies or Europeans, by tradition or common assumptions.

But Do the Utopians Have an Answer to Machiavelli?

The Florentine Machiavelli wrote *The Prince* in 1513, two years prior to *Utopia* – though it was not published until 1532. Central to this landmark work is the contention that in military and political affairs leaders must not concern themselves with morals but with hard realities, "what is done" rather than "what ought to be done."

> Because I want to write what will be useful to anyone who understands, it seems to me better to concentrate on what really happens rather than on theories or speculations. *For many have imagined republics and principalities that have never been seen or known to exist.* However, how men live is so diffe ent from how they should live that a ruler who does not do what is

> generally done, but persists in doing what ought to be done, will undermine his power rather than maintain it. If a ruler who wants always to act honorably is surrounded by many unscrupulous men his downfall is inevitable. Therefore, a ruler who wishes to maintain his power must be prepared to act immorally when this becomes necessary. (Italics mine)[50]

Following abstract moral virtue may lead to ruin, even the loss of one's kingdom, whereas what is considered vice, he goes on to say, "may strengthen one's position and cause one to flourish. [51] What is expedient, that is, may have nothing in common with abstract precepts.

It now seems clear that Machiavelli was mainly responding to the "mirror-for-princes" works of contemporary humanists that depicted, based in particular on Seneca's *De Clementia* (an early work), ideal ways a prince should behave in all circumstances.[52] In criticizing these "mirror-for-princes" works and those who "have imagined republics and principalities that have never been seen or known to exist," was he not also criticizing – however unknowingly – *Utopia*?

Actually Machiavelli's criticism is little relevant to the meaning of *Utopia*. The Utopians would not be happy with either the mirror-for-princes treatises or Machiavelli's alternative. They would see in the former an abstract one-dimensional view and in the latter a worldly one-dimensional view. Nowhere would they see anything of their unitarily two-dimensional outlook.

Before detailing diffe ences between *Utopia* and *The Prince* some relationships need to be pointed out.

Similarities between the Utopians and Machiavelli

Utopia can be compared to *The Prince* in that both are concerned with what is "seen" and "exists," actual practice and experience, and what

50 Machiavelli, *The Prince*, trans. and ed. Skinner and Price, chapter 15.

51 Machiavelli, *The Prince*, trans. and ed. Skinner and Price, chapter 15.

52 Among others, the following individuals produced idealistic treatises on princely rule: Bartolomeo Sacchi (1471), Diomede Carafa (c. 1480), Platina (c. 1481), Giuniano Majo (c. 1492), Francesco Patrizi (c. 1494), Giovanni Pontano (c. 1503), Poggio Bracciolini (1504), Filippo Beroaldo (c. 1509). Stacey shows in his *Roman Monarchy and the Renaissance Prince* that these mirror-for-princes treatises were primarily built from the thinking found in Seneca's *De clementia* and not, as had been believed, from (other than in secondary points) Cicero's *De officiis*. On the mirror-for-princes treatises and the one-dimensional Stoicism Machiavelli criticized, see Dealy, *Stoic Origins*, 39–45.

in this context would be expedient, against that which is merely imagined or ideal or "utopian" (in the modern meaning). While Plato took pride in creating in his *Republic* a state that never existed, Hythloday takes pride in describing a state that, according to him, actually existed (99).[53] And Hythloday was as experienced as he was learned (32/18–21, 54/15–16, 244/31–246/1). His recounting of Utopia is not based on books but on what "he had long experienced personally" and "had taken in directly with his own eyes" (21/28–9).[54] Regarding Hythloday's "experience" in the New World and elsewhere, two further points stand out: (1) He was the world's greatest traveller (21/29–33, 49/30–2) and (2) he adhered to an experientially based epistemology. Knowledge depends on personal experience. Ideas or contentions not based on experience are not knowledge, not certainly in the face of ideas or contentions which are based on experience. Hythloday insists that, had he not been in the New World and personally witnessed what goes on in Utopia, he would never have been able to believe what he saw had he learned about it from someone else's account (107/17–23, 151/5–12, 39–153/4).[55]

Correlating with Hythloday's contention that the abstract truths he has discovered from observing the Utopians cannot be applied to European realities, Machiavelli is convinced that attempting to practise abstract truth in the everyday world is self-defeating.[56] Both *Utopia* and *The Prince* derive from deep concerns with finding ways to handle and overcome the world that is, a world of unmitigated self-interest (as perceived), a world where individuals, as the song goes, do "what comes naturally." Both books are much concerned with cases of extreme necessity and emphasize the need to learn from the everyday world and seek

---

53 See also the introductions to *Utopia*: 19/24–5, 21/5–8, 253/17–20.

54 In his conclusion to the English version of *Richard III*, More states that Morton, his hero, had drunk deeply from "experience – the very mother and mistress of wisdom" (Kendall ed., 110). On "experience" in the Renaissance, see Haydn, *The Counter-Renaissance*, 176–92.

55 Compare Hythloday's view with that of Vasco de Quiroga (see 254n106 above). Quiroga recognizes in his *Información en derecho* (written in 1535) that Thomas More had never been to the New World, yet insists that More's "intention," in "considering, affirming, and setting down" his epublic, was to reveal "a thing seen, done, and experienced for he believed that if this republic [i.e., the Utopian state] was not once experienced it could not be believed, but he who has experienced it puts no doubt in it." "Nothing has to be believed if not experienced and seen." See Quiroga, *Información en derecho*, 467–8 and 497.

56 The diffe ence, of course, is that Hythloday argues in his debate with "More" that abstract truth is entirely relevant to worldly conditions, even if envy and pride keep rulers from accepting this reality, whereas Machiavelli belittles the relevance of abstract truth.

solutions that are useful and workable. Like Machiavelli, the Utopians are focused on "what is done" rather than – seen in rigid, abstract, and one-dimensional terms – "what ought to be done." While Machiavelli wishes true followers of *virtù* to imitate evildoers where necessary, the Utopians systematically study the behaviour of evildoers in order to master the tools needed to defeat them. Both works emphasize the importance of a powerful and effective military force. While Machiavelli wants to see a citizen army rather than an army composed of mercenaries (Ch. 12), the Utopians have a highly trained citizen army and hold mercenaries in contempt.[57] Rather than being at the mercy of private armies, the Utopians use and abuse them and then when necessary take direct control of the battlefield. Both Machiavelli and the Utopians emphasize the need to fit action to the times and the situation

Differences between the Utopians and Machiavelli

Readers have imagined that the Utopian state was meant to be an ideal state (at least where war is not an issue) – a "utopia" in the modern meaning – and as such represents everything Machiavelli opposed. In fact, the Utopian state does not in itself represent an ideal. What is ideal is only the Utopian *honestum/utile* way of confronting the situations found in their society and in their part of the world. And the most profound demonstration of these situations and Utopian reactions is precisely the war discussions. Utopian warfare is not a falling down from an ideal but a supreme representation of that ideal.

Giving a variant of the accepted view, Wegemer holds that "Utopia is a case study in disguised tyranny beneath a rhetoric of peace and *respublica*."[58] As demonstrated at length above, nothing could be further from the truth. The Utopians are at no time tyrannical. At no time do they reject or override the principles and rules that govern their lives. It may be objected that the Utopian "no advantage [commoda] at the expense [incommoda] of others" precept, based on Cicero (*Off.* 3.21),[59] does not hold, in that against their barbarous and unprincipled opponents, peoples devoid of all lawful or ethical behaviour, they clearly advantage themselves at the expense of others. There is, however, a

57 Machiavelli's *The Art of War*, published in 1521, was more popular among contemporaries than even *The Prince*. On the use of mercenaries in fifteenth-century Florentine affairs and the objections of humanists such as Petra ch, Boccaccio, Salutati, Bruni, Biondo, Patrizi, Platina, and Machiavelli, see Bayley, *War and Society in Renaissance Florence*.

58 Wegemer, *Young Thomas More and the Arts of Liberty*, 158.

59 See above 253–6 passim and below, 323n23.

simple explanation. Cicero maintains that in the killing of tyrants, "fie ce and savage monsters in human form" who serve not laws or justice but only a lust for power, the *honestum is* the *utile* (*Off.* 3.19, 32). Unlike all other situations, advantage at the expense of others is here necessary and even a requirement of the *honestum/utile* mindset (*Off.* 3.26). Without question, Thomas More's view was entirely in sync with Cicero's view. From early on More had been consumed with hatred for tyrants, as so evident in his epigrams and poems and most notably in his 1506 declamation in reply to Lucian, where he very explicitly approves the right to kill a tyrant.[60] His *Richard III* seethes with contempt for the evil and tyrannical cunning and deceit practised by players in the events of 1483–5 which led to Richard's downfall (above, 62–8). The brutish opponents of the Utopians are one with all of this. Over and over Cicero had shown that the *utile* separate from the *honestum* invariably results in immorality, and the opponents of the Utopians confirm in situation after situation the truth of this contention. They practise decorum and the indirect approach brilliantly, but evilly, separate from all higher thought. In short, they are masters at everything the Lesbian rule epitomizes. And yet in dealing with these abominable people – employing their own brilliantly decorous and indirect approaches – the Utopians always hold inseparably to their absolutes, including their "utter loathing of war." They disadvantage their depraved opponents without ever giving in to the outlook or behaviour of their opponents.

The goal of the Utopians is never vengeance but only the rectificatio of evil. They never do more than a situation or justice requires. When, for example, they lose their goods through fraud, "their anger [in contrast to practices of their enemies and Europeans] goes no further than abstention from trade with that nation until satisfaction is made" (Y203/28–35). They go to war "only to protect their own territory or to drive an invading enemy out of their friends' lands or, in pity for a people oppressed by tyranny, to deliver them by force of arms from the yoke and slavery of the tyrant, a course prompted by human sympathy" (Y201/5–9).

Far from what Machiavelli envisions, it is precisely the union of expedient procedures and unbending precepts that allows the Utopians to win wars. They know that there are no truly decorous practices lacking absolutes and that applying truly decorous (and therewith proportionate) practices to the world of affairs works.[61] They never fight for

60 See CWM 3.1, 109, 123, 127 and above, 60–1.

61 Contradicting the Peripatetic view, and in accord with Cicero, they never allow that something may be expedient (*utile*) and not *honestum* (*Off.* 3.20). Nor is their thinking in sync with Augustine's contention (a) that as long as God's truth is not an issue there is little diffe ence between the worldly goals of Christians and pagans

untoward advantage at the expense of others; never practise expedients for the sake of expedients; never fight wars for the sake of figh - ing wars; never fight wars motivated by self-centred personal desires. In short, the *honestum/utile* mindset makes the Lesbian rule impossible and therewith makes outcomes as positive as possible. As illustrated at length above, the discussions of Utopian warfare work out the viability of this way of thinking in context after context – a way of thinking that the author first glimpsed in late 1504

The Utopians would find Machiavelli's belief that "the means may justify the end" totally wrong, from the standpoint of both "means" and "end." Throughout the discourse on Utopia, "end" and "means" reflect a singular mindset. The "end" is not simply holding on to power, by any means, but *honestum.* At every step, the means (*utilia*) are demonstrably in accord with absolute principles. Therewith there is as much justice in the means as in the end. The Utopians employ stratagem and cunning and at times even assassination to overcome evil and rectify situations, but this never entails – unlike in Machiavelli's *Prince*[62] – that the means are not honourable.[63] Their purposes diverge entirely from Machiavelli's purposes. While Machiavelli describes the procedures needed to advantage a prince and disadvantage potential rivals, the Utopians see their own advantage as directly tied to the advantage of society as a whole. Thus, their goal is not to profit from evil but to rectify it. Both Machiavelli and Hythloday are contemptuous of what goes on in the councils of princes or kings, the ever-present ulterior motives of courtiers, but the Utopians demonstrate (in effect) what is wrong with both Machiavelli's uber-involvement as a counsellor and Hythloday's rejection of involvement. What works is only the unitary two-dimensional mindset. Were the Utopians to confront Machiavelli, they would point out that he has no abstract principles to guide and control action and that, this being the case, his objectives are little more justifiable than the practices he criticizes and would overcome (as Cicero shows again and again regarding Roman society). More than that, they would show him that the one-dimensional actions he takes in support of his objectives are in the long run always ineffective (as Cicero also

and (b) that members of the City of God enter into worldly affairs "like captives and strangers" and "only because they must" (19.17). See my discussion of *City of God*, above, 53 and 67–8. Truth for the Utopians is by its very nature unitarily both/and, worldly and otherworldly.

62 Machiavelli, *The Prince*, trans. and ed. Skinner and Price, chapter 18, 63.

63 Referring to the assassination of kings and the like, and implicitly to the entire Utopian enterprise in war (Y202/29f), Surtz states, contrarily, that "the Utopians have a laudatory end to justify the means" (Y502).

demonstrates). They are ineffective because there is no way to discover and act on truly decorous procedures lacking abstract principles. Take, for example, Machiavelli's contention that "deceit is detestable in all things, yet in war it is laudable and honorable."[64] Deceit is "laudable and honorable" – and ultimately successful – in war (as elsewhere) *only* if it is located on the decorum side of a unitary *honestum/utile* mindset.[65]

In short the Utopians never, at odds with Machiavelli's strictures, "act immorally when this becomes necessary." And were Machiavelli to respond, as he would, that, even if his prescriptions are not moral (and Christian), they are necessary, in that they allow a ruler to retain power and authority, the Utopians would find this expedience only apparent. True expedience, true self-interest, requires at all times the unitary two-dimensional mindset – and this being the case the Utopians never, unlike Machiavelli, frame their ever so inventive solutions in bad/good terms. What the harsh and particular situations found in the real world demand is not the abandoning of morals (and Christianity) but a new and correct understanding of what morality is all about. Morality – seen in unitarily two-dimensional terms – works in the real world. Immorality does not.

What Machiavelli advocates, the Utopians would say, is simply a perfecting of the Lesbian rule practices that everywhere currently exist. Pitting evil expedience against evil expedience never has a positive outcome, as evidenced

a by the vices fighting the vices in the games played by the Utopians
b by Hythloday's descriptions of what goes on in the councils of kings, and
c by More's descriptions of the many masters of cunning and deceit vying with each other in *Richard III*.

All of which hammers home the fact that the diffe ence between *The Prince* and *Utopia* is not, as has always been believed, that one is "realistic" and the other "utopian." Machiavelli works out a worldly methodology in *The Prince* and More works out a worldly methodology in *Utopia*. Both books are reactions to specific contemporary issues. Machiavelli wants to show us how to respond to "what really happens" in worldly affairs and so too do the Utopians. Machiavelli describes actions that need to be taken by leaders in a rough world, but More's Utopians demonstrate that "expedient" practices lacking oneness with absolutes are not truly expedient. The question modern readers may

64 *Discourses on the First Ten Books of Livy*, III, 40. Cf. *The Prince*, chapter 18.

65 Cf. the positive deceit practised by Morton against the evil deceit of Richard III (above, 193 and 281).

want to ask themselves is which book, *The Prince* or *Utopia*, actually sets forth the more realistic methodology? Was it the book written by the free-thinking Machiavelli or the book written by Thomas More, a book built (however brilliant and inventive) on a way of thinking worked out over and over in Greek and Roman philosophic and political thought.

At root that which diffe entiates Machiavelli and the Utopians, it may appear, are radically diffe ent understandings and employments of Stoicism. The many humanist "mirror-for-princes" treatises then circulating were modelled in particular on the Stoic Seneca's *De clementia* (an early work), which seems to argue that abstract truths should and can be imposed on the world *as is*, and it is this outlook that Machiavelli rejects (see above, 303). The Utopian state, in contrast, is built from a much more authentic two-dimensional understanding of Stoicism, discussed and exemplified by Cicero in *De officiis*, *De finibus*, and *Tusculan Disputations*, and by Seneca in *Epistulae Morales* and in many essays, such as *De tranquillitate animi*, *De vita beata*, and *De beneficiis* – and worked out by Erasmus in his edition of *De officiis*, *De taedio Iesu*, the *Enchiridion*, and *The Praise of Folly*, and by More in his *Lucian*. The author of *Utopia* was determined to show that the Utopians work out, at one with Nature, the Stoic *honestum/utile* way of thinking and, by implication, that this way of thinking was the base from which Christianity was built.[66] Ultimately only Christianity – a particular understanding of Christianity, that is – can effectively deal with "the green world." Joining the one-dimensional green world, as Hythloday accused "More" of advocating – and Machiavelli actually did advocate – is as self-defeating, in the minds of the Utopians, as Hythloday's abstract one-dimensional outlook.

The Utopians put their entire way of living and thinking on the line at every moment. Unlike practitioners of the Lesbian rule, who for self-serving ends see reality as they want to see it, the Utopians never deceive themselves. They have absolutely no illusions regarding what they are dealing with, the extreme difficultie and uncertainties that exist. They are realists in that their views and actions are in no way escapist. The world for them is a very harsh place. Their successes have come only because they, more than any other people, have come to deeply understand the mechanisms that govern the ever-present green world, the very world that they themselves long ago emerged from. The factors that allowed them to understand and deal with their society are the same factors that allow them to understand and deal so inventively and effectively with alien countries

Again, the book *Utopia* is not, as always believed, about a "utopian" ideal state. Unlike modern utopian thinking, the Utopians hold that

66 Part VIII below develops at length this implication.

truth that is not manifestly workable is not truth. Unlike modern utopian thinking, they show us not only what truth is but precisely how it works – in the present world. Central to the discussions on war, as with everything else in the discourse on Utopia, is the laying bare of this *how*. What is ideal, what others need to copy, is the Utopian way of dealing with worldly situations – no matter how common or how uncommon these situations may be.

While Erasmus had shown by many routes – often employing war metaphors – that one must be prepared, whatever situation may arise, to hold tenaciously to the philosophy of Christ (a philosophy built from Stoicism), More takes this thinking a step further. Though not yet arriving at Christianity, the Utopians throughout work out and implement unitary two-dimensional game plans – game plans that often go beyond anything conceptualized by Erasmus. And perhaps this is nowhere more evident than in their thinking on physical warfare, a subject dealt with by Erasmus in book after book. Although Erasmus argues that war must be waged "with Christian minds and with Christ's own weapons" – holding unbendingly to Christ's absolute prohibition of war while making war less attractive, less practised, and less evil by carrying out, in accord with the bending side of Christ's teachings, decorous, prudent, and expedient actions[67] – he never imagined a Christian need for continuous mental and physical training in the actual methods of war. He never saw that spiritual warfare might in itself *require* deep study of Lesbian rule practices; might in itself *require* extreme cunning and deceit (albeit decorous); might in itself *require* proficiency in the usage of physical force (albeit proportionate). That which evil men value more than anything the Utopians use against them – always governed by a radically diffe ent mindset.[68] Highest spirituality is demonstrated precisely where Utopian knowledge of evil is most profound; where their involvement with evil is greatest. Whether or not fully appreciated by Erasmus, the Utopians are embryonic soldiers of Christ – people transformed and therewith, whatever the situation, armed for real-world battle.

67 See Dealy, *Stoic Origins*, 520–5 and above, 276n16 and 283.

68 In *Antibarbarorum liber* (c. 1489–95), it may be noted, Erasmus had referred to the need to use the learning and oratory, the "arms and weapons," of the pagans to overcome pagan outlooks, "cut the enemy's throat with his own sword, as they say" (CWE 23, 25/16–19). Compare the *Enchiridion* (1503): "When you do battle with the enemy [employing the Christian unitary two-dimensional mindset], do not be satisfied with deflecting his blow or even epelling his attack, but bravely seizing the weapon, turn it back upon the attacker, cutting his throat with his own sword" (CWE 66, 107).

PART VIII

What Wiseman Hythloday Did Not Understand

Considering the author's systematic unitary both/and, *honestum/utile*, rendering of Utopian pleasure philosophy and Utopian warfare in Book II, what are we to make of the debate between Hythloday and "More" in Book I – Hythloday's abstract truth versus "More's" worldly "indirect" approach?

The Link between Justice and Expedience: Rhetoric in the Service of Philosophy

Note first that Hythloday's discussion of justice and expedience, which takes up a good part of Book I (55–77),[1] ties in not only with what was shown in Parts VI and VII about the thinking that guides Utopian pleasure philosophy and Utopian warfare but also with everything shown in Parts III–V about the author's mindset – beginning in late 1504. Here too we find two types of abstract value and two types of worldly value, and that truth is found only when the positive type of justice and the positive type of expedience are inseparable. So why does "More" criticize Hythloday and why does Hythloday object to this criticism?

The two types of abstract value described by Hythloday:

(a) One type advocates rigid justice. Even the slightest infraction of the law, according to an expert on the laws of England, necessitates the death penalty in that, were this penalty not in place, there would be even more criminals (55). The death penalty for theft is thus entirely appropriate.[2]

---

1 In Part VIII (as in Part VI) I employ, unless otherwise noted, the Cambridge edition of *Utopia*.

2 Seventy-two thousand thieves were hanged in the reign of Henry VIII, according to the sixteenth-century chronicler Holinshed. See "Henry VIII – Crime and Punishment," http://www.spartacus.schoolnet.co.uk/TUDhenry8.htm.

(b) The other type holds that "Nothing in the world that fortune can bestow can be put on a par with a human life," and, for Christians, this belief is further strengthened by the fact that "God has forbidden us to kill anyone" (69). In short, no killing of humans for theft can ever be justifiable

The two types of worldly value described by Hythloday:

(a) One type contends that there is no diffe ence between infractions, no diffe ence between theft and other types of crime, even murder (69).

(b) The other type holds that there is every diffe ence between crimes and degrees of culpability (69, 71).

Incompatible abstract and worldly values:

Comparing to the illustrations so extensively worked out in *The Praise of Folly*, Hythloday contrasts negative abstract value (a), the rigid justice principle, with positive worldly value (b), the multitudes of real-world types of crime and degrees of culpability. From an opposite standpoint, also worked out in *The Praise of Folly*, Hythloday contrasts negative worldly value (a), the Stoic contention that worldly crimes are equal,[3] with positive abstract value (b), the belief that killing for theft is never justifie [4] – and that, added to this, God has forbidden us to kill and called for mercy.

Compatible abstract and worldly values:

Hythloday shows that positive abstract value (b), the belief that no killing of humans for theft can ever be justifiable (considering that nothing "can be put on a par with a human life"), is one with positive worldly value (b), the contention that there is every diffe ence between crimes and theft must be judged accordingly. Adding to the positive abstract value, Christian teaching holds that God has forbidden all killing and Christians must judge crimes, including theft, with Christian mercy.[5]

Expedient solutions to life's problems are discussed at considerable length in Book I – within the unitary abstract values/worldly values

3 Cf. *Par.* 3, *Fin.* 3.48, 4.21, *Mur.* 61. Although in Stoicism virtue and vice are not subject to degree, progress towards virtue or vice is possible employing the preferred/dispreferred type of value. See Cicero, *On Moral Ends* [*De finibus*], ed. Annas, 80n28 (on 3.48), and 98n17 (on 4.21).

4 Hythloday states that extreme justice is extreme injury, which calls up the ancient proverb, "summum ius summa iniuria" (cf. *Off.* 1.33). See Fleisher, *Radical Reform and Political Persuasion in the Life and Writings of Thomas More*, 20–4.

5 Cf. the Utopian "utter loathing of warfare" precept (Part VII above). Without the precept (cf. "forbidding all killing"), appropriate ways of dealing with warfare (cf. "killing") would be impossible. Neither type of value can exist by itself. On the two types of unbending principles and two types of expedience at play in Utopian warfare, see above, 280.

(*honestum/utile*) frame. Just as lawyer Cicero diffe entiates in *De officiis* between actions that are expedient and those that only appear to be such, so too does lawyer Thomas More – through Hythloday's exemplifications. But beyond Cicero and beyond Erasmus, More was bent on discovering and working out new ways of responding expediently to worldly problems – with examples not found in England or Europe or ancient Rome. At centre court here are the practices of the Polylerites (meaning "People of Much Nonsense"), a people allegedly living in a remote area of central Asia surrounded by mountains. Superior to even the methods of punishment of the ancient Romans, "who were most expert in the arts of government" (71),[6] the Polylerites had worked out in detail, Hythloday reveals, procedures and laws that are "mild and practical" and do not take away all hope (75). The aim of the Polylerites (part of their conception of justice) is "to destroy vices and save the persons" (75). To this end they have found ways to rehabilitate thieves and at the same time to repay society. As one aspect of these procedures, monetary restitution is not made to the prince but to the person stolen from – unlike in Europe, where princes can gain financially from punishments (advantaging themselves at the expense of others) (71–2).[7] All of which shows that the strict justice advocated by the English lawyer "may look superficially like justice, but in reality it is neither just nor expedient [aut iustam aut utilem]" (67). Although some of the ways the Polylerites control their criminals may seem to modern ears quite harsh (73), we have to agree with Hythloday that the methods proposed are far better than the wholesale death penalties approved of by the lawyer. The core point is that Polylerite practices tie together justice and usefulness.[8] Were a valid conception of justice not in place, useful worldly practices would be impossible.

6 The Utopians (to be discussed in Book II) had learned from and then gone beyond some Romans and Egyptians who had been cast ashore some twelve hundred years earlier (c. 300 CE) (107). "Their records began 1,760 years ago with the conquest of the island" (c. 250 BCE) (121). Giles thinks there has been no one born like Hythloday in the last eight hundred years (i.e., since 700 CE) (25).

7 Compare the Utopian-based rule of Vasco de Quiroga in the Spanish New World, above, 254n106.

8 Logan, like others, makes a cardinal error in believing that Hythloday's justice/expedience discussion of the Polylerites and Utopians "originates in rhetorical theory" (Utopia, 2016 ed., xxv). In Book I the author works out the issue by means of rhetoric, but the issue itself is not for him rhetorical. Logan sees a relationship to Stoic "identity" of the moral and the expedient, but sees here and elsewhere the "identity" (in line with fifteenth-century humanists) as one-dimensional rather than two-dimensional (xxvi).

The Debate between Wiseman Hythloday and "More"

Consider now the relationship of Hythloday's *honestum/utile* (in effect) discussion, centring on the Polylerites, to the debate between Hythloday and "More" that surrounds it.

"More" wants Hythloday to apply his unequalled experience and learning to public affairs. The most helpful thing here would be to join the council of a great prince (53).

But Hythloday insists with great passion that this is impossible. Contrary to what Peter Giles surmises, there is no way that he can help his relatives or friends or the public by joining the council of a king (51). His "contemplative leisure [otium]" is not compatible with "active endeavor [negotium]" (52/17). Consequently he lives as he pleases ("nunca sic vivo ut volo," 50/28), separate from friends, family, and public affairs – a thesis that ties with the one-dimensional wisemen described in Cicero's *Paradoxa Stoicorum,* who defines freedom as "the power to live as you will [potestas vivendi ut velis]" (5.33), but contrasts with *De officiis,* where Cicero juxtaposes pejoratively those philosophers who live "just as they please [vivere ut velis]," divorced from politics, with the two-dimensional mindset statecraft requires (1.70–2, cf. 1.19).

A speaker of truth, Hythloday continues, can accomplish nothing in the councils of kings. In support, he describes at length the shenanigans that go on in these councils, outlooks and practices that are entirely at odds with what would be truly advantageous for a king and his people (85–95).[9] Envy makes these evil self-centred practices all the more irremediable. Should someone propose something diffe ent and positive, it would be immediately ridiculed (53). Plato was right: rulers will not accept philosophy unless they themselves become philosophers (*Rep.* 5.473c–d). For good reason Plato himself failed when he tried to implement philosophy in his trip to Syracuse (Plato, *Ep.* 7) (83). "Now, don't you suppose if I set these ideas and others like them before men strongly inclined to the contrary, they would turn deaf ears to me [quam surdis essem narraturus fabulam]?" (95).

"More" agrees entirely. "'Stone deaf, indeed, there's no doubt about it', I said, 'and by heaven it's no wonder! ... This academic philosophy [philosophia scholastica] is pleasant enough in the private conversation of close friends, but in the councils of kings, where great matters

9 Summarized above, Part VII, 275–6. Cf. Seneca's *De otio* and *De tranquillitate animi,* above, Introduction, 33–4.

are debated with great authority, there is no room for it.'"[10] Academic philosophy is not suitable because it "supposes every topic suitable for every occasion [quidvis putet ubivis convenire]" (95). "But there is another philosophy, more practical for statesmen [alia philosophia civilior], which knows its state, adapts itself to the play in hand, and performs its role neatly and appropriately [cum decoro]. This is the philosophy which you must employ" (Y99/12–16).

What precisely is "More" thinking of when he refers to Hythloday's academic philosophy ("philosophia scholastica")? Clearly, he is holding in mind the humanist belief that scholastic philosophers fail, with their logicizing, to consider context. Believing "every topic suitable for every occasion," they want to impose abstractly conceived academic solutions on worldly situations. Though "More" nowhere ties Hythloday's "academic philosophy" to actual scholastic discussions, he is intent on seeing Hythloday's rigid, abstract, and one-dimensional conceptualization of truth in scholastic terms. Hythloday's thinking is "scholastic" in that he believes that the Polylerite outlook and practices are totally superior constructs and as such are applicable *as is* to European affairs, and that councillors of kings should be expected to immediately accept and implement these constructs – though, being thoroughly corrupt, they won't. Thinking scholastically, Hythloday ties the Polylerite system and his conviction that councillors to kings would have nothing to do with this system, however superior, to Plato's abstract view of truth and Plato's contention that rulers will not accept philosophy unless they themselves become philosophers – proven by Plato's failure at Syracuse to implement his thinking.

"More's" "Indirect Approach" Is Not a Product of Rhetoric, As Everywhere Believed, but Philosophy

Of core importance – entirely misunderstood by modern readers – is "More's" statement that "there is another philosophy, more practical for statesmen, which knows its state, adapts itself to the play in hand, and performs its role neatly and appropriately [est alia philosophia civilior quae suam novit scaenam, eique sese accommodans, in ea fabula quae in manibus est suas partes concinne et cum decoro tutatur]" (Y99/12–16, C94/32–96/2). In line with accepted opinion, the Cambridge editors state

10 Cf. Cicero's *De oratore*. Abstract philosophical ideas, such as the justice Plato describes in his "new kind of republic," are anathema to the lives and customs of ordinary humans, and this being the case the orator will not mention such (*De or.* 1.224; cf. 2.178).

that this whole argument "reflects the ancient conflict between rhetoric and philosophy, which centers in the tension between persuasion and truth" (95n76; 2016 edition, 36n81). Hythloday, that is, speaks truth, while "More" thinks Hythloday should take a rhetorical approach and bend his thinking in ways that a particular audience can grasp – which, according to Hythloday, necessarily results in getting into bed with evil (97–8). Note Socrates' deprecation of rhetoric, as in *Gorgias* 453a, 455a, and 458e. The rhetorician Gorgias is tied with those who have no principles and judge things only in terms of opinion, experience, and pleasure (465a).[11] In point of fact, however, "More" refers here not to rhetoric but to "another philosophy." Should we take this "another philosophy" seriously or not? Is "another philosophy" just loose wording, imagining that a rhetorical approach is a type of philosophy? If "More" is not seeing adapting "to the play at hand" as rhetoric opposing philosophy but as one actual philosophy opposing another actual philosophy, what philosophy is he referring to? And what could be the role of decorum, adapting to the situation at hand, the "indirect approach" (97), in that philosophy? If he is seeing the indirect approach as relating to a philosophy, he is by definition, it would seem, not seeing this approach as opposed to truth – contrary to what Hythloday surmises. No actual philosophy sees the indirect approach as a standalone, separate from larger truths. What "More" is seeing in this "another philosophy" is a diffe ent type of truth. Clearly, he is bringing to mind Stoicism. Decorum (inseparable from *honestum*, *Off.* 1.94) is as central to Stoic philosophy as it is to rhetoric,[12] and he is pointing here to the philosophic meaning[13] – a meaning fundamentally at odds with Platonism. Unlike Plato, Stoics believed that by his very nature the philosopher enters into worldly affairs and deco ously implements truth.[14]

---

11 I will demonstrate elsewhere that More had analysed Plato's *Gorgias* and *Philebus* with great care. See above, 267–8.

12 See above, 20 and 192n100.

13 In the four sentences that immediately follow (C97; Y99/12–16), More builds up the case rhetorically by further employment of the word *fabula*, which compares closely to Folly's depiction of life as a stage play (*fabula*) (above, 173–5). But the thesis itself is no more rhetorical than is Folly's thesis. As Cicero argues and illustrates in many contexts, eloquence conjoined with philosophy "rushes along with the roar of a mighty stream" (*Or.* 97, cf. *De or.* 3.143).

14 Cf. *Fin.* 3.68, DL 7.121, 130, Introduction 8–11, 31, and below, 320n17. As Reydams-Schils comments, "The question which comes first, theory or practice, is not relevant to the Stoics, because philosophy is always inextricably linked to one's being in the world and in society." See *The Roman Stoics*, 90. In his *Enchiridion*, Erasmus had emphasized that Christianity without works is even worse than no Christianity in that this is evidence of deceit (CWE 66, 86). Contrast Plato's *Republic*. Philosophers, persons who consort "with what is ordered and divine," must be

The implications are all-encompassing. Assessing the issues in rhetorical either/or terms, modern readers have imagined that "More's" decorous "indirect approach" (97) is incompatible not just with Hythloday's rigid Platonist outlook but with the ideal societies Hythloday describes. This is not the case. *Of utmost importance, "More's" philosophy-based "indirect approach" is fundamental to all the societies and practices Hythloday describes.* Blinded by preconceptions, readers have simply passed over that which might otherwise have seemed obvious. "More" highlights with his "indirect approach [obliquo ductu]" the need to act appropriately, with decorum ("cum decoro") and tact, and to make things as little bad as possible ("et quod in bonum nequis vertere efficia saltem ut sit quam minime malum") (97), and in fact this is the very approach employed – within their *honestum/utile* outlook – by both the Polylerites in Book I and the Utopians in Book II (as with their stratagem and cunning in warfare, Part VII above). And nothing indicates that "More" is contrasting his view of decorum with the philosophical decorum of the Polylerites and Utopians. The decorous practices worked out by the Polylerites and Utopians are not rhetoric-based and neither is the decorum "More" advocates versus Hythloday. "More's" decorum is philosophical, and so too is the decorum found in the expedient/justice (*utile/honestum*) outlook. And not one passage indicates that "More" found anything wrong with this outlook.

Hythloday's Blindness: Truth Is Not One-Dimensional but Two-Dimensional

The problem "More" sees – and that the author expected readers to see – is that Hythloday does not grasp the scope and true meaning of the thinking he eulogizes. Hythloday's hold on absolute truth may seem admirable, initially, but seen in large his outlook turns out to be blind and something of a joke. Hythloday claims that "More's" indirect approach is unworkable and evil, but he himself shows that the Polylerite leaders are masters at finding decorous solutions to the problem of theft and that these solutions both (a) employ the indirect approach and (b) are one with the precepts that govern their lives – all of which makes

---

forced, "whether they want to or not," "to take charge of a city" (6.499). His famous cave analogy emphasizes the theme (esp. 7.517–19). Socrates contrasts those "who wander among the many things that vary in every sort of way" and philosophers, those who deal with the eternal and unchangeable (6.484b). Rhetoricians (Sophists) represent only common opinion but wrongly call this wisdom (6.493).

things as little bad as possible. And in Book II Hythloday will show that the Utopian leaders systematically work out decorous, prudent, and indirect solutions to every issue that comes up, whether this relates to philosophy or warfare (their war games focus on the "indirect" approach, as such, above, 277–82), or social and political arrangements – *always holding to their unbending values*. Had the author wanted Hythloday to understand the Polylerite and Utopian ways of dealing with issues, he most assuredly would not have had him criticize "More's" focus on the indirect approach. He would have simply had Hythloday point out that the indirect approach cannot stand alone, that it requires unbending values, as methodically illustrated by the Polylerites and Utopians.

In fact, however, "More" in no instance implies or indicates that "the indirect approach," as such, is at odds with abstract and unbending precepts – such as those employed by the Polylerites and Utopians. "More" is not rejecting abstract precepts. He is not contrasting decorous worldly and rhetorical needs with abstract precepts. He is not imagining that abstract precepts have no relationship to popular or common-sense conceptions. And he is not seeing decorum as something separate from abstract precepts. The Polylerites and Utopians are masters (like Erasmus' Folly) at adapting "to the drama [fabula] in hand" (96/1–2),[15] employing the indirect approach while *simultaneously* holding to abstract principles, and "More's" indirect approach is one with this outlook.

All Hythloday's exemplifications of truth tie with "More's" view, not Hythloday's. In denying "More's" view, Hythloday is in effect denying his own exemplifications of truth. This being the case, it is no wonder that Hythloday thinks what he has learned about the Polylerities and Utopians is inapplicable to the Old World. While his extensively worked out exemplifications show that their way of thinking adapts by its very nature to whatever situation arises, that "the indirect approach" is an inherent part of truth, he wants to believe, contradictorily, that these examples contrast, either/or, with Old World realities. He imagines that the outlook employed by the Polylerites and Utopians in responding to particular issues is something brittle, one-dimensional, and abstract, the results of which need to be applied *as is*.

At every turn, that is, Hythloday obstinately refuses to see the true meaning of the practices inaugurated by Polylerite and Utopian leaders. He assumes that the methodology employed by these leaders has nothing to do with himself and the approach he would need to take in

15 On relationships to Folly see 316n13 above.

the councils of kings. He contends that practising decorum, "More's" "indirect approach," in the councils of kings can only lead to evil in that one inevitably must bend truth. He imagines that practices such as those found among the Polylerites and Utopians need to be applied carte blanche in such councils, and, this being the case, implementation would never be possible. Since truth that is truth is rigid and abstract, the discoveries of the Polylerites and Utopians would have no impact on the nefarious worldly practices found in Europe, least of all the conniving that goes on in the councils of kings. In no instance does Hythloday recognize that his own illustrations systematically show that contemplative values and active values are always inseparable – as in Stoicism. At no time does he imagine that truth is about a methodology, much less a methodology that is inseparably bending and unbending, worldly and non-worldly – and that his own illustrations prove the point.

Not imagining that modern readers would see decorum only in rhetorical terms, the author expected perceptive readers to recognize – throughout all Hythloday's blustering and self-righteousness – that decorum, "the indirect approach," is inherent to the justice/expedience (*honestum/utile*) model and as such is as workable in the councils of kings as it is in Polylerite society. In short, the author assumed readers would see the obvious, that "More's" indirect approach is everywhere put into practice by the Polylerites and Utopians and that "More" does not deny the need for abstract and rigid principles; that what he objects to is only Hythloday's distorted, one-dimensional, outlook.

The Difference between True Decorum and Evil Decorum

In denying that the Polylerite and Utopian models could be applied in Europe, Hythloday sees only one type of decorum, evil decorum, the Lesbian (or Lydian) rule (making truth fit unprincipled worldly desires).[16] At no time does he explain the diffe ence between the positive decorum practised by the Utopians (holding to their precepts) and the evil decorum (lacking precepts) found in Europe, particularly in the courts of kings – and how, employing the Polylerite and Utopian way of thinking, evil decorum can be overcome. Pigheadedly refusing to allow that "More's" indirect approach can have any tie with truth, he contends that "More" is obviously cohabitating with evil. "More's"

16 I refer to the rule throughout Part VII, in discussing the attitudes and behaviour of enemies of the Utopians. Hythloday explicitly refers to the rule (99) (see below, 330–1). On Erasmus' definition of the Lesbian (or ydian) rule, see above Part VI, 223–4.

"philosophia civilior" is not a philosophy that can deal with the worldly *fabula* but is part of that diabolical *fabula* (97–101).

What author Thomas More assumed readers would see, in contrast, let us emphasize, is that "More's" decorum has nothing to do with Lesbian rule decorum and that "More" does not state, nor does he imagine or imply, that the indirect approach is something separate from abstract principles. And if "More's" decorum is not evil decorum, it is necessarily tied, the Polylerites and Utopians show us (as with Utopian warfare), with unbending precepts.[17] Added to this, the Polylerites and Utopians demonstrate throughout that abstract precepts that do not entail decorum do not represent truth. Nor is there any diffe ence between the unitary both/and methodology practised by the Polylerites and Utopians and the methodology that needs to be applied in the councils of kings. The Polylerite and Utopian leaders responded to particular and serious problems in their societies, and so too can councillors to kings. And a councillor can confront and overcome the destructive and negative attitudes of kings and other councillors by employing the same two-dimensional methodology.[18]

Notwithstanding the evidence provided massively by his own illustrations, that is, Hythloday passionately argues that one can hold to truth or to worldliness (and the decorous procedures found there) but not to both. There is no way to speak the truth in the councils of kings, considering the envy and Lesbian rule attitudes and practices of councillors, without joining the evil or going mad. "More's" "indirect" approach is about lying. "Whether it's the business of a philosopher to tell lies, I don't know, but it certainly isn't mine" (97–8). "In a council, there is no way to dissemble or look the other way. You must openly approve the worst proposals and endorse the most vicious policies" (99–100). All of which is of course true for a person like Hythloday, a person who is incapable of seeing that he himself must apply the *honestum/utile* mindset – a mindset, in the author's view, at the very heart of Christianity.

Not only does Hythloday not grasp that he needs to employ and can employ the *honestum/utile* mindset in advising councillors to kings, he

17 Cf. *De officiis*: *Decorum* is inseparable from moral goodness (*honestum*) (1.94). *Decorum* is a manifestation of action that accords with the virtues (1.95). "For whatever propriety [decorum] may be, it is manifested only when there is pre-existing moral rectitude [Quicquid est enim, quod deceat, id tum apparet, cum antegressa est honestas]" (1.94). Unseemly behaviour indicates the absence of *honestum* (1.94). See also 192n100 above.

18 Cf. 316n14 above and my Introduction (on Seneca), 36–7.

does not realize that it is not so much particular Polylerite and Utopian practices that councillors need to adopt as the way of thinking that created these practices. The Polylerites and Utopians work out the *honestum/utile* outlook in terms of their culture and their social and political situations – just as Cicero worked out this outlook in terms of Roman culture and Roman social and political situations – and then act on and successfully implement the results. So too, it follows, can Europeans apply this methodology to their culture and their particular social and political situations. Practices worked out by the Polylerites and Utopians may or may not have relevance to European realities, considering the vastly diffe ent social, political, and cultural environment. By its very nature the *honestum/utile* mindset constantly adjusts itself to meet differing or new situations – and is always about action. The realities faced by the Polylerites and Utopians (which were many and varied) were not the same, and neither were their solutions. What was the same in all cases was the *honestum/utile* methodology, a methodology equally applicable to contemporary Europe.[19]

Wiseman Hythloday's outlook is very obviously illusory and contradictory – and this is what the author assumed readers would see. Hythloday lauds the solutions to particular social and political problems found by the Polylerites and Utopians but is blind to the methodology they employ and, for greater reason, does not see that this methodology has anything to do with himself or that it could be reemployed in the councils of kings.

In short, "More" understands Hythloday's outlook but Hythloday does not understand "More's" outlook. Hythloday holds that truth is not implementable in the world that exists, that involvement in the world that exists helps nothing and always involves one in evil, and that "More" is on the one hand denying abstract truth and on the other advocating with his indirect approach the Lesbian rule. But "More" in response never denies the need for absolute and unbending precepts, and Hythloday's own illustrations show in situation after situation that the indirect approach advocated by "More" is something very positive and necessary and, properly practised, has nothing to do with the

19 Note the final sentence in Budé's long int oductory letter: "Our own age and ages to come will discover in his [More's] narrative a seedbed [seminarium], so to speak, of elegant and useful concepts from which they will be able to borrow practices to be introduced into their own several nations and adapted for use there" (19, 18/8–11). Though Budé may have grasped something of the Utopian way of thinking, no evidence indicates that any of the humanists who wrote the introductory letters, other than Erasmus, grasped the Stoic base.

Lesbian rule, that the indirect approach requires precepts and precepts require the indirect approach.[20]

The Game of Life

Repeatedly it has been alleged that "More's" "indirect approach," his advocating of a philosophy that "adapts itself to the drama at hand and acts its part neatly and appropriately" – seen in rhetorical terms – ties with a statement by Cicero in *De officiis*, but what has been missed is the context, and therewith the frame of thought within which "More's" view is embedded. The statement referred to is the following: "If at some time stress of circumstances shall thrust us aside into some uncongenial part, we must devote to it all possible thought, practice, and pains, that we may be able to perform it, if not with propriety [si non decore], at least with as little impropriety as possible" (*Off.* 1.114). In fact, this is only one side of Cicero's outlook here (as elsewhere). Humans have a particular character, but they also have a universal character (*Off.* 1.107). While the first persona, the universal, consists of reason, one with *honestum*, the second persona constitutes our unique characters as individuals. By definition, *honestum* is at all times inseparable from the active life. Cicero is here advising individuals to study their particular characteristics and to act as decorously as possible in dealing with worldly events while holding to the universal character, comprised of reason and other aspects of *honestum*. All of which is simply a restating of the unitary both/and, *honestum/utile*, *katorthoma/kathekon*, thesis argued by Stoics since Zeno. The propriety (decorum) that Cicero here refers to, that "More" was thinking of, is not rhetorical but deeply philosophical – and as such is not one-dimensional but two-dimensional.

The Stoic Seneca details this two-dimensional thinking in *De otio* and *De tranquillitate animi*, works which undoubtedly provided the base framework (though More was deeply familiar with many Stoic works) for the debate between Hythloday and "More." See above, 32–7. After describing two polar positions, positions that Hythloday and "More" can easily be identified with, Seneca leads us to the solution. Claiming

20 Erasmus shows over and over, similarly, that as such the prudential is laudable but, lacking unbending principles, people use prudence to live any way they want (the Lesbian rule). Lacking absolutes, we cannot even see what is truly prudent. See, for example, the colloquy Ἰχθυοφαγια (*A Fish Diet*) (1526), ASD I-3, 530/1304–11, CWE 40, 715/1–9. Christian decorum, on the other hand, "is the guiding principle not only in art but also in all the actions of life." We must adapt ourselves "to the prevailing circumstance" and learn "to perform the play of life." *Morae encomium* ASD IV-3, 96/443, 106/613–14, 619, Miller, 34, 44. Part V above works out the theme.

for virtue the entire earth (*Tr.* 4.4), the wiseman holds that there is no contemplation without action and no action without contemplation (*Ot.* 7.2). The wiseman is obligated to act, to enter into the game of life, to become involved in worldly affairs, including politics[21] – however uncertain the outcomes. He is an expert at coping with evil and change, at recognizing and dealing with the uncertainty of events, the possibilities of error, the obstacles that confront him (*Tr.* 14.1). He knows that the sea is often not calm and is sometimes swept by great storms (*Tr.* 11.7, *Ot.* 8.4). Although one must sometimes retire when faced with obstacles, any retreat must be gradual, "without surrendering the standards, without surrendering the honor of the soldier" (*Tr.* 4.1).[22]

This need of the wiseman to enter into the game of life, no matter the uncertainties and "great storms," is exactly "More's" meaning – likely holding in mind Seneca – when he tells Hythloday: "That's how things go in the commonwealth, and in the councils of princes. If you cannot pluck up bad ideas by the root, or cure long-standing evils to your heart's content, you must not therefore abandon the commonwealth. Don't give up the ship in a storm because you cannot hold back the winds" (97).

The Stoics are not "utopians" (in our meaning), and neither are the Polylerites and Utopians. The only utopian is Hythloday, the person who describes and eulogizes ideals that are, in his understanding, inapplicable to the existent world.

In dealing with the world, the Utopians hold rigidly to the virtue and reason found in *honestum* and its four components – wisdom, justice, courage, and decorum – expanded to include their "utter loathing of war" absolute and their "common-life" (no private property and no money) absolute. All-pervasive and directly reflecting core themes of *De officiis* 3 is their "no advantage at the expense of others" absolute and their unyielding denial that a practice or idea that is evil or dishonourable (not one with *honestum* and thus representative of the Lesbian rule) can be in any way expedient.[23] Tied to the Stoic belief that

21 See also 316n14 above and 324n24 below.

22 Relevant here are Seneca's discussions of "reservation" clauses. See above, 36–7, 169, 177, 247–8.

23 The Utopian "no advantage" absolute comprises Cicero's "formula," *De officiis* 3.21–32. The Utopian denial that something can be both *utile* and dishonourable is another rule that Cicero demonstrates at length in *De officiis* 3; see especially 3.35–42. For Cicero these two rules are ways of ensuring that the *honestum/utile* frame holds in all particular circumstances (*Off.* 3.19b). Cf. Dyck: "The *honestum* and (apparent) *utile* are conceived as rival litigants whose case is to be regulated by the [not advantage] *formula*" and absence of *turpe* is the test "of whether an act that seems *utile* is so in fact." See *A Commentary on Cicero, De Officiis*, 522 and 525.

honestum is one with the mind of god, the Utopians hold unbendingly to a religion that is serious and strict, almost stern and forbidding (161), and includes belief in divine providence, the immortality of the soul, and rewards in heaven for virtues and good deeds and punishments for sins. In no instance do the Utopians whittle away at their absolutes. In no instance do they bend absolutes to make them fit contrary worldly desires. Nor do they at any time find scholastic "conditions" under which one is not required to hold to – or even that one would be wrong to hold to – such absolutes.

"More's" View, As Distinct from Hythloday's Interpretation of That View, Is the Author's View

Although scholars have long seen the debate between Hythloday and "More" as an inconclusive version of the debate between philosophy and rhetoric in ancient times, the "two minds" thesis, only a few siding definitively with the views of either Hythloday or "More" (seen in one-dimensional terms), we can now put all previous discussions to rest. *The author's view is represented by "More" but not the "More" Hythloday sees.* Initially it may appear that "More's" position is one-dimensional and the polar opposite of Hythloday's one-dimensional postion, but what we quickly discover is that his position is two-dimensional, unitarily both/and, *honestum/utile*.[24] With his philosophically based "indirect approach," "More" is not advocating the telling of "lies" regarding truth. He is not advocating an evil one-dimensional decorum, the Lesbian rule. At no time does "More" see the indirect approach as something separate from highest truth. At no time does he deny the need for hard precepts. In short, his view is one with the two-dimensional outlook and practices demonstrated throughout by the Polylerites and Utopians. And once we understand "More's" true view, we can see that this is the view of the author and therewith the meaning and purpose of the entire book. Thomas More would have been shocked, we may think, to learn that modern readers – blinded by rhetorical understandings of decorum and the indirect approach – have speculated unendingly about the meaning of the work and have failed to see the obvious, that the Polylerites and Utopians everywhere represent the

24 As shown in my introduction above, 32–7, the debate between the wiseman and the worldly man in Seneca's *De otio* and *De tranquillitate animi* is resolved by the Stoic uniting of the contemplative and the active and the active and the contemplative. A diffe ence from the author of *Utopia* is that the latter has "More" represent not just the worldly position, against Hythloday, but, implicitly, the both/and position.

way of thinking advocated by "More" and that this is the author's view. A deeper problem, of course, is that readers have not come near deciphering (as shown in Parts VI and VII) the two-dimensional Utopian way of thinking.

All of which ties in with the approach to worldly affairs that Erasmus had found so unique and admirable about the person Thomas More (Part IV above) – and had worked out throughout *The Praise of Folly* (Part V above). More is simultaneously both a Democritus, a person who sees everything from a non-worldly prospect, and "a man for all seasons." If More were not a Democritus he would *not* be "a man for all seasons"; he would be exactly what Hythloday sees with the councillors of princes, merely an expert practitioner of evil decorum, the Lesbian rule. Exuding from the very depth of his soul this unitary two-dimensional outlook, he has a matchless ability to deal directly and pleasantly (a disposition philosophically developed by the Utopians in their rendering of pleasure philosophy) with all the variables of persons and situations that come before him and to move everything towards the good. In short, the Thomas More Erasmus describes in 1510 is not a person who simply draws up models of the *honestum/utile* outlook – as does More in his *Lucian* (and as More would do in his discussions of the Polylerites and Utopians). He is a person who in real life uniquely represents this outlook in dealing with all types of persons and happenings.

Hythloday, in contrast, is in no way "a man for all seasons." Indeed, he openly disdains worldly involvement. He is said to be the world's greatest traveller (21/29–33, 49/30–2) and therewith as experienced as learned (32/18–21, 54/15–16, 244/31–246/1), but this experience, by his own accounting, was only observational, what he "had taken in directly with his own eyes" (21/28–9) (see above, 304). Unlike Thomas More, Hythloday had never become seriously involved in anything. He had denied that he could help even family and friends, at one point referring to Plato and the philosopher who, unable to remedy the folly of others, simply stays home and at least keeps himself safe (101; *Rep.* 6.496d–e). In contrast, those who wrote the introductions to the work marvel, as good humanists, at Thomas More's ability to handle both scholarly endeavours and involvement in important affairs of state.[25] Unlike Hythloday, Thomas More was not a foreigner observing the

25 On More's uniting of scholarship and worldly affairs, see the int oductory statements of Erasmus (4/14–17), Budé (8/7–9), Giles (26/7–10), Busleyden (250/16–19), Desmarez (260/16–18), and More himself in a letter to Giles (30/14–32/23). On related fifteenth-century views, see Dealy, *Stoic Origins*, 38.

world from an abstract standpoint. And more than merely being both learned and involved, his outlook reflected at all times the unitary *honestum/utile* way of thinking – the roots of which, and precise meaning of which, were little grasped by those, other than Erasmus, who wrote the introductions.

The true wiseman is Thomas More. More's *Lucian*, Erasmus' *Praise of Folly*, and More's *Utopia* all work out – albeit in very diffe ent contexts – More's transit from an either/or understanding of Christianity to a unitary both/and understanding, and in all three works the hero and true wiseman is Thomas More himself.

Not without cause, the authors of the letters that introduce *Utopia* emphasize that More's view is superior to that of Hythloday. Budé thus attributes the discovery of Utopia to Hythloday but holds that it is Thomas More himself who is the "adorner" of its "holy institutions," "this model of the happy life and rule for living well [beatae vitae exemplar ac vivendi praescriptum]" (17, 16/4). Rhenanus ridicules in Greek those, "not just ordinary dolts but men of standing and trained theologians," who imagine that all More did was write down what Hythloday said (259). Giles states that, although he had heard, like More, Hythloday's own words, he does not believe that Hythloday "saw as much in the five years he lived on the island as can be seen in More's description" (27). Giles believes the Utopian state is superior to Plato's Republic and therewith admires More's ability (beyond Hythloday's) to show the sources of "the evils that arise in commonwealths and the blessings that could arise in them" (27).[26]

"More's" rejection of Hythloday's view and implicit support of an *honestum/utile* outlook ties with everything shown in Parts VI and VII regarding Utopian thinking and action. With regard to philosophy, the author shows with all care the ways Epicurean pleasure, *voluptas*, as refined, can add to the *utile* side of the *honestum/utile* frame. Just as worldly "advantage" and "pleasure" are inseparable from *honestum*, *honestum* is inseparable from considerations of actual advantage and of actual pleasure. Regarding warfare, one of the most discussed issues

26 The *Summa* to which lawyer Vasco de Quiroga often refers in discussing his Utopian-based New World communities in his *Información en derecho* (written 1535, above, 254n106) is a work edited and published in 1517 by Giles, an intimate friend of Erasmus and More as well as an important character in *Utopia*. The *Summa sive argumenta legum diversorum imperatorum* is not generically related to the Justinian corpus, so thoroughly analysed by scholastic legists, but is a compendium of the *Breviarium* (506 CE) of Alaric II, the Visigoth. See my "Vasco de Quiroga's *Regula Ubi Commodum*, the Utopian Roots," 11–14. I know of no modern scholar who has seen ties between Giles' edition of the *Breviarium* and *Utopia*.

in the entire volume, he shows in context after context the diffe ence between how the Utopians think about and carry out warfare (employing their "indirect approach") and how their opponents think about and carry out warfare. The diffe ence, never understood by readers, is that the Utopians hold at all times to a unitary two-dimesnional outlook whereas their opponents are merely brilliant masters of decorum, one-dimensional decorum, evil decorum, the Lesbian rule. Even where the decorous procedures of the Utopians seem extreme and harsh, analysis shows that these measures are never at odds with their precepts – precepts that their opponents do not have. Clearly, the Utopian leaders do not – unlike Hythloday – just sit back in their war thinking and accept that they can do nothing. They are masters at solving problems, holding tight their unitary both/and outlook. While the social and political situations in Utopia and surrounding countries were radically diffe ent from situations found in England and the Old World, and, this being the case, many particulars of their practices of warfare were clearly not transmissible, what is entirely transmissible, in the author's view, is the Utopian *honestum/utile* way of dealing with war – and other social and political problems. The Utopians never seek perfection in dealing with problems and neither should that councillor who would hold to the *honestum/utile* mindset in the councils of kings. As both Cicero and Seneca advised, such a councillor would simply make the best of situations.

Hythloday's Jealousy and Pride

Problems with Hythloday's outlook and personality are revealed yet again in his discussion of Cardinal Morton. Although he claims that councillors to kings will never listen to truth, much less implement truth, he had earlier noted, not recognizing the contradiction, that Morton had been Lord Chancellor of England "and the king depended greatly on his advice" (55). He now shows that Morton is one councillor to a king who in fact was open to trying out models that are superior. In response to Hythloday's belief that the Polylerite way of dealing with criminals could be adopted in England were it not for envy and Lesbian rule attitudes, Morton suggests that the system could be tried out in England and that if it didn't work the old system could be easily revived (75–7). Morton adds that vagabonds could perhaps be treated in the same way if it should work. All of which ties in with Thomas More's actual view of Morton – and disproves Hythloday's thesis. In the author's mind, Morton reflected to some degree, though he was not a scholar and not versed in Stoicism, the *honestum/utile*, non-worldly/worldly, mindset – as evidenced particularly by the discussion of Morton in *Richard III* (above, 193, 281).[27] It was thus entirely fitting that Morton was open to considering the workability of the Polylerite system in England.

Hythloday notes that Morton had treated with all prudence and decorum the ridiculous and humorous arguments and behaviour of a fool who was a friar. When Morton ultimately found that there was no end to the nonsense, he had "nodded to the fool to leave and tactfully turned the conversation to another matter" (81). But what Hythloday takes from all this is opposite from the reality. The problem he now wants to believe is not with councillor Morton but with onlookers. He contends that the conversation proves that no one will listen to truth in that "those who rejected what I had said approved it immediately afterwards, when they saw the Cardinal did not disapprove." But it was precisely because the Cardinal had gained unequalled respect as a councillor to the king that onlookers were moved by his views. So in fact Morton proves that some councillors are willing to learn from superior ways of doing things and that councillors can have an effect on both the affairs of kings and ordinary humans. Note also the eagerness of "More" and Peter Giles at the end of Book I to hear what Hythloday has to say about the Utopians – against his contention that individuals who need to learn the truth do not want to listen to contrary views and are envious (107).

The Utopians are always open to new ideas – whether these ideas relate to customs or politics or religion or literature or nature or practical skills (105–7, 179, 181–5, 219–20, 239–41)[28] – and so too is Morton. So why does Hythloday not recognize that Morton disproves his claim that councillors won't listen to truth? Why does he try to reinterpret what he sees directly in front of him? Note the reasons for the openness of the Utopians: they are open because they think in unitary both/and terms and

27 More had served as a page in Morton's household between the ages of twelve and fourteen, and he would never admire any political figu e more than Morton (above, 48, 62). Morton had been instrumental in the defeat of Richard III and the ascendance of the Tudor Henry VII.

28 On Utopian openness, note also the poem of three sentences, written in the Utopian language (23), that Hythloday handed to Giles (letter to Busyleden, C27). A literal reading of the second and third sentences is as follows: "Alone of all lands, without the aid of abstract philosophy [absque philosophia], I have represented for mortals the philosophical city [civitatem philosophicam]. Ungrudgingly do I share my benefits with others; undemurringly do I adopt whatever is better f om others" (Y19/24–7). Erasmus holds that the philosopher ("in practice the same as being a Christian") is "one who casts aside false pseudo realities and with open mind seeks and follows the truth" (*Education of the Christian Prince*, CWE 27, 214). From beginning to end, *The Praise of Folly* describes the "open mind," a mind that separates truth from myriads of "false pseudo realities" (Part V above).

thus lack the jealousy and pride found elsewhere (cf. 13–15, 53, 67, 137–9, 247). Just as Hythloday eulogizes the Utopian way of thinking without understanding it, so too does he eulogize the Utopian lack of jealousy and pride while personally exhibiting jealousy and pride – as exemplified by his efusal to see that Morton destroys his entire argument.

Regarding Hythloday's jealousy and pride, consider the conclusion to his discourse on Utopia (Book II) and "More's" response. Hythloday reckons that the whole world would have come to adopt Utopian-type institutions were it not for pride. "Pride measures her prosperity not by what she has but by what others lack [non suis commodis prosperitatem, sed ex alienis metitur incommodes]" (247).[29] "Pride is a serpent from hell that twines itself around the hearts of men, acting like a suckfish to draw and hold them back from choosing a better way of life" (247). And yet "More" states in a follow-up, the penultimate paragraph of the book, that he hesitates to ask any more questions of Hythloday because "I was not sure he could take contradiction in these matters, particularly when I recalled that he had reproached certain people [courtiers, 53] who were afraid they might not appear knowing enough unless they found something to criticize in the ideas of others" (249). Like the courtiers he so criticizes, Hythloday is prevented by jealousy and pride from seeing a larger view – the view tacitly represented throughout the book by "More."[30]

29 Here the "advantage" is found not simply in achieving things in a way that "disadvantages" others but, more perversely, in measuring prosperity not by one's own advantages but by others' disadvantages. The description of "pride" ties with the "envy" described by Hythloday in Book I (53). Compare the Stoic disorder of envy, described as "distress [aegritudo] incurred by reason of a neighbor's good fortune, though it does no harm to the envious person" (*Tusc.* 4.17). Cf. DL 7.111; Seneca *Tr.* 2. 10, 15.5; Stobaeus 2.90, quoted LS 412.

30 Readers have often taken seriously the statement by More that immediately precedes his referral to Hythloday's pride: "(1) When Raphael [Hythloday] had finished his stor , I was left thinking that not a few of the laws and customs he had described as existing among the Utopians were really absurd. These included their methods of waging war, their religious practices, as well as other customs of theirs; (2) but my chief objection was to the basis of their whole system, that is, their communal living and their moneyless economy. This one thing alone utterly subverts all the nobility, magnificence, splendor and majesty which (in the popular view) a e the true ornaments and glory of any commonwealth" (247).

(1) If many features of the Utopian commonwealth are "absurd" from a European standpoint, not least being "their methods of waging war," what is not absurd is the *honestum/utile* frame that governs these features (see also 331n34, "What needs ..." below). The final sentence of the book, following the eferral to Hythloday's blindness from pride, affirms that "in the Utopian commonwealth th e are very many features [*honestum/utile* features] that in our own societies I would wish rather than expect to see" (249).

The introductory letters make an issue of Hythloday's jealousy and pride. In his letter to Giles, More wants Giles to find out if Hythloday is annoyed by the fact that he has written down what Hythloday told him. More maintains that he would be sorry if, in publicizing Utopia, he had "robbed him [Hythloday] and his story of the flower of novelty" (37).[31] Building on Hythloday's outlook, More facetiously describes the ingratitude and disdain of those mortals who will receive such a work – concluding that it is "[too] late to be wise now" (39). Regarding Hythloday's wanting credit and glory for his discoveries, Budé in his letter to Lupset states sarcastically, in Greek, that "Such a conviction is characteristic of wise and virtuous men" (17).[32]

Hythloday's Faulty Understanding of Christianity

Leaving aside Hythloday's jealousy and pride, nothing more powerfully illustrates what is wrong with his outlook than his contention that "More's" view is invalid because Christ ordered that his teachings not be dissembled but "preached openly from the housetops [Matt. 10:27, Luke 12:3]."

> Most of his [Christ's] teachings are far more alien from the common customs of mankind than my discourse was. But preachers, like the crafty fellows they are, have found that people would rather not change their lives to fit Christ's rule [Christi normam], and so, following your advice, I suppose, they have adjusted his teaching to the way people live, as if it

---

(2) In Book I we remember that "More" had validated the traditional negative view of communism, seen as one-dimensional (C105, above, 259–60), against Hythloday's view – only to support throughout Book II Utopian two-dimensional communism. The statement at hand merely resurrects, playfully ("my chief objection"), his earlier support for the traditional criticism of communal living, seen as one-dimensional, and just as playfully agrees with "popular" glorification of nobilit , wealth, and magnificence – attributes which a e in Utopian two-dimensional thinking false pleasures, albeit "common opinion" (C153, 167–73 [above, 236–7]). See also above, 265 ("How could ..."). On More's rejection in *Utopia* and elsewhere of such "popular" views, see Thomas I. White, "Festivitas, Utilitas, et Opes," 139–42.

31 Speculating on Hythloday's whereabouts in his letter to Busleyden, Giles reports that some people are asserting "that he got home [to Portugal] but could not bear the ways of his countrymen, retained his old hankering for Utopia, and so made his way back there" (27) – which reminds us of the wiseman who escaped from the cave in Plato's *Republic*, a wiseman so in love with the beauty of absolute truth that he would never have wished to return to the world of affairs (7.517b–c)

32 On the superiority, according to the introductory letters, of More's understanding of Utopia vis-à-vis Hythloday's, see above, 326.

> were a leaden yardstick [regulam plumbeam]. At least in that way they can get the two things to correspond in some way or other. The only real thing they accomplish that I can see is to make people feel more secure about doing evil. (99)[33]

Hythloday is here merely spouting the understanding of Christianity that had so polarized the author's mind prior to late 1504: Christianity as an either/or proposition.[34] On one side are the monastic concepts and on the other the world. On the one side is "the rule [normam] of Christ" and on the other side "the rule of soft lead," the *regulam plumbeam* (or Lesbian rule) – the bending of truth to fit unprincipled worldly desires. Like Hythloday, Thomas More was deeply convinced before late 1504 that there is no way to join the world of affairs, particularly political affairs, without becoming inextricably involved with evil. Christianity is one thing, the world something else. Everywhere one sees only the Lesbian rule. The indirect approach and its decorous practices can never lead to anything other than evil. Look again at Part I above regarding his lectures on Augustine and in particular his despairing letter to Colet (74–5) – which includes, as above, a referral to Lesbian rule "preachers" – written immediately before he read (I have given reason to believe) Erasmus' *De taedio Iesu* and *Enchiridion*.

The discussions of Utopian pleasure philosophy (Part VI above) and Utopian warfare (Part VII above) show at length the ways in which the unitary both/and, *honestum/utile*, way of addressing issues makes actions

---

33 Earlier we read: "If mutual consent to certain laws about killing one another has such force that it entitles men to exempt their agents from this command [as in scholastic thought] and allows them to kill those condemned by human decrees where God has given us no precedent, what is this but giving that command of God only as much force as human laws allow? The result will be that in every situation men will decide for themselves how far it suits them to observe the laws of God [the *regulam plumbean*, Lesbian rule]" (69). Cf. Erasmus' denial in his many books on war, versus scholastics, of any diffe ence between precepts and counsels, "between those things which are to be kept in spirit only and what is to be done externally." See Dealy, *Stoic Origins*, 323–4.

34 Seeing no larger context for Hythloday's statement, Baker focuses interpretation on Hythloday's surname, Raphael, which ties him to the archangel Raphael, a guide and healer. Therewith Baker believes that Hythloday hovers "between divulgation and secrecy." See *Divulging Utopia*, 51–62 at 59. What needs to be pointed out here is that the name Hythloday was created from Greek words meaning "Speaker of Nonsense" and that his discussions of Utopian pleasure philosophy and warfare were nonsense only for those who did not grasp the *honestum/utile* mindset. Similarly, the name Polylerites means "People of Much Nonsense," but here too we find an ou - look that is the opposite of nonsense.

guided by the Lesbian rule impossible in that decorous actions (practising "the indirect approach") are never separate from unbending precepts, and yet Hythloday sees nothing of this when it comes to the nature of Christianity or to his own actions or to becoming involved in the councils of kings. Hythloday sees the Lesbian rule, but not how that rule is overcome. He sees decorum and expedience in one-dimensional Lesbian rule terms and contrasts this with a one-dimensional view of Christianity. But for the author, building on Erasmus' *De taedio Iesu* and *Enchiridion*, Christianity is about the methods that need to be employed in one's own life and in worldly affairs, methods which require inseparably Christian unbending precepts and Christian decorum, expedience, and mercy. Precepts require decorous practices and decorous practices require precepts.

In short, Hythloday not only misunderstands the nature of Christianity – as seen by the author – but therewith denies the applicability of Christianity. Christ wanted not only certain precepts shouted from the rooftops but also direct involvement by the person shouting in a world that is inherently imperfect, employing positive decorum. If Hythloday were a true Christian, he would take on the task, however difficult of dealing in a unitary both/and manner with the world of affairs. Instead, all Hythloday does is pontificate about something that he does not understand – or does not want to understand. In claiming that he would get nowhere in the councils of princes with decorum and tact, "More's" "indirect approach," and that the only solution is to reject what the known world is about in favour of a one-dimensional utopia, Hythloday clearly shows that he is incapable of thinking like a true Christian. Christianity is something very diffe ent – and radical, beyond Hythloday's comprehension. Christians as Christians must apply the unitary *honestum/utile* mindset to the real world. The *honestum/utile* mindset requires implementation and so too does the Christianity that builds on this mindset.

In the conclusion to Book I, Hythloday avers that only a revolutionary abolishing of private property, to be exemplified by the Utopians in Book II, could ever lead to the implementation of truth (101–5). But what kind of truth, what kind of communism, is he going to lay out? Hythloday ties Christ directly to the common life in both Book I (99) and Book II (221, 247), but here too there is a major problem. If Hythloday does not understand the nature of Christianity, as shown above, from this standpoint also how should we understand his descriptions of specific common-life practices found in Utopia? Did Christ see the common life in one-dimensional terms, as Hythloday contends in Book I, or in two-dimensional terms? If Hythloday believes wrongly that Christianity is one-dimensional, an either/or proposition, does he not believe just as erroneously that the common life advocated by Christ is an either/or proposition?[35] Hythloday may believe (as "More" surmises, C105) that the common life reflects truth that is one-dimensional, and that Christ saw the common life in this way, but there is every reason to believe that in actual fact the Utopians see the common life in two-dimensional, unitarily both/and, terms.[36]

Platonism Is Also at Odds with Truth and Christianity

Early in Book I we are told that Hythloday's sailing had been like that of Plato and that, being a philosopher, he had studied Greek more than Latin (45). Later he prefaces his lengthy discussion showing that kings of Europe will never listen to good counsel (83–95) by affirmin Plato's contention that "commonwealths will be happy only when philosophers become kings or kings become philosophers" (*Rep.* 5.473c–d) – the truth of which Plato himself learned on his unsuccessful trips to Syracuse (81–3). In so many words, Hythloday holds that the Utopians are governed by leaders who became philosophers, which allowed them to see the truth in Plato's claim that a just distribution of goods is possible only where private property is abolished (101–5).

Hythloday assures us that what Plato imagines in his republic is what the Utopians put in practice in their republic (99). Believing Hythloday, readers have assumed that Utopian ideas and practices are meant to reflect and actually do reflect Plato's way of thinking, but this is not the case – even if with regard to specific "common-life" practices the author sometimes brings in ideas that can be related to Plato's *Republic* (above, 265–6). Plato did not think in the two-dimensional terms that had so encased More's mind. Note first that no relationship to Platonism was

---

35 In discussing Utopian religion, Hythloday notes that the Utopians were "much influenced by the fact that Christ app oved of his followers' communal way of life [Acts 2:44–5], and that among the truest groups of Christians the practice still prevails" (221). But what Hythloday does not grasp is that Utopian religion is not a rudimentary form of monasticism but is unitarily both/and, non-worldly/worldly, *honestum/utile*. Consider not only much of the discussion of their pleasure philosophy (specificall , 213–27 above) but particular religious beliefs and practices (see above, 264–5 and 299–301.

36 See above, 264–7. In his "Letter to a Monk," written in 1519, More clearly sees the common life "instituted" by Christ as two-dimensional. Unless a person abides by Christ's precepts, one being the common life, one's own "ceremonies" are useless. The problem is not with ceremonies as such but with the fact that Christians do not hold to the precepts and thus do not align ceremonies with them and work for the common good. CWM 15, 197–311, esp. 279–81.

found in Utopian discussions of pleasure philosophy in Part VI or of warfare or religion (as exhibited in particular by their priests) in Part VII. Hythloday sees advantage at the expense of others as everywhere endemic and holds that only a Platonist-type revolution can change things, but what Book II unfolds is a Stoic revolution. Elsewhere it will be shown (outlined above, 267–8) that the goal of the Utopians in their silent discussions of Plato's "mixed" and "unmixed" pleasures and health is not just to correct Plato on a few points but to tear down the entire edifice of his thought

That More's thinking on "the common life," as such, was very consciously not built from Platonism but from the Stoic *honestum/utile* frame has in one context already been demonstrated. It was shown in discussing their philosophy that the Utopians carefully work out the common life in two-dimensional Stoic terms – with no mention of Plato (252–63). Therewith they describe in Stoic terms "public laws which control the distribution of vital goods" (C165, above, 254–6). Earlier they had worked out specifics of "their system of distributing goods" (C135, 137–45). There is every reason to believe that these specifics reflect a Stoic two-dimensional common-life/*utile* mindset and that this is how we should understand all the discussions of Utopian officials occupations, and social relations, as at 121–55 and 185–201.[37]

Regarding Hythloday's "Platonism," the secondary literature seems never to have noticed the correspondences between Hythloday's uncompromising character (far from Plato) and the one-dimensional portrait of the Stoic wiseman found in Cicero's *Paradoxa Stoicorum*, which was firs printed along with *De officiis* in 1465 and went through more editions (sixty-nine) before 1500 than even *De officiis* (sixty-four). The wiseman caricatured here has a "heaven-sent firmness of mind" (*Par.* 4.29) and cannot be conquered by human vicissitudes or the irrational fools surrounding him (4.27). He and he alone has the power and disposition to live as he wills ("vivendi ut velis"), doing nothing against his will (5.33); in no way controlled by worldly practices and worldly desires (5.34), the everyday cheating, trickery, plundering, and defrauding (6.43). Character and conduct are what count, not place of birth, race, or locality (4.29).[38]

As was noted earlier regarding the debate between Hythloday and "More" (314), Hythloday insists with great passion that there is no

37 See above, 265–6.

38 Hythloday was "more concerned about his travels than his tomb. He would often say, 'The man who has no grave is covered by the sky' [Lucan, *Pharsalia*, 7.819], and 'Wherever you start from, the road to heaven is the same length' [Cf. *Tusc.* 1.104]" (45).

way that he can help his relatives or friends or the public by joining the council of a king (51). His "contemplative leisure [otium]" is not compatible with "active endeavor [negotium]" (52/17). Consequently he lives as he pleases ("nunca sic vivo ut volo," 50/28), separate from friends, family, and public affairs – a thesis that ties with the one-dimensional wisemen described in *Paradoxa Stoicorum*, who defines freedom as "the power to live as you will [potestas vivendi ut velis]" (5.33). Significantl , in *De officiis* Cicero contrasts pejoratively those philosophers who live "just as they please [vivere ut velis]," divorced from politics, with the two-dimensional mindset statecraft requires (1.70–2) – an opinion that connects with Stoic views[39] and with the classical Stoic *katorthoma/kathekon, honestum/utile,* understanding of truth. As has been shown in so many ways, *Utopia* is all about what is wrong with Hythloday's rigid, self-centred, self-righteous, one-dimensional, abstract, Platonist view of truth.

In shaping *Utopia,* Thomas More clearly had in mind the procedure Erasmus employs throughout *The Praise of Folly,* revealed in Part V above. On the one hand, Erasmus has Folly unrelentingly ridicule the Stoic wiseman, a wiseman caricatured in *Paradoxa Stoicorum* – a work that related directly to the one-dimensional view of the Stoic wiseman held by virtually all fourteenth- and fifteenth-century humanists.[40] On the other hand, Erasmus shows us through Folly that truth accords with the two-dimensional *honestum/utile* (*katorthoma/kathekon*) mindset, as set forth by Cicero and Seneca and many other available ancient authors.[41] Just as Folly mocks the Stoic wiseman seen in one-dimensional terms, devoid of friends and worldliness (above, 167–70), only to set forth Stoic-based *honestum/utile* understandings of truth, "More" emphatically rejects Hythloday's one-dimensional (*Paradoxa Stoicorum* and "Platonist"-tied) mindset only to implicitly set forth with his indirect

---

39 Cf. *De finibus*: "Since we see that man is designed by nature to safeguard and protect his fellows, it follows from this natural disposition, that the wise man should desire to engage in politics and government, and also to live in accordance with nature by taking to himself a wife and desiring to have children by her" (*Fin.* 3.68). For the Stoic Epictetus, being "a citizen of the world" (contrast Hythloday's citizen of the world outlook, *Utopia* 43–7) meant looking out for one's relatives and other humans (*Disc.* 2.10). Likewise Seneca (see Introduction, 32–7): The need is to be more useful to friends, relatives, countrymen, and all mankind (*Tr.* 1.10, *Ot.* 3.5). Were virtue to consist of contemplation without action, it would be "an imperfect and spiritless good" (*Ot.* 6.3).

40 See Dealy, *Stoic Origins*, Part I.

41 For a list of available ancient authors who discuss the Stoic mindset, see above, 12n31.

approach an *honestum/utile* understanding of truth and to recognize – as Hythloday does not – that the Utopians detail throughout Stoic-based *honestum/utile* exemplifications of truth. Like Folly, who replaces Plato's myth of the cave with a Stoic myth and therewith the outlook of Christ himself (above, 175–84), Thomas More was fixated on working out the ramifications (in a social/political context) of truth that is "truer than truth itself."

CONCLUSION

Published in 1516, *Utopia* develops a way of thinking that in late 1504 had radicalized the author's mind. Inspired by Erasmus, More had come to see Christianity in terms of the unitary two-dimensional outlook at the heart of ancient Stoicism. His *Lucian*, 1506, works out this way of thinking, and Erasmus describes in detail specifics of More's newfound mindset in a 1510 letter and throughout his *Praise of Folly*, 1511. In *Utopia* More applies his ground-breaking Stoic/Christian frame of thought to major worldly issues, not least being behaviour in the councils of kings, warfare, and philosophy. All of which demonstrates that *Utopia* is not, as has been believed, a rhetorical jeu d'esprit. It was built from a deeply learned ancient philosophy.

Prior to late 1504, Thomas More saw Christianity as an ideal at odds with worldly affairs, most particularly sex and marriage and involvement in politics – an outlook at one with that of his spiritual advisor at the time, Colet. Christianity was an either/or proposition and monasticism was the ideal. While St Augustine had described in his *City of God* (426 CE) two cities, one earthly, built from Roman paganism, and one eternal, and had worked out the interactions between them, More was struck by the diffe ence between Augustine's world and the world that surrounded him, a world ostensibly built on Christianity – unlike Rome – but everywhere, he believed, lacking Christianity. Epitomizing everything was the brilliant cunning and deceit of King Richard III. Though More had trained for a legal career and was greatly interested in politics, he did not believe that he could be a true Christian and obtain eternal life through enmeshment in worldly affairs – most particularly high-level governmental affairs. He was convinced that involvement by its very nature meant contamination, as evidenced for one thing by the immoral and unbounded scheming of courtiers in the orbit of Richard III. Torn, that is, by an either/or way of thinking, either the world or the monastery, he had long suffe ed from extreme anxiety and despair, which is highlighted in an October 1504 letter to Colet.

But More's anguish and outlook on life and Christianity were suddenly transformed, evidence shows, on reading in late 1504 Erasmus' *De taedio Iesu* and *Enchiridion* (published together in 1503), both books built from the Stoic *katorthoma/kathekon* (*honestum/utile*) mindset. What he learned in these works is that there is no necessary contradiction between worldly involvements and eternal truths and that in fact worldliness is inherent to Christianity. What matters is only how worldly issues are addressed. Directly answering to More's desire to drum out worldly urges, particularly his desires for sex and for political and humanistic involvements, *De taedio Iesu* shows (inspired by Stoic *oikeiosis*) that such desires are natural instincts. Natural instincts and character traits are outside the realm of human control – and yet all-important, indispensable components of what it means to be human and Christian. In choosing human nature, Christ accepted his own involuntary natural instincts. Nor was Christ a martyr. In not going beyond his human nature and natural instincts, he did not in his Passion feel the joy that martyrs feel. The *Enchiridion* explains why joining a religious order, even the strictest, does not in itself make one holy and, for most people, is unsuitable. Spirituality depends on "each person's physical and mental constitution," a constitution that must be studied in depth and then built upon – as one holds unbendingly to the precepts of the faith. Erasmus' short biography of More shows just how deeply More had taken Erasmus' two-dimensional Stoic/Christian outlook to heart and applied it to his own particular instincts and situations.

Contrary to what has been believed, More did not in his January 1505 marriage make a choice between two polar views. Worldly and otherworldly, he now saw, are not two separate things. Joining the Carthusian monastery would have been for him not a greater thing but a lesser thing. And we can now comprehend how it came about that More was working with Erasmus, filled with joy and good spirits, shortly after his marriage.

More worked out his new life-transforming way of thinking while working alongside Erasmus – for months – interpreting and translating (from the Greek) writings of Lucian, the second-century CE satirist and social commentator. The evidence is found in the three dialogues of Lucian he published in 1506. The choice of these particular dialogues from the great number available and the way he orders them and the meaning he gives them show that More was thinking of the order and meaning of the three books of Cicero's *De officiis*. His short introduction, which builds on *De officiis* as well as Cicero's *Tusculan Disputations*, describes – far from both Lucian's meaning and anything he had previously written – the three dialogues. While the first dialogue (*Cynicus*) represents in his rendering contemplative (non-worldly) thinking and the second (*Menippus*) represents in his rendering active life (worldly) thinking, the third (*Philopseudes*) represents in his rendering a resolution of the two contradictory outlooks. The two contradictory views are united, his discussion reveals, by the Stoic *honestum/utile* mindset – worked out in Christian terms. While holding unquestioningly to the accounts found in divine scripture (aspects of *honestum*), we must accept or reject humanly created narratives (aspects of *utile*) based – after careful study – on whether they are one with divine scripture. Where this unity does not exist, Christianity does not exist. The contemplative and the active are aspects of a singular truth.

More certainly knew from the care he had taken with his translations that he was largely rewriting Lucian's outlook. While Tychiades, the hero of Lucian's *Philopseudes,* ridicules all abstract truth and sees magic and superstition everywhere in society, even among philosophers, More considers abstract truth, comprising "the principal mysteries of the Christian faith," an irreducible necessity of thought. Against Tychiades' belief that reason and truth are found only in worldly experience and common sense, More contends that reason requires a methodology and that this methodology cannot work lacking absolute standards. Truth is not "common sense." Some worldly contentions are true and some false, and it is not obvious which is which, lacking principles. The truth or falsity of statements can be discovered only by meticulously working out the Stoic unitary two-dimensional, *honestum/utile,* mindset. Worldly and non-worldly *are* bridgeable. Indeed, they require each other. At play is both a positive and a negative type of abstraction and both a positive and a negative type of worldliness. What needs to be unified, in all situations, is the positive type of abstraction and the positive type of worldliness.

A consequence of the combining of worldly and otherworldly is that we free ourselves from "anxiety," "gloomy untruths," and "superstitious dread." At one point More refers to Book 5 of Cicero's *Tusculan Disputations,* a book which focuses on the Stoic contention that vice produces misery while virtue produces happiness. More undoubtedly identified "vice" and its misery with the extreme either/or anxiety he had felt before late 1504 (so evident in his letter to Colet) and "virtue" and its happiness with the joy that encompassed him on discovering that truth is not either/or but both/and, *honestum/utile.* Getting rid of superstition doesn't simply clear our minds, as with Lucian; it deeply affects our emotional state

While Tychiades is mystified as to why people make up magical stories and then lie, Thomas More is not mystified. Unlike Tychiades, who recognizes only gullibility, he sees deliberate deceit. Persons who are Christians in name only have deliberately inserted false stories into books on the lives of saints in order to get around recognizing and accepting "truth unadorned, "the principal mysteries." These persons include members of the Carthusian order, the very order More before late 1504 had considered joining. "Under the guise of religion," they have silently replaced "truth unadorned" with magic and superstition, a move which makes the Stoic/Christian *honestum/utile* mindset impossible in that the hard side (*honestum*) has been falsified

In a 1510 letter, which serves as the preface to his *Praise of Folly* (1511), Erasmus describes More as "a man for all seasons," incredibly affable and easygoing, and this characterization is standard fare in the secondary literature. But Erasmus in the same statement refers to More as a Democritus, a person who ridicules and dissents sharply from what goes on in worldly affairs – a statement little explained in the secondary literature. Aren't these two characterizations contradictory? How, opposite other humans, could a person be both affable and easygoing and hard and unbendable? Could Erasmus be implying that More vacillates, as a rhetorician, from one pole to the other? Analysis shows that Erasmus sees in More two types of value that are opposites and yet inseparable components of a unitary both/and, *honestum/utile*, mindset. More would not be "a man for all seasons" were he not inseparably an unbending Democritus.

Never realized, *The Praise of Folly* is not a rhetorical jeu d'esprit but from cover to cover a working out of More's life-transforming outlook. The rhetoric is brilliant, but throughout it serves a Stoic/Christian philosophy. In multiple contexts the work lays out two sides to abstract folly, one negative and one positive, and two sides to worldly folly, one negative and one positive, and shows that Folly the person, like Thomas More, unites – overcoming either/or thinking – true abstract folly and true worldly folly. One side of Folly shows what is right about rigid abstract values and what is wrong about bending worldly values (comparing to More's rendering of *Cynicus*), and another side shows what is right about bending worldly values and what is wrong about rigid abstract values (comparing to More's rendering of *Menippus*). What valid abstract values oppose are false worldly values. What valid worldly values oppose are false abstract values. But the worldly values rejected (pretence, false adulation, cheating, etc.) are not the same as the worldly values admired (based on natural instinct), and the rigid abstract values condemned (exemplified by the Stoic wiseman and scholastics) are not the same as those praised (exemplified by Democritus and pious persons). The repeated attacks on the Stoic wiseman, seen as one-dimensionally rigid, abstract, and unfeeling, reflect the view of this wiseman held by all of Erasmus' contemporaries, not least Italian humanists. Erasmus, then the world's greatest expert on Stoicism, and in his wake Thomas More, had uncovered a deeper two-dimensional understanding of Stoicism and the Stoic wiseman – which is worked out by Folly the person.

A major thesis is that there is not just one type of reality but two. In this regard, Folly objects to Plato's myth of the cave and the idea that what is "real" is only found outside the cave. She shows that the worldly truth of those within the cave is as indispensable as invisible truth. Truth is "truer than truth itself," and in fact those who wish to reach the heights of wisdom can do so only with the help of worldly values. Bodily and external factors, emotions, and all the variables of life comprise an indispensable part of truth – and, thus, "the very inner sanctum of happiness." Happiness, that is, is not found in abstract ideas alone. As Erasmus had already shown at length in *De taedio* and the *Enchiridion*, truth is not one-dimensional but two-dimensional. *De taedio Iesu* had been about proving – against a thousand years of theology – that Christ was incapable of separating himself and did not want to separate himself from natural instincts and worldly realities, notwithstanding that he was the wisdom of the Father, and *The Praise of Folly* comes back to this thesis: "Though Christ was the wisdom of the Father," he became somehow foolish "when he took on human nature." Like Christ, St Paul recognized human limitations and entered into human affairs "with a spirit of openminded generosity" – and Folly the person, like Thomas More, "embraces everyone equally with ready and easy generosity," not concerned about points of ceremony.

There is all the diffe ence, Folly shows, between apparent prudence and true prudence. "Just as nothing is more foolish than misplaced wisdom, so too, is nothing more imprudent than perverse prudence." True prudence arises out of actual worldly issues, not rigid or abstract rules, and effectively deals with these issues, but it would not be true prudence and would not be effective were it at odds with the unbending precepts of the faith. Conversely, where true unseen values are actually in place, so too is true worldly prudence (Stoic *honestum* requires appropriate action). Unfortunately, what goes on in the world is for the most part only apparent prudence, not true prudence, and is both self-destructive and socially destructive. The prudent practitioner of Christianity always holds to a both/and (Democritus/"man for all seasons") frame of mind, whereas the false practitioner sees no connection between worldly and non-worldly or, if a connection is seen, judges the relationship in either/or terms – as had Thomas More before late 1504.

Compare also what Folly has to say about flattery with More's Democritus/"man for all seasons" ability to interact with anyone and to enjoy doing so. Noting that Plato separated flattery and rhetoric from philosophy, Folly does not doubt the power of flattery to move "that enormous and powerful monster, the mob," but there is all the diffe ence between positive and negative flatter , and this diffe ence is not explained by common sense or rhetoric, as such, but by the Stoic philosophical mindset. False flattery is one-dimensional, true flattery is unitarily two-dimensional. Noteworthy is Folly's description of the false flattery that goes on in the courts of kings (illustrated at length by Hythloday in Book I of *Utopia*).

Scholars have believed that *Utopia*, like in their view *The Praise of Folly*, is a work built around rhetorical debate, and, this being the case, they find ambiguous meanings throughout the work. Utopian pleasure philosophy is a case in point. According to one recent assessment, More's discussion of pleasure is filled with twists and turns, Lucianic irony, humour, exaggerations, and contradictions, all of which illustrate More's desire "to encourage reflection and stud ."

Deep analysis shows something else. There is a very carefully developed and logical rationale behind every statement made in the philosophy section. Every issue is systematically worked out in terms of a pre-existing way of thinking. Here (and elsewhere in *Utopia*) the accuracy of Erasmus' detailed illustrations of More's Democritus/"man for all seasons" mindset in *The Praise of Folly* is fully borne out. This notwithstanding that the New World setting and subject matter differ radically.

What stands out, first of all, is that More had carefully studied both Epicurean pleasure philosophy and Stoic philosophy – philosophies in the ancient world considered incompatible. He was particularly impressed by the fact that Epicurus' pleasure philosophy is one-dimensional whereas Stoic philosophy is two-dimensional. For Epicurus, pleasure (*voluptas*), as defined, determines what is virtuous and what isn't – not abstract reason. For Stoics, virtue is impossible lacking unbending abstract truths. *Voluptas*, that is, is utilitarian while *honestum* is abstract and rigid – albeit worldly as well.

More was intrigued by pleasure philosophy because he was by nature pleasure-loving and "enjoyed," according to Erasmus, playing "the man for all seasons with all men." But he also believed that there is no truth outside the Stoic two-dimensional outlook and that, this being the case, pleasure calculations may have a role to play; but by themselves they can never lead to virtue. He solved the problem by expanding the *utile* side of the Stoic frame to include *voluptas*. In this context, the ways Utopians diffe entiate between pleasures are not unrelated to Stoic diffe entiations between "preferred indiffe ents" and "dispreferred indiffe ents" or "things expedient" and "things not expedient." He recognized in expanding the Stoic frame that Stoics were not inattentive to the mental state of others in that they considered it a duty to remove the distress and misery of fellow humans, and to comfort them, but he was determined to take their outlook one step further: Humans must be restored to "enjoyment." The problem here, he shows, is that others cannot be truly restored to joy unless we ourselves are joyful, and not (as Stoics tend to be) solemn and severe.

Deeply knowledgeable of the intricacies of Epicurean and Stoic thought, More works out unitary both/and solutions with all determination and care, in situation after situation – building from a frame of thought that is fundamentally Stoic. Just as in his *Lucian* and Erasmus' *Praise of Folly*, there are both valid and invalid renderings of abstract truth and there are both valid and invalid renderings of worldly truth. Crucially, valid abstract truths and valid worldly truths are never such considered by themselves. In working all this out, we learn why it is that Utopian religion is "serious and strict, almost harsh and rigid" (comparing to Stoic *honestum*), notwithstanding the softness of their pleasure thinking; and why reason is weak and defective without religious and moral principles (such as belief in immortality of the soul); and why invariably there is evil and deceit where the *utile* (including *voluptas*) is not one with the principles (*honestum*). Distinguishing false principles from true and false *utile* from true is made doubly difficul by the fact that so-called Christians everywhere invent rationalizations to cover non-Christian and non-natural desires and actions.

At centre court in Utopian philosophy is the core Stoic doctrine, emphasized by Cicero in many books, that humans have by nature a common humanity, and, this being the case, nothing can be more harmful than to seek advantage at the expense of others. Making money by trickery destroys the very basis of civilization, "the law of nature," "a bond of fellowship uniting all men." Even loss of children, kin, or friends should be valued less, contends Cicero, than an act of injustice against another human. Readers have always imagined that the Utopians are somehow reworking Plato's thinking on the common life, but this is not the case. Although More clearly knew a lot about Plato's reasoning, his Utopians very explicitly reject Plato's conception of the common life, which they see in abstract and one-dimensional terms. Never previously pointed out, they show that the "no advantage at the expense of others" precept (an aspect of *honestum*) can be added just as easily to a locality governed by a common-life precept as to localities governed (as traditionally) by a private property precept. In either case the unitary two-dimensional, *honestum/utile*, mindset applies – albeit the results are radically diffe ent. Noteworthy, the Utopians focus not only on what the "no advantage at the expense of others" precept disallows, but also on what by default it allows – not just in a private property society (as worked out by Stoics) but in a "common-life" society (as elsewhere evidenced by Utopian social practices).

Believing that the book *Utopia* is about a "utopian" ideal state, many scholars have simply passed over the lengthy discussions of Utopian warfare, deeming them dystopian – possibly a giving in by the author to worldly realities. Those who have discussed Utopian warfare have almost always (since even the nineteenth century) seen this warfare in Machiavellian terms. Don't the Utopians in fact use any means available to win wars and don't they continually prepare for war? Don't they overcome their enemies by extreme cunning, stratagem, and deceit while now and then willing to fight to death? Then too, how could there be any diffe ence between Utopian warfare and the warfare in Europe so criticized by Hythloday in Book I – not to mention More's powerful descriptions of the malevolent cunning and deceit surrounding King Richard III in his *Richard III*? All this and yet we are told – contradictorily it is believed – that the Utopians "utterly loathe war"!

Actually, there is no better example of the Utopian mindset in the entire volume than the discussions of warfare. Highest spirituality is demonstrated precisely where Utopian knowledge of evil is most profound and where their involvement with evil is greatest. Not grasped by readers, the Utopians respond to all circumstances, no matter how horrendous, with a unitary two-dimensional, *honestum/utile*, methodology. In no instance do they contradict themselves. In no instance is their thinking not serious or inconsistent or rhetorical. They overcome the cunning, stratagem, pretence, indirection, and savagery of their opponents by perfecting the indirect methods of their opponents, but unlike their opponents, who lack all honour or principles, they hold unbendingly to absolute precepts – which ties with the way the Utopians correct Epicurus' one-dimensional pleasure philosophy. The flexible worldly methods they decide on, in accord with one type of value, are never in contradiction with their unflinching hold on another type of value – their non-worldly precepts, one of which is their "utter loathing of war." Their goal is never vengeance but only the rectification of evil. They seek no gain from war and respond to all situations proportionately. They seek not perfect solutions but only the best possible solutions. They know (as Cicero had demonstrated) that there are no truly expedient practices lacking absolutes, that applying truly expedient practices to the world of affairs works. More than this, they recognize that the *honestum/utile* outlook allows as well as disallows. Holding to this outlook allows them to think creatively, not bound by tradition or common assumptions – unlike their enemies or Europeans. As a result, the types of cunning and deceit they practise are unparalleled as are also, for example, their elaborate employments of money – which they themselves have no use for.

The Utopians would have found equally wrong and unworkable the abstract (one-dimensional) idealistic rules for leaders of states espoused by contemporary humanists and the worldly (one-dimensional) "realism" found in Machiavelli's harsh strictures – in correction of the humanists – on how to overcome those who would threaten a prince (*The Prince*, 1513, published 1532). They would find that Machiavelli actually lacked realism, not to mention spirituality, in that he recognized no unbending precepts and did not understand that expedient practices lacking oneness with absolutes are not truly expedient. They would not simply assert that Machiavelli's ideas are wrong, they would show him in detail the way of thinking that has allowed them to triumph over all their barbarous opponents. Truth works.

Although Erasmus describes the steps Christians need to take with regard to war, he never saw that spiritual warfare might in itself *require* deep study of the skilfully crafted cunning and deceit of one's opponents; might in itself *require* the employment of extreme cunning and deceit (albeit decorous); might in itself *require* proficiency in the usage of physical force (albeit proportionate). In short, Erasmus never saw that what evil men value more than anything must be used against them – always governed by a radically diffe ent mindset. And yet, Utopian warfare is clearly a development of Erasmus' "philosophy of Christ." The Utopians are embryonic soldiers of Christ – people transformed by the *honestum/utile* mindset and thus, whatever the situation, armed for real-world battle.

And yet, an important question remains. How does the Book I either/or debate between Hythloday and persona "More" fit into what Book II tells us about the Utopian mentality? Specialists have long believed that the essential meaning of the book *Utopia*, whatever the particular interpretation, is not found in the Book II discussions of the Utopians (which, as shown above, they do not understand) but in the Book I debate. They have seen the debate as a playing out of the opposition in ancient times between the philosophic and rhetorical traditions – and have concluded that the author simply couldn't make up his mind which route to follow. Philosopher Hythloday self-righteously represents abstract truth and sees "More's" worldly "indirect approach" as nothing but a giving in to evil, while rhetorician "More," it is believed, is willing to bend truth to fit worldly circumstances – and from this stance criticizes Hythloday's abstract philosophic outlook.

Scholars have here – unanimously – made a fundamental and far-reaching mistake. What hasn't been seen is that persona "More" demonstrably does not represent the rhetorical tradition but the Stoic two-dimensional understanding of truth – like More the real-life person described over and over by Erasmus. The accepted interpretation hinges on "More's" statement, in response to Hythloday, that "there is another philosophy, more practical for statesmen, which knows its state, adapts itself to the play in hand, and performs its role neatly and appropriately [est alia philosophia civilior quae suam novit scaenam, eique sese accommodans, in ea fabula quae in manibus est suas partes concinne et cum decoro tutatur]." Blinded by preconceptions and not seeing what "another philosophy, more practical for statesmen" could refer to, readers far and wide have simply assumed, without discussion even, that "another philosophy" is a metaphor for rhetoric. As the editors of the Cambridge editions of *Utopia* so cavalierly emphasize, the author was simply putting new life into the long-standing ancient debates between the disciplines of rhetoric and philosophy. In fact, "More" is referring to a real "philosophy," a philosophy little understood by Renaissance scholars. "More" – one with real-life Thomas More – is contrasting Stoic two-dimensional philosophy with Hythloday's Platonism and refusal to enter into politics and worldly affairs

Believing that "More's" decorous "indirect approach" is a tool of rhetoric, and as such not attached to higher truths, researchers have found this approach incompatible not just with Hythloday's personal view but with Hythloday's extensive descriptions of the practices of the Utopians in Book II. In fact, "More's" philosophy-based "indirect approach" is demonstrably fundamental to the outlook and practices of the Utopians. The author expected readers to see the obvious, that Hythloday's arrogant and self-righteous outlook is contradicted throughout by the Utopian practices he describes. As my analyses of Utopian philosophy and Utopian warfare have shown, the Utopians are masters at adapting, as in "More's" Book I statement above, "to the play in hand," employing the indirect approach while simultaneously holding to abstract principles. Likewise, the Stoic-based indirect approach "More" advocates in Book I is (by clear implication) one with abstract principles. The author expected readers to see that Hythloday's view throughout the book is misguided, un-Christian, and something of a joke. What the author would never have imagined is that modern readers would reinterpret "More's" "philosophy" in terms of rhetoric.

This fundamental mistake has led to unending speculations by scholars (most of them residing in literature departments, the home of rhetoric) regarding the meaning of *Utopia*. Thomas More would have been astonished and dismayed to see that readers have not only misunderstood the debate between Hythloday and "More" but have also been carried away by the strange practices of the Utopians and have missed the overriding meaning and purpose of these practices. Again, the central objective of the book was to demonstrate the necessity and workability of the Stoic *honestum/utile* mindset in all situations – a way of thinking for which Christianity, correctly understood, is the perfect exemplar.

What mattered most for the author – in line with Stoics – was how issues are addressed. Whether the issues before them relate to philosophy or war or religion or the common life or something else, the Utopians respond with exquisitely crafted decorous solutions, at one with their absolutes. As is so evident in their lengthy discussions of warfare, in no situation, no matter how dire, do they make truth fit immoral desires – "the Lesbian rule" – and in each instance we are shown why their tactics are both appropriate and admirable. Where their decorous and expedient procedures are one with their rigid absolutes, including an "utter loathing of war," Lesbian rule practices are impossible. More than this, in holding that any indirect solution is allowable if developed in accord with nature and the absolutes, the Utopians are at every step forced to think creatively, "outside the box." Employing their unitary unbending/bending methodology, they make things in their part of the world "as little bad as possible" – just as "More" had advised Hythloday to do. If only Europeans would apply this methodology – as Christian soldiers – to the very diffe ent conditions found in their area of the world and likewise make things "as little bad as possible"!

What can transfer from one society to another is the *honestum/utile* methodology, not the way the methodology works out in divergent settings. Even within the Utopian state, the *honestum/utile* frame of thought is applied not only to philosophy and warfare but to all aspects of life – social, political, and religious. Expanding out from the Utopian state, it seems clear that the way the Utopians think about and practise warfare absolutely needs to be transferred to the Old World – as distinct from warfare practices worked out by their methodology that are relevant only to New World situations. Similarly, the Polylerites discussed in Book I use the *honestum/utile* method in finding better ways of punishing criminals, and Europeans need to build – with open mind – on their achievements. If specific "common-life" practices have often disturbed modern readers, in that they have seemed overly rigid and to limit individuality, what matters (as with the specific warfare practices readers have abhorred) is the governing rationale. Transferred to the Old World, how would a Stoic-based common-life/decorum, unbending/bending, methodology work out?

Our word *utopia* derives in large from a misunderstanding. Unlike the vast and multifaceted utopian literature that has come into existence in the intervening centuries, More's Utopia is not about an ideal place as such but about an ideal methodology, a methodology considered eminently practicable in the real world. The debate between Hythloday and "More" in Book I and the discussions of Utopian philosophy and warfare in Book II – and behind all this More's work on *Lucian*, Erasmus' description of More's personality, and Erasmus' working out of More's unitary both/and mindset in *The Praise of Folly* – show us that the Utopian state is not about a conglomeration of more or less ideal practices, customs, and institutions but about a way of solving problems. The author considered Utopian methodology not just true but profoundly realistic and applicable to any culture and any political or social situation – had humans the necessary understanding, ability, will, and religiosity. *De officiis*, Book 3, describes the workings of the *honestum/utile* way of thinking in Roman society, and *Utopia*, fifteen hundred years later, illustrates in great detail the workings of this outlook in an imaginary New World society. Would only Europeans copy the Utopian mindset.

Once we see what More was actually doing in composing *Utopia*, that the work was not an off-the-cuff rhetorical hodgepodge about a fixed ideal state but a profoundly learned and creative systematic working out of Stoic-based philosophy, in multiple contexts, we can better appreciate Colet's belief that More was the only true genius in all of England.

The background to the book is all-important. Not grasped by scholars, wiseman Hythloday represents the author's view prior to late 1504, the belief that worldly involvement necessitates bending truth to fit immoral desires (the Lesbian rule) and that consequently one must make an either/or choice between abstract (Christian) truth or worldliness. Take your pick. Also not grasped by scholars, persona "More's" view, correctly understood, represents the actual and complete view of the author. There is no need for quotation marks. In late 1504, influenced by Erasmus, More's mind was transformed by the deep conviction that the unitary two-dimensional mindset developed by the Stoics was in fact a precursor of the mind of Christ, and he was determined from this time onward to demonstrate for himself and others this outlook against either/or, non-worldly versus worldly, thinking. He believed the only thing lacking with the Utopian way of thinking (as distinct from particular practices) was the addition of Christ's wisdom on the *honestum* side and Christ's humanity on the *utile* side.

In joining the court of Henry VIII in 1518, two years after the publication of *Utopia*, More was not denying the meaning of the work but representing it. Joining the court was an eminently logical extension of years invested in working out in multifarious contexts the oneness, correctly understood, of two radically diffe ent types of value. Consequently, he knew exactly how he needed to act in the councils of kings – giving no thought to wiseman Hythloday. If in his 1501 lectures on Augustine's *City of God* More had no answer to the tyranny of Richard III, other than joining in the evil or retreating to the Carthusian monastery, the situation now was entirely diffe ent.

Bibliography

Primary Sources

Aquinas, Thomas. *Summa Theologiae*. Trans. the Dominican Fathers. 60 vols. London: Blackfriars, 1964.
Aristotle. *The Complete Works of Aristotle: The Revised Oxford Translation*. Ed. Jonathan Barnes. Bollingen Series. 2 vols. Princeton: Princeton University Press, 1984.
Augustine. *The City of God against the Pagans*. Ed. and trans. R.W. Dyson. Cambridge: Cambridge University Press, 1998.
Aurelius, Marcus. *Meditations*. Ed. and trans. C.R. Haines. Loeb Classical Library. London and Cambridge, MA: Harvard University Press, 1916.
Buck, George. *The History of King Richard III* (1619). Ed. Arthur N. Kincaid. Gloucester: A. Sutton, 1979.
Budé, Guillaume. *Annotationes in XXIV libros Pandectarum*. Paris, 1508.
Caxton, William. *The Golden Legend; or, Lives of the saints, as Englished by William Caxton*. 7 vols. London: J.M. Dent, 1931–9.
Cicero. *Brutus. Orator*. Trans. G.L. Hendrickson and H.M. Hubbell. Loeb Classical Library. Cambridge, MA: Harvard University Press, 1939.
– *De finibus bonorum et malorum*. Trans. H. Rackham. Loeb Classical Library. 2nd ed. London and Cambridge, MA: Harvard University Press, 1931.
– *De inventione*. Trans. H.M. Hubbell. Loeb Classical Library. London and Cambridge, MA: Harvard University Press, 1949.
– *De natura deorum*. Trans. H. Rackham. Loeb Classical Library. London and Cambridge, MA: Harvard University Press, 1951.
– *De officiis*. Trans. W. Miller. Loeb Classical Library. London and Cambridge, MA: Harvard University Press, 1913.
– *De oratore, books I, II*. Trans. E.W. Sutton and H. Rackham. Loeb Classical Library. London and Cambridge, MA: Harvard University Press, 1942.

– *De oratore, book III*. Trans. H. Rackham. Loeb Classical Library. London and Cambridge, MA: Harvard University Press, 1942.
– *How to Be a Friend [De amicitia]*. Trans. P. Freeman. Princeton: Princeton University Press, 2018.
– *In Catilinam 1–4. Pro Murena. Pro Sulla. Pro Flacco*. Trans. C. MacDonald. Loeb Classical Library. Cambridge, MA: Harvard University Press, 1976.
– *Letters to Atticus*. Vol. 5. Ed. and trans. D.R. Shackleton Bailey. Cambridge: Cambridge University Press, 1966.
– *Lucullus*. Book 2 of Cicero, *Academica*. Trans. H. Rackham. Loeb Classical Library. Cambridge, MA: Harvard University Press, 1933.
– *On Duties*. Ed. M.T. Griffin and E.M Atkins. Cambridge: Cambridge University Press, 1991.
– *On Moral Ends* [*De finibus*]. Ed. J. Annas. Trans. R. Woolf. Cambridge: Cambridge University Press, 2001.
– *On the Republic. On the Laws*. Trans. C.W. Keyes. Loeb Classical Library. Cambridge, MA: Harvard University Press, 1928.
– *Orator*. Trans. G.L. Hendrickson and H.M. Hubbell. Loeb Classical Library. London and Cambridge, MA: Harvard University Press, 1942.
– *Paradoxa Stoicorum*. Trans. H. Rackham. Loeb Classical Library. London and Cambridge, MA: Harvard University Press, 1942.
– *Posterior Academics*. Book I of Cicero, *Academica*. Trans. H. Rackham. Loeb Classical Library. Cambridge, MA: Harvard University Press, 1933.
– *Tusculan Disputations*. Trans. J.E. King. Loeb Classical Library. Rev. ed. London and Cambridge, MA: Harvard University Press, 1945.
Cicero [pseudo.] *Rhetorica ad Herennium*. Trans. Harry Caplan. Loeb Classical Library. London and Cambridge, MA: Harvard University Press, 1954.
Colet, John. *An Exposition of St. Paul's Epistle to the Romans* (5 ch. version). In *Letters to Radulphus*. Ed. J.H. Lupton. London: G. Bell, 1876.
– *An Exposition of St. Paul's Epistle to the Romans* (16 ch. version). Ed. J.H. Lupton. London: G. Bell, 1873.
– *An Exposition of St. Paul's First Epistle to the Corinthians*. Ed. J.H. Lupton. London: G. Bell, 1874.
– *John Colet on the Ecclesiastical Hierarchy of Dionysius*. Ed. and trans. Daniel J. Nodes and Daniel Lochman. Leiden: Brill, 2013.
– *Letters to Radulphus on the Mosaic Account of the Creation*. Ed. J.H. Lupton. London: G. Bell, 1876; repr. Ridgewood, NJ, 1966.
The Crowland Chronicle Continuations, 1459–1486. Ed. Nicholas Pronay and John Cox. London: Alan Sutton Publishing, 1986.
Empiricus, Sextus. *Against the Ethicists: (Adversus Mathematicos XI)*. Ed. Richard Bett. Oxford: Oxford University Press, 1997.
Epictetus. *Discourses*. Trans. William A. Oldfather. 2 vols. Loeb Classical Library. London and Cambridge, MA: Harvard University Press, 1925.

– *Discourses, Book I.* Ed. Robert F. Dobbin. Oxford: Oxford Univesity Press, 1998.
– *Enchiridion.* Trans. William A. Oldfather. Loeb Classical Library. London and Cambridge, MA: Harvard University Press, 1928.
Epicurus. *The Epicurus Reader.* Translations by B. Inwood and L.P. Gerson. Indianapolis: Hackett, 1994.
– *Principal Doctrines.* In Diogenes Laertius, *Lives*, 10.139–54.
Erasmus, Desiderius. *Antibarbarorum liber.* Ed. Kazimierz Kumaniecki. ASD I-1. Trans. Margaret M. Phillips, CWE 23.
– *Christian Humanism and the Reformation: Selected Writings of Erasmus.* Ed. and trans. John C. Olin. New York: Harper and Row, 1965.
– *Collected Works of Erasmus* (CWE). Toronto: University of Toronto Press, 1974–.
– *Desiderius Erasmus Roterodamus: Ausgewählte Werke.* Ed. Hajo Holborn and Annemarie Holborn. Munich: Beck, 1933
– *Disputatiuncula de taedio, pavore, tristitia Jesu, instante supplicio crucis: Deque verbis, quibus visus est mortem deprecari, Pater, si fieri potest, transeat a me calix iste.* LB 5, 1265A–1292A [also ASD vol. 7 (2013)].
– *Dulce bellum inexpertis.* Ed. R. Hoven, ASD II-7. Trans. Denis L. Drysdall, CWE 35.
– *Ecclesiastes.* Ed. Jacques Chomarat. ASD V-4 and 5.
– *Enchiridion Militis Christiani.* In *Desiderius Erasmus Roterodamus Ausgewählte Werke*, ed. Hajo Holborn and Annemarie Holborn, 22–136. Munich: Beck, 1933. Trans. Charles Fantazzi, CWE 66.
– *Encomium matrimonii (The Praise of Matrimony).* ASD I-2, 400–29, CWE 25, 129–44.
– *The Handbook of the Christian Soldier/Enchiridion Militis Christiani.* Trans. Charles Fantazzi, CWE 66, 24–127.
– *Moriae encomium id est Stultitiae Laus.* Ed. Clarence Miller. ASD IV-3.
– *Opera omnia.* Ed. J. Leclerc. 10 vols. Leiden: Van der Aa, 1703–6.
– *Opera omnia Desiderii Erasmi Roterodami.* Amsterdam: Brill, 1969–.
– *Opus epistolarum Des. Erasmi Roterodami.* Ed. P.S. Allen, H.M. Allen, and H.W. Garrod. 12 vols. Oxford: Clarendon Press, 1906–58. Trans. various scholars, CWE 1974–.
– *Opuscula: A Supplement to the Opera Omnia.* Ed. W.K. Ferguson. The Hague: Nijhoff, 1933
– *The Praise of Folly.* Trans. Hoyt H. Hudson. Princeton: Princeton University Press, 1941.
– *The Praise of Folly.* Trans. Clarence H. Miller. New Haven: Yale University Press, 1979.
– *The Praise of Folly.* Trans. Betty Radice, CWE 27.
– *A Short Debate Concerning the Distress, Alarm, and Sorrow of Jesus As the Crucifixion Drew Nigh; and Concerning the Words in Which He Seemed to Pray*

for Deliverance From Death: "Father, If It Be Possible, Let This cup Pass from Me." Trans. Michael J. Heath, CWE 70, 13–67.

– *Utilissima consultatio de bello Turcis inferendo.* Ed. A.G. Weiler, ASD V-3. Trans. Betty Radice, CWE 27.

Erasmus, Desiderius, ed. *De officiis Marci Tullii Ciceronis libri tres.* [London]: Ioannem Kyngstonem, 1574.

Ficino, Marsilio. *The Letters of Marsilio Ficino.* Trans. School of Economic Science, London. London: Shepheard-Walwyn Publishers, 1975.

– *Opera Omnia.* 2 vols. Basle, 1576; repr. Turin, 1959.

– *Platonic Theology: On the Immortality of Souls.* Ed. and trans. J. Hankins, W. Bowen, M.J.B. Allen, J. Warden. 6 vols. Cambridge, MA: Harvard University Press, 2001–6.

Froissart, Jean. *Froissart's Chronicles.* Ed. and trans. John Jolliffe. London: Harvill Press, 1967.

Gellius, Aulus. *Noctes Atticae.* Ed. P.K. Marshall. 3 vols. Oxford: Oxford University Press, 1990.

– *Noctes Atticae.* Trans. John C. Rolfe. 3 vols. Loeb Classical Library. London and Cambridge, MA: Harvard University Press, 1927.

Giles, Peter. *Summa sive argumenta legum diversorum imperatorum.* Antwerp or Louvain, 1517.

Harpsfield, Nicholas. *The Life and Death of Sir Thomas More* (c. 1557). In *Lives of Saint Thomas More,* trans. Philip E. Hallett, ed. E.E. Reynolds, 51–157. London: Dent, 1963.

The Hellenistic Philosophers. Ed. and trans. A.A. Long and D.N. Sedley. 2 vols. Cambridge: Cambridge University Press, 1987.

Horace. *The Complete Odes and Satires.* Trans. Sidney Alexander. Princeton: Princeton University Press, 1999.

– *Satires, Epistles and Ars Poetica.* Trans. H. Rushton Fairclough. London and Cambridge, MA: Harvard University Press, 1955.

Innocent III, Pope. *De miseria humane conditionis.* Ed. M. Maccarrone. Lugano: Thesaurus Mundi, 1955. Trans. Bernard Murchland in *Two Views of Man.* New York: Ungar, 1966.

Justinian. *Institutes.* Trans. J.B. Moyle. Oxford: Oxford University Press, 1911.

Knowledge, Goodness, and Power: The Debate over Nobility among Quattrocento Italian Humanists. Ed. and trans. Albert Rabil, Jr. Binghamton, NY: Medieval and Renaissance Texts and Studies, 1991.

Laertius, Diogenes. *Lives of Eminent Philosophers.* Trans. R.D. Hicks. 2 vols. Loeb Classical Library. London and Cambridge, MA: Harvard University Press, 1972.

Listrius, Gerardus. *Commentary on The Praise of Folly* (1515). In Erasmus, *Opera omnia,* ed. J. Clericus, vol. 4, cols. 401–504.

Lucian. *Lucian, Vols. 1–8*. Trans. A.M. Harmon and M.D. MacLeod. Loeb Classical Library. Cambridge, MA: Harvard University Press, 1913–67.

Lucretius. *On the Nature of Things (De rerum natura)*. Loeb Classical Library. Trans. W.H.D. Rouse, revised by M.F. Smith. Cambridge, MA: Harvard University Press, 1992.

Machiavelli. *Discourses on Livy*. Trans. H.C. Mansfield and N. arcov. Chicago: University of Chicago Press, 1996.

– *The Prince*. Trans. and ed. Quentin Skinner and Russell Price. Cambridge: Cambridge University Press, 1988.

Mancini, Dominic. *The Usurpation of Richard III*. Ed. and trans. C.A.J. Armstrong. 2nd edition. Oxford: Oxford University Press, 1969.

Manetti, Giannozzo. *De dignitate et excellentia hominis*. Ed. E.R. Leonard. Padua: Antenore, 1975.

– *Two Views of Man: Pope Innocent III: On the Misery of Man; Giannozzo Manetti: On the Dignity of Man*. Trans. Bernard Murchland. New York: Ungar, 1966.

Mirk, John. *John Mirk's "Festial": A Collection of Homilies*. Ed. Theodore Erbe. London: Early English Text Society (vol. 96), 1905; rpt. 1987.

More, Cresacre. *The Life and Death of Sir Thomas Moore* (1627). London: William Pickering, 1828.

More, Thomas. *The Complete Works of St. Thomas More*. 15 volumes. New Haven: Yale University Press, 1963–97.

– *The Confutation of Tyndale's Answer*. CWM 8, Pt. 1.

– *The Correspondence of Sir Thomas More*. Ed. E.F. Rogers. Princeton: Princeton University Press, 1947.

– *Historia Richardi Tertii*. Ed. and trans. Daniel Kinney. CWM 15, 313–485.

– *History of King Richard III*. Ed. Paul Murray Kendall. In Kendall, *Richard III: The Great Debate*, 31–112. New York: Norton, 1965.

– *The History of King Richard III*. Ed. R.S. Sylvester. CWM 2.

– "Letter to a Monk." CWM 15, 197–311.

– *Luciani opuscula ... ab Erasmo Roterodamo et Thoma Moro ... in Latinorum linguam traducta*. Paris: J. Bade, 13 November 1506. ASD I-1, pp. 361–627; CWM 3, Pt. 1.

– *St. Thomas More: Selected Letters*. Ed. E.F. Rogers. New Haven: Yale University Press, 1961.

– *Utopia*. Ed. George M. Logan. Trans. Robert M. Adams. Third edition. Cambridge: Cambridge University Press, 2016.

– *Utopia*. Ed. George M. Logan, Robert M. Adams, and Clarence H. Miller. Cambridge: Cambridge University Press, 1995.

– *Utopia*. Ed. Edward Surtz, SJ, and J.H. Hexter. CWM 4.

– *L'Utopie de Thomas More*. Ed. André Prévost. Paris: Mame, 1978.

Pace, Richard. *De fructu qui ex doctrina percipitur* (*The Benefit of a Liberal Education*) (1517). Ed. and trans. Frank Manley and Richard S. Sylvester. New York: Ungar, 1967.

Pico della Mirandola, Giovanni. *Opera Omnia*, vol. 1 (1557–73). Repr. Hildesheim: G. Olms, 1969.

Plato. *Complete Works*. Ed. John M. Cooper. Indianapolis: Hackett, 1997.

Plutarch. *De communibus notitiis contra Stoicos*. Trans. H. Cherniss. In *Moralia*, vol. 13, pt. 2, 622–827.

– *De Stoicorum repugnantiis*. Trans. H. Cherniss. In *Moralia*, vol. 13, pt. 2, 369–603.

– *Moralia*. 16 vols. Loeb Classical Library. London and Cambridge, MA: Harvard University Press, 1927–2004.

Quintilian. *The Orator's Education* (*Institutio Oratoria*). Trans. Donald A. Russell. Loeb Classical Library. 5 vols. Cambridge, MA: Harvard University Press, 2002.

Quiroga, Vasco de. *Información en derecho* (written in 1535). In *Collección de documentos inéditos relativos al descubrimiento, conquista, y organizacion de las antiguas posesiones españoles de América y Oceanía*, vol. 10, 333–525. Madrid: Manuel G. Hernández, 1868.

Ro Ba. *The Lyfe of Syr Thomas More* (completed 1599). Ed. E.V. Hitchcock and P.E. Hallett. London: Oxford University Press, 1950.

Roper, William. *The Life of Sir Thomas More* (c. 1556). In *Two Early Tudor Lives*, ed. Richard S. Sylvester and Davis P. Harding. London and New Haven: Yale University Press, 1962.

Seneca. *Ad Lucilium Epistulae Morales*. Trans. Richard M. Gummere. 3 vols. Loeb Classical Library. London and Cambridge, MA: Harvard University Press, 1917–25.

– *De otio, De brevitate vitae*. Ed. G.S. Williams. Cambridge: Cambridge University Press, 2003.

– *Moral Essays*. Trans. John W. Basore. 3 vols. Loeb Classical Library. London and Cambridge, MA: Harvard University Press, 1932.

The South English Legendary. Ed. Charlotte D'Evelyn and Anna J. Mills. London: Early English Text Society (vols. 235, 236, 244), 1956–9.

Speculum Sacerdotale. Ed. Edward H. Weatherly. London: Early English Text Society (vol. 200), 1936.

St. Patrick's Purgatory: Two Versions of "Owayne Miles" and "The Vision of William of Stranton" together with the Long Text of the "Tractatus de Purgatorio Sancti Patricii". Ed. R.B. Easting. London: Early English Text Society (298), 1991.

Stapleton, Thomas. *De universa justificationis doctrina hodie controversa*. Paris: Michael Sonnius, 1582.

– *The Life and Illustrious Martyrdom of Sir Thomas More* (1588). Trans. Philip E. Hallett. Ed. E.E. Reynolds. London: Burns and Oates, 1966.

– *Principiorum fidei doctrinalium demonstratio methodica.* Paris: Michael Sonnius, 1578.
– *Vita Thomae Mori.* Frankfurt, 1689; repr. Frankfurt, 1964.
Valla, Lorenzo. *De vero falsoque bono.* Ed. M. de P. Lorch. Bari: Adriatica, 1970.
– *On Pleasure/De voluptate.* Trans. A. Kent Hieatt and Maristella Lorch. New York: Abaris Books, 1977.
Voragine, Jacobus de. *Legenda aurea.* 2nd edition. 2 vols. Ed. G.P. Magioni. Florence: SISMEL, 1998.
– *The Golden Legend: Readings on the Saints.* 2 vols. Translated by Granger Ryan. Princeton: Princeton University Press, 1993.
Waldseemüller, Martin. *Quattuor navigations* (c. 1504). Includes English translation by Joseph Fischer and Franz von Wiser. New York: US Catholic Historical Society, 1907; Rpt. Ann Arbor, 1966.
Whittington, Robert. *Vulgaria* (1520). Ed. Beatrice White. London: *Early English Text Society* (orig. ser. no. 187), 1932.

Secondary Sources

Abou-El-Haj, Barbara. *The Medieval Cult of Saints: Formations and Transformations.* Cambridge: Cambridge University Press, 1994.
Ackroyd, Peter. *The Life of Thomas More.* New York: Anchor, 1999.
Adams, Robert P. *The Better Part of Valor: More, Erasmus, Colet, and Vives, on Humanism, War, and Peace, 1496–1535.* Seattle: University of Washington Press, 1962.
Altman, Joel B. *The Tudor Play of Mind: Rhetorical Enquiry and the Development of Elizabethan Drama.* Los Angeles: University of California Press, 1978.
Anderson, Graham. *Lucian: Theme and Variation in the Second Sophistic.* Lugduni: Brill, 1976.
Annas, Julia. *The Morality of Happiness.* New York: Oxford University Press, 1993.
Arnold, E. Vernon. *Roman Stoicism.* Cambridge: Cambridge University Press, 1911.
Arnold, Jonathan. *Dean John Colet of St. Paul's: Humanism and Reform in Early Tudor England.* London: I.B. Taurus, 2007.
– "Humanist Ecclesiology in Theory: The Dating of John Colet's Written Works." *Moreana* 52 (2015): 237–72.
– "John Colet, Preaching, and Reform at St. Paul's Cathedral, 1505–19." *Historical Research* 76 (2003): 450–68.
Atkins, Jed W. *Cicero on Politics and the Limits of Reason: The Republic and Law.* Cambridge: Cambridge University Press, 2013.
Avineri, Shlomo. "War and Slavery in More's Utopia." *International Review of Social History* 7 (1962): 260–90.

Baker, David Weil. *Divulging Utopia: Radical Humanism in Sixteenth-Century England*. Amherst: University of Massachusetts Press, 1999.
– "Jacobean Historiography and the Election of Richard III." *Huntington Library Quarterly* 70 (2007): 311–42.
Baker-Smith, Dominic. "*Civitas philosophica*: Ideas and Community in Thomas More." In *A Companion to Thomas More*, 165–77.
– *More's Utopia*. London: Unwin, 1991; rpt. 2000.
– "Reading *Utopia*." In *The Cambridge Companion to Thomas More*, 141–67.
– "Uses of Plato by Erasmus and More." In *Platonism and the English Imagination*, ed. Anna Baldwin and Sarah Hutton, 86–99. Cambridge: Cambridge University Press, 1994.
– "Who Went to Thomas More's Lectures on St. Augustine's *De Civitate Dei*." *Church History and Religious Culture* 87 (2007): 145–60.
Baraz, Yelena. *A Written Republic: Cicero's Philosophical Politics*. Princeton: Princeton University Press, 2012.
Baschet, Jérôme. *Les justices de l'au-delà. Les représentations de l'enfer en France et en Italie (XIIe–XVe siècle)*. Rome: École Française de Rome, 1993.
Bayley, C.C. *War and Society in Renaissance Florence: The De Militia of Leonardo Bruni*. Toronto: University of Toronto Press, 1961.
Bené, Charles. *Erasme et Saint Augustin*. Geneva: Droz, 1969.
Bernstein, Alan E. *The Formation of Hell: Death and Retribution in the Ancient and Early Christian Worlds*. Ithaca: Cornell University Press, 1993.
Bietenholz, Peter G. *Encounters with a Radical Erasmus: Erasmus' Work as a Source of Radical Thought in Early Modern Europe*. Toronto: University of Toronto Press, 2009.
Blanchard, W. Scott. *Scholars' Bedlam: Menippean Satire in the Renaissance* Lewisburg, PA: Bucknell University Press, 1995.
Blum, Paul Richard. "The Immortality of the Soul." In *The Cambridge Companion to Renaissance Philosophy*, ed. J. Hankins, 211–33. Cambridge: Cambridge University Press, 2007.
Bolchazy, Ladislaus J., ed. *A Concordance to the Utopia of St. Thomas More and a Frequency Word List*. Hildesheim: Olms, 1978.
Bompaire, Jacques. *Lucien, écrivain, imitation et creation*. Paris: Ed. de Boccard, 1958.
Borchardt, Frank L. "The Magus as Renaissance Man." *Sixteenth-Century Journal* 21 (1990): 57–76.
Boyle, Marjorie O'Rourke. *Christening Pagan Mysteries: Erasmus in Pursuit of Wisdom*. Toronto: University of Toronto Press, 1981.
– "Folly Plus: Moria and More." *Journal of Religious History* 15 (1989): 436–47.
Branham, R.B. *Unruly Eloquence: Lucian and the Comedy of Traditions*. Cambridge, MA: Harvard University Press, 1989.
– "Utopian Laughter: Lucian and Thomas More." *Moreana* 86 (1985): 23–43.

Branham, R.B., and M. Goulet-Cazé, eds. *The Cynics: The Cynic Movement in Antiquity and Its Legacy*. Berkeley: University of California Press, 1996.

Brann, Noel L. *Trithemius and Magical Theology*. Albany: SUNY Press, 1999.

Brennan, Tad. *The Stoic Life: Emotions, Duties, and Fate*. Oxford: Clarendon Press, 2005.

Bridgett, T.E. *Life and Writings of Sir Thomas More*. London: Burns and Oates, 1891.

Brown, Peter. *Augustine of Hippo: A Biography*. Berkeley: University of California Press, 1967.

– *The Body and Society: Men, Women, and Sexual Renunciation in Early Christianity*. 2nd ed. New York: Columbia University Press, 2008.

– *The Cult of the Saints*. Chicago: University of Chicago Press, 1981.

Burgess, Theodore C. *Epideictic Literature*. Chicago: University of Chicago Press, 1902.

Bynum, Caroline Walker, and Paul Freedman, eds. *Last Things: Death and the Apocalypse in the Middle Ages*. Philadelphia: University of Pennsylvania Press, 2000.

The Cambridge Companion to Thomas More. Ed. George M. Logan. Cambridge: Cambridge University Press, 2011.

The Cambridge Companion to Utopian Literature. Ed. Gregory Claeys. Cambridge: Cambridge University Press, 2010.

The Cambridge History of Renaissance Philosophy. Ed. C.B. Schmitt and Q. Skinner. Cambridge: Cambridge University Press, 1988.

Campbell, W.E. *Erasmus, Tyndale and More*. London: Eyre and Spottiswoode, 1949.

Carpenter, Nan C. "A Song for All Seasons: Sir Thomas More and Music." *Comparative Literature* 33 (1981): 113–36.

Cartwright, Jane, ed. *Celtic Hagiography and Saints' Cults*. Cardiff: University of Wales Press, 2003.

Cave, Terence, ed. *Thomas More's Utopia in Early Modern Europe: Paratexts and Contexts*. Manchester: Manchester University Press, 2008.

Celenza, Christopher S. *Piety and Pythagoras in Renaissance Florence: The Symbolum Nesianum*. Leiden: Brill, 2001.

Center for Thomas More Studies: Library Index. See thomasmorestudies.org.

Chambers, R.W. *Thomas More* (1935). Ann Arbor: University of Michigan Press, 1958.

Chomarat, Jacques. *Grammaire et rhétorique chez Erasme*. 2 vols. Paris: Les Belles Lettres, 1981.

– "L''Eloge de la Folie' et Quintilien." *Information littéraire* 2 (1972): 77–82.

Christ-Von Wedel, Christine. *Erasmus of Rotterdam: Advocate of a New Christianity*. Toronto: University of Toronto Press, 2013.

Christian, Linda G. "The Metamorphoses of Erasmus' 'Folly.'" *Journal of the History of Ideas* 32 (1997): 289–94.

Clay, Jenny Strauss. *Hesiod's Cosmos*. Cambridge: Cambridge University Press, 2003.

Clayton, Mary, and Hugh Magennis. *The Old English Lives of St Margaret*. Cambridge: Cambridge University Press, 1994.

Cohn, Norman. *The Pursuit of the Millennium*. Revised edition. New York: Oxford University Press, 1970.

Coletti, Theresa. *Mary Magdalene and the Drama of Saints: Theater, Gender, and Religion in Late Medieval England*. Philadelphia: University of Pennsylvania Press, 2004.

Colie, Rosalie L. *Paradoxia Epidemica: The Renaissance Tradition of Paradox*. Princeton: Princeton University Press, 1966.

Colish, Marcia L. *The Stoic Tradition from Antiquity to the Early Middle Ages*. 2 vols. Leiden: Brill, 1985.

A Companion to Thomas More. Ed. A.D. Cousins and D. Grace. Teaneck, NJ: Fairleigh Dickinson University, 2009.

Connolly, Joy. *The State of Speech: Rhetoric and Political Thought in Ancient Rome*. Princeton: Princeton University Press, 2007.

Contemporaries of Erasmus: A Biographical Register of the Renaissance and Reformation. Ed. Peter G. Bietenholz and Thomas B. Deutscher. 3 vols. Toronto: Univesity of Toronto Press, 1985–7.

Copenhaver, Brian. "Scholastic Philosophy and Renaissance Magic in the *De Vita* of Marsilio Ficino." *Renaissance Quarterly* 37 (1984): 523–54.

– "Studied as an Oration: Readers of Pico's Letters, Ancient and Modern." In *Laus Platonici Philosophi: Marsilio Ficino and His Influence*, ed. S. Clucas, P.J. Forshaw, and V. Rees, 151–91. Leiden: Brill, 2011.

Cox, Virginia. "Machiavelli and the *Rhetorica ad Herennium*: Deliberative Rhetoric in *The Prince*." *Sixteenth-Century Journal* 28 (1997): 1109–41.

Craig, Christopher P. "Cato's Stoicism and the Understanding of Cicero's Speech for Murena." *Transactions of the American Philological Association* 116 (1986): 229–39.

Craig, Leon H. *The War Lover: A Study of Plato's Republic*. Toronto: University of Toronto Press, 1994.

Curtis, Cathy. "'The Best State of the Commonwealth': Thomas More and Quentin Skinner." In *Rethinking the Foundations of Modern Political Thought*, ed. A. Brett and J. Tully, 93–112. Cambridge: Cambridge University Press, 2006.

– "From Sir Thomas More to Robert Burton: The Laughing Philosopher in the Early Modern Period." In *The Philosophy of Early Modern Europe*, ed. C. Condren et al., 90–112. Cambridge: Cambridge University Press, 2006.

– "Richard Pace's *De fructu* and Early Tudor Pedagogy." In Woolfson, ed., *Reassessing Tudor Humanism*, 43–77.

Curtius, Ernest. *European Literature and the Latin Middle Ages*. New York: Bollingen, 1953.

Curtright, Travis. *The One Thomas More*. Washington, DC: Catholic University of America Press, 2012.

Daly, Saralyn R. "Peter Comestor: Master of Histories." *Speculum* 32 (1957): 62–73.

Davidson, Cliffo d, and Thomas H. Seiler, eds. *The Iconography of Hell*. Kalamazoo: Medieval Institute Publications, Western Michigan University, 1992.

Davis, J.C. "Thomas More's *Utopia*: Sources, Legacy and Interpretation." In *The Cambridge Companion to Utopian Literature*, 28–50.

Dawson, Doyne. *Cities of the Gods: Communist Utopias in Greek Thought*. New York: Oxford University Press, 1992.

De Smet, Ingred A.R. *Menippean Satire and the Republic of Letters, 1581–1655*. Geneva: Droz, 1996.

Dealy, Ross. "The Dynamics of Erasmus' Thought on War." *Erasmus of Rotterdam Society Yearbook* 4 [now *Erasmus Studies*] (1984): 53–67.

– *The Politics of an Erasmian Lawyer, Vasco de Quiroga*. Los Angeles: Undena (UCLA Center for Medieval and Renaissance Studies, Humana Civilitas 3), 1976.

– *The Stoic Origins of Erasmus' Philosophy of Christ*. Toronto: University of Toronto Press, 2017.

– "Vasco de Quiroga's *Regula Ubi Commodum*, the Utopian Roots." In *Materiali per una Storia della Cultura Giuridica* VIII.2, ed. G. Tarello, 7–26. Bologna: Società editrice il Mulino, 1978.

Dean, James. "The World Grown Old and Genesis in Middle English Historical Writings." *Speculum* 57 (1982): 548–68.

Dean, Leonard F. "Literary Problems in More's *Richard III*." In *Essential Articles*, 315–25.

Dean, Paul. "Tudor Humanism and the Roman Past: A Background to Shakespeare." *Renaissance Quarterly* 41 (1988): 84–111.

Delany, Sheila. *Impolitic Bodies: Poetry, Saints, and Society in Fifteenth-Century England*. Oxford: Oxford University Press, 1998.

Delehaye, Hippolyte. *The Legends of the Saints* (1905). New York: Fordham University Press, 1962.

Delumeau, Jean. *Sin and Fear: The Emergence of a Western Guilt Culture, 13th–18th Centuries*, trans. E. Nicholson. New York: St Martin's Press, 1990.

Dinzelbacher, Peter. *Vision und Visionsliteratur im Mittelalter*. Stuttgart: Anton Hiersemann, 1981.

Di Scipio, Giuseppe C. "*De Re Militari* in Machiavelli's *Prince* and More's *Utopia*." *Moreana* 77 (1983): 11–22.

Dominik, William, and Jon Hall, eds. *A Companion to Roman Rhetoric*. Malden, MA: Blackwell, 2007.

Donner, H.W. *Introduction to Utopia*. London: Folcroft, 1945; rpt. 1969.

Donno, Elizabeth Story. "Thomas More and Richard III." *Renaissance Quarterly* 35 (1982): 401–47.

Dorsch, T.S. "Sir Thomas More and Lucian: An Interpretation of *Utopia*." *Archiv für das Studium der Neueren Sprachen und Literaturen* 203 (1966): 345–63.

Duff , Eamon. "'The comen knowen multytude of crysten men': *A Dialogue Concerning Heresies* and the Defence of Christendom." In *The Cambridge Companion to Thomas More*, 191–215.

– *The Stripping of the Altars: Traditional Religion in England 1400–1580*. New Haven: Yale University Press, 1992.

Dugan, John. *Making a New Man: Ciceronian Self-Fashioning in the Rhetorical Works*. Oxford: Oxford University Press, 2005.

Dyck, Andrew R. *A Commentary on Cicero, De Legibus*. Ann Arbor: University of Michigan Press, 2004.

– *A Commentary on Cicero, De Officiis*. Ann Arbor: University of Michigan Press, 1996.

Ebner, M., H. Gzella, H.-G. Nesselrath, and E. Ribbat. *Lukian: Die Lügenfreunde, oder Der Ungläubige. Eingeleitet, übersetzt und mit interpretierenden.* Darmstadt: Wissenschaftliche Buchgesellschaft, 2001.

Eden, Kathy. *Friends Hold All Things in Common: Tradition, Intellectual Property, and the "Adages" of Erasmus*. New Haven: Yale University Press, 2001.

Elton, G.R. "Thomas More, Councillor." In Elton, *Studies in Tudor and Stuart Politics and Government* vol. 1, 129–54. Cambridge: Cambridge University Press, 1974.

Engberg-Pedersen, T. "Discovering the Good: *Oikeiosis* and *Kathekonta* in Stoic Ethics." In *Norms of Nature: Studies in Hellenistic Ethics*, ed. Malcolm Schofiel and Gisela Striker, 145–83. Cambridge: Cambridge University Press, 1986.

Essential Articles for the Study of Thomas More. Ed. R.S. Sylvester and G.P. Marc'hadour. Hamden, CT: Archon, 1977.

Farmer, S.A. *Syncretism in the West: Pico's 900 Theses (1486): The Evolution of Traditional Religious and Philosophical Systems, with Text, Translation, and Commentary*. Tempe, AZ: Medieval and Renaissance Texts and Studies, 1998.

Fenlon, Dermont. "Thomas More and Tyranny." *Journal of Ecclesiastical History* 32 (1981): 453–76.

Fernandez-Santamaria, J.A. *The State, War and Peace*. Cambridge: Cambridge University Press, 1977.

Field, Arthur. *The Origins of the Platonic Academy of Florence*. Princeton: Princeton University Press, 1989.

Fleisher, Martin. *Radical Reform and Political Persuasion in the Life and Writings of Thomas More*. Geneva: Librairie Droz, 1973.

Flint, Valerie I.J. *The Rise of Magic in Early Medieval Europe*. Princeton: Princeton University Press, 1991.

Fox, Alastair. *Thomas More: History and Providence*. Oxford: Blackwell, 1982.

– *Utopia: An Elusive Vision*. New York: Twayne, 1993.

Frank, Jill. "Wages of War: On Judgment in Plato's *Republic*." *Political Theory* 35.4 (2007): 443–67.

Frazier, Alison Knowles. *Possible Lives: Authors and Saints in Renaissance Italy*. New York: Columbia University Press, 2005.

French, Katherine L. *The People of the Parish: Community Life in a Late Medieval English Diocese*. Philadelphia: University of Pennsylvania Press, 2001.

Furey, Constance M. *Erasmus, Contarini, and the Religious Republic of Letters*. Cambridge: Cambridge University Press, 2006.

Garcia Gomez, Angel M. *The Legend of the Laughing Philosopher and Its Presence in Spanish Literature (1500–1700)*. Cordoba: Servicio de Publicaciones, Universidad de Córdoba, 1984.

Gavin, J. Austin, and Thomas M. Walsh. "*The Praise of Folly* in Context: The Commentary of Girardus Listrius." *Renaissance Quarterly* 24 (1971): 193–209.

Gibson, R.W., and J.M. Patrick, eds. *St. Thomas More: A Preliminary Bibliography of His Works and of Moreana to the Year 1750*. New Haven: Yale University Press, 1961.

Gill, Christopher. *The Structured Self in Hellenistic and Roman Thought*. Oxford: Oxford University Press, 2006.

Gleason, John B. *John Colet*. Berkeley: University of California Press, 1989.

Glucker, J.E. "Critolaus' Scale and Philo." *Classical Quarterly* n.s. 42 (1992): 142–6.

Goldhill, Simon. *Who Needs Greek?: Contests in the Cultural History of Hellenism*. Cambridge: Cambridge University Press, 2002.

Gordon, Walter M. *Humanist Play and Belief: The Seriocomic Art of Desiderius Erasmus*. Toronto: University of Toronto Press, 1990.

Gorlach, Manfred. *The Textual Tradition of the South English Legendary*. Leeds: University of Leeds, School of English, 1974.

Grace, Damian. "*Utopia*." In *A Companion to Thomas More*, 178–207.

Gransden, Antonia. *Historical Writing in England*, vol. 2. Ithaca: Cornell University Press 1982.

Grant, Patrick. "Thomas More's Richard III: Moral Narration and Humanist Method." *Renaissance and Reformation* n.s. 7 (1983): 157–72.

Grassi, Ernesto, and Maristella Lorch. *Folly and Insanity in Renaissance Literature*. Binghamton, NY: Medieval and Renaissance Texts and Studies, 1986.

Graver, Margaret. *Stoicism and Emotion*. Chicago: University of Chicago Press, 2007.

Greenblatt, Stephen. *Renaissance Self-Fashioning: From More to Shakespeare*. Chicago: University of Chicago Press, 1980.

– *The Swerve: How the World Became Modern*. New York: Norton, 2011.

– "Utopian Pleasure." In *Cultural Reformations: Medieval and Renaissance in Literary History*, ed. B. Cummings and J. Simpson, 305–20. Oxford: Oxford University Press, 2010.

Griffin, Miriam. "Political Thought in th Age of Nero." In *Neronia VI: Rome à l' époque néronienne*, ed. Jean-Michel Croisille et Yves Perrin, Collection Latomus, vol. 268, 325–37. Brussels: Peeters, 2002.

– *Seneca, A Philosopher in Politics*. New York: Oxford University Press, 1976.

Griffiths, Jane. "Glossing the Spoken ord: Erasmus' *Moriae Encomium* and Chaloner's *Praise of Folie*." In Griffiths *Diverting Authorities: Experimental Glossing Practices in Manuscript and Print*, 103–22. Oxford: Oxford University Press, 2014.

Guy, John. *The Public Career of Sir Thomas More*. New Haven: Yale University Press, 1980.

– *Thomas More*. London: Arnold; New York: Oxford University Press, 2000.

– "Thomas More and Tyranny." *Moreana* 49 (2012): 157–88.

Haarberg, Jon. *Parody and "The Praise of Folly"*. Oslo: Scandinavian University Press, 1998.

Hahm, David E. "Critolaus and Late Hellenistic Peripatetic Philosophy." In *Pyrrhonists, Patricians, Platonizers: Hellenistic Philosophy in the Period 155–86 BC*, ed. A.M. Ioppolo and D.N. Sedley, 47–101. Naples: Bibliopolis, 2007.

Hall, Jennifer. *Lucian's Satire*. New York: Arno, 1981.

Hanham, Alison. *Richard III and His Early Historians, 1483–1535*. Oxford: Clarendon Press, 1975.

Hankins, James. "Humanism and the Origins of Modern Political Thought." In *The Cambridge Companion to Renaissance Humanism*, ed. J. Kraye, 118–41. Cambridge: Cambridge University Press, 1996.

– "Pico della Mirandola, Giovanni (1463–94)." In *Routledge Encyclopedia of Philosophy*, 386–92. London: Routledge, 1998.

– *Plato in the Italian Renaissance*. 2 vols. Leiden: Brill, 1990.

Hankins, James, and Ada Palmer. *The Recovery of Ancient Philosophy in the Renaissance: A Brief Guide*. Florence: Leo S. Olschki, 2008.

Harari, Yuval Noah. *Special Operations in the Age of Chivalry, 1100–1500*. Rochester, NY: Boydell, 2007.

Haren, Michael, and Yolande de Pontfarcy, eds. *The Medieval Pilgrimage to St. Patrick's Purgatory: Lough Derg and the European Tradition*. Enniskillen: Clogher Historical Society, 1990.

Hastings, Margaret. "The Ancestry of Sir Thomas More." In *Essential Articles*, 92–103.

Hathaway, Ronald F. *Hierarchy and the Definition of Order in the Letters of Pseudo-Dionysius*. The Hague: Springer, 1969.

Hay, Denys. *Polydore Vergil: Renaissance Historian and Man of Letters*. Oxford: Clarendon Press, 1952.

Haydn, Hiram. *The Counter-Renaissance*. New York: Scribner, 1950.

Heffernan, Thomas J. *Sacred Biography: Saints and Their Biographers in the Middle Ages*. Oxford: Oxford University Press, 1988.

Hexter, J.H. *More's Utopia: The Biography of an Idea*. Princeton: Princeton University Press, 1952.

Hindman, Sandra. "Dutch Bible Illustration and the *Historia Scholastica*." *Journal of the Warburg and Courtauld Institutes* 37 (1974): 131–44.

Hitchcock, James. "Thomas More and the *Sensus Fidelium*." *Theological Studies* 36 (1975), 145–54.

Hughes, Robert. *Heaven and Hell in Western Art*. New York: Stein and Day, 1968.

Inwood, Brad. "Rules and Reasoning in Stoic Ethics." In *Topics in Stoic Philosophy*, ed. Katerina Ierodiakonou, 94–127. Oxford: Oxford University Press, 1999.

Jankofsky, Klaus P., ed. *The South English Legendary: A Critical Assessment*. Tubingen: Franke, c. 1992.

Jardine, Lisa. *Erasmus, Man of Letters: The Construction of Charisma in Print*. Princeton: Princeton University Press, 1993.

Jayne, Sears. *John Colet and Marsilio Ficino*. Oxford: Oxford University Press, 1963.

Jones, C.P. *Culture and Society in Lucian*. Cambridge, MA: Harvard University Press, 1986.

Joost-Gaugier, Christine L. *Pythagoras and Renaissance Europe: Finding Heaven*. Cambridge: Cambridge University Press, 2009.

Kahn, Victoria. *Rhetoric, Prudence, and Skepticism in the Renaissance*. Ithaca: Cornell University Press, 1985.

– "*Stultitia* and *Diatribe*: Erasmus' Praise of Prudence." *German Quarterly* 55 (1982): 349–69.

Kaiser, Walter. *Praisers of Folly: Erasmus–Rabelais–Shakespeare*. Cambridge, MA: Harvard University Press, 1963.

Kaufman, Peter Iver. "John Colet's *Opus de sacramentis* and Clerical Anticlericalism: The Limitations of 'Ordinary Wayes.'" *Journal of British Studies* 22 (1982): 1–22.

Kautsky, Karl. *Thomas More and His Utopia* (1888). Trans. H.J. Stenning, 1927. Rpt. New York: Russell and Russell, 1959.

Kay, David. "Erasmus' Learned Joking: The Ironic Use of Classical Wisdom in *The Praise of Folly*." *Texas Studies in Literature and Language* 19 (1977): 247–67.

Kelly, Donald R. "The Science of Philology: Guillaume Budé Begins the Restoration of Roman Law." In Kelly, *Foundations of Modern Historical Scholarship*, 53–86. New York: Columbia University Press, 1970.

Kendall, Paul M., ed. *Richard III: The Great Debate*. New York: Norton, 1965.

Kennedy, George A. *A New History of Classical Rhetoric*. Princeton: Princeton University Press, 1994.

Kerferd, G.B. *The Sophistic Movement*. Cambridge: Cambridge University Press, 1981.

Kidd, I.G. "Moral Actions and Rules in Stoic Ethics." In *The Stoics*, ed. John M. Rist, 247–58. Berkeley: University of California Press, 1978.

Kieckhefer, Richard. *Magic in the Middle Ages.* Cambridge: Cambridge University Press, 1990.

– "The Specific Rationality of Medieval Magic." *American Historical Review* 99 (1994): 813–36.

Kincaid, Arthur N. "The Dramatic Structure of Sir Thomas More's History of Richard III." *Studies in English Literature* 12 (1972): 223–42.

Kinney, Arthur. *Humanist Poetics: Thought, Rhetoric, and Fiction in Sixteenth-Century England.* Amherst: University of Massachusetts Press, 1986.

Kinney, Daniel. "Heirs of the Dog: Cynic Selfhood in Medieval and Renaissance Culture." In Branham and Goulet-Cazé, eds., *The Cynics*, 294–328.

Knox, Dilwyn. *Ironia: Medieval and Renaissance Ideas on Irony.* Leiden: Brill, 1989.

Knox, Norman. *The Word "Irony" and Its Context, 1500–1755.* Durham, NC: Duke University Press, 1961.

Kochin, M.S. "War, Class, and Justice in Plato's Republic." *Review of Metaphysics* 53 (1999): 403–23.

Könneker, Barbara. *Wesen und Wandlung der Narrenidé im Zeitalter des Humanismus: Brant–Murner–Erasmus.* Wiesbaden: Steiner, 1966.

Kristeller, Paul O. *Renaissance Thought and Its Sources.* New York: Columbia University Press, 1979.

– *Renaissance Thought II: Papers on Humanism and the Arts.* New York: Harper and Row, 1965.

Kurz, Otto. "Filippino Lippi's Worship of the Apis." *Burlington Magazine for Connoisseurs* 89 (1947): 144–7.

Laks, André, and Malcolm Schofield, eds. *Justice and Generosity: Studies in Hellenistic Social and Political Philosophy.* Cambridge: Cambridge University Press, 1995.

Lauvergnat-Gagnière, Christiane. *Lucien de Samosate et le lucianisme en France au XVIe siècle: Athéisme et polémique.* Geneva: Droz, 1988.

Lehmberg, S.E. "Sir Thomas More's Life of Pico della Mirandola." *Studies in the Renaissance* 3 (1956): 61–74.

Leushuis, Reinier. "The Mimesis of Marriage: Dialogue and Intimacy in Erasmus's Matrimonial Writings." *Renaissance Quarterly* 57 (2004): 1278–1307.

Levin, Harry. *The Myth of the Golden Age in the Renaissance.* Bloomington: Indiana University Press, 1969.

Logan, George M. *The Meaning of More's Utopia.* Princeton: Princeton University Press, 1983; rpt. 2014.

– "More on Tyranny: *The History of King Richard the Third*." In *The Cambridge Companion to Thomas More*, 168–90.

– "*Utopia* and Deliberative Rhetoric." *Moreana* 31 (1994): 103–20.

Long, A.A. "Cicero's Politics in *De Officiis*." In Laks and Schofield, eds., *Justice and Generosity*, 213–40.

– "Hierocles on *Oikeiosis* and Self-Perception." In Long, *Stoic Studies*, 250–63. Cambridge: Cambridge University Press, 1996.

Love, Rosalind C., ed. and trans. *Goscelin of Saint-Bertin: The Hagiography of the Female Saints of Ely*. Oxford: Clarendon Press, 2004.

Lovejoy, Arthur O., and George Boas. *A Documentary History of Primitivism and Related Ideas*, vol. 1. Baltimore: Johns Hopkins University Press, 1935.

Luscombe, David. "Peter Comestor." In *The Bible in the Medieval World: Essays in Memory of Beryl Smalley*, ed. K. Walsh and D. Wood, 109–29. London: Blackwell, 1985.

Luthy, Christoph. "The Fourfold Democritus on the Stage of Early Modern Science." *Isis* 91 (2000): 443–79.

Mansfield, B uce. "Erasmus and More: Exploring Vocations." In *A Companion to Thomas More*, 145–64.

Marc'hadour, Germain. "Latin Lives of Thomas More." In *A Companion to Thomas More*, 21–38.

– "*Omnium Horarum Homo*: 'A Man For All Seasons.'" *Erasmus Yearbook One* (1981): 141–7.

– "Thomas More on the Agony of Christ." In *Concordia Discors, studi su Niccolò Cusano e L'Umanesimo Europeo Offerti a Giovanni Santinello*, ed. Gregorio Piaia, 487–504. Padua: Antenore, 1993.

Marius, Richard. *Thomas More: A Biography*. New York: Knopf, 1984.

– "Thomas More and the Early Church Fathers." *Traditio* 24 (1968): 379–407.

Marrou, H.I. *A History of Education in Antiquity*. Trans. George Lamb. Madison: University of Wisconsin Press, 1956.

Marsh, David. *Lucian and the Latins: Humor and Humanism in the Early Renaissance*. Ann Arbor: University of Michigan Press, 1998.

Martin, Terence J. *Truth and Irony: Philosophical Meditations on Erasmus*. Washington, DC: Catholic University Press of America, 2015.

Matton, Sylvain. "Cynicism and Christianity from the Middle Ages to the Renaissance." In Branham and Goulet-Cazé, eds., *The Cynics*, 240–64.

McConica, James. "The Recusant Reputation of Thomas More." In *Essential Articles*, 136–49.

– "Thomas More as Humanist." In *The Cambridge Companion to Thomas More*, 22–45.

McCutcheon, Elizabeth. "More's Rhetoric." In *The Cambridge Companion to Thomas More*, 46–68.

– "More's *Utopia* and Cicero's *Paradoxa Stoicorum*." *Moreana*, no. 86 (1985): 3–22.

– "War Games in Utopia." In *The Portrayal of Life Stages in English Literature, 1500–1800: Infancy, Youth, Marriage, Aging, Death, Martyrdom*, ed. Jeanie Watson, 29–56. Lewiston, NY: Mellen, 1989.

McDonagh, Patrick. "Holy Fools, Witty Fools, Depraved Fools: Folly, Innocence and Sin." In McDonagh, *Idiocy: A Cultural History*, 129–51. Liverpool: Liverpool University Press, 2008.

Mebane, John S. *Renaissance Magic and the Return of the Golden Age*. Lincoln: University of Nebraska Press, 1989.

Mermel, Jerry. "Preparations for a Politic Life: Sir Thomas More's Entry into The King's Service." *Journal of Medieval and Renaissance Studies* 7 (1977): 53–66.

Miles, Leland. *John Colet and the Platonic Tradition*. La Salle, IL: Open Court, 1961.

Miller, Clarence H. Introduction to his translation of *Utopia*, vii–xxiii. New Haven: Yale University Press, 2001; 2nd edition 2014.

– "The Logic and Rhetoric of Proverbs in Erasmus' *Praise of Folly*." In *Essays on the Works of Erasmus*, ed. Richard L. DeMolen, 83–98. New Haven: Yale University Press, 1978.

Miller, Henry Knight. "The Paradoxical Encomium with Special Reference to Its Vogue in England, 1600–1800." *Modern Philology* 53 (1956): 145–78.

Mitsis, Phillip. "Seneca on Reason, Rules, and Moral Development." In *Passions and Perceptions: Studies in Hellenistic Philosophy of Mind*, ed. J. Brunschwig and M. Nussbaum, 285–312. Cambridge: Cambridge University Press, 1993.

Moles, J.L. "The Cynics and Politics." In Laks and Schofield, eds., *Justice and Generosity*, 120–58.

Monfasani, John. "Episodes of Anti-Quintilianism in the Italian Renaissance: Quarrels on the Orator as a *Vir bonus* and Rhetoric as the *Scientia Bene Dicendi*." *Rhetorica* 10 (1992): 127–35.

– "Humanism and Rhetoric." In Rabil, ed., *Renaissance Humanism*, vol. 3, 171–235.

Morey, James H. "Peter Comestor, Biblical Paraphrase, and the Medieval Popular Bible." *Speculum* 68 (1993): 6–35.

Morgan, Alison. *Dante and the Medieval Other World*. Cambridge: Cambridge University Press, 1990.

Morison, Stanley. *The Likeness of Thomas More*. London: Burns and Oates, 1963.

Muecke, D.C. *The Compass of Irony*. London: Routledge, 1983.

Müllenbrock, Hans-Joachim. "Krieg in Morus' Utopia." *Anglia: Zeitschrift für englishe philologie* 120 (2002): 1–29.

Nelson, Eric. "Greek *Nonsense* in More's *Utopia*." In Nelson, *The Greek Tradition in Republican Thought*, 19–48. Cambridge: Cambridge University Press, 2004.
– "Utopia through Italian Eyes: Thomas More and the Critics of Civic Humanism." *Renaissance Quarterly* 59 (2006): 1029–57.
Newman, Barbara J. "On the Threshold of the Dead: Purgatory, Hell, and Religious Women." In Newman, *From Virile Woman to WomanChrist: Studies in Medieval Religion and Literature*, 108–36. Philadelphia: University of Pennsylvania Press, 1995.
Nicgorski, Walter. "Cicero's Paradoxes and His Idea of Utility." *Political Theory* 12 (1984): 557–78.
O'Connell, Marvin Richard. *Thomas Stapleton and the Counter Reformation*. New Haven: Yale University Press, 1964.
Ogden, Daniel. *Search of the Sorcerer's Apprentice: The Traditional Tales of Lucian's Lover of Lies*. Swansea: Classical Press of Wales, 2007.
Ogle, Marbury B. "Petrus Comestor, Methodius, and the Saracens." *Speculum* 21 (1946): 318–24.
O'Malley, John W. *Praise and Blame in Renaissance Rome: Rhetoric, Doctrine, and Reform in the Sacred Orators of the Papal Court, c. 1450–1521*. Durham, NC: Duke University Press, 1979.
Oncken, Henry. *Die Utopia des Thomas Morus und das Machtproblem in der Staatslehre*. Heidelberg: C. Winter, 1922.
Pabel, Hilmar M. "Reading Jerome in the Renaissance: Erasmus' Reception of the *Adversus Jovinianum*." *Renaissance Quarterly* 55 (2002): 470–97.
Pangle, Thomas L. "Roman Cosmopolitanism: The Stoics and Cicero." In *Cosmopolitanism in the Age of Globalization: Citizens without States*, ed. L. Trepanier and K. Habib, 40–69. Lexington: University of Kentucky Press, 2011.
Parks, George B. "Pico della Mirandola in Tudor Translation." In *Philosophy and Humanism: Renaissance Essays in Honor of Paul Oskar Kristeller*, ed. Edward Mahoney, 352–69. Leiden: Brill, 1976.
Parrish, John M. "A New Source for More's *Utopia*." *Historical Journal* 40 (1997): 493–8.
Patch, Howard Rollin. *The Other World, According to Descriptions in Medieval Literature*. Cambridge: Cambridge University Press, 1950.
Patterson, A.M. *Hermogenes and the Renaissance: Seven Ideas of Style*. Princeton: Princeton University Press, 1970.
Pawlowski, Mary. "Thomas More's Mis-translations of Lucian's *Cynic*, *Menippus*, and *Tyrannicide*." *Moreana* 47 (2010): 85–101.
Pease, Arthur S. "Things without Honor." *Classical Philology* 21 (1926): 27–42.
Perl, Eric D. *Theophany: The Neoplatonic Philosophy of Dionysius the Areopagite*. Albany: SUNY Press, 2007.

Pernot, Laurent. *Rhetoric in Antiquity*. Trans. W.E. Higgins. Washington, DC: Catholic University of America Press, 2005.

Peters, Edward. *The Magician, the Witch and the Law.* Philadelphia: University of Pennsylvania Press, 1978.

Pollard, A.J. "The Making of Sir Thomas More's Richard III" (1933). In *Essential Articles*, 421–31.

– *Richard III and the Princes in the Tower.* New York: St Martin's Press, 1991.

Powell, J.G.F. "Cicero's Translations from the Greek." In *Cicero the Philosopher: Twelve Papers*, ed. J.G.F. Powell, 273–300. Oxford: Oxford University Press, 1995.

Price, Simon. *Religions of the Ancient Greeks.* Cambridge: Cambridge University Press, 1999.

Pyle, Cynthia M. *Milan and Lombardy in the Renaissance: Essays in Cultural History*. Rome: La Fenice, 1997.

Quillen, Carol Everhart. *Rereading the Renaissance: Petrarch, Augustine, and the Language of Humanism.* Ann Arbor: University of Michigan Press, 1998.

Rabil, Albert, Jr, ed. and trans. *Knowledge, Goodness, and Power: The Debate over Nobility among Quattrocento Italian Humanists.* Binghamton, NY: Medieval and Renaissance Texts and Studies, 1991.

– ed. *Renaissance Humanism: Foundations, Forms, and Legacy*. 3 vols. Philadelphia: University of Pennsylvania Press, 1988.

Ramsay, Nigel, Margaret Sparks, and Tim Tatton-Brown, eds. *St. Dunstan: His Life, Times and Cult*. Woodbridge, UK: Boydell, 1992.

Rawson, Elizabeth. "Roman Rulers and the Philosophic Adviser." In *Philosophia Togata*, ed. M.T. Griffin and J. Barnes, 233–57. Ne York: Oxford University Press, 1989.

Reames, Sherry L. *The Legenda Aurea: A Re-examination of Its Paradoxical History.* Madison: University of Wisconsin Press, 1985.

Rebhorn, Wayne. "The Metamorphoses of Moria: Structure and Meaning in *The Praise of Folly*." *Publications of the Modern Language Association* 89 (1974): 463–76.

Reese, A.W. "Learning Virginity: Erasmus' Ideal of Christian Marriage." *Bibliothèque d'Humanisme et Renaissance* 57 (1995): 551–67.

Reiss, Edmond. "Medieval Irony." *Journal of the History of Ideas* 42 (1981): 209–26.

Relihan, Joel C. *Ancient Menippean Satire.* Baltimore: Johns Hopkins University Press, 1993.

– "Menippus in Antiquity and the Renaissance." In Branham and Goulet-Cazé, eds., *The Cynics*, 265–93.

Remer, Gary. *Humanism and the Rhetoric of Toleration.* University Park: Pennsylvania State University Press, 1996.

Reydams-Schils, Gretchen. *The Roman Stoics: Self, Responsibility, and Affection.* Chicago: University of Chicago Press, 2005.

Reynolds, E.E. *The Field Is Won: The Life and Death of St Thomas More.* London: Bruce Publishing, 1968.

Rice, Eugene F., Jr. "John Colet and the Annihilation of the Natural." *Harvard Theological Review* 45 (1952): 141–63.

Ridyard, Susan J. *The Royal Saints of Anglo-Saxon England: A Study of West Sax and East Anglian Cults.* Cambridge: Cambridge University Press, 1988.

Ritter, Gerhard. *The Corrupting Influence of Power.* Hadleigh, UK: Tower Bridge, 1952.

– *Machstaat und Utopie: Vom Streit und die Dämonie der Macht seit Machiavelli und Morus.* Munich: Oldenbourg, 1940.

Robinson, Christopher. *Lucian and His Influence in Europe.* Chapel Hill: University of North Carolina Press, 1979.

Rollason, David. *Saints and Relics in Anglo-Saxon England.* Oxford: Blackwell, 1989.

Roller, Matthew B. "Color-Blindness: Cicero's Death, Declamation, and the Production of History." *Classical Philology* 92 (1997): 109–30.

Ronnick, Michele V. "A Note Concerning Elements of Tacitus' Depiction of Nero in Thomas More's *Historia Richardi Regis Angliae.*" *Moreana* 36 (1999): 63–5.

Rorem, Paul. *Pseudo-Dionysius: A Commentary on the Texts and an Introduction to Their Influence.* New York: Oxford University Press, 1993.

Ross, Charles. *Richard III.* Berkeley: University of California Press, 1981.

Rummel, Erika. *Erasmus and His Catholic Critics.* 2 vols. Nieuwkoop: Brill, 1989.

Rummel, Erika, ed. *Erasmus on Women.* Toronto: University of Toronto Press, 1996.

Rütten, Thomas. *Demokrit – Lachender Philosoph und Sanguinischer Melancholiker.* Leiden: Brill, 1992.

Saul, Nigel. *The Three Richards: Richard I, Richard II and Richard III.* London: Hambledon, 2005.

Schmidt, Gary D. *The Iconography of the Mouth of Hell: Eighth-Century Britain to the Fifteenth-Century.* Selinsgrove, PA: Susquehanna University Press, 1995.

Schoeck, R.J. "More, Plutarch, and King Agis: Spartan History and the Meaning of *Utopia*" (1956). *Essential Articles*, 275–80.

– "Telling More from Erasmus: An Essay in Renaissance Humanism." *Moreana* 23.91–2 (1986): 11–19.

Schofield, Malcolm. *The Stoic Idea of the City.* Cambridge: Cambridge University Press, 1991.

– "Two Stoic Approaches to Justice." In Laks and Schofield, eds., *Justice and Generosity*, 191–212.

Schutzeichel, Heribert. *Wesen und Gegenstand der kirchlichen Lehrautorität nach Thomas Stapleton.* Trier: Paulinus, 1966.

Screech, Michael A. *Erasmus: Ecstasy and the Praise of Folly.* London: Duckworth, 1980.

Scribner, Robert W. "The Reformation, Popular Magic, and the 'Disenchantment of the World.'" *Journal of Interdisciplinary History* 23 (1993): 475–94.

Sellars, John. *The Art of Living: The Stoics on the Nature and Function of Philosophy.* Aldershot: Ashgate, 2003.

Semler, L.E. "Virtue, Transformation, and Exemplarity in *The Lyfe of Johan Picus.*" In *A Companion to Thomas More*, 95–113.

Seward, Desmond. *The War of the Roses: Through the Lives of Five Men and Women of the Fifteenth Century.* New York: Viking, 1995.

Shereshevsky, Esra. "Hebrew Traditions in Peter Comestor's *Historia Scholastica*: I. Genesis." *Jewish Quarterly Review* n.s. 59 (1969): 268–89.

Sherman, Nancy. *Stoic Warriors: The Ancient Philosophy behind the Military Mind.* Oxford: Oxford University Press, 2005.

Simpson, James. "Rhetoric, Conscience, and the Playful Positions of Sir Thomas More." In *The Oxford Handbook of Tudor Literature, 1485–1603,* ed. M. Pincombe and C. Shrank, 121–36. Oxford: Oxford University Press, 2009.

Skinner, Quentin. "Ambrogio Lorenzetti and the Portrayal of Virtuous Government." In Skinner, *Visions of Politics*, vol. 2, 39–92.

– *The Foundations of Modern Political Thought*. Vol. 1. Cambridge: Cambridge University Press, 1978.

– *Liberty before Liberalism.* Cambridge: Cambridge University Press, 1998.

– *Machiavelli: A Very Short Introduction.* Oxford: Oxford University Press, 2000.

– *Reason and Rhetoric in the Philosophy of Hobbes.* Cambridge: Cambridge University Press, 1996.

– "Sir Thomas More's *Utopia* and the Language of Renaissance Humanism." In *The Languages of Political Theory in Early Modern Europe*, ed. Anthony Pagden, 123–57. Cambridge: Cambridge University Press, 1987.

– "Thomas More's *Utopia* and the Virtue of True Nobility." In Skinner, *Visions of Politics*, Vol. 2, 213–44.

– *Visions of Politics.* Vol. 1, *Regarding Method*. Cambridge: Cambridge University Press, 2002.

– *Visions of Politics.* Vol. 2, *Renaissance Virtues*. Cambridge: Cambridge University Press, 2002.

Smalley, Beryl. *The Gospels in the Schools, c. 1100–c. 1280.* London: A&C Black, 1985.

– *The Study of the Bible in the Middle Ages.* Notre Dame: University of Notre Dame Press, 1964.

Smith, Constance. *An Updating of R.W. Gibson's "St. Thomas More: A Preliminary Bibliography."* St Louis: Center for Reformation Research, 1981.

Smith, Julia M.H. "Oral and Written: Saints, Miracles, and Relics in Brittany, c. 850–1250." *Speculum* 65 (1990): 309–43.

Sowards, J.K. "The Two Lost Years of Erasmus: Summary, Review, and Speculation." *Studies in the Renaissance* 9 (1962): 161–86.

Spencer, Theodore. "Chaucer's Hell: A Study in Mediaeval Convention." *Speculum* 2 (1927): 177–200.

Stacey, Peter. *Roman Monarchy and the Renaissance Prince.* Cambridge: Cambridge University Press, 2007.

Starnes, Colin. *The New Republic: A Commentary on Book I of More's Utopia Showing Its Relation to Plato's Republic.* Waterloo, ON: Wilfrid Laurier University Press, 1990.

Stem, Rex. "Cicero as Orator and Philosopher: The Value of the *Pro Murena* for Ciceronian Political Thought." *Review of Politics* 68.2 (Spring, 2006): 206–31.

Stenger, Genevieve. "*The Praise of Folly* and Its Parerga." *Medievalia et Humanistica* n.s. 2 (1971): 97–117.

Stewart, Alan. "The Trouble with English Humanism: Tyndale, More and Darling Erasmus." In Woolfson, ed., *Reassessing Tudor Humanism*, 78–98.

Striker, Gisela. "Cicero and Greek Philosophy." *Harvard Studies in Classical Philology* 97 (1995): 53–61.

– "Following Nature: A Study in Stoic Ethics." In Striker, *Essays on Hellenistic Epistemology and Ethics*, 221–80. Cambridge: Cambridge University Press, 1996.

Surtz, Edward. *The Praise of Pleasure: Philosophy, Education, and Communism in More's* Utopia. Cambridge, MA: Harvard University Press, 1957.

– "Richard Pace's Sketch of Thomas More." In *Essential Articles*, 180–8.

Suzuki, Yoshinori. "Thomas More on Politics as a Profession." *Moreana* 97 (1988): 125–32.

Swain, Barbara. *Fools and Folly during the Middle Ages and the Renaissance.* New York: Columbia University Press, 1932.

Sylvester, Richard S. "The 'Man for All Seasons' Again: Robert Whittington's Verses to Sir Thomas More." *Huntington Library Quarterly* 26.2 (1963): 147–54.

Telle, Emile V. *Érasme de Rotterdam et Le Septième Sacrement.* Geneva: Droz, 1954.

Thomas, Keith. *Religion and the Decline of Magic: Studies in Popular Beliefs in Sixteenth and Seventeenth Century England.* New York: Scribner, 1971.

Thompson, Anne B. *Everyday Saints and the Art of Narrative in the South English Legendary*. Aldershot: Ashgate, 2003.

Thompson, Geraldine. *Under Pretext of Praise: Satiric Mode in Erasmus' Fiction.* Toronto: University of Toronto Press, 1973.

Tinkler, John F. "Praise and Advice: Rhetorical Approaches in More's *Utopia* and Machiavelli's *The Prince*." *Sixteenth-Century Journal* 29 (1988): 187–207.

Trapp, J.B. "An English Late Medieval Cleric and Italian Thought: The Case of John Colet, Dean of St. Paul's (1467–1519)." In *Medieval English Religious and Ethical Literature: Essays in Honour of G.H. Russell*, ed. Gregory Kratzman and James Simpson, 233–50. Dover, NH: Brewer, 1986.

– *Erasmus, Colet and More: The Early Tudor Humanists and Their Books*. London: British Library, 1991.

Trinkaus, Charles. "Thomas More and the Humanist Tradition: Martyrdom and Ambiguity." In Trinkaus, *The Scope of Renaissance Humanism*, 422–36. Ann Arbor: University of Michigan Press, 1983.

Turner, Alice K. *The History of Hell*. New York: Harcourt, 1993.

Twomey, Michael W. "Falling Giants and Floating Lead: Scholastic History in the Middle English 'Cleanness.'" In *Marvels, Monsters, and Miracles*, ed. Timothy S. Jones and David A. Sprunger, 141–65. Kalamazoo, MI: Medieval Institute Publications, 2002.

van der Poel, M. "For Freedom of Opinion: Erasmus' Defense of the *Encomium matrimonii*." *Erasmus of Rotterdam Society Yearbook* [now *Erasmus Studies*] 25 (2005): 1–17.

van Oort, Johannes. *Jerusalem and Babylon: A Study into Augustine's City of God and the Sources of His Doctrine of the Two Cities*. Leiden: Brill, 1991.

Van Ruler, Han, and Giulia Sissa, eds. *Utopia 1516–2016: More's Eccentric Essay and Its Activist Aftermath*. Amsterdam: Amsterdam University Press, 2017.

Vauchez, André. *Sainthood in the Later Middle Ages*. Trans. Jean Birrell. Cambridge: Cambridge University Press, 1997.

Vieira, Fátima. "The Concept of Utopia." In *The Cambridge Companion to Utopian Literature*, 2–27.

Vickers, Brian. *In Defence of Rhetoric*. Oxford: Clarendon Press, 1988.

Vitz, Evelyn Birge. "From the Oral to the Written in Medieval and Renaissance Saints' Lives." In *Images of Sainthood in Medieval Europe*, ed. R. Blumenfeld-Kosinski and T.K. Szell, 97–114. Ithaca: Cornell University Press, 1991.

Vogt, Katja Maria. *Law, Reason, and the Cosmic City: Political Philosophy in the Early Stoa*. Oxford: Oxford University Press, 2008.

Walker, D.P. *Spiritual and Demonic Magic from Ficino to Campanella*. London: Warburg Institute, 1958.

Wallace-Hadrill, Andrew. "Rhetoric and Myth-Making at the Court of Nero." In *Neronia VI: Rome à l' époque néronienne*, ed. Jean-Michel Croisille et Yves Perrin, Collection Latomus, vol. 268, 472–8. Brussels: Peeters, 2002.

Walzer, Arthur E. "Quintilian's 'Vir Bonus' and the Stoic Wise Man." *Rhetoric Society Quarterly* 33 (2003): 25–41.

Ward, John O. "From Antiquity to the Renaissance: Glosses and Commentaries on Cicero's *Rhetorica*." In *Medieval Eloquence*, ed. James J. Murphy, 25–67. Berkeley: University of California Press, 1978.
– "Quintilian and the Rhetorical Revolution of the Middle Ages." *Rhetorica* 13 (1995): 231–84.
– "Renaissance Commentators on Ciceronian Rhetoric." In *Renaissance Eloquence*, ed. James J. Murphy, 126–73. Berkeley: Univeristy of California Press, 1983.
Warnicke, Retha M. "More's Richard III and the Mystery Plays." *Historical Journal* 35 (1992): 761–78.
Watson, Donald G. "Erasmus' Praise of Folly and the Spirit of Carnival." *Renaissance Quarterly* (1979): 333–53.
Webb, Diana. "Eloquence and Education: A Humanist Approach to Hagiography." *Journal of Ecclesiastical History* 31 (1980): 19–39.
Wegemer, Gerard B. *Thomas More on Statesmanship*. Washington, DC: Catholic University Press of America, 1996.
– "Thomas More's 'Rule' of Pleasure before, after, and in *Utopia*." *Moreana* 54.1 (2017): 36–56.
– *Young Thomas More and the Arts of Liberty*. Cambridge: Cambridge University Press, 2011.
Weinstein, Donald, and Rudolph M. Bell. *Saints and Society: The Two Worlds of Western Christendom, 1000–1700*. Chicago: University of Chicago Press, 1982.
Weir, Alison. *The Princes in the Tower*. New York: Random House, 1992.
Wesseling, Ari. "Dutch Proverbs and Ancient Sources in Erasmus' *Praise of Folly*." *Renaissance Quarterly* 47 (1994): 351–78.
White, Nicholas P. *A Companion to Plato's Republic*. Indianapolis: Hackett, 1979.
White, Thomas I. "Aristotle and *Utopia*." *Renaissance Quarterly* 29 (1976): 635–75.
– "Festivitas, Utilitas, et Opes: The Concluding Irony and Philosophical Purpose of Thomas More's *Utopia*." *Albion* 10 (1978), 135–50.
– "Legend and Reality: The Friendship between More and Erasmus." In *Supplementum Festivum: Studies in Honor of Paul Oskar Kristeller*, ed. J. Hankins, J. Monfasani and F. Purnell, Jr, 489–504. Binghamton, NY: Medieval and Renaissance Texts and Studies, 1987.
– "Pride and the Public Good: Thomas More's Use of Plato in *Utopia*." *Journal of the History of Philosophy* 20 (1982): 329–54.
Whitfield, B.G. " irgil and the Bees: A Study in Ancient Apicultural Lore." *Greece and Rome*, second series, 3 (1956): 99–117.
Whitmarsh, Tim. *Greek Literature and the Roman Empire: The Politics of Imitation*. Oxford: Oxford University Press, 2001.
Wind, E. "The Christian Democritus." *Journal of the Warburg Institute* 1 (1937): 180–2.

Winstead, Karen A. *Virgin Martyrs: Legends of Sainthood in Late Medieval England*. Ithaca: Cornell University Press, 1997.

Winterbottom, Michael. "Quintilian and the *Vir Bonus*." *Journal of Roman Studies* 54 (1964): 90–7.

Winterbottom, M., and R.M. Thomson, eds. and trans. William of Malmesbury, *Saints' Lives*. Oxford: Clarendon Press, 2002.

Witchcraft and Magic in Europe: Volume 3, The Middle Ages. Ed. K. Jolly, C. Raudvere, and E. Peters. London: Athlone Press, 2002.

Wood, James. "Sir Thomas More: A Man for One Season." In Wood, *The Broken Estate: Essays on Literature and Belief*, 3–15. New York: Random House, 1999.

Woolfson, Jonathan, ed. *Reassessing Tudor Humanism*. New York: Palgrave Macmillan, 2002.

Wootton, David. "Friendship Portrayed: A New Account of Utopia." *History Workshop Journal* 45 (1989): 28–47.

– Introduction. In *Thomas More's "Utopia" with Erasmus' "Sileni Alcibiades"*, ed. and trans. D. Wootton, 1–34. Indianapolis: Hackett, 1999.

Yates, Frances Amelia. *Giordano Bruno and the Hermetic Tradition*. Chicago: University of Chicago Press, 1964.

Yoran, Hanan. *Between Utopia and Dystopia: Erasmus, Thomas More, and the Humanist Republic of Letters*. Lanham, MD: Lexington Books, 2010.

Zaleski, Carol G. "St. Patrick's Purgatory: Pilgrimage Motifs in a Medieval Otherworld Vision." *Journal of the History of Ideas* 46 (1985): 467–85.

Zatta, Claudia. "Democritus and Folly: The Two Wise Fools." *Bibliothèque d'Humanisme et Renaissance* 63.3 (2001): 533–49.

Index

www.ingramcontent.com/pod-product-compliance
Lightning Source LLC
LaVergne TN
LVHW090146080826
844660LV00013B/693/J

* 9 7 8 1 4 8 7 5 0 6 5 9 9 *